THE ENCYCLOPÆDIA BRITANNICA
VOLUME V SLICE III

Capefigue to Carneades

CAPEFIGUE, JEAN-BAPTISTE HONORÉ RAYMOND (1801-1872), French historian and biographer, was born at Marseilles in 1801. At the age of twenty he went to Paris to study law; but he soon deserted law for journalism. He became editor of the *Quotidienne*, and was afterwards connected, either as editor or leading contributor, with the *Temps*, the *Messager des Chambres,* the *Révolution de 1848* and other papers. During the ascendancy of the Bourbons he held a post in the foreign office, to which is due the royalism of some of his newspaper articles. Indeed all Capefigue's works receive their colour from his legitimist politics; he preaches divine right and non-resistance, and finds polite words even for the profligacy of Louis XV. and the worthlessness of his mistresses. He wrote biographies of Catherine and Marie de' Medici, Anne and Maria Theresa of Austria, Catherine II. of Russia, Elizabeth of England, Diana of Poitiers and Agnes Sorel—for he delighted in passing from "queens of the right hand" to "queens of the left." His historical works, besides histories of the Jews from the fall of the Maccabees to the author's time, of the first four centuries of the Christian church, and of European diplomatists, extend over the whole range of French history. He died at Paris in December 1872.

The general catalogue of printed books for the Bibliothèque Nationale contains no fewer than seventy-seven works (145 volumes) published by Capefigue during forty years. Of these only the *Histoire de Philippe-Auguste*(4 vols., 1829) and the *Histoire de la réforme, de la ligue et du règne de Henri IV* (8 vols., 1834-1835) perhaps deserve still to be remembered. For Capefigue's style bears evident marks of haste, and although he had access to an exceptionally large number of sources of information, including the state papers, neither his accuracy nor his judgment was to be trusted.

CAPEL (OF HADHAM), **ARTHUR CAPEL,** BARON (fl. 1640-1649), English royalist, son of Sir Henry Capel of Rayne Hall, 249Essex, and of Theodosia, daughter of Sir Edward Montagu of Broughton, Northamptonshire, was elected a member of the Short and Long Parliaments in 1640 for Hertfordshire. He at first supported the opposition to Charles's arbitrary government, but soon allied himself with the king's cause, on which side his sympathies were engaged, and was raised to the peerage by the title of Baron Capel of Hadham on the 6th of August 1641. On the outbreak of the war he was appointed lieutenant-general of Shropshire, Cheshire and North Wales, where he rendered useful military services, and later was made one of the prince of Wales's councillors, and a commissioner at the negotiations at Uxbridge in 1645. He attended the queen in her flight to France in 1646, but disapproved of the prince's journey thither, and retired to Jersey, subsequently aiding in the king's escape to the Isle of Wight. He was one of the chief leaders in the second Civil War, but met with no success, and on the 27th of August, together with Lord Norwich, he surrendered to Fairfax at Colchester on promise of quarter for life.1 This assurance, however, was afterwards interpreted as not binding the civil authorities, and his fate for some time hung in the balance. He succeeded in escaping from the Tower, but was again captured, was condemned to death by the new "high court of justice" on the 8th of March 1649, and was beheaded together with the duke of Hamilton and Lord Holland the next day. He married Elizabeth, daughter and heir of Sir Charles Morrison of Cassiobury, Hertfordshire, through whom that estate passed into his family, and by whom besides four daughters he had five sons, the eldest Arthur being created earl of Essex at the Restoration. Lord Capel, who was much beloved, and who was a man of deep religious feeling and exemplary life, wrote *Daily Observations or Meditations: Divine, Morall,* published with some of his letters in 1654, and reprinted, with a short life of the author, under the title *Excellent Contemplations,* in 1683.

1Gardiner's *Hist. of the Civil War,* iv. 206; cf. article on Fairfax by C.H. Frith in the *Dict. of Nat. Biog.*

CAPEL CURIG, a tourist resort in Carnarvonshire, North Wales, 14½ m. from Bangor. It is a collection of a few houses, too scattered to form a village properly so called. At the Roberts hotel is shown on a window pane the supposed signature of Wellington. The road from Bettws y coed, past the Swallow Falls to Capel Curig, and thence to Llanberis and

Carnarvon, is very interesting, grand and lonely. Excellent fishing is to be had here, chiefly for trout. In summer, coaching tours discharge numbers of visitors daily; the railway station is Bettws (London & North-Western railway). Capel Curig means "chapel of Curig," a British saint mentioned in Welsh poetry. The place is a centre for artists, geologists and botanists, for the ascent of Snowdon, Moel Siabod, Glydyr Fawr, Glydyr Fach, Tryfan, &c., and for visiting Llyn Ogwen, Llyn Idwal, Twll du (Devil's Kitchen), Nant Ffrancon and the Penrhyn quarries.

CAPELL, EDWARD (1713-1781), English Shakespearian critic, was born at Troston Hall in Suffolk on the 11th of June 1713. Through the influence of the duke of Grafton he was appointed to the office of deputy-inspector of plays in 1737, with a salary of £200 per annum, and in 1745 he was made groom of the privy chamber through the same influence. In 1760 appeared his *Prolusions, or Select Pieces of Ancient Poetry*, a collection which included *Edward III.*, placed by Capell among the doubtful plays of Shakespeare. Shocked at the inaccuracies which had crept into Sir Thomas Hanmer's edition of Shakespeare, he projected an entirely new edition, to be carefully collated with the original copies. After spending three years in collecting, and comparing scarce folio and quarto editions, he published his own edition in 10 vols. 8vo (1768), with an introduction written in a style of extraordinary quaintness, which was afterwards appended to Johnson's and Steevens's editions. Capell published the first part of his commentary, which included notes on nine plays with a glossary, in 1774. This he afterwards recalled, and the publication of the complete work, *Notes and Various Readings of Shakespeare* (1779-1783), the third volume of which bears the title of *The School of Shakespeare*, was completed, under the superintendence of John Collins, in 1783, two years after the author's death. It contains the results of his unremitting labour for thirty years, and throws considerable light on the history of the times of Shakespeare, as well as on the sources from which he derived his plots. Collins asserted that Steevens had stolen Capell's notes for his own edition, the story being that the printers had been bribed to show Steevens the sheets of Capell's edition while it was passing through the press. Besides the works already specified, he published an edition of *Antony and Cleopatra*, adapted for the stage with the help of David Garrick in 1758. His edition of Shakespeare passed through many editions (1768, 1771, 1793, 1799, 1803, 1813). Capell died in the Temple on the 24th of February 1781.

CAPELLA, MARTIANUS MINNEUS FELIX, Latin writer, according to Cassiodorus a native of Madaura in Africa, flourished during the 5th century, certainly before the year 439. He appears to have practised as a lawyer at Carthage and to have been in easy circumstances. His curious encyclopaedic work, entitled *Satyricon*, or *De Nuptiis Philologiae et Mercurii et de septem Artibus liberalibus libri novem*, is an elaborate allegory in nine books, written in a mixture of prose and verse, after the manner of the Menippean satires of Varro. The style is heavy and involved, loaded with metaphor and bizarre expressions, and verbose to excess. The first two books contain the allegory proper—the marriage of Mercury to a nymph named Philologia. The remaining seven books contain expositions of the seven liberal arts, which then comprehended all human knowledge. Book iii. treats of grammar, iv. of dialectics, v. of rhetoric, vi. of geometry, vii. of arithmetic, viii. of astronomy, ix. of music. These abstract discussions are linked on to the original allegory by the device of personifying each science as a courtier of Mercury and Philologia. The work was a complete encyclopaedia of the liberal culture of the time, and was in high repute during the middle ages. The author's chief sources were Varro, Pliny, Solinus, Aquila Romanus, and Aristides Quintilianus. His prose resembles that of Apuleius (also a native of Madaura), but is even more difficult. The verse portions, which are on the whole correct and classically constructed, are in imitation of Varro and are less tiresome.

A passage in book viii. contains a very clear statement of the heliocentric system of astronomy. It has been supposed that Copernicus, who quotes Capella, may have received from this work some hints towards his own new system.

Editio princeps, by F. Vitalis Bodianus, 1499; the best modern edition is that of F. Eyssenhardt (1866); for the relation of Martianus Capella to Aristides Quintilianus see H.

Deiters, *Studien zu den griechischen Musikern*(1881). In the 11th century the German monk Notker Labeo translated the first two books into Old High German.

CAPE MAY, a city and watering-place of Cape May county, New Jersey, U.S.A., on the Atlantic coast, 2 m. E.N.E. of Cape May, the S. extremity of the state, and about 80 m. S. by E. of Philadelphia. Pop. (1890) 2136; (1900) 2257; (1905) 3006; (1910) 2471. Cape May is served by the Maryland, Delaware & Virginia (by ferry to Lewes, Delaware), the West Jersey & Seashore (Pennsylvania system), and the Atlantic City (Reading system) railways, and, during the summer season, by steamboat to Philadelphia. The principal part of the city is on a peninsula (formerly Cape Island) between the ocean and Cold Spring inlet, which has been dredged and is protected by jetties to make a suitable harbour. The further improvement of the inlet and the harbour was authorized by Congress in 1907. On the ocean side, along a hard sand beach 5 m. long, is the Esplanade. There are numerous hotels and handsome cottages for summer visitors, who come especially from Philadelphia, from New York, from the South and from the West. Cape May offers good bathing, yachting and fishing, with driving and hunting in the wooded country inland from the coast. At Cape May Point is the Cape May lighthouse, 145 ft. high, built in 1800 and rebuilt in 1859. In the city are canneries of vegetables and fruit, glass-works and a gold-beating establishment. Fish and oysters are exported. Cape May was named by Cornelis Jacobsen Mey, director of the Prince Hendrick (Delaware) river for the West India Company of 250Holland, who took possession of the river in 1623, and planted the short-lived colony of Fort Nassau 4 m. below Philadelphia, near the present Gloucester City, N.J. Cape May was settled about 1699,—a previous attempt to settle here made by Samuel Blommaert in 1631 was unsuccessful. It was an important whaling port early in the 18th century, and became prominent as a watering-place late in that century. It was incorporated as the borough of Cape Island in 1848, and chartered as the city of Cape Island in 1851; in 1869 the name was changed to Cape May.

CAPENA, an ancient city of southern Etruria, frequently mentioned with Veii and Falerii. Its exact site is, however, uncertain. According to Cato it was a colony of the former, and in the wars between Veii and Rome it appears as dependent upon Veii, after the fall of which town, however, it became subject to Rome. Out of its territory the *tribus Stellatina* was formed in 367 B.C. In later republican times the city itself is hardly mentioned, but under the empire a*municipium Capenatium foederatum* is frequently mentioned in inscriptions. Of these several were found upon the hill known as Civitucola, about 4 m. north-east of the post station of *ad Vicesimum* on the ancient Via Flaminia, a site which is well adapted for an ancient city. It lies on the north side of a dried-up lake, once no doubt a volcanic crater. Remains of buildings of the Roman period also exist there, while, in the sides of the hill of S. Martino which lies on the north-east,1 rock-cut tombs belonging to the 7th and 6th centuries B.C. but used in Roman times for fresh burials, were excavated in 1859-1864, and again in 1904. Inscriptions in early Latin and in local dialect were also found (W. Henzen, *Bullettino dell' Istituto*, 1864, 143; R. Paribeni, *Notizie degli Scavi*, 1905, 301). Similar tombs have also been found on the hills south of Civitucola. G.B. de Rossi, however, supposed that the games of which records (fragments of the *fasti ludorum*) were also discovered at Civitucola, were those which were celebrated from time immemorial at the Lucus Feroniae, with which he therefore proposed to identify this site, placing Capena itself at S. Oreste, on the south-eastern side of Mount Soracte. But there are difficulties in the way of this assumption, and it is more probable that the Lucus Feroniae is to be sought at or near Nazzano, where, in the excavation of a circular building which some conjecture to have been the actual temple of Feronia, inscriptions relating to a municipality were found. Others, however, propose to place Lucus Feroniae at the church of S. Abbondio, 1 m. east of Rignano and 4 m. north-north-west of Civitucola, which is built out of ancient materials. On the Via Flaminia, 26 m. from Rome, near Rignano, is the Christian cemetery of Theodora.

See R. Lanciani, *Bullettino dell' Istituto*, 1870, 32; G.B. de Rossi, *Annali dell' Istituto*, 1883, 254; *Bullettino Cristiano*, 1883, 115; G. Dennis, *Cities and Cemeteries of Etruria* (London, 1883), i. 131; E. Bormann, *Corpus Inscriptionum Latinarum* (Berlin, 1888), xi. 571; H. Nissen, *Italische Landeskunde* (Berlin, 1902), ii. 369; R. Paribeni, in *Monumenti dei Lincei*, xvi. (1906), 277 seq.

1Some writers wrongly speak as though the two hills were identical.

CAPER, FLAVIUS, Latin grammarian, flourished during the and century. He devoted special attention to the early Latin writers, and is highly spoken of by Priscian. Caper was the author of two works—*De Lingua Latina* and *De Dubiis Generibus.* These works in their original form are lost; but two short treatises entitled *De Orthographia* and *De Verbis Dubiis* have come down to us under his name, probably excerpts from the original works, with later additions by an unknown writer.

See F. Osann, *De Flavio Capro* (1849), and review by W. Christ in*Philologus*, xviii. 165-170 (1862), where several editions of other important grammarians are noticed; G. Keil, "De Flavio Grammatico," in*Dissertationes Halenses*, x. (1889); text in H. Keil's *Grammatici Latini*, vii.

CAPERCALLY, or CAPERKALLY,1 a bird's name commonly derived from the Gaelic *capull*, a horse (or, more properly, a mare), and *coille*, a wood, but with greater likelihood, according to the opinion of Dr M'Lauchlan, from*cabher*, an old man (and, by metaphor, an old bird), and *coille*, the name of*Tetrao urogallus*, the largest of the grouse family (*Tetraonidae*), and a species which was formerly indigenous to Scotland and Ireland. The word is frequently spelt otherwise, as capercalze, capercailzie (the z, a letter unknown in Gaelic, being pronounced like y), and capercaillie, and the English name of wood-grouse or cock-of-the-wood has been often applied to the same bird. The earliest notice of it as an inhabitant of North Britain seems to be by Hector Boethius, whose works were published in 1526, and it can then be traced through various Scottish writers, to whom, however, it was evidently but little known, for about 200 years, or may be more, and by one of them only, Bishop Lesley, in 1578, was a definite *habitat* assigned to it:—"In Rossia quoque Louguhabria [Lochaber], atque aliis montanis locis" (*De Origine Moribus et rebus gestis Scotorum.* Romae: ed. 1675, p. 24). Pennant, during one of his tours in Scotland, found that it was then (1769) still to be met with in Glen Moriston and in The Chisholm's country, whence he saw a cock-bird. We may infer that it became extinct about that time, since Robert Gray (*Birds of the West of Scotland*, p. 229) quotes the Rev. John Grant as writing in 1794: "The last seen in Scotland was in the woods of Strathglass about thirty-two years ago." Of its existence in Ireland we have scarcely more details. If we may credit the *Pavones sylvestres* of Giraldus Cambrensis with being of this species, it was once abundant there, and Willughby (1678) was told that it was known in that kingdom as the "cock-of-the-wood." A few other writers mention it by the same name, and John Rutty, in 1772, says (*Nat. Hist. Dublin*, i.p. 302) that "one was seen in the county of Leitrim about the year 1710, but they have entirely disappeared of late, by reason of the destruction of our woods." Pennant also states that about 1760 a few were to be found about Thomastown in Tipperary, but no later evidence is forthcoming, and thus it would seem that the species was exterminated at nearly the same period in both Ireland and Scotland.

When the practice of planting was introduced, the restoration of this fine bird to both countries was attempted. In Ireland the trial, of which some particulars are given by J. Vaughan Thompson (*Birds of Ireland*, ii. 32), was made at Glengariff, but it seems to have utterly failed, whereas in Scotland, where it was begun at Taymouth, it finally succeeded, and the species is now not only firmly established, but is increasing in numbers and range. Mr L. Lloyd, the author of several excellent works on the wild sports and natural history of Scandinavia, supplied the stock from Sweden, but it must be always borne in mind that the original British race was wholly extinct, and no remains of it are known to exist in any museum.

This species is widely, though intermittently, distributed on the continent of Europe, from Lapland to the northern parts of Spain, Italy and Greece, but is always restricted to pine-forests, which alone afford it food in winter. Its bones have been found in the kitchen-middens of Denmark, proving that country to have once been clothed with woods of that kind. Its remains have also been recognized from the caves of Aquitaine. Its eastern or southern limits in Asia cannot be precisely given, but it certainly inhabits the forests of a great part of Siberia. On the Stannovoi Mountains, however, it is replaced by a distinct though nearly allied species, the *T. urogalloides* of Dr von Middendorff,2 which is smaller with a slenderer bill but longer tail.

The cock-of-the-wood is remarkable for his large size and dark plumage, with the breast metallic green. He is polygamous, and in spring mounts to the topmost bough of a tall tree, whence he challenges all comers by extraordinary sounds and gestures; while the hens, which are much smaller and mottled in colour, timidly abide below the result of the frequent duels, patiently submitting themselves to the victor. While this is going on it is the practice in many countries, though generally in defiance 251of the law, for the so-called sportsman stealthily to draw nigh, and with well-aimed gun to murder the principal performer in the scene. The hen makes an artless nest on the ground, and lays therein from seven to nine or even more eggs. The young are able to fly soon after they are hatched, and towards the end of summer and beginning of autumn, from feeding on the fruit and leaves of the bilberries and other similar plants, which form the undercovert of the forests, get into excellent condition and become good eating. With the first heavy falls of snow they betake themselves to the trees, and then, feeding on the pine-leaves, their flesh speedily acquires so strong a flavour of turpentine as to be distasteful to most palates. The usual method of pursuing this species on the continent of Europe is by encouraging a trained dog to range the forest and spring the birds, which then perch on the trees; while he is baying at the foot their attention is so much attracted by him that they permit the near approach of his master, who thus obtains a more or less easy shot. A considerable number, however, are also snared. Hybrids are very frequently produced between the capercally and the black grouse (*T. tetrix*), and the offspring has been described by some authors under the name of *T. medius*, as though a distinct species.

(A. N.)

1This is the spelling of the old law-books, as given by Pennant, the zoologist, who, on something more than mere report, first included this bird among the British fauna. The only one of the "Scots Acts," however, in which the present writer has been able to ascertain that the bird is named is No. 30 of James VI. (1621), which was passed to protect "powties, partrikes, moore foulles, blakcoks, gray hennis, termigantis, quailzies, *capercailzies*," &c.

2Not to be confounded with the bird so named previously by Prof. Nilsson, which is a hybrid.

CAPERN, EDWARD (1819-1894), English poet, was born at Tiverton, Devonshire, on the 21st of January 1819. From an early age he worked in a lace factory, but owing to failing eyesight he had to abandon this occupation in 1847 and he was in dire distress until he secured an appointment to be "the Rural Postman of Bideford," by which name he is usually known. He occupied his leisure in writing occasional poetry which struck the popular fancy. Collected in a volume and published by subscription in 1856, it received the warm praise of the reviews and many distinguished people. *Poems, by Edward Capern*, was followed by *Ballads and Songs* (1858), *The Devonshire Melodist* (a collection of the author's songs, some of them to his own music) and *Wayside Warbles*(1865), and resulted in a civil list pension being granted him by Lord Palmerston. He died on the 5th of June 1894.

CAPERNAUM (Καπερναούμ; probably, "the village of Naḥum"), an ancient city of Galilee. More than any other place, it was the home of Jesus after he began his mission; there he preached, called several of his disciples, and did many works, but without meeting with much response from the inhabitants, over whom he pronounced the heavy denunciation:—"And thou, Capernaum, which art exalted unto heaven, shalt be brought down to hell." The site of the city has been a matter of much dispute,—one party, headed by Dr E. Robinson, maintaining an identification with Khan Minyeh at the north-west corner of the Sea of Galilee, and another, represented especially by Sir C.W. Wilson, supporting the claims of Tell Hum, midway between Khan Minyeh and the mouth of the Jordan. Khan Minyeh is beautifully situated in a "fertile plain formed by the retreat of the mountains about

5

the middle of the western shore" of the Sea of Galilee. Its ruins are not very extensive, though they may have been despoiled for building the great Saracenic Khan from which they take their name. In the neighbourhood is a water-source, *Ain et-Tābighah*, an Arabic corruption of *Heptapegon* or Seven Springs (referred to by Josephus as being near Capernaum). Tell Hum lies about 3 m. north of Khan Minyeh, and its ruins, covering an area of "half a mile long by a quarter wide," prove it to have been the site of no small town. It must be admitted that if it be not Capernaum it is impossible to say what ancient place it represents. But it is doubtful whether Tell Hūm can be considered as a corruption of *Kefr Nahum*, the Semitic name which the Greek represents: and there is not here, as at Khan Minyeh, any spring that can be equated to the Heptapegon of Josephus. On the whole the probabilities of the two sites seem to balance, and it is practically impossible without further discoveries to decide between them. The sites of the neighbouring cities of Bethsaida and Chorazin are probably to be sought respectively at El-Bateiha, a grassy plain in the north-east corner of the lake, and at Kerazeh, 2 m. north of Tell Hum. According to the so-called *Pseudo-Methodius* there was a tradition that Antichrist would be born at Chorazin, educated at Bethsaida and rule at Capernaum—hence the curse of Jesus upon these cities.

On the site of Capernaum see especially W. Sanday in *Journal of Theological Studies*, vol. v. p. 42.

(R. A. S. M.)

CAPERS, the unexpanded flower-buds of *Capparis spinosa*, prepared with vinegar for use as a pickle. The caper plant is a trailing shrub, belonging to the Mediterranean region, resembling in habit the common bramble, and having handsome flowers of a pinkish white, with four petals, and numerous long tassel-like stamens. The leaves are simple and ovate, with spiny stipules. The plant is cultivated in Sicily and the south of France; and in commerce capers are valued according to the period at which the buds are gathered and preserved. The finest are the young tender buds called "nonpareil," after which, gradually increasing in size and lessening in value, come "superfine," "fine," "capucin" and "capot." Other species of *Capparis* are similarly employed in various localities, and in some cases the fruit is pickled.

CAPET, the name of a family to which, for nearly nine centuries, the kings of France, and many of the rulers of the most powerful fiefs in that country, belonged, and which mingled with several of the other royal races of Europe. The original significance of the name remains in dispute, but the first of the family to whom it was applied was Hugh, who was elected king of the Franks in 987. The real founder of the house, however, was Robert the Strong (*q.v.*), who received from Charles the Bald, king of the Franks, the countships of Anjou and Blois, and who is sometimes called duke, as he exercised some military authority in the district between the Seine and the Loire. According to Aimoin of Saint-Germain-des-Prés, and the chronicler, Richer, he was a Saxon, but historians question this statement. Robert's two sons, Odo or Eudes, and Robert II., succeeded their father successively as dukes, and, in 887, some of the Franks chose Odo as their king. A similar step was taken, in 922, in the case of Robert II., this too marking the increasing irritation felt at the weakness of the Carolingian kings. When Robert died in 923, he was succeeded by his brother-in-law, Rudolph, duke of Burgundy, and not by his son Hugh, who is known in history as Hugh the Great, duke of France and Burgundy, and whose domain extended from the Loire to the frontiers of Picardy. When Louis V., king of the Franks, died in 987, the Franks, setting aside the Carolingians, passed over his brother Charles, and elected Hugh Capet, son of Hugh the Great, as their king, and crowned him at Reims. Avoiding the pretensions which had been made by the Carolingian kings, the Capetian kings were content, for a time, with a more modest position, and the story of the growth of their power belongs to the history of France. They had to combat the feudal nobility, and later, the younger branches of the royal house established in the great duchies, and the main reason for the permanence of their power was, perhaps, the fact that there were few minorities among them. The direct line ruled in France from 987 to 1328, when, at the death of King Charles

6

IV., it was succeeded by the younger, or Valois, branch of the family. Philip VI., the first of the Valois kings, was a son of Charles I., count of Valois and grandson of King Philip III. (see VALOIS). The Capetian-Valois dynasty lasted until 1498, when Louis, duke of Orleans, became king as Louis XII., on the death of King Charles VIII. (see ORLEANS). Louis XII. dying childless, the house of Valois-Angoulême followed from Francis I. to the death of Henry III. in 1589 (see ANGOULÊME), when the last great Capetian family, the Bourbons (*q.v.*) mounted the throne.

Scarcely second to the royal house is the branch to which belonged the dukes of Burgundy. In the 10th century the duchy of Burgundy fell into the hands of Hugh the Great, father of Hugh Capet, on whose death in 956 it passed to his son Otto, and, in 965, to his son Henry. In 1032 Robert, the second son of Robert the Pious, king of the Franks, and grandson of Hugh Capet, founded the first ducal house, which ruled until 1361. For two years the duchy was in the hands of the crown, but in 1363, the second ducal house, also Capetian, was founded by Philip the Bold, son of John II., king of France. This branch 252of the Capetians is also distinguished by its union with the Habsburgs, through the marriage of Mary, daughter of Charles the Bold, duke of Burgundy, with Maximilian, afterwards the emperor Maximilian I. Of great importance also was the house of the counts of Anjou, which was founded in 1246, by Charles, son of the French king Louis VIII., and which, in 1360, was raised to the dignity of a dukedom (see ANJOU). Members of this family sat upon the thrones of two kingdoms. The counts and dukes of Anjou were kings of Naples from 1265 to 1442. In 1308 Charles Robert of Anjou was elected king of Hungary, his claim being based on the marriage of his grandfather Charles II., king of Naples and count of Anjou, with Maria, daughter of Stephen V., king of Hungary. A third branch formed the house of the counts of Artois, which was founded in 1238 by Robert, son of King Louis VIII. This house merged in that of Valois in 1383, by the marriage of Margaret, daughter of Louis, count of Artois, with Philip the Bold, duke of Burgundy. The throne of Navarre was also filled by the Capetians. In 1284 Jeanne, daughter and heiress of Henry I., king of Navarre, married Philip IV., king of France, and the two kingdoms were united until Philip of Valois became king of France as Philip VI. in 1328, when Jeanne, daughter of King Louis X., and heiress of Navarre, married Philip, count of Evreux (see NAVARRE).

In the 13th century the throne of Constantinople was occupied by a branch of the Capetians. Peter, grandson of King Louis VI., obtained that dignity in 1217 as brother-in-law of the two previous emperors, Baldwin, count of Flanders, and his brother Henry. Peter was succeeded successively by his two sons, Robert and Baldwin, from whom in 1261 the empire was recovered by the Greeks.

The counts of Dreux, for two centuries and a half (1132-1377), and the counts of Evreux, from 1307 to 1425, also belonged to the family of the Capets,—other members of which worthy of mention are the Dunois and the Longuevilles, illegitimate branches of the house of Valois, which produced many famous warriors and courtiers.

CAPE TOWN, the capital of the Cape Province, South Africa, in 33° 56′ S., 18° 28′ E. It is at the north-west extremity of the Cape Peninsula on the south shore of Table Bay, is 6181 m. by sea from London and 957 by rail south-west of Johannesburg. Few cities are more magnificently situated. Behind the bay the massive wall of Table Mountain, 2 m. in length, rises to a height of over 3500 ft., while on the east and west projecting mountains enclose the plain in which the city lies. The mountain to the east, 3300 ft. high, which projects but slightly seawards, is the Devil's Peak, that to the west the Lion's Head (over 2000 ft. high), with a lesser height in front called the Lion's Rump or Signal Hill. The city, at first confined to the land at the head of the bay, has extended all round the shores of the bay and to the lower spurs of Table Mountain.

The purely Dutch aspect which Cape Town preserved until the middle of the 19th century has disappeared. Nearly all the stucco-fronted brick houses, with flat roofs and cornices and wide spreading *stoeps*, of the early Dutch settlers have been replaced by shops, warehouses and offices in styles common to English towns. Of the many fine public buildings which adorn the city scarcely any date before 1860. The mixture of races among the inhabitants, especially the presence of numerous Malays, who on all festive occasions appear in gorgeous raiment, gives additional animation and colour to the street scenes. The mosques with their cupolas and minarets, and houses built in Eastern fashion contrast curiously with the Renaissance style of most of the modern buildings, the medieval aspect of the castle and the quaint appearance of the Dutch houses still standing.

Chief Public Buildings.—The castle stands near the shore at the head of the bay. Begun in 1666 its usefulness as a fortress has long ceased, but it serves to link the city to its past. West of the castle is a large oblong space, the Parade Ground. A little farther west, at the foot of the central jetty is a statue of Van Riebeek, the first governor of the Cape. In a line with the jetty is Adderley Street, and its continuation Government Avenue. Adderley Street and the avenue make one straight road a mile long, and at its end are "the Gardens," as the suburbs built on the rising ground leading to Table Mountain are called. The avenue itself is fully half a mile long and is lined on either side with fine oak trees. In Adderley Street are the customs house and railway station, the Standard bank, the general post and telegraph offices, with a tower 120 ft. high, and the Dutch Reformed church. The church dates from 1699 and is the oldest church in South Africa. Of the original building only the clock tower (sent from Holland in 1727) remains. Government Avenue contains, on the east side, the Houses of Parliament, government house, a modernized Dutch building, and the Jewish synagogue; on the west side are the Anglican cathedral and grammar schools, the public library, botanic gardens, the museum and South African college. Many of these buildings are of considerable architectural merit, the material chiefly used in their construction being granite from the Paarl and red brick. The botanic gardens cover 14 acres, contain over 8000 varieties of trees and plants, and afford a magnificent view of Table Mountain and its companion heights. In the gardens, in front of the library is a statue of Sir George Grey, governor of the Cape from 1854 to 1861. The most valuable portion of the library is the 5000 volumes presented by Sir George Grey. In Queen Victoria Street, which runs along the west side of the gardens, are the Cape University buildings (begun in 1906), the law courts, City club and Huguenot memorial hall. The Anglican cathedral, begun in 1901 to replace an unpretentious building on the same site, is dedicated to St George. It lies between the library and St George's Street, in which are the chief newspaper offices, and premises of the wholesale merchants. West of St George's Street is Greenmarket Square, the centre of the town during the Dutch period. From the balcony of the town house, which overlooks the square, proclamations were read to the burghers, summoned to the spot by the ringing of the bell in the small-domed tower. Still farther west, in Riebeek Square, is the old slave market, now used as a church and school for coloured people.

Facing the north side of the Parade Ground are the handsome municipal buildings, completed in 1906. The most conspicuous feature is the clock tower and belfry, 200 ft. high. The hall is 130 ft. by 62, and 55 ft. high. Opposite the main entrance is a statue of Edward VII. by William Goscombe John, unveiled in 1905. The opera house occupies the north-west corner of the Parade Ground. Plein Street, which leads south from the Parade Ground, is noted for its cheap shops, largely patronized on Saturday nights by the coloured inhabitants. In Sir Lowry Road, the chief eastern thoroughfare, is the large vegetable and fruit market. Immediately west of the harbour are the convict station and Somerset hospital. They are built at the town end of Greenpoint Common, the open space at the foot of Signal Hill. Cape Town is provided with an excellent water supply and an efficient drainage system.

The Suburbs.—The suburbs of Cape Town, for natural beauty of position, are among the finest in the world. On the west they extend about 3 m., by Green Point to Sea Point, between the sea and the foot of the Lion's Rump; on the east they run round the foot of the Devil's Peak, by Woodstock, Mowbray, Rondebosch, Newlands, Claremont, &c., to Wynberg, a distance of 7 m. Though these are managed by various municipalities, there is practically no break in the buildings for the whole distance. All the parts are connected by the suburban railway service, and by an electric tramway system. A tramway also runs from the town over the Kloof, or pass between Table Mountain and the Lion's Head, to Camp's Bay, on the west coast south of Sea Point, to which place it is continued, the tramway thus completely circling the Lion's Head and Signal Hill. Of the suburbs mentioned, Green Point and Sea Point are seaside resorts, Woodstock being both a business and residential quarter.

Woodstock covers the ground on which the British, in 1806, defeated the Dutch, and contains the house in which the articles of capitulation were signed. Another seaside suburb is Milnerton on the north-east shores of Table Bay at the mouth of the Diep river. Near Maitland, and 3 m. from the city, is the Cape Town observatory, built in 25?1820 and maintained by the British government. Rondebosch, 5 m. from the city, contains some of the finest of the Dutch mansions in South Africa. Less than a mile from the station is Groote Schuur, a typical specimen of the country houses built by the Dutch settlers in the 17th century. The house was the property of Cecil Rhodes, and was bequeathed by him for the use of the prime minister of Federated South Africa. The grounds of the estate extend up the slopes of Table Mountain. At Newlands is Bishop's Court, the home of the archbishop of Cape Town. More distant suburbs to the south-east are Constantia, with a famous Dutch farm-house and wine farm, and Muizenberg and Kalk Bay, the two last villages on the shore of False Bay. At Muizenberg Cecil Rhodes died, 1902. Facing the Atlantic is Hout's Bay, 10 m. south-south-west of Wynberg.

Most of the suburbs and the city itself are exposed to the south-east winds which, passing over the flats which join the Cape Peninsula to the mainland, reach the city sand-laden. From its bracing qualities this wind, which blows in the summer, is known as the "Cape Doctor." During its prevalence Table Mountain is covered by a dense whitish-grey cloud, overlapping its side like a tablecloth.

The Harbour.—Table Bay, 20 m. wide at its entrance, is fully exposed to north and north-west gales. The harbour works, begun in 1860, afford sheltered accommodation for a large number of vessels. From the west end of the bay a breakwater extends north-east for some 4000 ft. East of the breakwater and parallel to it for 2700 ft. is the South pier. From breakwater and pier arms project laterally. In the area enclosed are the Victoria basin, covering 64 acres, the Alfred basin of 8½ acres, a graving dock 529 ft. long and a patent slip for vessels up to 1500 tons. There is good anchorage outside the Victoria basin under the lee of the breakwater, and since 1904 the foreshore east of the south pier has been reclaimed and additional wharfage provided. Altogether there are 2½ m. of quay walls, the wharfs being provided with electrical cranage. Cargo can be transferred direct from the ship into railway trucks. Vessels of the deepest draught can enter into the Victoria basin, the depth of water at low tide ranging from 24 to 36 ft.

Trade and Communication.—The port has a practical monopoly of the passenger traffic between the Cape and England. Several lines of steamers—chiefly British and German—maintain regular communication with Europe, the British mail boats taking sixteen days on the journey. By its railway connexions Cape Town affords the quickest means of reaching, from western Europe, every other town in South Africa. In the import trade Cape Town is closely rivalled by Port Elizabeth, but its export trade, which includes diamonds and bar gold, is fully 70% of that of the entire colony. In 1898, the year before the beginning of the Anglo-Boer war, the volume of trade was:—Imports £5,128,292, exports £15,881,952. In 1904, two years after the conclusion of the war the figures were:—imports £9,070,757; exports £17,471,760. In 1907 during a period of severe and prolonged trade depression the imports had fallen to £5,263,930, but the exports owing entirely to the increased output of gold from the Rand mines had increased to £37,994,658; gold and diamonds represented over £37,000,000 of this total. The tonnage of ships entering the harbour in 1887 was 801,033. In 1904 it had risen to 4,846,012 and in 1907 was 4,671,146. The trade of the port in tons was 1,276,350 in 1899 and 1,413,471 in 1904. In 1907 it had fallen to 658,721.

Defence.—Cape Town, being in the event of the closing of the Suez Canal on the main route of ships from Europe to the East, is of considerable strategic importance. It is defended by several batteries armed with modern heavy guns. It is garrisoned by Imperial and local troops, and is connected by railway with the naval station at Simon's Town on the east of the Cape Peninsula.

Population.—The Cape electoral division, which includes Cape Town, had in 1865 a population of 50,064, in 1875 57,319, in 1891 97,238, and in 1904 213,167, of whom 120,475 were whites. Cape Town itself had a population in 1875 of 33,000, in 1891 of 51,251 and in 1904 of 77,668. Inclusive of the nearer suburbs the population was 78,866 in 1891 and 170,083 in 1904. Of the inhabitants of the city proper 44,203 were white (1904). Of the coloured inhabitants 6561 were Malays; the remainder being chiefly of mixed blood. The most populous suburbs in 1904 were Woodstock with 28,990 inhabitants, and Wynberg with 18,477.

History and Local Government.—Cape Town was founded in 1652 by settlers sent from Holland by the Netherlands East India Co., under Jan van Riebeek. It came definitely into the possession of Great Britain in 1806. Its political history is indistinguishable from that of Cape Colony (*q.v.*). The town was granted municipal institutions in 1836. (Among the councillors returned at the election of 1904 was Dr Abdurrahman, a Mahommedan and a graduate of Edinburgh, this being, it is believed, the first instance of the election of a man of colour to any European representative body in South Africa.) The municipality owns the water and lighting services. The municipal rating value was, in 1880 £2,054,204, in 1901 £9,475,260, in 1908 (when the rate levied was 3d. in the £) £14,129,439. The total rateable value of the suburbs, not included in the above figures, is over £8,000,000. Rates are based on capital, not annual, value. The control of the port is vested in the Harbour and Railway Board of the Union.

Cape Town is the seat of the legislature of the Union of South Africa, of the provincial government, of the provincial division of the Supreme Court of South Africa, and of the Cape University; also of an archbishop of the Anglican and a bishop of the Roman Catholic churches.

CAPE VERDE ISLANDS (*Ilhas do Caba Verde*), an archipelago belonging to Portugal; off the West African coast, between 17° 13′ and 14° 47′ N. and 22° 40′ and 25° 22′ W. Pop. (1905) about 138,620; area, 1475 sq. m. The archipelago consists of ten islands:— Santo Antão (commonly miswritten St Antonio), São Vicente, Santa Luzia, São Nicolao, Sal, Boa Vista, Maio, São Thiago (the St Jago of the English), Fogo, and Brava, besides four uninhabited islets. It forms a sort of broken crescent, with the concavity towards the west. The last four islands constitute the leeward (Sotavento) group and the other six the windward (Barlavento). The distance between the coast of Africa and the nearest island (Boa Vista) is about 300 m. The islands derive their name, frequently but erroneously written "Cape Verd," or "Cape de Verd" Islands, from the African promontory off which they lie, known as Cape Verde, or the Green Cape. The entire archipelago is of volcanic origin, and on the island of Fogo there is an active volcano. No serious eruption has taken place since 1680, and the craters from which the streams of basalt issued have lost their outline.

Climate.—The atmosphere of the islands is generally hazy, especially in the direction of Africa. With occasional exceptions during summer and autumn, the north-east trade is the prevailing wind, blowing most strongly from November to May. The rainy season is during August, September and October, when there is thunder and a light variable wind from south-east or south-west. The Harmattan, a very dry east wind from the African continent, occasionally makes itself felt. The heat of summer is high, the thermometer ranging from 80° to 90° Fahr. near the sea. The unhealthy season is the period during and following the rains, when vegetation springs up with surprising rapidity, and there is much stagnant water, poisoning the air on the lower grounds. Remittent fevers are then common. The people of all the islands are also subject in May to an endemic of a bilious nature called locally *levadias*, but the cases rarely assume a dangerous form, and recovery is usually attained in three or four days without medical aid. On some of the islands rain has occasionally not fallen for three years. The immediate consequence is a failure of the crops, and this is followed by the death of great numbers from starvation, or the epidemics which usually break out afterwards.

Flora.—Owing largely to the widespread destruction of timber for fuel, and to the frequency of drought, the flora of the islands is poor when compared with that of the Canaries, the Azores or Madeira. It is markedly tropical in character; and although some seventy wild-flowers, grasses, ferns, &c., are peculiar to the archipelago, the majority of plants are those found on the neighbouring African littoral. Systematic afforestation has not been attempted, but the Portuguese have introduced a few trees, such as the baobab, eucalyptus and dragon-tree, besides many plants of economic value. Coffee-growing, an industry dating from 1790, is the chief resource of the people of Santo Antão, Fogo and São Thiago; maize, millet, sugar-cane, manioc, excellent oranges, pumpkins, sweet potatoes, and, to a less extent, tobacco and cotton are produced. On most of the islands coco-nut and date palms, tamarinds and bananas may be seen; orchil is gathered; and indigo and castor-oil are produced. Of considerable importance is the physic-nut (*Jatropha curcas*), which is exported.

Fauna.—Quails are found in all the islands; rabbits in Boa Vista, São Thiago and Fogo; wild boars in São Thiago. Both black and grey rats are common. Goats, horses and asses are reared, and goatskins are exported. The neighbouring sea abounds with fish, and coral fisheries are carried on by a colony of Neapolitans in São Thiago. Turtles come from the African coast to lay their eggs on the sandy shores. The Ilheu Branco, or White Islet, between São Nicolao and Santa Luzia, is remarkable as containing a variety of puffin unknown elsewhere, and a species of large lizard (*Macroscinctus coctei*) which feeds on plants.

Inhabitants.—The first settlers on the islands imported negro slaves from the African coast. Slavery continued in full force until 1854, when the Portuguese government freed the public slaves, and ameliorated the conditions of private ownership. In 1857 arrangements were made for the gradual abolition of slavery, and by 1876 the last slave had been liberated. The transportation of convicts from Portugal, a much-dreaded punishment, was continued until the closing years of the 19th century. It was the coexistence of these two forms of servitude, even more than the climate, which prevented any large influx of Portuguese colonists. Hence the blacks and mulattoes far outnumber the white inhabitants. They are, as a rule, taller than the Portuguese, and are of fine physique, with regular features but woolly hair. Slavery and the enervating climate have left their mark on the habits of the people, whose indolence and fatalism are perhaps their most obvious qualities. Their language is a bastard Portuguese, known as the *lingua creoula*. Their religion is Roman Catholicism, combined with a number of pagan beliefs and rites, which are fostered by the *curandeiros* or medicine men. These superstitions tend to disappear gradually before the advance of education, which has progressed considerably since 1867, when the first school, a lyceum, was opened in Ribeira Brava, the capital of São Nicolao. On all the inhabited islands, except Santa Luzia, there are churches and primary schools, conducted by the government or the priests. The children of the wealthier classes are sent to Lisbon for their education.

Government.—The archipelago forms one of the foreign provinces of Portugal, and is under the command of a governor-in-chief appointed by the crown. There are two principal judges, one for the windward and another for the leeward group, the former with his residence at São Nicolao, and the latter at Praia; and each island has a military commandant, a few soldiers, and a number of salaried officials, such as police, magistrates and custom-house directors. There is also an ecclesiastical establishment, with a bishop, dean and canons.

Industries.—The principal industries, apart from agriculture, are the manufacture of sugar, spirits, salt, cottons and straw hats and fish-curing. The average yearly value of the exports is about £60,000; that of the imports (including £200,000 for coal), about £350,000. The most important of the exports are coffee, physic-nuts, millet, sugar, spirits, salt, live animals, skins and fish. This trade is principally carried on with Lisbon and the Portuguese possessions on the west coast of Africa, and with passing vessels. The imports consist principally of coal, textiles, food-stuffs, wine, metals, tobacco, machinery, pottery and vegetables. Over 3000 vessels, with a total tonnage exceeding 3,500,000, annually enter the ports of the archipelago; the majority call at Mindello, on São Vicente, for coal, and do not receive or discharge any large quantities of cargo.

Santo Antão (pop. 25,000), at the extreme north-west of the archipelago, has an area of 265 sq. m. Its surface is very rugged and mountainous, abounding in volcanic craters, of which the chief is the Topoda Coroa (7300 ft.), also known as the Sugar-loaf. Mineral springs exist in many places. The island is the most picturesque, the healthiest, and, on its north-western slope, the best watered and most fertile of the archipelago. The south-eastern slope, shut out by lofty mountains from the fertilizing moisture of the trade-winds, has an entirely different appearance, black rocks, white pumice and red clay being its most characteristic features. Santo Antão produces large quantities of excellent coffee, besides sugar and fruit. It has several small ports, of which the chief are the sheltered and spacious Tarrafal Bay, on the south-west coast, and the more frequented Ponta do Sol, on the north-east, 8 m. from the capital, Ribeira Grande, a town of 4500 inhabitants. Cinchona is cultivated in the neighbourhood. In 1780 the slaves on Santo Antão were declared free, but this decree was not carried out. About the same time many white settlers, chiefly from the Canaries, entered the island, and introduced the cultivation of wheat.

São Vicente, or *St Vincent* (8000), lies near Santo Antão, on the south-east, and has an area of 75 sq. m. Its highest point is Monte Verde (2400 ft.). The whole island is as arid and sterile as the south-eastern half of Santo Antão, and for the same reason. It was practically uninhabited until 1795; in 1829 its population numbered about 100. Its harbour, an extinct crater on the north coast, with an entrance eroded by the sea, affords complete shelter from every wind. An English speculator founded a coaling station here in 1851, and the town of Mindello, also known as Porto Grande or St Vincent, grew up rapidly, and became the commercial centre of the archipelago. Most of the business is in English hands, and nine-tenths of the inhabitants understand English. Foodstuffs, wood and water are imported from Santo Antão, and the water is stored in a large reservoir at Mindello. São Vicente has a station for the submarine cable from Lisbon to Pernambuco in Brazil.

Santa Luzia, about 5 m. south-east, has an area of 18 sq. m., and forms a single estate, occupied only by the servants or the family of the proprietor. Its highest point is 885 ft. above sea-level. On the south-west it has a good harbour, visited by whaling and fishing boats. Much orchil was formerly gathered, and there is good pasturage for the numerous herds of cattle. A little to the south are the uninhabited islets of Branco and Razo.

São Nicolao, or *Nicolau* (12,000), a long, narrow, crescent-shaped island with an area of 126 sq. m., lies farther east, near the middle of the archipelago. Its climate is not very healthy. Maize, kidney-beans, manioc, sugar-cane and vines are cultivated; and in ordinary years grain is exported to the other islands. The interior is mountainous, and culminates in two peaks which can be seen for many leagues; one has the shape of a sugar-loaf, and is near the middle of the island; the other, Monte Gordo, is near the west end, and has a height of 4280 ft. All the other islands of the group can be seen from São Nicolao in clear weather. Vessels frequently enter Preguiça, or Freshwater Bay, near the south-east extremity of the island, for water and fresh provisions; and the custom-house is here. The island was one of the first colonized; in 1774 its inhabitants numbered 13,500, but famine subsequently caused a great decrease. The first capital, Lapa, at the end of a promontory on the south, 255was abandoned during the period of Spanish ascendancy over Portugal (1580-1640) in favour of Ribeira Brava (4000), on the north coast, a town which now has a considerable trade.

Sal (750), in the north-east of the archipelago, has an area of 75 sq. m. It was originally named *Lana*, or *Lhana* ("plain"), from the flatness of the greater part of its surface. It derives its modern name from a natural salt-spring, but most of the salt produced here is now obtained from artificial salt-pans. Towards the close of the 17th century it was inhabited only by a few shepherds, and by slaves employed in the salt-works. In 1705 it was entirely abandoned, owing to drought and consequent famine; and only in 1808 was the manufacture of salt resumed. A railway, the first built in Portuguese territory, was opened in 1835. The hostile Brazilian tariffs of 1889 for a time nearly destroyed the salt trade. Whales, turtles and fish are abundant, and dairy-farming is a prosperous industry. There are many small harbours, which render every part of the island easily accessible.

Boa Vista (2600), the most easterly island of the archipelago, has an area of 235 sq. m. It was named São Christovão by its discoverers in the 15th century. Its modern name, meaning "fair view," is singularly inappropriate, for with the exception of a few coco-nut trees there is no wood, and in the dry season the island seems nothing but an arid waste. The little vegetation that exists is in the bottom of ravines, where corn, beans and cotton are cultivated. The springs of good water are few. The coast is indented by numerous shallow bays, the largest of which is the harbour of the capital, Porto Sal-Rei, on the western side (pop. about 1000). A chain of heights, flanked by inferior ranges, traverses the middle of Boa Vista, culminating in Monte Gallego (1250 ft.), towards the east. In the north-western angle of the island there is a low tract of loose sand, which is inundated with water during the rainy season; and here are some extensive salt-pans, where the sea-water is evaporated by the heat of the sun. Salt and orchil are exported. A good deal of fish is taken on the coast and supplies the impoverished islanders with much of their food.

Maio (1000) has an area of 70 sq. m., and resembles Sal and Boa Vista in climate and configuration, although it belongs to the Sotavento group. Its best harbour is that of Nossa Senhora da Luz, on the south-west coast, and is commonly known as Porto Inglez or English Road, from the fact that it was occupied until the end of the 18th century by the British, who based their claim on the marriage-treaty between Charles II. and Catherine of Braganza (1662). The island is a barren, treeless waste, surrounded by rocks. Its inhabitants, who live chiefly by the manufacture of salt, by cattle-farming and by fishing, are compelled to import most of their provisions from São Thiago, with which, for purposes of local administration, Maio is included.

São Thiago (63,000) is the most populous and the largest of the Cape Verde Islands, having an area of 350 sq. m. It is also one of the most unhealthy, except among the mountains over 2000 ft. high. The interior is a mass of volcanic heights, formed of basalt covered with chalk and clay, and culminating in the central Pico da Antonia (4500 ft.), a sharply pointed cone. There are numerous ravines, furrowed by perennial streams, and in these ravines are grown large quantities of coffee, oranges, sugar-cane and physic-nuts, besides a variety of tropical fruits and cereals. Spirits are distilled from sugar-cane, and coarse sugar is manufactured. The first capital of the islands was Ribeira Grande, to-day called Cidade Velha or the Old City, a picturesque town with a cathedral and ruined fort. It was built in the 15th century on the south coast, was made an episcopal see in 1532, and became capital of the archipelago in 1592. In 1712 it was sacked by a French force, but despite its poverty and unhealthy situation it continued to be the capital until 1770, when its place was taken by Praia on the south-east. Praia (often written Praya) has a fine harbour, a population of 21,000 and a considerable trade. It contains the palace of the governor-general, a small natural history museum, a meteorological observatory and an important station for the cables between South America, Europe and West Africa. It occupies a basalt plateau, overlooking the bay (Porto da Praia), and has an attractive appearance, with its numerous coco-nut trees and the peak of Antonia rising in the background above successive steps of tableland. Its unhealthiness has been mitigated by the partial drainage of a marsh lying to the east.

Fogo (17,600) is a mass of volcanic rock, almost circular in shape and measuring about 190 sq. m. In the centre a still active volcano, the Pico do Cano, rises to a height of about 10,000 ft. Its crater, which stands within an older crater, measures 3 m. in circumference and is visible at sea for nearly 100 m. It emits smoke and ashes at intervals; and in 1680, 1785, 1799, 1816, 1846, 1852 and 1857 it was in eruption. After the first and most serious of these outbreaks, the island, which had previously been called São Felippe, was renamed Fogo, *i.e.* "Fire." The ascent of the mountain was first made in 1819 by two British naval officers, named Vidal and Mudge. The island is divided, like Santo Antão, into a fertile and a sterile zone. Its northern half produces fine coffee, beans, maize and sugar-cane; the southern half is little better than a desert, with oases of cultivated land near its few springs. São Felippe or Nossa Senhora da Luz (3000), on the west coast, is the capital. The islanders claim to be the aristocracy of the archipelago, and trace their descent from the original Portuguese settlers. The majority, however, are negroes or mulattoes. Drought and famine, followed by severe epidemics, have been especially frequent here, notably in the years 1887-1889.

Brava (9013), the most southerly of the islands, has an area of 23 sq. m. Though mountainous, and in some parts sterile, it is very closely cultivated, and, unlike the other islands, is divided into a multitude of small holdings. The desire to own land is almost universal, and as the population numbers upwards of 380 per sq. m., and the system of tenure gives rise to many disputes, the peasantry are almost incessantly engaged in litigation. The women, who are locally celebrated for their beauty, far outnumber the men, who emigrate at an early age to America. These emigrants usually return richer and better educated than the peasantry of the neighbouring islands. To the north of Brava lie a group of reefs among which two islets (Ilheus Seccos or Ilheus do Rombo) are conspicuous. These are usually known as the Ilheu de Dentro (Inner Islet) and the Ilheu de Fóra (Outer Islet).

The first is used as a shelter for whaling and fishing vessels, and as pasturage for cattle; the second has supplied much guano for export.

History.—The earliest known discovery of the islands was made in 1456 by the Venetian captain Alvise Cadamosto (*q.v.*), who had entered the service of Prince Henry the Navigator. The archipelago was granted by King Alphonso V. of Portugal to his brother, Prince Ferdinand, whose agents completed the work of discovery. Ferdinand was an absolute monarch, exercising a commercial monopoly. In 1461 he sent an expedition to recruit slaves on the coast of Guinea and thus to people the islands, which were almost certainly uninhabited at the time. On his death in 1470 his privileges reverted to the crown, and were bestowed by John II. on Prince Emanuel, by whose accession to the throne in 1495 the archipelago finally became part of the royal dominions. Its population and importance rapidly increased; its first bishop was consecrated in 1532, its first governor-general appointed about the end of the century. It was enriched by the frequent visits of Portuguese fleets, on their return to Europe laden with treasure from the East, and by the presence of immigrants from Madeira, who introduced better agricultural methods and several new industries, such as dyeing and distillation of spirits. The failure to maintain an equal rate of progress in the 18th and 19th centuries was due partly to drought, famine and disease—in particular, to the famines of 1730-1733 and 1831-1833—and partly to gross misgovernment by the Portuguese officials.

The best general account of the islands is given in vols. xxiii. and xxvii. of the *Boletim* of the Lisbon Geographical Society (1905 and 1908), and in*Madeira, Cabo Verde, e Guiné,* by J.A. Martins (Lisbon, 1891). Official statistics are published in Lisbon at irregular intervals. See also *Über die Capverden* (Leipzig, 1884) and *Die Vulcane der Capverden* (Graz, 1882), both by C. Dölter. A useful map, entitled *Ocean Atlantico Norte, Archipelago do Cabo Verde,* was issued in 1900 by the *Commissão de Cartographia,* Lisbon.

CAPGRAVE, JOHN (1393-1464), English chronicler and hagiologist, was born at Lynn in Norfolk on the 21st of April 1393. He became a priest, took the degree of D.D. at Oxford, where he lectured on theology, and subsequently joined the order of Augustinian hermits. Most of his life he spent in the house of the order at Lynn, of which he probably became prior; he was certainly provincial of his order in England, which involved visits to other friaries, and he made at least one journey to Rome. He died on the 12th of August 1464.

Capgrave was an indefatigable student, and was reputed one of the most learned men of his age. The bulk of his works are theological: sermons, commentaries and lives of saints. His reputation as a hagiologist rests on his*Nova legenda Angliae,* or *Catalogus* of the English saints, but this was no more than a recension of the *Sanctilogium* which the chronicler John of Tinmouth, a monk of St Albans, had completed in 1366, which in its turn was largely borrowed from the *Sanctilogium* of Guido, abbot of St Denis. The *Nova legenda*was printed by Wynkyn de Worde in 1516 and again in 1527. Capgrave's historical works are *The Chronicle of England* (from the Creation to 1417), written in English and unfinished at his death, and the *Liber de illustribus Henricis,* completed between 1446 and 1453. The latter is a collection of lives of German emperors (918-1198), English kings (1100-1446) and other famous Henries in various parts of the world (1031-1406). The portion devoted to Henry VI. of England is a contemporary record, but consists mainly of ejaculations in praise of the pious king. The accounts of the 256other English Henries are transferred from various well-known chroniclers. The *Chronicle* was edited for the "Rolls" Series by Francis Charles Hingeston (London, 1858); the *Liber de illustrious Henricis* was edited (London, 1858) for the same series by F.C. Hingeston, who published an English translation the same year. The editing of both the works is very uncritical and bad.

See Potthast, *Bibliotheka Med. Aev.*; and U. Chevalier, *Répertoire des sources hist. Bio-bibliographie, s.v.*

CAP HAITIEN, CAPE HAÏTIEN or HAYTIEN, a seaport of Haiti West Indies. Pop. about 15,000. It is situated on the north coast, 90 m. N. of Port au Prince, in 19° 46' N. and

72° 14′ W. Its original Indian name was Guarico, and it has been known, at various times, as Cabo Santo, Cap Français and Cape Henri, while throughout Haiti it is always called Le Cap. It is the most picturesque town in the republic, and the second in importance. On three sides it is hemmed in by lofty mountains, while on the fourth it overlooks a safe and commodious harbour. Under the French rule it was the capital of the colony, and its splendour, wealth and luxury earned for it the title of the "Paris of Haiti." It was then the see of an archbishop and possessed a large and flourishing university. The last remains of its former glory were destroyed by the earthquake of 1842 and the British bombardment of 1865. Although now but a collection of squalid wooden huts, with here and there a well-built warehouse, it is the centre of a thriving district and does a large export trade. It was founded by the Spaniards about the middle of the 17th century, and in 1687 received a large French colony. In 1695 it was taken and burned by the British, and in 1791 it suffered the same fate at the hands of Toussaint L'Ouverture. It then became the capital of King Henri Christophe's dominions, but since his fall has suffered severely in numerous revolutions.

CAPILLARY ACTION.1 A tube, the bore of which is so small that it will only admit a hair (Lat. *capilla*), is called a capillary tube. When such a tube of glass, open at both ends, is placed vertically with its lower end immersed in water, the water is observed to rise in the tube, and to stand within the tube at a higher level than the water outside. The action between the capillary tube and the water has been called capillary action, and the name has been extended to many other phenomena which have been found to depend on properties of liquids and solids similar to those which cause water to rise in capillary tubes.

The forces which are concerned in these phenomena are those which act between neighbouring parts of the same substance, and which are called forces of cohesion, and those which act between portions of matter of different kinds, which are called forces of adhesion. These forces are quite insensible between two portions of matter separated by any distance which we can directly measure. It is only when the distance becomes exceedingly small that these forces become perceptible. G.H. Quincke (*Pogg. Ann.* cxxxvii. p. 402) made experiments to determine the greatest distance at which the effect of these forces is sensible, and he found for various substances distances about the twenty-thousandth part of a millimetre.

Historical.—According to J.C. Poggendorff (*Pogg. Ann.* ci. p. 551), Leonardo da Vinci must be considered as the discoverer of capillary phenomena, but the first accurate observations of the capillary action of tubes and glass plates were made by Francis Hawksbee (*Physico-Mechanical Experiments*, London, 1709, pp. 139-169; and *Phil. Trans.*, 1711 and 1712), who ascribed the action to an attraction between the glass and the liquid. He observed that the effect was the same in thick tubes as in thin, and concluded that only those particles of the glass which are very near the surface have any influence on the phenomenon. Dr James Jurin (*Phil. Trans.*, 1718, p. 739, and 1719, p. 1083) showed that the height at which the liquid is suspended depends on the section of the tube at the surface of the liquid, and is independent of the form of the lower part of the tube. He considered that the suspension of the liquid is due to "the attraction of the periphery or section of the surface of the tube to which the upper surface of the water is contiguous and coheres." From this he showed that the rise of the liquid in tubes of the same substance is inversely proportional to their radii. Sir Isaac Newton devoted the 31st query in the last edition of his *Opticks* to molecular forces, and instanced several examples of the cohesion of liquids, such as the suspension of mercury in a barometer tube at more than double the height at which it usually stands. This arises from its adhesion to the tube, and the upper part of the mercury sustains a considerable tension, or negative pressure, without the separation of its parts. He considered the capillary phenomena to be of the same kind, but his explanation is not sufficiently explicit with respect to the nature and the limits of the action of the attractive force.

It is to be observed that, while these early speculators ascribe the phenomena to attraction, they do not distinctly assert that this attraction is sensible only at insensible distances, and that for all distances which we can directly measure the force is altogether insensible. The idea of such forces, however, had been distinctly formed by Newton, who

15

gave the first example of the calculation of the effect of such forces in his theorem on the alteration of the path of a light-corpuscle when it enters or leaves a dense body.

Alexis Claude Clairault (*Théorie de la figure de la terre*, Paris, 1808, pp. 105, 128) appears to have been the first to show the necessity of taking account of the attraction between the parts of the fluid itself in order to explain the phenomena. He did not, however, recognize the fact that the distance at which the attraction is sensible is not only small but altogether insensible. J.A. von Segner (*Comment. Soc. Reg. Götting.* i. (1751) p. 301) introduced the very important idea of the surface-tension of liquids, which he ascribed to attractive forces, the sphere of whose action is so small "ut nullo adhuc sensu percipi potuerit." In attempting to calculate the effect of this surface-tension in determining the form of a drop of the liquid, Segner took account of the curvature of a meridian section of the drop, but neglected the effect of the curvature in a plane at right angles to this section.

The idea of surface-tension introduced by Segner had a most important effect on the subsequent development of the theory. We may regard it as a physical fact established by experiment in the same way as the laws of the elasticity of solid bodies. We may investigate the forces which act between finite portions of a liquid in the same way as we investigate the forces which act between finite portions of a solid. The experiments on solids lead to certain laws of elasticity expressed in terms of coefficients, the values of which can be determined only by experiments on each particular substance. Various attempts have also been made to deduce these laws from particular hypotheses as to the action between the molecules of the elastic substance. We may therefore regard the theory of elasticity as consisting of two parts. The first part establishes the laws of the elasticity of a finite portion of the solid subjected to a homogeneous strain, and deduces from these laws the equations of the equilibrium and motion of a body subjected to any forces and displacements. The second part endeavours to deduce the facts of the elasticity of a finite portion of the substance from hypotheses as to the motion of its constituent molecules and the forces acting between them. In like manner we may by experiment ascertain the general fact that the surface of a liquid is in a state of tension similar to that of a membrane stretched equally in all directions, and prove that this tension depends only on the nature and temperature of the liquid and not on its form, and from this as a secondary physical principle we may deduce all the phenomena of capillary action. This is one step of the investigation. The next step is to deduce this surface-tension from a hypothesis as to the molecular constitution of the liquid and of the bodies that surround it. The scientific importance of this step is to be measured by the degree of insight which it affords or promises into the molecular constitution of real bodies by the suggestion of experiments by which we may discriminate between rival molecular theories.

257

In 1756 J.G. Leidenfrost (*De aquae communis nonnullis qualitatibus tractatus*, Duisburg) showed that a soap-bubble tends to contract, so that if the tube with which it was blown is left open the bubble will diminish in size and will expel through the tube the air which it contains. He attributed this force, however, not to any general property of the surfaces of liquids, but to the fatty part of the soap which he supposed to separate itself from the other constituents of the solution, and to form a thin skin on the outer face of the bubble.

In 1787 Gaspard Monge (*Mémoires de l'Acad. des Sciences*, 1787, p. 506) asserted that "by supposing the adherence of the particles of a fluid to have a sensible effect only at the surface itself and in the direction of the surface it would be easy to determine the curvature of the surfaces of fluids in the neighbourhood of the solid boundaries which contain them; that these surfaces would be *lineariae* of which the tension, constant in all directions, would be everywhere equal to the adherence of two particles, and the phenomena of capillary tubes would then present nothing which could not be determined by analysis." He applied this principle of surface-tension to the explanation of the apparent attractions and repulsions between bodies floating on a liquid.

In 1802 John Leslie (*Phil. Mag.*, 1802, vol. xiv. p. 193) gave the first correct explanation of the rise of a liquid in a tube by considering the effect of the attraction of the solid on the very thin stratum of the liquid in contact with it. He did not, like the earlier speculators, suppose this attraction to act in an upward direction so as to support the fluid directly. He showed that the attraction is everywhere normal to the surface of the solid. The

16

direct effect of the attraction is to increase the pressure of the stratum of the fluid in contact with the solid, so as to make it greater than the pressure in the interior of the fluid. The result of this pressure if unopposed is to cause this stratum to spread itself over the surface of the solid as a drop of water is observed to do when placed on a clean horizontal glass plate, and this even when gravity opposes the action, as when the drop is placed on the under surface of the plate. Hence a glass tube plunged into water would become wet all over were it not that the ascending liquid film carries up a quantity of other liquid which coheres to it, so that when it has ascended to a certain height the weight of the column balances the force by which the film spreads itself over the glass. This explanation of the action of the solid is equivalent to that by which Gauss afterwards supplied the defect of the theory of Laplace, except that, not being expressed in terms of mathematical symbols, it does not indicate the mathematical relation between the attraction of individual particles and the final result. Leslie's theory was afterwards treated according to Laplace's mathematical methods by James Ivory in the article on capillary action, under "Fluids, Elevation of," in the supplement to the fourth edition of the *Encyclopaedia Britannica*, published in 1819.

In 1804 Thomas Young (Essay on the "Cohesion of Fluids," *Phil. Trans.*, 1805, p. 65) founded the theory of capillary phenomena on the principle of surface-tension. He also observed the constancy of the angle of contact of a liquid surface with a solid, and showed how from these two principles to deduce the phenomena of capillary action. His essay contains the solution of a great number of cases, including most of those afterwards solved by Laplace, but his methods of demonstration, though always correct, and often extremely elegant, are sometimes rendered obscure by his scrupulous avoidance of mathematical symbols. Having applied the secondary principle of surface-tension to the various particular cases of capillary action, Young proceeded to deduce this surface-tension from ulterior principles. He supposed the particles to act on one another with two different kinds of forces, one of which, the attractive force of cohesion, extends to particles at a greater distance than those to which the repulsive force is confined. He further supposed that the attractive force is constant throughout the minute distance to which it extends, but that the repulsive force increases rapidly as the distance diminishes. He thus showed that at a curved part of the surface, a superficial particle would be urged towards the centre of curvature of the surface, and he gave reasons for concluding that this force is proportional to the sum of the curvatures of the surface in two normal planes at right angles to each other.

The subject was next taken up by Pierre Simon Laplace (*Mécanique céleste*, supplement to the tenth book, pub. in 1806). His results are in many respects identical with those of Young, but his methods of arriving at them are very different, being conducted entirely by mathematical calculations. The form into which he threw his investigation seems to have deterred many able physicists from the inquiry into the ulterior cause of capillary phenomena, and induced them to rest content with deriving them from the fact of surface-tension. But for those who wish to study the molecular constitution of bodies it is necessary to study the effect of forces which are sensible only at insensible distances; and Laplace has furnished us with an example of the method of this study which has never been surpassed. Laplace investigated the force acting on the fluid contained in an infinitely slender canal normal to the surface of the fluid arising from the attraction of the parts of the fluid outside the canal. He thus found for the pressure at a point in the interior of the fluid an expression of the form

$$p = K + \tfrac{1}{2}H(1/R + 1/R'),$$

where K is a constant pressure, probably very large, which, however, does not influence capillary phenomena, and therefore cannot be determined from observation of such phenomena; H is another constant on which all capillary phenomena depend; and R and R' are the radii of curvature of any two normal sections of the surface at right angles to each other.

In the first part of our own investigation we shall adhere to the symbols used by Laplace, as we shall find that an accurate knowledge of the physical interpretation of these symbols is necessary for the further investigation of the subject. In the *Supplement to the Theory of Capillary Action*, Laplace deduced the equation of the surface of the fluid from the condition that the resultant force on a particle at the surface must be normal to the surface. His explanation, however, of the rise of a liquid in a tube is based on the *assumption* of the constancy of the angle of contact for the same solid and fluid, and of this he has nowhere given a satisfactory proof. In this supplement Laplace gave many important applications of the theory, and compared the results with the experiments of Louis Joseph Gay Lussac.

The next great step in the treatment of the subject was made by C.F. Gauss (*Principia generalia Theoriae Figurae Fluidorum in statu Aequilibrii*, Göttingen, 1830, or *Werke*, v. 29, Göttingen, 1867). The principle which he adopted is that of virtual velocities, a principle which under his hands was gradually transforming itself into what is now known as the principle of the conservation of energy. Instead of calculating the direction and magnitude of the resultant force on each particle arising from the action of neighbouring particles, he formed a single expression which is the aggregate of all the potentials arising from the mutual action between pairs of particles. This expression has been called the force-function. With its sign reversed it is now called the potential energy of the system. It consists of three parts, the first depending on the action of gravity, the second on the mutual action between the particles of the fluid, and the third on the action between the particles of the fluid and the particles of a solid or fluid in contact with it.

The condition of equilibrium is that this expression (which we may for the sake of distinctness call the potential energy) shall be a minimum. This condition when worked out gives not only the equation of the free surface in the form already established by Laplace, but the conditions of the angle of contact of this surface with the surface of a solid.

Gauss thus supplied the principal defect in the great work of Laplace. He also pointed out more distinctly the nature of the assumptions which we must make with respect to the law of action of the particles in order to be consistent with observed phenomena. He did not, however, enter into the explanation of particular phenomena, as this had been done already by Laplace, but he pointed out to physicists the advantages of the 258method of Segner and Gay Lussac, afterwards carried out by Quincke, of measuring the dimensions of large drops of mercury on a horizontal or slightly concave surface, and those of large bubbles of air in transparent liquids resting against the under side of a horizontal plate of a substance wetted by the liquid.

In 1831 Siméon Denis Poisson published his *Nouvelle Théorie de l'action capillaire*. He maintained that there is a rapid variation of density near the surface of a liquid, and he gave very strong reasons, which have been only strengthened by subsequent discoveries, for believing that this is the case. He proceeded to an investigation of the equilibrium of a fluid on the hypothesis of uniform density, and arrived at the conclusion that on this hypothesis none of the observed capillary phenomena would take place, and that, therefore, Laplace's theory, in which the density is supposed uniform, is not only insufficient but erroneous. In particular he maintained that the constant pressure K, which occurs in Laplace's theory, and which on that theory is very large, must be in point of fact very small, but the equation of equilibrium from which he concluded this is itself defective. Laplace assumed that the liquid has uniform density, and that the attraction of its molecules extends to a finite though insensible distance. On these assumptions his results are certainly right, and are confirmed by the independent method of Gauss, so that the objections raised against them by Poisson fall to the ground. But whether the assumption of uniform density be physically correct is a very different question, and Poisson rendered good service to science in showing how to carry on the investigation on the hypothesis that the density very near the surface is different from that in the interior of the fluid.

The result, however, of Poisson's investigation is practically equivalent to that already obtained by Laplace. In both theories the equation of the liquid surface is the same, involving a constant H, which can be determined only by experiment. The only difference is in the manner in which this quantity H depends on the law of the molecular forces and the law of density near the surface of the fluid, and as these laws are unknown to us we cannot obtain any test to discriminate between the two theories.

We have now described the principal forms of the theory of capillary action during its earlier development. In more recent times the method of Gauss has been modified so as to

18

take account of the variation of density near the surface, and its language has been translated in terms of the modern doctrine of the conservation of energy.2

J.A.F. Plateau (*Statique expérimentale et théorique des liquides*), who made elaborate study of the phenomena of surface-tension, adopted the following method of getting rid of the effects of gravity. He formed a mixture of alcohol and water of the same density as olive oil, and then introduced a quantity of oil into the mixture. It assumes the form of a sphere under the action of surface-tension alone. He then, by means of rings of iron-wire, disks and other contrivances, altered the form of certain parts of the surface of the oil. The free portions of the surface then assume new forms depending on the equilibrium of surface-tension. In this way he produced a great many of the forms of equilibrium of a liquid under the action of surface-tension alone, and compared them with the results of mathematical investigation. He also greatly facilitated the study of liquid films by showing how to form a liquid, the films of which will last for twelve or even for twenty-four hours. The debt which science owes to Plateau is not diminished by the fact that, while investigating these beautiful phenomena, he never himself saw them, having lost his sight in about 1840.

G.L. van der Mensbrugghe (*Mém. de l'Acad. Roy. de Belgique*, xxxvii., 1873) devised a great number of beautiful illustrations of the phenomena of surface-tension, and showed their connexion with the experiments of Charles Tomlinson on the figures formed by oils dropped on the clean surface of water.

Athanase Dupré in his 5th, 6th and 7th Memoirs on the Mechanical Theory of Heat (*Ann. de Chimie et de Physique*, 1866-1868) applied the principles of thermodynamics to capillary phenomena, and the experiments of his son Paul were exceedingly ingenious and well devised, tracing the influence of surface-tension in a great number of very different circumstances, and deducing from independent methods the numerical value of the surface-tension. The experimental evidence which Dupré obtained bearing on the molecular structure of liquids must be very valuable, even if our present opinions on this subject should turn out to be erroneous.

F.H.R. Lüdtge (*Pogg. Ann.* cxxxix. p. 620) experimented on liquid films, and showed how a film of a liquid of high surface-tension is replaced by a film of lower surface-tension. He also experimented on the effects of the thickness of the film, and came to the conclusion that the thinner a film is, the greater is its tension. This result, however, was tested by Van der Mensbrugghe, who found that the tension is the same for the same liquid whatever be the thickness, as long as the film does not burst. [The continued coexistence of various thicknesses, as evidenced by the colours in the same film, affords an instantaneous proof of this conclusion.] The phenomena of very thin liquid films deserve the most careful study, for it is in this way that we are most likely to obtain evidence by which we may test the theories of the molecular structure of liquids.

Sir W. Thomson (afterwards Lord Kelvin) investigated the effect of the curvature of the surface of a liquid on the thermal equilibrium between the liquid and the vapour in contact with it. He also calculated the effect of surface-tension on the propagation of waves on the surface of a liquid, and determined the minimum velocity of a wave, and the velocity of the wind when it is just sufficient to disturb the surface of still water.

THEORY OF CAPILLARY ACTION

When two different fluids are placed in contact, they may either diffuse into each other or remain separate. In some cases diffusion takes place to a limited extent, after which the resulting mixtures do not mix with each other. The same substance may be able to exist in two different states at the same temperature and pressure, as when water and its saturated vapour are contained in the same vessel. The conditions under which the thermal and mechanical equilibrium of two fluids, two mixtures, or the same substance in two physical states in contact with each other, is possible belong to thermodynamics. All that we have to observe at present is that, in the cases in which the fluids do not mix of themselves, the potential energy of the system must be greater when the fluids are mixed than when they are separate.

It is found by experiment that it is only very close to the bounding surface of a liquid that the forces arising from the mutual action of its parts have any resultant effect on one of its particles. The experiments of Quincke and others seem to show that the extreme range of the forces which produce capillary action lies between a thousandth and a twenty-thousandth part of a millimetre.

We shall use the symbol ε to denote this extreme range, beyond which the action of these forces may be regarded as insensible. If χ denotes the potential energy of unit of mass of the substance, we may treat χ as sensibly constant except within a distance ε of the bounding surface of the fluid. In the interior of the fluid it has the uniform value $\chi 0$. In like manner the density, ρ, is sensibly equal to the constant quantity $\rho 0$, which is its value in the interior of the liquid, except within a distance ε of the bounding surface. Hence if V is the volume of a mass M of liquid bounded by a surface whose area is S, the integral

$$M = \iiint \rho \, dxdydz, \qquad (1)$$

where the integration is to be extended throughout the volume 259V, may be divided into two parts by considering separately the thin shell or skin extending from the outer surface to a depth ε, within which the density and other properties of the liquid vary with the depth, and the interior portion of the liquid within which its properties are constant.

Since ε is a line of insensible magnitude compared with the dimensions of the mass of liquid and the principal radii of curvature of its surface, the volume of the shell whose surface is S and thickness ε will be Sε, and that of the interior space will be V − Sε.

If we suppose a normal v less than ε to be drawn from the surface S into the liquid, we may divide the shell into elementary shells whose thickness is dv, in each of which the density and other properties of the liquid will be constant.

The volume of one of these shells will be Sdv. Its mass will be Sρdv. The mass of the whole shell will therefore be $S \int \varepsilon 0 \, \rho dv$, and that of the interior part of the liquid (V − Sε)$\rho 0$. We thus find for the whole mass of the liquid

$$M = V \, \rho 0 - S \int \varepsilon 0 (\rho 0 - \rho) \, dv. \qquad (2)$$

To find the potential energy we have to integrate

$$\iiint \chi \rho \, dxdydz. \qquad (3)$$

Substituting $\chi \rho$ for ρ in the process we have just gone through, we find

$$E = V \chi 0 \rho 0 - S \int \varepsilon 0 \, (\chi 0 \rho 0 - \chi \rho) \, dv. \qquad (4)$$

Multiplying equation (2) by $\chi 0$, and subtracting it from (4),

$$E - M \chi 0 = S \int \varepsilon 0 \, (\chi - \chi 0) \, \rho dv \qquad (5)$$

In this expression M and $\chi 0$ are both constant, so that the variation of the right-hand side of the equation is the same as that of the energy E, and expresses that part of the energy which depends on the area of the bounding surface of the liquid. We may call this the surface energy.

The symbol χ expresses the energy of unit of mass of the liquid at a depth v within the bounding surface. When the liquid is in contact with a rare medium, such as its own vapour or any other gas, χ is greater than $\chi 0$, and the surface energy is positive. By the principle of the conservation of energy, any displacement of the liquid by which its energy is diminished will tend to take place of itself. Hence if the energy is the greater, the greater the area of the exposed surface, the liquid will tend to move in such a way as to diminish the area of the exposed surface, or, in other words, the exposed surface will tend to diminish if it can do so consistently with the other conditions. This tendency of the surface to contract itself is called the surface-tension of liquids.

FIG. 1.

Dupré has described an arrangement by which the surface-tension of a liquid film may be illustrated. A piece of sheet metal is cut out in the form AA (fig. 1). A very fine slip of metal is laid on it in the position BB, and the whole is dipped into a solution of soap, or M. Plateau's glycerine mixture. When it is taken out the rectangle AACC if filled up by a liquid film. This film, however, tends to contract on itself, and the loose strip of metal BB will, if it is let go, be drawn up towards AA, provided it is sufficiently light and smooth.

Let T be the surface energy per unit of area; then the energy of a surface of area S will be ST. If, in the rectangle AACC, AA = a, and AC = b, its area is S = ab, and its energy Tab. Hence if F is the force by which the slip BB is pulled towards AA,

$$\overline{} \quad Tab = Ta,$$
$$= \quad \quad \quad (6)$$
$$b$$

or the force arising from the surface-tension acting on a length a of the strip is Ta, so that T represents the surface-tension acting transversely on every unit of length of the periphery of the liquid surface. Hence if we write

$$T = \int \varepsilon 0 \ (\chi - \chi 0) \ \rho \ dv, \quad \quad (7)$$

we may define T either as the surface-energy per unit of area, or as the surface-tension per unit of contour, for the numerical values of these two quantities are equal.

If the liquid is bounded by a dense substance, whether liquid or solid, the value of χ may be different from its value when the liquid has a free surface. If the liquid is in contact with another liquid, let us distinguish quantities belonging to the two liquids by suffixes. We shall then have

$$E1 - M1 \ \chi 01 = S \int \varepsilon 10 \ (\chi 1 - \chi 01) \ \rho 1 \ dv1, \quad \quad (8)$$
$$E2 - M2 \ \chi 02 = S \int \varepsilon 20 \ (\chi 2 - \chi 02) \ \rho 2 \ dv2. \quad \quad (9)$$

Adding these expressions, and dividing the second member by S, we obtain for the tension of the surface of contact of the two liquids

$$T1 \cdot 2 = \int \varepsilon 10 \ (\chi 1 - \chi 01) \ \rho 1 \ dv1 + \int \varepsilon 20 \ (\chi 2 - \chi 02) \ \rho 2 \ dv2. \quad \quad (10)$$

If this quantity is positive, the surface of contact will tend to contract, and the liquids will remain distinct. If, however, it were negative, the displacement of the liquids which tends to enlarge the surface of contact would be aided by the molecular forces, so that the liquids, if not kept separate by gravity, would at length become thoroughly mixed. No instance, however, of a phenomenon of this kind has been discovered, for those liquids which mix of themselves do so by the process of diffusion, which is a molecular motion, and not by the spontaneous puckering and replication of the bounding surface as would be the case if T were negative.

It is probable, however, that there are many cases in which the integral belonging to the less dense fluid is negative. If the denser body be solid we can often demonstrate this; for the liquid tends to spread itself over the surface of the solid, so as to increase the area of the surface of contact, even although in so doing it is obliged to increase the free surface in opposition to the surface-tension. Thus water spreads itself out on a clean surface of glass. This shows that $\int \varepsilon 0 \ (\chi - \chi 0) \rho dv$ must be negative for water in contact with glass.

On the Tension of Liquid Films.—The method already given for the investigation of the surface-tension of a liquid, all whose dimensions are sensible, fails in the case of a liquid film such as a soap-bubble. In such a film it is possible that no part of the liquid may be so far from the surface as to have the potential and density corresponding to what we have called the interior of a liquid mass, and measurements of the tension of the film when drawn out to different degrees of thinness may possibly lead to an estimate of the range of the molecular forces, or at least of the depth within a liquid mass, at which its properties become sensibly uniform. We shall therefore indicate a method of investigating the tension of such films.

Let S be the area of the film, M its mass, and E its energy; σ the mass, and e the energy of unit of area; then

$$M = S\sigma, \quad \quad (11)$$
$$E = Se. \quad \quad (12)$$

Let us now suppose that by some change in the form of the boundary of the film its area is changed from S to S + dS. If its tension is T the work required to effect this increase of surface will be T dS, and the energy of the film will be increased by this amount. Hence

$$TdS = dE = Sde + edS. \quad \quad (13)$$

But since M is constant,

$$dM = Sd\sigma + \sigma dS = 0. \quad \quad (14)$$

Eliminating dS from equations (13) and (14), and dividing by S, we find

$$\frac{T}{\sigma} = e - \sigma\,\frac{e}{\sigma}$$

In this expression σ denotes the mass of unit of area of the film, and e the energy of unit of area.

If we take the axis of z normal to either surface of the film, the radius of curvature of which we suppose to be very great compared with its thickness c, and if ρ is the density, and χ the energy of unit of mass at depth z, then

$$\sigma = \int_c^0 \rho\,dz, \qquad (16)$$

and

$$e = \int_c^0 \chi\rho\,dz. \qquad (17)$$

Both ρ and χ are functions of z, the value of which remains the same when $z - c$ is substituted for z. If the thickness of the film is greater than 2ε, there will be a stratum of thickness $c - 2\varepsilon$ in the middle of the film, within which the values of ρ and χ will be ρ0 and χ0. In the two strata on either side of this the law, according to which ρ and χ depend on the depth, will be the same as in a liquid mass of large dimensions. Hence in this case

$$\sigma = (c - 2\varepsilon)\,\rho0 + 2\int_\varepsilon^0 \rho\,dv, \qquad (18)$$
$$e = (c - 2\varepsilon)\,\chi0\rho0 + 2\int_\varepsilon^0 \chi\rho\,dv, \qquad (19)$$

$$\frac{\sigma}{c} = \rho0, \qquad \frac{e}{c} = \chi0\rho0, \quad \therefore \quad \frac{e}{\sigma} = \chi0,$$

$$T = 2\int_\varepsilon^0 \chi\rho\,dv - 2\chi0\int_\varepsilon^0 \rho\,dv = 2\int_\varepsilon^0 (\chi - \chi0)\,\rho\,dv. \qquad (20)$$

Hence the tension of a thick film is equal to the sum of the tensions of its two surfaces as already calculated (equation 7). On the hypothesis of uniform density we shall find that this is true for films whose thickness exceeds ε.

The symbol χ is defined as the energy of unit of mass of the substance. A knowledge of the absolute value of this energy is not required, since in every expression in which it occurs it is under the 260form $\chi - \chi0$, that is to say, the difference between the energy in two different states. The only cases, however, in which we have experimental values of this quantity are when the substance is either liquid and surrounded by similar liquid, or gaseous and surrounded by similar gas. It is impossible to make direct measurements of the properties of particles of the substance within the insensible distance ε of the bounding surface.

When a liquid is in thermal and dynamical equilibrium with its vapour, then if ρ′ and χ′ are the values of ρ and χ for the vapour, and ρ0 and χ0 those for the liquid,

$$\chi' - \chi0 = JL - p(1/\rho' - 1/\rho0), \qquad (21)$$

where J is the dynamical equivalent of heat, L is the latent heat of unit of mass of the vapour, and p is the pressure. At points in the liquid very near its surface it is probable that χ is greater than χ0, and at points in the gas very near the surface of the liquid it is probable that χ is less than χ′, but this has not as yet been ascertained experimentally. We shall therefore endeavour to apply to this subject the methods used in Thermodynamics, and where these fail us we shall have recourse to the hypotheses of molecular physics.

We have next to determine the value of χ in terms of the action between one particle and another. Let us suppose that the force between two particles m and m' at the distance f is

$$F = mm'\,(\varphi(f) + Cf\text{-}2), \qquad (22)$$

being reckoned positive when the force is attractive. The actual force between the particles arises in part from their mutual gravitation, which is inversely as the square of the distance. This force is expressed by $m\,m'\,Cf\text{-}2$. It is easy to show that a force subject to this law would not account for capillary action. We shall, therefore, in what follows, consider only that part of the force which depends on $\varphi(f)$, where $\varphi(f)$ is a function of f which is insensible for all sensible values of f, but which becomes sensible and even enormously great when f is exceedingly small.

If we next introduce a new function of f and write

$$\int_\infty^f \varphi(f)\, df = \Pi(f), \qquad (23)$$

then $m\, m'\, \Pi(f)$ will represent—(I) The work done by the attractive force on the particle m, while it is brought from an infinite distance from m' to the distance f from m'; or (2) The attraction of a particle m on a narrow straight rod resolved in the direction of the length of the rod, one extremity of the rod being at a distance f from m, and the other at an infinite distance, the mass of unit of length of the rod being m'. The function $\Pi(f)$ is also insensible for sensible values of f, but for insensible values of f it may become sensible and even very great.

If we next write

$$\int_\infty^f f\Pi(f)\, df = \psi(z), \qquad (24)$$

then $2\pi m\sigma\psi(z)$ will represent—(1) The work done by the attractive force while a particle m is brought from an infinite distance to a distance z from an infinitely thin stratum of the substance whose mass per unit of area is σ; (2) The attraction of a particle m placed at a distance z from the plane surface of an infinite solid whose density is σ.

FIG. 2

Let us examine the case in which the particle m is placed at a distance z from a curved stratum of the substance, whose principal radii of curvature are R1 and R2. Let P (fig. 2) be the particle and PB a normal to the surface. Let the plane of the paper be a normal section of the surface of the stratum at the point B, making an angle ω with the section whose radius of curvature is R1. Then if O is the centre of curvature in the plane of the paper, and BO = u,

$$\frac{\cos^2\omega}{1} + \frac{\sin^2\omega}{2} \qquad (25)$$

Let

$$POQ = \theta, \quad PO = r, \quad PQ = f, \quad BP = z,$$
$$f^2 = u^2 + r^2 - 2ur\cos\theta. \qquad (26)$$

The element of the stratum at Q may be expressed by

$$\sigma u^2 \sin\theta\, d\theta d\omega,$$

or expressing $d\theta$ in terms of df by (26),

$$\sigma ur\text{-}1\, f\, df\, d\theta.$$

Multiplying this by m and by $\pi(f)$, we obtain for the work done by the attraction of this element when m is brought from an infinite distance to P1,

$$m\sigma ur\text{-}1\, f\Pi(f)\, df d\omega.$$

Integrating with respect to f from $f = z$ to $f = a$, where a is a line very great compared with the extreme range of the molecular force, but very small compared with either of the radii of curvature, we obtain for the work

$$\int m\sigma ur\text{-}1\, (\psi(z) - \psi(a))\, d\omega,$$

and since $\psi(a)$ is an insensible quantity we may omit it. We may also write

$$ur\text{-}1 = 1 + zu\text{-}1 + \&c.,$$

since z is very small compared with u, and expressing u in terms of ω by (25), we find

$$\int_0^{2\pi} m\sigma\, \psi(z)\left\{ 1 + z\left(\frac{\cos^2\omega}{1} + \frac{\sin^2\omega}{2} \right)\right\} d\omega = 2\pi m\sigma\, \psi(z)\left\{ 1 + \left(\frac{}{1} + \frac{}{2} \right)\right\}.$$

This then expresses the work done by the attractive forces when a particle m is brought from an infinite distance to the point P at a distance z from a stratum whose surface-density is σ, and whose principal radii of curvature are R1 and R2.

To find the work done when m is brought to the point P in the neighbourhood of a solid body, the density of which is a function of the depth v below the surface, we have only to write instead of σ ρdz, and to integrate

$$2\pi m \int^{\infty}_{z} \rho\psi(z)\,dz \quad \underset{1}{\text{———}} \quad \underset{2}{\text{———}} \quad) \int^{\infty}_{z} \rho z$$
$$+ \pi m (\qquad\qquad\qquad \psi(z)\,dz,$$

where, in general, we must suppose ρ a function of z. This expression, when integrated, gives (1) the work done on a particle m while it is brought from an infinite distance to the point P, or (2) the attraction on a long slender column normal to the surface and terminating at P, the mass of unit of length of the column being m. In the form of the theory given by Laplace, the density of the liquid was supposed to be uniform. Hence if we write

$$K = 2\pi \int^{\infty}_{0} \psi(z)\,dz, \qquad H = 2\pi \int^{\infty}_{0} z\psi(z)\,dz,$$

the pressure of a column *of the fluid itself* terminating at the surface will be

$$\rho^2 \{K + \tfrac{1}{2}H (1/R1 + 1/R2) \},$$

and the work done by the attractive forces when a particle m is brought to the surface of the fluid from an infinite distance will be

$$m\rho \{K + \tfrac{1}{2}H (1/R1 + 1/R2) \}.$$

If we write

$$\int^{\infty}_{z} \psi(z)\,dz = \theta(z),$$

then $2\pi m\rho\theta(z)$ will express the work done by the attractive forces, while a particle m is brought from an infinite distance to a distance z from the plane surface of a mass of the substance of density ρ and infinitely thick. The function $\theta(z)$ is insensible for all sensible values of z. For insensible values it may become sensible, but it must remain finite even when z = 0, in which case $\theta(0) = K$.

If χ' is the potential energy of unit of mass of the substance in vapour, then at a distance z from the plane surface of the liquid

$$\chi = \chi' - 2\pi\rho\theta(z).$$

At the surface

$$\chi = \chi' - 2\pi\rho\theta(0).$$

At a distance z within the surface

$$\chi = \chi' - 4\pi\rho\theta(0) + 2\pi\rho\theta(z).$$

If the liquid forms a stratum of thickness c, then

$$\chi = \chi' - 4\pi\rho\theta(0) + 2\pi\rho\theta(z) + 2\pi\rho\theta(z - c).$$

The surface-density of this stratum is σ = cρ. The energy per unit of area is

$$e = \int c0 \chi\rho\,dz = c\rho (\chi' - 4\pi\rho\theta(0)) + 2\pi\rho^2 \int c0\ \theta(z)\,dz + 2\pi\rho^2 \int c0\ \theta(z - c)\,dz.$$

Since the two sides of the stratum are similar the last two terms are equal, and

$$e = c\rho (\chi' - 4\pi\rho\theta(0)) + 4\pi\rho^2 \int c0\ \theta(z)\,dz.$$

Differentiating with respect to c, we find

$$\frac{\sigma}{c} = \frac{e}{c} \rho, = \rho (\chi' - 4\pi\rho\theta(0)) + 4\pi\rho^2\theta(c).$$

Hence the surface-tension

$$\frac{T}{\sigma} = e - \sigma \frac{e}{\sigma} \qquad 4\pi\rho^2 (\int c0\ \theta(z)\,dz - c\theta(c)).$$

Integrating the first term within brackets by parts, it becomes

$$c\theta(c) - 0\theta(0)$$

$$-\int_{c}^{0} z \quad \theta \quad z.$$

$$z$$

Remembering that $\theta(0)$ is a finite quantity, and that $d\theta/dz = -\psi(z)$, we find

$$T = 4\pi\rho^2 \int_{c}^{0} z\psi(z) \, dz. \quad (27)$$

When c is greater than ε this is equivalent to 2H in the equation of Laplace. Hence the tension is the same for all films thicker than ε, the range of the molecular forces. For thinner films

$$\frac{T}{c} = 4\pi\rho^2 c\psi(c).$$

Hence if $\psi(c)$ is positive, the tension and the thickness will increase together. Now $2\pi m\rho\psi(c)$ represents the attraction between a particle m and the plane surface of an infinite mass of the liquid, when the distance of the particle outside the surface is c. Now, the force between the particle and the liquid is certainly, on the whole, attractive; but if between any two small values of c it should be repulsive, then for films whose thickness lies between these values the tension will increase as the thickness diminishes, but for all other cases the tension will diminish as the thickness diminishes.

We have given several examples in which the density is assumed to be uniform, because Poisson has asserted that capillary 261 phenomena would not take place unless the density varied rapidly near the surface. In this assertion we think he was mathematically wrong, though in his own hypothesis that the density does actually vary, he was probably right. In fact, the quantity $4\pi\rho2K$, which we may call with van der Waals the molecular pressure, is so great for most liquids (5000 atmospheres for water), that in the parts near the surface, where the molecular pressure varies rapidly, we may expect considerable variation of density, even when we take into account the smallness of the compressibility of liquids.

The pressure at any point of the liquid arises from two causes, the external pressure P to which the liquid is subjected, and the pressure arising from the mutual attraction of its molecules. If we suppose that the number of molecules within the range of the attraction of a given molecule is very large, the part of the pressure arising from attraction will be proportional to the square of the number of molecules in unit of volume, that is, to the square of the density. Hence we may write

$$p = P + A\rho^2,$$

where A is a constant [equal to Laplace's intrinsic pressure K. But this equation is applicable only at points in the interior, where ρ is not varying.]

[The intrinsic pressure and the surface-tension of a uniform mass are perhaps more easily found by the following process. The former can be found at once by calculating the mutual attraction of the parts of a large mass which lie on opposite sides of an imaginary plane interface. If the density be σ, the attraction between the whole of one side and a layer upon the other distant z from the plane and of thickness dz is $2\pi\sigma^2\psi(z)\,dz$, reckoned per unit of area. The expression for the intrinsic pressure is thus simply

$$K = 2\pi\sigma^2 \int_{\infty}^{0} \psi(z) \, dz. \quad (28)$$

In Laplace's investigation σ is supposed to be unity. We may call the value which (28) then assumes K0, so that as above

$$K0 = 2\pi \int_{\infty}^{0} \psi(z) \, dz. \quad (29)$$

The expression for the superficial tension is most readily found with the aid of the idea of superficial energy, introduced into the subject by Gauss. Since the tension is constant, the work that must be done to extend the surface by one unit of area measures the tension, and the work required for the generation of any surface is the product of the tension and the area. From this consideration we may derive Laplace's expression, as has been done by Dupre (*Théorie mécanique de la chaleur*, Paris, 1869), and Kelvin ("Capillary Attraction," *Proc. Roy. Inst.*, January 1886. Reprinted, *Popular Lectures and Addresses*, 1889). For imagine a small cavity to be formed in the interior of the mass and to be gradually expanded in such a shape that the walls consist almost entirely of two parallel planes. The distance between the planes is supposed to be very small compared with their ultimate diameters, but at the same time large enough to exceed the range of the attractive forces. The work required to produce this crevasse is twice the product of the tension and the area of one of the faces. If we now suppose the crevasse produced by direct separation of its walls, the work necessary must be the same as before, the initial and final configurations being identical; and we recognize that the tension may be measured by half the work that must be done per unit of area against the mutual attraction in order to separate the two portions which lie upon opposite sides of an ideal plane to a distance from one another which is outside the range of the forces. It only remains to calculate this work.

If $\sigma1$, $\sigma2$ represent the densities of the two infinite solids, their mutual attraction at distance z is per unit of area

$$2\pi\sigma1\sigma2 \int\infty0 \, \psi(z) \, dz, \qquad (30)$$

or $2\pi\sigma1\sigma2\theta(z)$, if we write

$$\int\infty0 \, \psi(z) \, dz = \theta(z) \qquad (31)$$

The work required to produce the separation in question is thus

$$2\pi\sigma1\sigma2 \int\infty0 \, \theta(z) \, dz; \qquad (32)$$

and for the tension of a liquid of density σ we have

$$T = \pi\sigma^2 \int\infty0 \, \theta(z) \, dz. \qquad (33)$$

The form of this expression may be modified by integration by parts. For

$$\int\theta(z) \, dz = \frac{\theta(z)}{z} \qquad dz = \theta(z)\,z +$$
$$\theta(z)\,z - \int z \qquad\qquad \int z\psi(z) \, dz.$$

Since $\theta(0)$ is finite, proportional to K, the integrated term vanishes at both limits, and we have simply

$$\int\infty0 \, \theta(z) \, dz = \int\infty0 \, z\psi(z) \, dz, \qquad (34)$$

and

$$T = \pi\sigma^2 \int\infty0 \, z\psi(z) \, dz. \qquad (35)$$

In Laplace's notation the second member of (34), multiplied by 2π, is represented by H.

As Laplace has shown, the values for K and T may also be expressed in terms of the function φ, with which we started. Integrating by parts, we get

$$\int\psi(z) \, dz = z \, \psi(z) + 1/3 \, z3 \, \Pi(z) + 1/3 \int z3 \, \varphi(z) \, dz,$$
$$\int z\psi(z) \, dz = 1/2 \, z2\psi(z) + 1/8 \, z4 \, \Pi(z) + 1/8 \int z4 \, \varphi(z) \, dz.$$

In all cases to which it is necessary to have regard the integrated terms vanish at both limits, and we may write

$$\int\infty0 \, \psi(z) \, dz = 1/3 \int\infty2 \, z3 \, \varphi(z) \, dz, \qquad \int\infty0 \, z\psi(z) \, dz = 1/8 \int\infty0 \, z4 \, \varphi(z) \, dz; \qquad (36)$$

so that

$$0 = \frac{\pi}{} \qquad \frac{\int\infty0 \, z3 \, \varphi(z) \, dz,}{T0 =} \qquad \frac{\int\infty0 \, z4 \, \varphi(z) \, dz.}{} \qquad (37)$$

A few examples of these formulae will promote an intelligent comprehension of the subject. One of the simplest suppositions open to us is that

$$\varphi(f) = e\beta f. \qquad (38)$$

From this we obtain

$$\Pi(z) = \beta\text{-}1 \, e\text{-}\beta z, \quad \psi(z) = \beta\text{-}3 \, (\beta z + 1)e\text{-}\beta z, \qquad (39)$$
$$K0 = 4\pi\beta\text{-}4, \quad T0 = 3\pi\beta\text{-}5. \qquad (40)$$

The range of the attractive force is mathematically infinite, but practically of the order β-1, and we see that T is of higher order in this small quantity than K. That K is in all cases of the fourth order and T of the fifth order in the range of the forces is obvious from (37) without integration.

An apparently simple example would be to suppose $\varphi(z) = zn$. We get

26

$$(z) = -\ \frac{n+1}{+1}\qquad \psi(z) = \ \frac{zn+3}{n+3\,n+1}$$

$$0 = \ \frac{2\pi zn+4}{n+4\,n+3\,n+1}\ \Big|^{\infty}0 \tag{41}$$

The intrinsic pressure will thus be infinite whatever n may be. If n + 4 be positive, the attraction of infinitely distant parts contributes to the result; while if n + 4 be negative, the parts in immediate contiguity act with infinite power. For the transition case, discussed by William Sutherland (*Phil. Mag.* xxiv. p. 113, 1887), of n + 4 = 0, K0 is also infinite. It seems therefore that nothing satisfactory can be arrived at under this head.

As a third example, we will take the law proposed by Young, viz.

$\varphi(z) = 1$ from z = 0 to z = a,

$\varphi(z) = 0$ from z = a to z = ∞; \qquad (42)

and corresponding therewith,

$\Pi(z) = a - z$ from z = 0 to z = a,

$\Pi(z) = 0$ \quad from z = a to z = ∞, \qquad (43)

$\psi(z) = \tfrac{1}{2}\,a(a^2 - z^2)$

$= \tfrac{1}{3}(a^3 - z^3)$ \qquad from z = 0 to z = a, \qquad (44)

$\psi(z) = 0$ \quad from z = a to z = ∞,

Equations (37) now give

$$0 = \ \frac{\pi}{}\ \int_0^{\infty} z3\ dz = \ \frac{a4}{}\ , \tag{45}$$

$$0 = \ \frac{}{}\ \int_0^{\infty} z4\ dz = \ \frac{a5}{0}\ . \tag{46}$$

The numerical results differ from those of Young, who finds that "*the contractile force is one-third of the whole cohesive force of a stratum of particles, equal in thickness to the interval to which the primitive equable cohesion extends*," viz. T = 1/3 aK; whereas according to the above calculation T = 3/20 aK. The discrepancy seems to depend upon Young having treated the attractive force as operative in one direction only. For further calculations on Laplace's principles, see Rayleigh, *Phil. Mag.*, Oct. Dec. 1890, or *Scientific Papers*, vol. iii. p. 397.]

ON SURFACE-TENSION

Definition.—*The tension of a liquid surface across any line drawn on the surface is normal to the line, and is the same for all directions of the line, and is measured by the force across an element of the line divided by the length of that element.*

Experimental Laws of Surface-Tension.—1. For any given liquid surface, as the surface which separates water from air, or oil from water, the surface-tension is the same at every point of the surface and in every direction. It is also practically independent of the curvature of the surface, although it appears from the mathematical theory that there is a slight increase of tension where the mean curvature of the surface is concave, and a slight diminution where it is convex. The amount of this increase and diminution is too small to be directly measured, though it has a certain theoretical importance in the explanation of the equilibrium of the superficial layer of the liquid where it is inclined to the horizon.

2. The surface-tension diminishes as the temperature rises, and when the temperature reaches that of the critical point at which the distinction between the liquid and its vapour ceases, it has been observed by Andrews that the capillary action also vanishes. The early writers on capillary action supposed that the diminution of capillary action was due simply to the change of density corresponding to the rise of temperature, and, therefore, assuming the surface-tension to vary as the square of the 262density, they deduced its variations from the observed dilatation of the liquid by heat. This assumption, however, does not appear to be verified by the experiments of Brunner and Wolff on the rise of water in tubes at different temperatures.

3. The tension of the surface separating two liquids which do not mix cannot be deduced by any known method from the tensions of the surfaces of the liquids when separately in contact with air.

When the surface is curved, the effect of the surface-tension is to make the pressure on the concave side exceed the pressure on the convex side by T $(1/R1 + 1/R2)$, where T is the intensity of the surface-tension and R1, R2 are the radii of curvature of any two sections normal to the surface and to each other.

Fig. 3.

If three fluids which do not mix are in contact with each other, the three surfaces of separation meet in a line, straight or curved. Let O (fig. 3) be a point in this line, and let the plane of the paper be supposed to be normal to the line at the point O. The three angles between the tangent planes to the three surfaces of separation at the point O are completely determined by the tensions of the three surfaces. For if in the triangle abc the side ab is taken so as to represent on a given scale the tension of the surface of contact of the fluids a and b, and if the other sides bc and ca are taken so as to represent on the same scale the tensions of the surfaces between b and c and between c and a respectively, then the condition of equilibrium at O for the corresponding tensions R, P and Q is that the angle ROP shall be the supplement of abc, POQ of bca, and, therefore, QOR of cab. Thus the angles at which the surfaces of separation meet are the same at all parts of the line of concourse of the three fluids. When three films of the same liquid meet, their tensions are equal, and, therefore, they make angles of 120° with each other. The froth of soap-suds or beaten-up eggs consists of a multitude of small films which meet each other at angles of 120°.

If four fluids, a, b, c, d, meet in a point O, and if a tetrahedron ABCD is formed so that its edge AB represents the tension of the surface of contact of the liquids a and b, BC that of b and c, and so on; then if we place this tetrahedron so that the face ABC is normal to the tangent at O to the line of concourse of the fluids abc, and turn it so that the edge AB is normal to the tangent plane at O to the surface of contact of the fluids a and b, then the other three faces of the tetrahedron will be normal to the tangents at O to the other three lines of concourse of the liquids, and the other five edges of the tetrahedron will be normal to the tangent planes at O to the other five surfaces of contact.

If six films of the same liquid meet in a point the corresponding tetrahedron is a regular tetrahedron, and each film, where it meets the others, has an angle whose cosine is −1/3. Hence if we take two nets of wire with hexagonal meshes, and place one on the other so that the point of concourse of three hexagons of one net coincides with the middle of a hexagon of the other, and if we then, after dipping them in Plateau's liquid, place them horizontally, and gently raise the upper one, we shall develop a system of plane laminae arranged as the walls and floors of the cells are arranged in a honeycomb. We must not, however, raise the upper net too much, or the system of films will become unstable.

28

When a drop of one liquid, B, is placed on the surface of another, A, the phenomena which take place depend on the relative magnitude of the three surface-tensions corresponding to the surface between A and air, between B and air, and between A and B. If no one of these tensions is greater than the sum of the other two, the drop will assume the form of a lens, the angles which the upper and lower surfaces of the lens make with the free surface of A and with each other being equal to the external angles of the triangle of forces. Such lenses are often seen formed by drops of fat floating on the surface of hot water, soup or gravy. But when the surface-tension of A exceeds the sum of the tensions of the surfaces of contact of B with air and with A, it is impossible to construct the triangle of forces; so that equilibrium becomes impossible. The edge of the drop is drawn out by the surface-tension of A with a force greater than the sum of the tensions of the two surfaces of the drop. The drop, therefore, spreads itself out, with great velocity, over the surface of A till it covers an enormous area, and is reduced to such extreme tenuity that it is not probable that it retains the same properties of surface-tension which it has in a large mass. Thus a drop of train oil will spread itself over the surface of the sea till it shows the colours of thin plates. These rapidly descend in Newton's scale and at last disappear, showing that the thickness of the film is less than the tenth part of the length of a wave of light. But even when thus attenuated, the film may be proved to be present, since the surface-tension of the liquid is considerably less than that of pure water. This may be shown by placing another drop of oil on the surface. This drop will not spread out like the first drop, but will take the form of a flat lens with a distinct circular edge, showing that the surface-tension of what is still apparently pure water is now less than the sum of the tensions of the surfaces separating oil from air and water.

The spreading of drops on the surface of a liquid has formed the subject of a very extensive series of experiments by Charles Tomlinson; van der Mensbrugghe has also written a very complete memoir on this subject (*Sur la tension superficielle des liquides*, Bruxelles, 1873).

FIG. 4.

When a solid body is in contact with two fluids, the surface of the solid cannot alter its form, but the angle at which the surface of contact of the two fluids meets the surface of the solid depends on the values of the three surface-tensions. If a and b are the two fluids and c the solid then the equilibrium of the tensions at the point O depends only on that of thin components parallel to the surface, because the surface-tensions normal to the surface are balanced by the resistance of the solid. Hence if the angle ROQ (fig. 4) at which the surface of contact OP meets the solid is denoted by α,
$$Tbc - Tca - Tab \cos \alpha = 0,$$
Whence
$$\cos \alpha = (Tbc - Tca) / Tab.$$

As an experiment on the angle of contact only gives us the difference of the surface-tensions at the solid surface, we cannot determine their actual value. It is theoretically probable that they are often negative, and may be called surface-pressures.

The constancy of the angle of contact between the surface of a fluid and a solid was first pointed out by Dr Young, who states that the angle of contact between mercury and glass is about 140°. Quincke makes it 128° 52′.

If the tension of the surface between the solid and one of the fluids exceeds the sum of the other two tensions, the point of contact will not be in equilibrium, but will be dragged towards the side on which the tension is greatest. If the quantity of the first fluid is small it will stand in a drop on the surface of the solid without wetting it. If the quantity of the second fluid is small it will spread itself over the surface and wet the solid. The angle of contact of the first fluid is 180° and that of the second is zero.

If a drop of alcohol be made to touch one side of a drop of oil on a glass plate, the alcohol will appear to chase the oil over the plate, and if a drop of water and a drop of bisulphide of carbon be placed in contact in a horizontal capillary tube, the bisulphide of carbon will chase the water along the tube. In both cases the liquids move in the direction in which the surface-pressure at the solid is least.

[In order to express the dependence of the tension at the interface of two bodies in terms of the forces exercised by the bodies upon themselves and upon one another, we cannot do better than follow the method of Dupré. If T12 denote the interfacial tension, the energy corresponding to unit of area of the interface 263is also T12, as we see by considering the introduction (through a fine tube) of one body into the interior of the other. A comparison with another method of generating the interface, similar to that previously employed when but one body was in question, will now allow us to evaluate T12.

The work required to cleave asunder the parts of the first fluid which lie on the two sides of an ideal plane passing through the interior, is per unit of area 2T1, and the free surface produced is two units in area. So for the second fluid the corresponding work is 2T2. This having been effected, let us now suppose that each of the units of area of free surface of fluid (1) is allowed to approach normally a unit area of (2) until contact is established. In this process work is gained which we may denote by 4T'12, 2T'12 for each pair. On the whole, then, the work expended in producing two units of interface is 2T1 + 2T2 − 4T'12, and this, as we have seen, may be equated to 2T12. Hence

$$T12 = T1 + T2 - 2T'12 \qquad (47)$$

If the two bodies are similar,

$$T1 = T2 = T'12;$$

and T12 = 0, as it should do.

Laplace does not treat systematically the question of interfacial tension, but he gives incidentally in terms of his quantity H a relation analogous to (47).

If 2T'12 > T1 + T2, T12 would be negative, so that the interface would of itself tend to increase. In this case the fluids must mix. Conversely, if two fluids mix, it would seem that T'12 must exceed the mean of T1 and T2; otherwise work would have to be *expended* to effect a close alternate stratification of the two bodies, such as we may suppose to constitute a first step in the process of mixture (Dupré, *Théorie mécanique de la chaleur*, p. 372; Kelvin, *Popular Lectures*, p. 53).

The value of T'12 has already been calculated (32). We may write

$$T'12 = \pi\sigma1\sigma2 \int\infty0\ \theta(z)\ dz = 1/8\ \pi\sigma1\sigma2 \int\infty0\ z4\varphi(z)\ dz; \qquad (48)$$

FIG. 5.

and in general the functions θ, or φ, must be regarded as capable of assuming different forms. Under these circumstances there is no limitation upon the values of the interfacial tensions for three fluids, which we may denote by T12, T23, T31. If the three fluids can remain in contact with one another, the sum of any two of the quantities must exceed the third, and by Neumann's rule the directions of the interfaces at the common edge must be parallel to the sides of a triangle, taken proportional to T12, T23, T31. If the above-mentioned condition be not satisfied, the triangle is imaginary, and the three fluids cannot rest in contact, the two weaker tensions, even if acting in full concert, being incapable of balancing the strongest. For instance, if T31 > T12 + T23, the second fluid spreads itself indefinitely upon the interface of the first and third fluids.

The experimenters who have dealt with this question, C.G.M. Marangoni, van der Mensbrugghe, Quincke, have all arrived at results inconsistent with the reality of Neumann's triangle. Thus Marangoni says (*Pogg. Annalen*, cxliii. p. 348, 1871):—"Die gemeinschaftliche Oberfläche zweier Flüssigkeiten hat eine geringere Oberflächenspannung als die Differenz der Oberflächenspannung der Flüssigkeiten selbst (mit Ausnahme des Quecksilbers)." Three pure bodies (of which one may be air) cannot accordingly remain in contact. If a drop of oil stands in lenticular form upon a surface of water, it is because the water-surface is already contaminated with a greasy film.

On the theoretical side the question is open until we introduce some limitation upon the generality of the functions. By far the simplest supposition open to us is that the functions are the same in all cases, the attractions differing merely by coefficients analogous to densities in the theory of gravitation. This hypothesis was suggested by Laplace, and may conveniently be named after him. It was also tacitly adopted by Young, in connexion with the still more special hypothesis which Young probably had in view, namely that the force in each case was constant within a limited range, the same in all cases, and vanished outside that range.

As an immediate consequence of this hypothesis we have from (28),

$$K = K_0\sigma^2, \qquad (49)$$
$$T = T_0\sigma^2, \qquad (50)$$

where K_0, T_0 are the same for all bodies.

But the most interesting results are those which Young (*Works*, vol. i. p. 463) deduced relative to the interfacial tensions of three bodies. By (37), (48),

$$T'_{12} = \sigma_1\sigma_2 T_0; \qquad (51)$$

so that by (47), (50),

$$T_{12} = (\sigma_1 - \sigma_2)^2\, T_0 \qquad (52)$$

According to (52), the interfacial tension between any two bodies is proportional to the square of the difference of their densities. The densities σ_1, σ_2, σ_3 being in descending order of magnitude, we may write

$$T_{31} = (\sigma_1 - \sigma_2 + \sigma_2 - \sigma_3)^2\, T_0 = T_{12} + T_{23} + 2(\sigma_1 - \sigma_2)\,(\sigma_2 - \sigma_3)T_0;$$

so that T_{31} necessarily exceeds the sum of the other two interfacial tensions. We are thus led to the important conclusion that according to this hypothesis Neumann's triangle is necessarily imaginary, that one of three fluids will always spread upon the interface of the other two.

Another point of importance may be easily illustrated by this theory, viz. the dependency of capillarity upon abruptness of transition. "The reason why the capillary force should disappear when the transition between two liquids is sufficiently gradual will now be evident. Suppose that the transition from 0 to σ is made in two equal steps, the thickness of the intermediate layer of density $\frac{1}{2}\sigma$ being large compared to the range of the molecular forces, but small in comparison with the radius of curvature. At each step the difference of capillary pressure is only one-quarter of that due to the sudden transition from 0 to σ, and thus altogether half the effect is lost by the interposition of the layer. If there were three equal steps, the effect would be reduced to one-third, and so on. When the number of steps is infinite, the capillary pressure disappears altogether." ("Laplace's Theory of Capillarity," Rayleigh, *Phil. Mag.*, 1883, p. 315.)

According to Laplace's hypothesis the whole energy of any number of contiguous strata of liquids is least when they are arranged in order of density, so that this is the disposition favoured by the attractive forces. The problem is to make the sum of the interfacial tensions a minimum, each tension being proportional to the square of the difference of densities of the two contiguous liquids in question. If the order of stratification differ from that of densities, we can show that each step of approximation to this order lowers the sum of tensions. To this end consider the effect of the abolition of a stratum σ_{n+1}, contiguous to σ_n and σ_{n+2}. Before the change we have $(\sigma_n - \sigma_{n+1})^2 + (\sigma_{n+1} - \sigma_{n+2})^2$, and afterwards $(\sigma_n - \sigma_{n+2})^2$. The second *minus* the first, or the increase in the sum of tensions, is thus

$$2(\sigma_n - \sigma_{n+1})\,(\sigma_{n+1} - \sigma_{n+2}).$$

Hence, if σ_{n+1} be intermediate in magnitude between σ_n and σ_{n+2}, the sum of tensions is increased by the abolition of the stratum; but, if σ_{n+1} be not intermediate, the sum is decreased. We see, then, that the removal of a stratum from between neighbours where it is out of order and its introduction between neighbours where it will be in order is doubly favourable to the reduction of the sum of tensions; and since by a succession of such steps we may arrive at the order of magnitude throughout, we conclude that this is the disposition of minimum tensions and energy.

So far the results of Laplace's hypothesis are in marked accordance with experiment; but if we follow it out further, discordances begin to manifest themselves. According to (52)

$$\sqrt{T31} = \sqrt{T12} + \sqrt{T23}, \qquad (53)$$

a relation not verified by experiment. What is more, (52) shows that according to the hypothesis T12 is necessarily positive; 264so that, if the preceding argument be correct, no such thing as mixture of two liquids could ever take place.

There are two apparent exceptions to Marangoni's rule which call for a word of explanation. According to the rule, water, which has the lower surface-tension, should spread upon the surface of mercury; whereas the universal experience of the laboratory is that drops of water standing upon mercury retain their compact form without the least tendency to spread. To Quincke belongs the credit of dissipating the apparent exception. He found that mercury specially prepared behaves quite differently from ordinary mercury, and that a drop of water deposited thereon spreads over the entire surface. The ordinary behaviour is evidently the result of a film of grease, which adheres with great obstinacy.

The process described by Quincke is somewhat elaborate; but there is little difficulty in repeating the experiment if the mistake be avoided of using a free surface already contaminated, as almost inevitably happens when the mercury is poured from an ordinary bottle. The mercury should be drawn from underneath, for which purpose an arrangement similar to a chemical wash bottle is suitable, and it may be poured into watch-glasses, previously dipped into strong sulphuric acid, rinsed in distilled water, and dried over a Bunsen flame. When the glasses are cool, they may be charged with mercury, of which the first part is rejected. Operating in this way there is no difficulty in obtaining surfaces upon which a drop of water spreads, although from causes that cannot always be traced, a certain proportion of failures is met with. As might be expected, the grease which produces these effects is largely volatile. In many cases a very moderate preliminary warming of the watch-glasses makes all the difference in the behaviour of the drop.

The behaviour of a drop of carbon bisulphide placed upon clean water is also, at first sight, an exception to Marangoni's rule. So far from spreading over the surface, as according to its lower surface-tension it ought to do, it remains suspended in the form of a lens. Any dust that may be lying upon the surface is not driven away to the edge of the drop, as would happen in the case of oil. A simple modification of the experiment suffices, however, to clear up the difficulty. If after the deposition of the drop, a little lycopodium be scattered over the surface, it is seen that a circular space surrounding the drop, of about the size of a shilling, remains bare, and this, however often the dusting be repeated, so long as any of the carbon bisulphide remains. The interpretation can hardly be doubtful. The carbon bisulphide is really spreading all the while, but on account of its volatility is unable to reach any considerable distance. Immediately surrounding the drop there is a film moving outwards at a high speed, and this carries away almost instantaneously any dust that may fall upon it. The phenomenon above described requires that the water-surface be clean. If a very little grease be present, there is no outward flow and dust remains undisturbed in the immediate neighbourhood of the drop.]

FIG. 6.

On the Rise of a Liquid in a Tube.—Let a tube (fig. 6) whose internal radius is r, made of a solid substance c, be dipped into a liquid a. Let us suppose that the angle of contact for this liquid with the solid c is an acute angle. This implies that the tension of the free surface of the solid c is greater than that of the surface of contact of the solid with the liquid a. Now consider the tension of the free surface of the liquid a. All round its edge there is a tension T acting at an angle a with the vertical. The circumference of the edge is $2\pi r$, so that the resultant of this tension is a force $2\pi r T \cos \alpha$ acting vertically upwards on the liquid. Hence the liquid will rise in the tube till the weight of the vertical column between the free surface and the level of the liquid in the vessel balances the resultant of the surface-tension. The upper surface of this column is not level, so that the height of the column cannot be directly measured, but let us assume that h is the mean height of the column, that is to say, the height of a column of equal weight, but with a flat top. Then if r is the radius of the tube at the top of the column, the volume of the suspended column is $\pi r^2 h$, and its weight is $\pi \rho g r^2 h$, when ρ is its density and g the intensity of gravity. Equating this force with the resultant of the tension

$$\pi \rho g r^2 h = 2\pi r T \cos \alpha,$$

or

$$h = 2T \cos \alpha / \rho g r.$$

Hence the mean height to which the fluid rises is inversely as the radius of the tube. For water in a clean glass tube the angle of contact is zero, and

$$h = 2T / \rho g r.$$

For mercury in a glass tube the angle of contact is 128° 52', the cosine of which is negative. Hence when a glass tube is dipped into a vessel of mercury, the mercury within the tube stands at a lower level than outside it.

Rise of a Liquid between Two Plates.—When two parallel plates are placed vertically in a liquid the liquid rises between them. If we now suppose fig. 6 to represent a vertical section perpendicular to the plates, we may calculate the rise of the liquid. Let l be the breadth of the plates measured perpendicularly to the plane of the paper, then the length of the line which bounds the wet and the dry parts of the plates inside is l for each surface, and on this the tension T acts at an angle α to the vertical. Hence the resultant of the surface-tension is 2lT cos α. If the distance between the inner surfaces of the plates is a, and if the mean height of the film of fluid which rises between them is h, the weight of fluid raised is $\rho g h l a$. Equating the forces—

$$\rho g h l a = 2 l T \cos \alpha,$$

whence

$$h = 2T \cos \alpha / \rho g a.$$

This expression is the same as that for the rise of a liquid in a tube, except that instead of r, the radius of the tube, we have a the distance of the plates.

Form of the Capillary Surface.—The form of the surface of a liquid acted on by gravity is easily determined if we assume that near the part considered the line of contact of the surface of the liquid with that of the solid bounding it is straight and horizontal, as it is when the solids which constrain the liquid are bounded by surfaces formed by horizontal and parallel generating lines. This will be the case, for instance, near a flat plate dipped into the liquid. If we suppose these generating lines to be normal to the plane of the paper, then all sections of the solids parallel to this plane will be equal and similar to each other, and the section of the surface of the liquid will be of the same form for all such sections.

FIG. 7.

Let us consider the portion of the liquid between two parallel sections distant one unit of length. Let P1, P2 (fig. 7) be two points of the surface; $\theta 1$, $\theta 2$ the inclination of the surface to the horizon at P1 and P2; y1, y2 the heights of P1 and P2 above the level of the liquid at a distance from all solid bodies. The pressure at any point of the liquid which is above this level is negative unless another fluid as, for instance, the air, presses on the upper surface, but it is only the difference of pressures with which we have to do, because two equal pressures on opposite sides of the surface produce no effect.

We may, therefore, write for the pressure at a height y

$$p = -\rho g y,$$

where ρ is the density of the liquid, or if there are two fluids the excess of the density of the lower fluid over that of the upper one.

The forces acting on the portion of liquid P1P2A2A1 are—first, the horizontal pressures, $-\frac{1}{2}\rho gy1^2$ and $\frac{1}{2}\rho gy2^2$; second, the surface-tension T acting at P1 and P2 in directions inclined $\theta1$ and $\theta2$ to the horizon. Resolving horizontally we find—

$$T(\cos\theta2 - \cos\theta1) + \frac{1}{2}g\rho(y2^2 - y1^2) = 0,$$

whence

$$\cos\theta2 = \frac{\rho y1^2}{T} \quad \frac{\rho y2^2}{T}$$
$$\cos\theta1 +$$

or if we suppose P1 fixed and P2 variable, we may write

$$\cos\theta = \text{constant} - \frac{1}{2}g\rho y^2 / T.$$

This equation gives a relation between the inclination of the curve to the horizon and the height above the level of the liquid.

FIG. 8.

Resolving vertically we find that the weight of the liquid raised above the level must be equal to $T(\sin\theta2 - \sin\theta1)$, and this is therefore equal to the area P1P2A2A1 multiplied by $g\rho$. The form of the capillary surface is identical with that of the "elastic curve," or the curve formed by a uniform spring originally straight, when its ends are acted on by equal and opposite forces applied either to the ends themselves or to solid pieces attached to them. Drawings of the different forms of the curve may be found in Thomson and Tait's *Natural Philosophy*, vol. i. p. 455.

We shall next consider the rise of a liquid between two plates of different materials for which the angles of contact are $\alpha1$ and $\alpha2$, the distance between the plates being a, a small quantity. Since the plates are very near one another we may use the following equation of the surface as an approximation:—

$$y = h1 + Ax + Bx^2, \quad h2 = h1 + Aa + Ba^2,$$

whence

$$\cot\alpha1 = -A, \quad \cot\alpha2 = A + 2Ba$$
$$T(\cos\alpha1 + \cos\alpha2) = \rho ga(h1 + \frac{1}{2}Aa + \frac{1}{3}Ba^2),$$

whence we obtain

$$1 = \frac{\overline{\quad}}{ga}(\cos\alpha1 + \cos\alpha2) + \overline{\quad}(2\cot\alpha1 - \cot\alpha2)$$

$$1 = \frac{\overline{\quad}}{ga}(\cos\alpha1 + \cos\alpha2) + \overline{\quad}(2\cot\alpha2 - \cot\alpha1).$$

Let X be the force which must be applied in a horizontal direction to either plate to keep it from approaching the other, then the forces acting on the first plate are $T + X$ in the negative direction, and $T\sin\alpha1 + \frac{1}{2}g\rho h1^2$ in the positive direction. Hence

$$X = \frac{1}{2}g\rho h1^2 - T(1 - \sin\alpha1).$$

For the second plate

$$X = \frac{1}{2}g\rho h2^2 - T(1 - \sin\alpha2).$$

Hence

$$X = \frac{1}{4}g\rho(h1^2 + h2^2) - T\{1 - \frac{1}{2}(\sin\alpha1 + \sin\alpha2)\},$$

or, substituting the values of h1 and h2,

$$(\cos\alpha1 + \cos\alpha2)^2 - T\{1 - \frac{1}{2}(\sin\alpha1 + \sin\alpha2) - \frac{1}{12}(\cos\alpha1 + \cos\alpha2)(\cot$$

$$\frac{\overline{\qquad}}{ga^2}(\alpha 1 + \cot \alpha 2)\},$$

the remaining terms being negligible when a is small. The force, therefore, with which the two plates are drawn together consists first of a positive part, or in other words an attraction, varying inversely as the square of the distance, and second, of a negative part of repulsion independent of the distance. Hence in all cases except that in which the angles $\alpha 1$ and $\alpha 2$ are supplementary to each other, the force is attractive when α is small enough, but when $\cos \alpha 1$ and $\cos \alpha 2$ are of different signs, as when the liquid is raised by one plate, and depressed by the other, the first term may be so small that the repulsion indicated by the second term comes into play. The fact that a pair of plates which repel one another at a certain distance may attract one another at a smaller distance was deduced by Laplace from theory, and verified by the observations of the abbé Haüy.

A Drop between Two Plates.—If a small quantity of a liquid which wets glass be introduced between two glass plates slightly inclined to each other, it will run towards that part where the glass plates are nearest together. When the liquid is in equilibrium it forms a thin film, the outer edge of which is all of the same thickness. If d is the distance between the plates at the edge of the film and Π the atmospheric pressure, the pressure of the liquid in the film is $\Pi - (2T \cos \alpha)/d$, and if A is the area of the film between the plates and B its circumference, the plates will be pressed together with a force

$$\frac{2A}{d}T \cos \alpha + BT \sin \alpha,$$

and this, whether the atmosphere exerts any pressure or not. The force thus produced by the introduction of a drop of water between two plates is enormous, and is often sufficient to press certain parts of the plates together so powerfully as to bruise them or break them. When two blocks of ice are placed loosely together so that the superfluous water which melts from them may drain away, the remaining water draws the blocks together with a force sufficient to cause the blocks to adhere by the process called *Regelation*.

[An effect of an opposite character may be observed when the fluid is mercury in place of water. When two pieces of flat glass are pressed together under mercury with moderate force they cohere, the mercury leaving the narrow crevasses, even although the alternative is a vacuum. The course of events is more easily followed if one of the pieces of glass constitutes the bottom, or a side, of the vessel containing the mercury.]

In many experiments bodies are floated on the surface of water in order that they may be free to move under the action of slight horizontal forces. Thus Sir Isaac Newton placed a magnet in a floating vessel and a piece of iron in another in order to observe their mutual action, and A.M. Ampère floated a voltaic battery with a coil of wire in its circuit in order to observe the effects of the earth's magnetism on the electric circuit. When such floating bodies come near the edge of the vessel they are drawn up to it, and are apt to stick fast to it. There are two ways of avoiding this inconvenience. One is to grease the float round its water-line so that the water is depressed round it. This, however, often produces a worse disturbing effect, because a thin film of grease spreads over the water and increases its surface-viscosity. The other method is to fill the vessel with water till the level of the water stands a little higher than the rim of the vessel. The float will then be repelled from the edge of the vessel. Such floats, however, should always be made so that the section taken at the level of the water is as small as possible.

[*The Size of Drops.*—The relation between the diameter of a tube and the weight of the drop which it delivers appears to have been first investigated by Thomas Tate (*Phil. Mag.* vol. xxvii. p. 176, 1864), whose experiments led him to the conclusion that "other things being the same, the weight of a drop of liquid is proportional to the diameter of the tube in which it is formed." Sufficient time must of course be allowed for the formation of the drops; otherwise no simple results can be expected. In Tate's experiments the period was never less than 40 seconds.

The magnitude of a drop delivered from a tube, even when the formation up to the phase of instability is infinitely slow, cannot be calculated a priori. The weight is sometimes equated to the product of the capillary tension (T) and the circumference of the tube ($2\pi a$), but with little justification. Even if the tension at the circumference of the tube acted vertically, and the whole of the liquid below this level passed into the drop, the calculation would still be vitiated by the assumption that the internal pressure at the level in question is atmospheric. It would be necessary to consider the curvatures of the fluid surface at the edge of attachment. If the surface could be treated as a cylindrical prolongation of the tube (radius a), the pressure would be T/a, and the resulting force acting downwards upon the drop would amount to one-half ($\pi a T$) of the direct upward pull of the tension along the circumference. At this 266rate the drop would be but one-half of that above reckoned. But the truth is that a complete solution of the statical problem for all forms up to that at which instability sets in, would not suffice for the present purpose. The detachment of the drop is a *dynamical* effect, and it is influenced by collateral circumstances. For example, the bore of the tube is no longer a matter of indifference, even though the attachment of the drop occurs entirely at the outer edge. It appears that when the external diameter exceeds a certain value, the weight of a drop of water is sensibly different in the two extreme cases of a very small and of a very large bore.

But although a complete solution of the dynamical problem is impracticable, much interesting information may be obtained from the principle of dynamical similarity. The argument has already been applied by Dupré (*Théorie mécanique de la chaleur*, Paris, 1869, p. 328), but his presentation of it is rather obscure. We will assume that when, as in most cases, viscosity may be neglected, the mass (M) of a drop depends only upon the density (σ), the capillary tension (T), the acceleration of gravity (g), and the linear dimension of the tube (a). In order to justify this assumption, the formation of the drop must be sufficiently slow, and certain restrictions must be imposed upon the shape of the tube. For example, in the case of water delivered from a glass tube, which is cut off square and held vertically, a will be the external radius; and it will be necessary to suppose that the ratio of the internal radius to a is constant, the cases of a ratio infinitely small, or infinitely near unity, being included. But if the fluid be mercury, the flat end of the tube remains unwetted, and the formation of the drop depends upon the internal diameter only.

The "dimensions" of the quantities on which M depends are:—

σ = (Mass)1 (Length)-3,

T = (Force)1 (Length)-1 =

(Mass)1 (Time)-2,

g = Acceleration = (Length)1 (Time)-

2,

of which M, a mass, is to be expressed as a function. If we assume

$$M \propto T^x \cdot g^y \cdot \sigma^z \cdot a^u,$$

we have, considering in turn length, time and mass,

$$y - 3z + u = 0, \quad 2x + 2y = 0, \quad x + z = 1;$$

so that

$$y = -x, \quad z = 1 - x, \quad u = 3 - 2x.$$

Accordingly

$$\propto \frac{a}{\sigma a^2} \, x{-}1.$$

Since x is undetermined, all that we can conclude is that M is of the form

$$\propto \frac{a}{\sigma a^2} \, F(\quad), \quad (1)$$

36

where F denotes an arbitrary function.

Dynamical similarity requires that $T/g\sigma a^2$ be constant; or, if g be supposed to be so, that a^2 varies as T/σ. If this condition be satisfied, the mass (or weight) of the drop is proportional to T and to a.

If Tate's law be true, that *ceteris paribus* M varies as a, it follows from (1) that F is constant. For all fluids and for all similar tubes similarly wetted, the weight of a drop would then be proportional not only to the diameter of the tube, but also to the superficial tension, and it would be independent of the density.

Careful observations with special precautions to ensure the cleanliness of the water have shown that over a considerable range, the departure from Tate's law is not great. The results give material for the determination of the function F in (1).

T /(9σa²)	g M/Ta
2.58	4.13
1.16	3.97
0.708	3.80
0.441	3.73
0.277	3.78
0.220	3.90
0.169	4.06

In the preceding table, applicable to thin-walled tubes, the first column gives the values of $T/g\sigma a^2$, and the second column those of gM/Ta, all the quantities concerned being in C.G.S. measure, or other consistent system. From this the weight of a drop of any liquid of which the density and surface tension are known, can be calculated. For many purposes it may suffice to treat F as a constant, say 3.8. The formula for the weight of a drop is then simply

$$Mg = 3.8Ta, \qquad (2)$$

in which 3.8 replaces the 2π of the faulty theory alluded to earlier (see Rayleigh, *Phil. Mag.*, Oct. 1899).]

Phenomena arising from the Variation of the Surface-tension.—Pure water has a higher surface-tension than that of any other substance liquid at ordinary temperatures except mercury. Hence any other liquid if mixed with water diminishes its surface-tension. For example, if a drop of alcohol be placed on the surface of water, the surface-tension will be diminished from 80, the value for pure water, to 25, the value for pure alcohol. The surface of the liquid will therefore no longer be in equilibrium, and a current will be formed at and near the surface from the alcohol to the surrounding water, and this current will go on as long as there is more alcohol at one part of the surface than at another. If the vessel is deep, these currents will be balanced by counter currents below them, but if the depth of the water is only two or three millimetres, the surface-current will sweep away the whole of the water, leaving a dry spot where the alcohol was dropped in. This phenomenon was first described and explained by James Thomson, who also explained a phenomenon, the converse of this, called the "tears of strong wine."

If a wine-glass be half-filled with port wine the liquid rises a little up the side of the glass as other liquids do. The wine, however, contains alcohol and water, both of which evaporate, but the alcohol faster than the water, so that the superficial layer becomes more watery. In the middle of the vessel the superficial layer recovers its strength by diffusion from below, but the film adhering to the side of the glass becomes more watery, and therefore has a higher surface-tension than the surface of the stronger wine. It therefore creeps up the side of the glass dragging the strong wine after it, and this goes on till the quantity of fluid dragged up collects into a drop and runs down the side of the glass.

The motion of small pieces of camphor floating on water arises from the gradual solution of the camphor. If this takes place more rapidly on one side of the piece of camphor than on the other side, the surface-tension becomes weaker where there is most camphor in solution, and the lump, being pulled unequally by the surface-tensions, moves off in the direction of the strongest tension, namely, towards the side on which least camphor is dissolved.

If a drop of ether is held near the surface of water the vapour of ether condenses on the surface of the water, and surface-currents are formed flowing in every direction away from under the drop of ether.

If we place a small floating body in a shallow vessel of water and wet one side of it with alcohol or ether, it will move off with great velocity and skim about on the surface of the water, the part wet with alcohol being always the stern.

The surface-tension of mercury is greatly altered by slight changes in the state of the surface. The surface-tension of pure mercury is so great that it is very difficult to keep it clean, for every kind of oil or grease spreads over it at once.

But the most remarkable effects of change of surface-tension are those produced by what is called the electric polarization of the surface. The tension of the surface of contact of mercury and dilute sulphuric acid depends on the electromotive force acting between the mercury and the acid. If the electromotive force is from the acid to the mercury the surface-tension increases; if it is from the mercury to the acid, it diminishes. Faraday observed that a large drop of mercury, resting on the flat bottom of a vessel containing dilute acid, changes its form in a remarkable way when connected with one of the electrodes of a battery, the other electrode being placed in the acid. When the mercury 267is made positive it becomes dull and spreads itself out; when it is made negative it gathers itself together and becomes bright again. G. Lippmann, who has made a careful investigation of the subject, finds that exceedingly small variations of the electromotive force produce sensible changes in the surface-tension. The effect of one of a Daniell's cell is to increase the tension from 30.4 to 40.6. He has constructed a capillary electrometer by which differences of electric potential less than 0.01 of that of a Daniell's cell can be detected by the difference of the pressure required to force the mercury to a given point of a fine capillary tube. He has also constructed an apparatus in which this variation in the surface-tension is made to do work and drive a machine. He has also found that this action is reversible, for when the area of the surface of contact of the acid and mercury is made to increase, an electric current passes from the mercury to the acid, the amount of electricity which passes while the surface increases by one square centimetre being sufficient to decompose .000013 gramme of water.

[The movements of camphor scrapings referred to above afford a useful test of the condition of a water surface. If the contamination exceed a certain limit, the scrapings remain quite dead. In a striking form of the experiment, the water is contained, to the depth of perhaps one inch, in a large flat dish, and the operative part of the surface is limited by a flexible hoop of thin sheet brass lying in the dish and rising above the water-level. If the hoop enclose an area of (say) one-third of the maximum, and if the water be clean, camphor fragments floating on the interior enter with vigorous movements. A touch of the finger will then often reduce them to quiet; but if the hoop be expanded, the included grease is so far attenuated as to lose its effect. Another method of removing grease is to immerse and remove strips of paper by which the surface available for the contamination is in effect increased.

The thickness of the film of oil adequate to check the camphor movements can be determined with fair accuracy by depositing a weighed amount of oil (such as .8 mg.) upon the surface of water in a large bath. Calculated as if the density were the same as in a normal state, the thickness of the film is found to be about two millionths of a millimetre.

Small as is the above amount of oil, the camphor test is a comparatively coarse one. Conditions of a contaminated surface may easily be distinguished, upon all of which camphor fragments spin vigorously. Thus, a shallow tin vessel, such as the lid of a biscuit box, may be levelled and filled with tap-water through a rubber hose. Upon the surface of the water a little sulphur is dusted. An application of the finger for 20 or 30 seconds to the under surface of the vessel will then generate enough heat to lower appreciably the surface-tension, as is evidenced by the opening out of the dust and the formation of a bare spot perhaps 1½ in. in diameter. When, however, the surface is but very slightly greased, a spot can no longer be cleared by the warmth of the finger, or even of a spirit lamp, held underneath. And yet the greasing may be so slight that camphor fragments move with apparently unabated vigour.

The varying degrees of contamination to which a water surface is subject are the cause of many curious phenomena. Among these is the *superficial viscosity* of Plateau. In his experiments a long compass needle is mounted so as to swing in the surface of the liquid under investigation. The cases of ordinary clean water and alcohol are strongly contrasted, the motion of the needle upon the former being comparatively sluggish. Moreover, a different behaviour is observed when the surfaces are slightly dusted over. In the case of water the whole of the surface in front of the needle moves with it, while on the other hand the dust floating on alcohol is scarcely disturbed until the needle actually strikes it. Plateau attributed these differences to a special quality of the liquids, named by him "superficial viscosity." It has been proved, however, that the question is one of contamination, and that a water surface may be prepared so as to behave in the same manner as alcohol.

Another consequence of the tendency of a moderate contamination to distribute itself uniformly is the calming effect of oil, investigated by B. Franklin. On pure water the propagation of waves would be attended by temporary extensions and contractions of the surface, but these, as was shown by O. Reynolds, are resisted when the surface is contaminated.

Indeed the possibility of the continued existence of films, such as constitute foam, depends upon the properties now under consideration. If, as is sometimes stated, the tension of a vertical film were absolutely the same throughout, the middle parts would of necessity fall with the acceleration of gravity. In reality, the tension adjusts itself automatically to the weight to be supported at the various levels.

Although throughout a certain range the surface-tension varies rapidly with the degree of contamination, it is remarkable that, as was first fully indicated by Miss Pockels, the earlier stages of contamination have little or no effect upon surface-tension. Lord Rayleigh has shown that the fall of surface-tension *begins* when the quantity of oil is about the half of that required to stop the camphor movements, and he suggests that this stage may correspond with a complete coating of the surface with a single layer of molecules.]

On the Forms of Liquid Films which are Figures of Revolution.— A soap bubble is simply a small quantity of soap-suds spread out so as to expose a large surface to the air. The bubble, in fact, has two surfaces, an outer and an inner *Spherical soap-bubble.* surface, both exposed to air. It has, therefore, a certain amount of surface-energy depending on the area of these two surfaces. Since in the case of thin films the outer and inner surfaces are approximately equal, we shall consider the area of the film as representing either of them, and shall use the symbol T to denote the energy of unit of area of the film, both surfaces being taken together. If T' is the energy of a single surface of the liquid, T the energy of the film is $2T'$. When by means of a tube we blow air into the inside of the bubble we increase its volume and therefore its surface, and at the same time we do work in forcing air into it, and thus increase the energy of the bubble.

That the bubble has energy may be shown by leaving the end of the tube open. The bubble will contract, forcing the air out, and the current of air blown through the tube may be made to deflect the flame of a candle. If the bubble is in the form of a sphere of radius r this material surface will have an area

$$S = 4\pi r^2. \qquad (1)$$

If T be the energy corresponding to unit of area of the film the surface-energy of the whole bubble will be

$$ST = 4\pi r^2 T. \qquad (2)$$

The increment of this energy corresponding to an increase of the radius from r to r + dr is therefore

$$TdS = 8\pi Tdr. \qquad (3)$$

Now this increase of energy was obtained by forcing in air at a pressure greater than the atmospheric pressure, and thus increasing the volume of the bubble.

Let Π be the atmospheric pressure and $\Pi + p$ the pressure of the air within the bubble. The volume of the sphere is

$$V = 4/3\ \pi r3, \qquad (4)$$

and the increment of volume is

$$dV = 4\pi r^2 dr. \qquad (5)$$

Now if we suppose a quantity of air already at the pressure $\Pi + p$, the work done in forcing it into the bubble pdV. Hence the equation of work and energy is

$$p\ dV = Tds \qquad (6)$$

or

$$4\pi p r^2 dr = 8\pi r dr T \qquad (7)$$

or

$$p = 2T/r. \qquad (8)$$

This, therefore, is the excess of the pressure of the air within the bubble over that of the external air, and it is due to the action of the inner and outer surfaces of the bubble. We may conceive this pressure to arise from the tendency which the bubble has to contract, or in other words from the surface-tension of the bubble.

If to increase the area of the surface requires the expenditure 268of work, the surface must resist extension, and if the bubble in contracting can do work, the surface must tend to contract. The surface must therefore act like a sheet of india-rubber when extended both in length and breadth, that is, it must exert surface-tension. The tension of the sheet of india-rubber, however, depends on the extent to which it is stretched, and may be different in different directions, whereas the tension of the surface of a liquid remains the same however much the film is extended, and the tension at any point is the same in all directions.

The intensity of this surface-tension is measured by the stress which it exerts across a line of unit length. Let us measure it in the case of the spherical soap-bubble by considering the stress exerted by one hemisphere of the bubble on the other, across the circumference of a great circle. This stress is balanced by the pressure p acting over the area of the same great circle: it is therefore equal to $\pi r^2 p$. To determine the intensity of the surface-tension we have to divide this quantity by the length of the line across which it acts, which is in this case the circumference of a great circle $2\pi r$. Dividing $\pi r^2 p$ by this length we obtain $\frac{1}{2}pr$ as the value of the intensity of the surface-tension, and it is plain from equation 8 that this is equal to T. Hence the numerical value of the intensity of the surface-tension is equal to the numerical value of the surface-energy per unit of surface. We must remember that since the film has two surfaces the surface-tension of the film is double the tension of the surface of the liquid of which it is formed.

FIG. 9.

To determine the relation between the surface-tension and the pressure which balances it when the form of the surface is not spherical, let us consider the following case:—

Let fig. 9 represent a section through the axis Cc of a soap-bubble in the form of a figure of revolution bounded by two circular disks AB and ab, and having the meridian section APa. Let PQN*on-spherical soap bubble.*be an imaginary section normal to the axis. Let the radius of this section PR bey, and let PT, the tangent at P, make an angle a with the axis.

Let us consider the stresses which are exerted across this imaginary section by the lower part on the upper part. If the internal pressure exceeds the external pressure by p, there is in the first place a force $\pi y^2 p$ acting upwards arising from the pressure p over the area of the section. In the next place, there is the surface-tension acting downwards, but at an angle a with the vertical, across the circular section of the bubble itself, whose circumference is $2\pi y$, and the downward force is therefore $2\pi yT \cos a$.

Now these forces are balanced by the external force which acts on the disk ACB, which we may call F. Hence equating the forces which act on the portion included between ACB and PRQ

$$\pi y^2 p - 2\pi yT \cos \alpha = -F \qquad (9).$$

If we make CR = z, and suppose z to vary, the shape of the bubble of course remaining the same, the values of y and of a will change, but the other quantities will be constant. In studying these variations we may if we please take as our independent variable the length s of the meridian section AP reckoned from A. Differentiating equation 9 with respect to s we obtain, after dividing by 2π as a common factor,

$$y\ \frac{y}{s}\ T\cos\alpha\ -\ \frac{y}{s}\ Ty\sin\alpha\ +\ \frac{\alpha}{s}\ = 0 \qquad (10).$$

Now

$$\frac{y}{s} = \sin\alpha \qquad (11).$$

The radius of curvature of the meridian section is

$$1 = -\ \frac{R\ s}{\alpha} \qquad (12)$$

The radius of curvature of a normal section of the surface at right angles to the meridian section is equal to the part of the normal cut off by the axis, which is

$$R2 = PN = y/\cos\alpha \qquad (13).$$

Hence dividing equation 10 by y sin α, we find

$$p = T(1/R1 + 1/R2) \qquad (14).$$

This equation, which gives the pressure in terms of the principal radii of curvature, though here proved only in the case of a surface of revolution, must be true of all surfaces. For the curvature of any surface at a given point may be completely defined in terms of the positions of its principal normal sections and their radii of curvature.

Before going further we may deduce from equation 9 the nature of all the figures of revolution which a liquid film can assume. Let us first determine the nature of a curve, such that if it is rolled on the axis its origin will trace out the meridian section of the bubble. Since at any instant the rolling curve is rotating about the point of contact with the axis, the line drawn from this point of contact to the tracing point must be normal to the direction of motion of the tracing point. Hence if N is the point of contact, NP must be normal to the traced curve. Also, since the axis is a tangent to the rolling curve, the ordinate PR is the perpendicular from the tracing point P on the tangent. Hence the relation between the radius vector and the perpendicular on the tangent of the rolling curve must be identical with the relation between the normal PN and the ordinate PR of the traced curve. If we write r for PN, then y = r cos α, and equation 9 becomes

$$^2\ (2\ \frac{}{r}\ 1) = \frac{}{p}$$

This relation between y and r is identical with the relation between the perpendicular from the focus of a conic section on the tangent at a given point and the focal distance of that point, provided the transverse and conjugate axes of the conic are 2a and 2b respectively, where

$$= \quad \frac{\overline{}}{} \quad \text{and } b^2 = \frac{\overline{}}{p}$$

Hence the meridian section of the film may be traced by the focus of such a conic, if the conic is made to roll on the axis.

On the different Forms of the Meridian Line.—1. When the conic is an ellipse the meridian line is in the form of a series of waves, and the film itself has a series of alternate swellings and contractions as represented in figs. 9 and 10. This form of the film is called the unduloid.

1a. When the ellipse becomes a circle, the meridian line becomes a straight line parallel to the axis, and the film passes into the form of a cylinder of revolution.

1b. As the ellipse degenerates into the straight line joining its foci, the contracted parts of the unduloid become narrower, till at last the figure becomes a series of spheres in contact.

In all these cases the internal pressure exceeds the external by 2T/a where a is the semi-transverse axis of the conic. The resultant of the internal pressure and the surface-tension is equivalent to a tension along the axis, and the numerical value of this tension is equal to the force due to the action of this pressure on a circle whose diameter is equal to the conjugate axis of the ellipse.

2. When the conic is a parabola the meridian line is a catenary (fig. 11); the internal pressure is equal to the external pressure, and the tension along the axis is equal to $2\pi Tm$ where m is the distance of the vertex from the focus.

3. When the conic is a hyperbola the meridian line is in the form of a looped curve (fig. 12). The corresponding figure of the film is called the nodoid. The resultant of the internal pressure and the surface-tension is equivalent to a pressure along the axis equal to that due to a pressure p acting on a circle whose diameter is the conjugate axis of the hyperbola.

When the conjugate axis of the hyperbola is made smaller and smaller, the nodoid approximates more and more to the series of spheres touching each other along the axis. When the conjugate axis of the hyperbola increases without limit, the loops of the nodoid are crowded on one another, and each becomes more nearly a ring of circular section, without, however, ever 269reaching this form. The only closed surface belonging to the series is the sphere.

These figures of revolution have been studied mathematically by C.W.B. Poisson,3 Goldschmidt,4 L.L. Lindelöf and F.M.N. Moigno,5 C.E. Delaunay,6A.H.E. Lamarle,7 A. Beer,8 and V.M.A. Mannheim,9 and have been produced experimentally by Plateau10 in the two different ways already described.

FIG. 10.—   FIG. 11.—   FIG. 12.—
Unduloid.   Catenoid.   Noboid.

The limiting conditions of the stability of these figures have been studied both mathematically and experimentally. We shall notice only two of them, the cylinder and the catenoid.

FIG. 13.

Stability of the Cylinder.—The cylinder is the limiting form of the unduloid when the rolling ellipse becomes a circle. When the ellipse differs infinitely little from a circle, the equation of the meridian line becomes approximately y = a + c sin (x/a) where c is small. This is a simple harmonic wave-line, whose mean distance from the axis is a, whose wave-length is 2πa and whose amplitude is c. The internal pressure corresponding to this unduloid is as before p = T/a. Now consider a portion of a cylindric film of length x terminated by two equal disks of radius r and containing a certain volume of air. Let one of these disks be made to approach the other by a small quantity dx. The film will swell out into the convex part of an unduloid, having its largest section midway between the disks, and we have to determine whether the internal pressure will be greater or less than before. If A and C (fig. 13) are the disks, and if x the distance between the disks is equal to πr half the wave-length of the harmonic curve, the disks will be at the points where the curve is at its mean distance from the axis, and the pressure will therefore be T/r as before. If A1, C1 are the disks, so that the distance between them is less than πr, the curve must be produced beyond the disks before it is at its mean distance from the axis. Hence in this case the mean distance is less than r, and the pressure will be greater than T/r. If, on the other hand, the disks are at A2 and C2, so that the distance between them is greater than πr, the curve will reach its mean distance from the axis before it reaches the disks. The mean distance will therefore be greater than r, and the pressure will be less than T/r. Hence if one of the disks be made to approach the other, the internal pressure will be increased if the distance between the disks is less than half the circumference of either, and the pressure will be diminished if the distance is greater than this quantity. In the same way we may show that if the distance between the disks is increased, the pressure will be diminished or increased according as the distance is less or more than half the circumference of either.

Now let us consider a cylindric film contained between two equal fixed disks. A and B, and let a third disk, C, be placed midway between. Let C be slightly displaced towards A. If AC and CB are each less than half the circumference of a disk the pressure on C will increase on the side of A and diminish on the side of B. The resultant force on C will therefore tend to oppose the displacement and to bring C back to its original position. The equilibrium of C is therefore stable. It is easy to show that if C had been placed in any other position than the middle, its equilibrium would have been stable. Hence the film is stable as regards longitudinal displacements. It is also stable as regards displacements transverse to the axis, for the film is in a state of tension, and any lateral displacement of its middle parts would produce a resultant force tending to restore the film to its original position. Hence if the length of the cylindric film is less than its circumference, it is in stable equilibrium. But if the length of the cylindric film is greater than its circumference, and if we suppose the disk C to be placed midway between A and B, and to be moved towards A, the pressure on the side next A will diminish, and that on the side next B will increase, so that the resultant force will tend to increase the displacement, and the equilibrium of the disk C is therefore unstable. Hence the equilibrium of a cylindric film whose length is greater than its circumference is unstable. Such a film, if ever so little disturbed, will begin to contract at one secton and to expand at another, till its form ceases to resemble a cylinder, if it does not break up into two parts which become ultimately portions of spheres.

Instability of a Jet of Liquid.—When a liquid flows out of a vessel through a circular opening in the bottom of the vessel, the form of the stream is at first nearly cylindrical though its diameter gradually diminishes from the orifice downwards on account of the increasing velocity of the liquid. But the liquid after it leaves the vessel is subject to no forces except gravity, the pressure of the air, and its own surface-tension. Of these gravity has no effect on the form of the stream except in drawing asunder its parts in a vertical direction, because the lower parts are moving faster than the upper parts. The resistance of the air produces little disturbance until the velocity becomes very great. But the surface-tension, acting on a cylindric column of liquid whose length exceeds the limit of stability, begins to produce enlargements and contractions in the stream as soon as the liquid has left the

43

orifice, and these inequalities in the figure of the column go on increasing till it is broken up into elongated fragments. These fragments as they are falling through the air continue to be acted on by surface-tension. They therefore shorten themselves, and after a series of oscillations in which they become alternately elongated and flattened, settle down into the form of spherical drops.

This process, which we have followed as it takes place on an individual portion of the falling liquid, goes through its several phases at different distances from the orifice, so that if we examine different portions of the stream as it descends, we shall find next the orifice the unbroken column, then a series of contractions and enlargements, then elongated drops, then flattened drops, and so on till the drops become spherical.

[The circumstances attending the resolution of a cylindrical jet into drops were admirably examined and described by F. Savart ("Mémoire sur la constitution des veines liquides lancées par des orifices circulaires en minces parois," *Ann. d. Chim.* t. liii., 1833) and for the most part explained with great sagacity by Plateau. Let us conceive an infinitely long circular cylinder of liquid, at rest (a motion common to every part of the fluid is necessarily without influence upon the stability, and may therefore be left out of account for convenience of conception and expression), and inquire under what circumstances it is stable or unstable, for small displacements, symmetrical about the axis of figure.

Whatever the deformation of the originally straight boundary of the axial section may be, it can be resolved by Fourier's theorem into deformations of the harmonic type. These component deformations are in general infinite in number, of very wave-length and of arbitrary phase; but in the first stages of the motion, with which alone we are at present concerned, each produces its effect independently of every other, and may be considered by itself. Suppose, therefore, that the equation of the boundary is

$$r = a + a \cos kz, \qquad (1)$$

where a is a small quantity, the axis of z being that of symmetry. 270The wave-length of the disturbance may be called λ, and is connected with k by the equation $k = 2\pi/\lambda$. The capillary tension endeavours to contract the surface of the fluid; so that the stability, or instability, of the cylindrical form of equilibrium depends upon whether the surface (enclosing a given volume) be greater or less respectively after the displacement than before. It has been proved by Plateau (*vide supra*) that the surface is greater than before displacement if ka > 1, that is, if λ < $2\pi a$; but less if ka < 1, or λ > $2\pi a$. Accordingly, the equilibrium is stable if λ be less than the circumference; but unstable if λ be greater than the circumference of the cylinder. Disturbances of the former kind lead to *vibrations* of harmonic type, whose amplitudes always remain small; but disturbances, whose wave-length exceeds the circumference, result in a greater and greater departure from the cylindrical figure. The analytical expression for the motion in the latter case involves exponential terms, one of which (except in case of a particular relation between the initial displacements and velocities) increases rapidly, being equally multiplied in equal times. The coefficient (q) of the time in the exponential term (eqt) may be considered to measure the degree of dynamical instability; its reciprocal 1/q is the time in which the disturbance is multiplied in the ratio 1 : e.

The degree of instability, as measured by q, is not to be determined from statical considerations only; otherwise there would be no limit to the increasing efficiency of the longer wave-lengths. The joint operation of superficial tension and *inertia* in fixing the wave-length of maximum instability was first considered by Lord Rayleigh in a paper (*Math. Soc. Proc.*, November 1878) on the "Instability of Jets." It appears that the value of q may be expressed in the form

$$= \sqrt{\left(\frac{q}{a^3}\right)} \cdot F(ka), \qquad (2)$$

where, as before, T is the superficial tension, ρ the density, and F is given by the following table: —

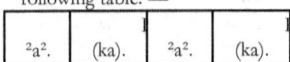

$^2a^2$.	(ka).	$^2a^2$.	(ka).

44

05	1536	4	3382
1	2108	5	3432
2	2794	6	3344
3	3182	8	2701
		9	2015

The greatest value of F thus corresponds, not to a zero value of k^2a^2, but approximately to $k^2a^2 = .4858$, or to $\lambda = 4.508 \times 2a$. Hence the maximum instability occurs when the wave-length of disturbance is about half as great again as that at which instability first commences.

Taking for water, in C.G.S. units, $T = 81$, $\rho = 1$, we get for the case of maximum instability

$$-1 = \frac{\frac{a3}{/2}}{81 \times .343} = .115d3/2 \qquad (3),$$

if d be the diameter of the cylinder. Thus, if $d = 1$, $q-1 = .115$; or for a diameter of one centimetre the disturbance is multiplied 2.7 times in about one-ninth of a second. If the disturbance be multiplied 1000 fold in time, t, $qt = 3\log_e 10 = 6.9$, so that $t = .79d3/2$. For example, if the diameter be one millimetre, the disturbance is multiplied 1000 fold in about one-fortieth of a second. In view of these estimates the rapid disintegration of a fine jet of water will not cause surprise.

The relative importance of two harmonic disturbances depends upon their initial magnitudes, and upon the rate at which they grow. When the initial values are very small, the latter consideration is much the more important; for, if the disturbances be represented by $\alpha 1 e^{q1t}$, $\alpha 2 e^{q2t}$, in which q1 exceeds q2, their ratio is $(\alpha 1/\alpha 2)e^{-(q1 - q2)t}$; and this ratio decreases without limit with the time, whatever be the initial (finite) ratio $\alpha 2 : \alpha 1$. If the initial disturbances are small enough, that one is ultimately preponderant for which the measure of instability is greatest. The smaller the causes by which the original equilibrium is upset, the more will the cylindrical mass tend to divide itself regularly into portions whose length is equal to 4.5 times the diameter. But a disturbance of less favourable wave-length may gain the preponderance in case its magnitude be sufficient to produce disintegration in a less time than that required by the other disturbances present.

The application of these results to actual jets presents no great difficulty. The disturbances by which equilibrium is upset are impressed upon the fluid as it leaves the aperture, and the continuous portion of the jet represents the distance travelled during the time necessary to produce disintegration. Thus the length of the continuous portion necessarily depends upon the character of the disturbances in respect of amplitude and wave-length. It may be increased considerably, as F. Savart showed, by a suitable isolation of the reservoir from tremors, whether due to external sources or to the impact of the jet itself in the vessel placed to receive it. Nevertheless it does not appear to be possible to carry the prolongation very far. Whether the residuary disturbances are of external origin, or are due to friction, or to some peculiarity of the fluid motion within the reservoir, has not been satisfactorily determined. On this point Plateau's explanations are not very clear, and he sometimes expresses himself as if the time of disintegration depended only upon the capillary tension, without reference to initial disturbances at all.

Two laws were formulated by Savart with respect to the length of the continuous portion of a jet, and have been to a certain extent explained by Plateau. For a given fluid and a given orifice the length is approximately proportional to the square root of the head. This follows at once from theory, if it can be assumed that the disturbances remain always of the same character, so that the *time* of disintegration is constant. When the head is given, Savart found the length to be proportional to the diameter of the orifice. From (3) it appears that the time in which a disturbance is multiplied in a given ratio varies, not as d, but as d3/2. Again, when the fluid is changed, the time varies as $\rho 1/2T -1/2$. But it may be doubted whether the length of the continuous portion obeys any very simple laws, even when external disturbances are avoided as far as possible.

When the circumstances of the experiment are such that the reservoir is influenced by the shocks due to the impact of the jet, the disintegration usually establishes itself with complete regularity, and is attended by a musical note (Savart). The impact of the regular series of drops which is at any moment striking the sink (or vessel receiving the water), determines the rupture into similar drops of the portion of the jet at the same moment passing the orifice. The pitch of the note, though not absolutely definite, cannot differ much from that which corresponds to the division of the jet into wave-lengths of maximum instability; and, in fact, Savart found that the frequency was directly as the square root of the head, inversely as the diameter of the orifice, and independent of the nature of the fluid— laws which follow immediately from Plateau's theory.

From the pitch of the note due to a jet of given diameter, and issuing under a given head, the wave-length of the nascent divisions can be at once deduced. Reasoning from some observations of Savart, Plateau finds in this way 4.38 as the ratio of the length of a division to the diameter of the jet. The diameter of the orifice was 3 millims., from which that of the jet is deduced by the introduction of the coefficient .8. Now that the length of a division has been estimated a priori, it is perhaps preferable to reverse Plateau's calculation, and to exhibit the frequency of vibration in terms of the other data of the problem. Thus

$$
\text{frequency} = \frac{(2gh)}{4} \quad (4)
$$
$$
.508d
$$

But the most certain method of obtaining complete regularity of resolution is to bring the reservoir under the influence of an external vibrator, whose pitch is approximately the same as that proper to the jet. H.G. Magnus (*Pogg. Ann.* cvi., 1859) employed a Neef's hammer, attached to the wooden frame which supported the reservoir. Perhaps an electrically maintained tuning-fork is still better. Magnus showed that the most important part of the effect is due to the forced vibration of that side of the vessel which contains the orifice, and that but little 271of it is propagated through the air. With respect to the limits of pitch, Savart found that the note might be a fifth above, and more than an octave below, that proper to the jet. According to theory, there would be no well-defined lower limit; on the other side, the external vibration cannot be efficient if it tends to produce divisions whose length is less than the circumference of the jet. This would give for the interval defining the upper limit π : 4.508, which is very nearly a fifth. In the case of Plateau's numbers (π : 4.38) the discrepancy is a little greater.

The detached masses into which a jet is resolved do not at once assume and retain a spherical form, but execute a series of vibrations, being alternately compressed and elongated in the direction of the axis of symmetry. When the resolution is effected in a perfectly periodic manner, each drop is in the same phase of its vibration as it passes through a given point of space; and thence arises the remarkable appearance of alternate swellings and contractions described by Savart. The interval from one swelling to the next is the space described by the drop during one complete vibration, and is therefore (as Plateau shows) proportional *ceteris paribus* to the square root of the head.

The time of vibration is of course itself a function of the nature of the fluid and of the size of the drop. By the method of dimensions alone it may be seen that the time of infinitely small vibrations varies directly as the square root of the mass of the sphere and inversely as the square root of the capillary tension; and it may be proved that its expression is

$$
= \sqrt{\left(\frac{r}{\pi \rho V} \right)}, \quad (5)
$$

46

T

V being the volume of the vibrating mass.

In consequence of the rapidity of the motion some optical device is necessary to render apparent the phenomena attending the disintegration of a jet. Magnus employed a rotating mirror, and also a rotating disk from which a fine slit was cut out. The readiest method of obtaining instantaneous illumination is the electric spark, but with this Magnus was not successful. The electric spark had, however, been used successfully for this purpose some years before by H. Buff (*Liebigs Ann.* lxxviii. 1851), who observed the *shadow* of the jet on a white screen. Preferable to an opaque screen is a piece of ground glass, which allows the shadow to be examined from the farther side (Lord Rayleigh). Further, the jet may be very well observed directly, if the illumination is properly managed. For this purpose it is necessary to place it between the source of light and the eye. The best effect is obtained when the light of the spark is somewhat diffused by being passed (for example) through a piece of ground glass.

The spark may be obtained from the secondary of an induction coil, whose terminals are in connexion with the coatings of a Leyden jar. By adjustment of the contact breaker the series of sparks may be made to fit more or less perfectly with the formation of the drops. A still greater improvement may be effected by using an electrically maintained fork, which performs the double office of controlling the resolution of the jet and of interrupting the primary current of the induction coil. In this form the experiment is one of remarkable beauty. The jet, illuminated only in one phase of transformation, appears almost perfectly steady, and may be examined at leisure. In one experiment the jet issued horizontally from an orifice of about half a centimetre in diameter, and almost immediately assumed a rippled outline. The gradually increasing amplitude of the disturbance, the formation of the elongated ligament, and the subsequent transformation of the ligament into a spherule, could be examined with ease. In consequence of the transformation being in a more advanced stage at the forward than at the hinder end, the ligament remains for a moment connected with the mass behind, when it has freed itself from the mass in front, and thus the resulting spherule acquires a backwards relative velocity, which of necessity leads to a collision. Under ordinary circumstances the spherule rebounds, and may be thus reflected backwards and forwards several times between the adjacent masses. Magnus showed that the stream of spherules may be diverted into another path by the attraction of a powerfully electrified rod, held a little below the place of resolution.

Very interesting modifications of these phenomena are observed when a jet from an orifice in a thin plate (Tyndall has shown that a pinhole gas burner may also be used with advantage) is directed obliquely upwards. In this case drops which break away with different velocities are carried under the action of gravity into different paths; and thus under ordinary circumstances a jet is apparently resolved into a "sheaf," or bundle of jets all lying in one vertical plane. Under the action of a vibrator of suitable periodic time the resolution is regularized, and then each drop, breaking away under like conditions, is projected with the same velocity, and therefore follows the same path. The apparent gathering together of the sheaf into a fine and well-defined stream is an effect of singular beauty.

In certain cases where the tremor to which the jet is subjected is compound, the single path is replaced by two, three or even more paths, which the drops follow in a regular cycle. The explanation has been given with remarkable insight by Plateau. If, for example, besides the principal disturbance, which determines the size of the drops, there be another of twice the period, it is clear that the alternate drops break away under different conditions and therefore with different velocities. Complete periodicity is only attained after the passage of a *pair* of drops; and thus the odd series of drops pursues one path, and the even series another.

Electricity, as has long been known, has an extraordinary influence upon the appearance of a fine jet of water ascending in a nearly perpendicular direction. In its normal state the jet resolves itself into drops, which even before passing the summit, and still more after passing it, are scattered through a considerable width. When a feebly electrified body

47

(such as a stick of sealing-wax gently rubbed upon the coat sleeve) is brought into its neighbourhood, the jet undergoes a remarkable transformation and appears to become coherent; but under more powerful electrical action the scattering becomes even greater than at first. The second effect is readily attributed to the mutual repulsion of the electrified drops, but the action of feeble electricity in producing apparent coherence was long unexplained.

It was shown by W. von Beetz that the coherence is apparent only, and that the place where the jet breaks into drops is not perceptibly shifted by the electricity. By screening the various parts with metallic plates in connexion with earth, Beetz further proved that, contrary to the opinion of earlier observers, the seat of sensitiveness is not at the root of the jet where it leaves the orifice, but at the place of resolution into drops. An easy way of testing this conclusion is to excite the extreme tip of a glass rod, which is then held in succession to the root of the jet, and to the place of resolution. An effect is observed in the latter, and not in the former position.

The normal scattering of a nearly vertical jet is due to the *rebound* of the drops when they come into collision with one another. Such collisions are inevitable in consequence of the different velocities acquired by the drops under the action of the capillary force, as they break away irregularly from the continuous portion of the jet. Even when the resolution is regularized by the action of external vibrations of suitable frequency, as in the beautiful experiments of Savart and Plateau, the drops must still come into contact before they reach the summit of their parabolic path. In the case of a continuous jet, the equation of continuity shows that as the jet loses velocity in ascending, it must increase in section. When the stream consists of drops following one another in single file, no such increase of section is possible; and then the constancy of the total stream requires a gradual approximation of the drops, which in the case of a nearly vertical direction of motion cannot stop short of actual contact. Regular vibration has, however, the effect of postponing the collisions and consequent scattering of the drops, and in the case of a direction of motion less nearly vertical, may prevent them altogether.

Under moderate electrical influence there is no material 272change in the resolution into drops, nor in the subsequent motion of the drops up to the moment of collision. The difference begins here. Instead of rebounding after collision, as the unelectrified drops of clean water generally, or always, do, the electrified drops *coalesce*, and then the jet is no longer scattered about. When the electrical influence is more powerful, the repulsion between the drops is sufficient to prevent actual contact, and then, of course, there is no opportunity for amalgamation.

These experiments may be repeated with extreme ease, and with hardly any apparatus. The diameter of the jet may be about 1/20 in., and it may issue from a glass nozzle. The pressure may be such as to give a fountain about 2 ft. high. The change in the sound due to the falling drops as they strike the bottom of the sink should be noticed, as well as that in the appearance of the jet.

The actual behaviour of the colliding drops becomes apparent under instantaneous illumination, *e.g.* by sparks from a Leyden jar. The jet should be situated between the sparks and the eye, and the observation is facilitated by a piece of ground glass held a little beyond the jet, so as to diffuse the light; or the *shadow* of the jet may be received on the ground glass, which is then held as close as possible on the side towards the observer.

In another form of the experiment, which, though perhaps less striking to the eye, lends itself better to investigation, the collision takes place between two still unresolved jets issuing horizontally from glass nozzles in communication with reservoirs containing water. One at least of the reservoirs must be insulated. In the absence of dust and greasy contamination, the obliquely colliding jets may rebound from one another without coalescence for a considerable time. In this condition there is complete electrical insulation between the jets, as may be proved by the inclusion in the circuit of a delicate galvanometer, and a low electromotive force. But if the difference of potential exceed a small amount (1 or 2 volts), the jets instantaneously coalesce. There is no reason to doubt that in the case of the fountain also, coalescence is due to *differences* of potential between colliding drops.

If the water be soapy, and especially if it contain a small proportion of milk, coalescence ensues without the help of electricity. In the case of the fountain the experiment may be made by leading tap-water through a Woulfe's bottle in which a little milk has been placed. As the milk is cleared out, the scattering of the drops is gradually re-established.

In attempting to explain these curious phenomena, it is well to consider what occurs during a collision. As the liquid masses approach one another, the intervening air has to be squeezed out. In the earlier stages of approximation the obstacle thus arising may not be important; but when the thickness of the layer of air is reduced to the point at which the colours of thin plates are visible, the approximation must be sensibly resisted by the viscosity of the air which still remains to be got rid of. No change in the capillary conditions can arise until the interval is reduced to a small fraction of a wave-length of light; but such a reduction, unless extremely local, is strongly opposed by the remaining air. It is true that this opposition is temporary. The question is whether the air can everywhere be squeezed out during the short time over which the collision extends.

It would seem that the forces of electrical attraction act with peculiar advantage. If we suppose that upon the whole the air cannot be removed, so that the mean distance between the opposed surfaces remains constant, the electric attractions tend to produce an instability whereby the smaller intervals are diminished while the larger are increased. Extremely local contacts of the liquids, while opposed by capillary tension which tends to keep the surfaces flat, are thus favoured by the electrical forces, which moreover at the small distances in question act with exaggerated power.

A question arises as to the mode of action of milk or soap turbidity. The observation that it is possible for soap to be in excess may here have significance. It would seem that the surfaces, coming into collision within a fraction of a second of their birth, would still be subject to further contamination from the interior. A particle of soap rising accidentally to the surface would spread itself with rapidity. Now such an outward movement of the liquid is just what is required to hasten the removal of intervening air. It is obvious that the effect would fail if the contamination of the surface had proceeded too far previously to the collision.

This view is confirmed by experiments in which other gases are substituted for air as the environment of colliding jets. Oxygen and coal-gas were found to be without effect. On the other hand, the more soluble gases, carbon dioxide, nitrous oxide, sulphur dioxide, and steam, at once caused union.]

Stability of the Catenoid.—When the internal pressure is equal to the external, the film forms a surface of which the mean curvature at every point is zero. The only surface of revolution having this property is the catenoid formed by the revolution of a catenary about its directrix. This catenoid, however, is in stable equilibrium only when the portion considered is such that the tangents to the catenary at its extremities intersect before they reach the directrix.

To prove this, let us consider the catenary as the form of equilibrium of a chain suspended between two fixed points A and B. Suppose the chain hanging between A and B to be of very great length, then the tension at A or B will be very great. Let the chain be hauled in over a peg at A. At first the tension will diminish, but if the process be continued the tension will reach a minimum value and will afterwards increase to infinity as the chain between A and B approaches to the form of a straight line. Hence for every tension greater than the minimum tension there are two catenaries passing through A and B. Since the tension is measured by the height above the directrix these two catenaries have the same directrix. Every catenary lying between them has its directrix higher, and every catenary lying beyond them has its directrix lower than that of the two catenaries.

Now let us consider the surfaces of revolution formed by this system of catenaries revolving about the directrix of the two catenaries of equal tension. We know that the radius of curvature of a surface of revolution in the plane normal to the meridian plane is the portion of the normal intercepted by the axis of revolution.

The radius of curvature of a catenary is equal and opposite to the portion of the normal intercepted by the directrix of the catenary. Hence a catenoid whose directrix coincides with the axis of revolution has at every point its principal radii of curvature equal and opposite, so that the mean curvature of the surface is zero.

The catenaries which lie between the two whose direction coincides with the axis of revolution generate surfaces whose radius of curvature convex towards the axis in the meridian plane is less than the radius of concave curvature. The mean curvature of these surfaces is therefore convex towards the axis. The catenaries which lie beyond the two generate surfaces whose radius of curvature convex towards the axis in the meridian plane is greater than the radius of concave curvature. The mean curvature of these surfaces is, therefore, concave towards the axis.

Now if the pressure is equal on both sides of a liquid film, and if its mean curvature is zero, it will be in equilibrium. This is the case with the two catenoids. If the mean curvature is convex towards the axis the film will move from the axis. Hence if a film in the form of the catenoid which is nearest the axis is ever so slightly displaced from the axis it will move farther from the axis till it reaches the other catenoid.

If the mean curvature is concave towards the axis the film will tend to approach the axis. Hence if a film in the form of the catenoid which is nearest the axis be displaced towards the axis, it will tend to move farther towards the axis and will collapse. Hence the film in the form of the catenoid which is nearest the axis is in unstable equilibrium under the condition that it is exposed to equal pressures within and without. If, however, the circular ends of the catenoid are closed with solid disks, so that the volume of air contained between these disks and the film is determinate, the film will be in stable equilibrium however large a portion of the catenary it may consist of.

273

The criterion as to whether any given catenoid is stable or not may be obtained as follows:—

FIG. 14.

Let PABQ and ApqB (fig. 14) be two catenaries having the same directrix and intersecting in A and B. Draw Pp and Qq touching both catenaries, Pp and Qq will intersect at T, a point in the directrix; for since any catenary with its directrix is a similar figure to any other catenary with its directrix, if the directrix of the one coincides with that of the other the centre of similitude must lie on the common directrix. Also, since the curves at P and p are equally inclined to the directrix, P and p are corresponding points and the line Pp must pass through the centre of similitude. Similarly Qq must pass through the centre of similitude. Hence T, the point of intersection of Pp and Qq, must be the centre of similitude and must be on the common directrix. Hence the tangents at A and B to the upper catenary must intersect above the directrix, and the tangents at A and B to the lower catenary must intersect below the directrix. The condition of stability of a catenoid is therefore that the tangents at the extremities of its generating catenary must intersect before they reach the directrix.

Stability of a Plane Surface.—We shall next consider the limiting conditions of stability of the horizontal surface which separates a heavier fluid above from a lighter fluid below. Thus, in an experiment of F. Duprez ("Sur un cas particulier de l'équilibre des liquides," *Nouveaux Mém. del' Acad. de Belgique, 1851 et 1853*), a vessel containing olive oil is placed with its mouth downwards in a vessel containing a mixture of alcohol and water, the mixture being denser than the oil. The surface of separation is in this case horizontal and stable, so that the equilibrium is established of itself. Alcohol is then added very gradually to the mixture till it becomes lighter than the oil. The equilibrium of the fluids would now be unstable if it were not for the tension of the surface which separates them, and which, when the orifice of the vessel is not too large, continues to preserve the stability of the equilibrium.

When the equilibrium at last becomes unstable, the destruction of equilibrium takes place by the lighter fluid ascending in one part of the orifice and the heavier descending in

50

the other. Hence the displacement of the surface to which we must direct our attention is one which does not alter the volume of the liquid in the vessel, and which therefore is upward in one part of the surface and downward in another. The simplest case is that of a rectangular orifice in a horizontal plane, the sides being a and b.

Let the surface of separation be originally in the plane of the orifice, and let the co-ordinates x and y be measured from one corner parallel to the sides a and b respectively, and let z be measured upwards. Then if ρ be the density of the upper liquid, and σ that of the lower liquid, and P the original pressure at the surface of separation, then when the surface receives an upward displacement z, the pressure above it will be $P - \rho gz$, and that below it will be $P - \sigma gz$, so that the surface will be acted on by an upward pressure $(\rho - \sigma)gz$. Now if the displacement z be everywhere very small, the curvature in the planes parallel to xz and yz will be d^2z/dx^2 and d^2z/dy^2 respectively, and if T is the surface-tension the whole upward force will be

$$T\left(\frac{d^2z}{dx^2} + \frac{d^2z}{dy^2}\right) + (\rho - \sigma)gz.$$

If this quantity is of the same sign as z, the displacement will be increased, and the equilibrium will be unstable. If it is of the opposite sign from z, the equilibrium will be stable. The limiting condition may be found by putting it equal to zero. One form of the solution of the equation, and that which is applicable to the case of a rectangular orifice, is

$$z = C \sin px \sin qy.$$

Substituting in the equation we find the condition

$$(p^2 + q^2)T - (\rho - \sigma)g = \begin{cases} \text{+ve stable.} \\ 0 \quad \text{neutral.} \\ \text{−ve unstable.} \end{cases}$$

That the surface may coincide with the edge of the orifice, which is a rectangle, whose sides are a and b, we must have

$$pa = m\pi, \quad qb = n\pi,$$

when m and n are integral numbers. Also, if m and n are both unity, the displacement will be entirely positive, and the volume of the liquid will not be constant. That the volume may be constant, either n or m must be an even number. We have, therefore, to consider the conditions under which

$$\pi^2\left(\frac{m^2}{a^2} + \frac{n^2}{b^2}\right)T - (\rho - \sigma)g$$

cannot be made negative. Under these conditions the equilibrium is stable for all small displacements of the surface. The smallest admissible value of $m^2/a^2 + n^2/b^2$ is $4/a^2 + 1/b^2$, where a is the longer side of the rectangle. Hence the condition of stability is that

$$\pi^2\left(\frac{4}{a^2} + \frac{1}{b^2}\right)T - (\rho - \sigma)g$$

is a positive quantity. When the breadth b is less than $\sqrt{[\pi^2T/(\rho - \sigma)g]}$ the length a may be unlimited.

When the orifice is circular of radius a, the limiting value of a is $\sqrt{[(T/g\rho)z]}$, where z is the least root of the equation

$$\frac{2J_1(z)}{z} = 1 - \frac{z^2}{2\cdot} - \frac{z^4}{\cdots} - \frac{z^6}{2\cdot} + \&c., = 0.$$

51

$$\cdot 4 \qquad \cdot 4^2 \cdot 6 \qquad 4^2 \cdot 6^2 \cdot 8$$

The least root of this equation is
$$z = 3.83171.$$

If h is the height to which the liquid will rise in a capillary tube of unit radius, then the diameter of the largest orifice is
$$2a = 3.83171 \ \sqrt{(2h)} = 5.4188 \ \sqrt{(h)}.$$

Duprez found from his experiments
$$2a = 5.485\sqrt{(h)}.$$

[The above theory may be well illustrated by a lecture experiment. A thin-walled glass tube of internal diameter equal to 14½ mm. is ground true at the lower end. The upper end is contracted and is fitted with a rubber tube under the control of a pinch-cock. Water is sucked up from a vessel of moderate size, the rubber is nipped, and by a quick motion the tube and vessel are separated, preferably by a downward movement of the latter. The inverted tube, with its suspended water, being held in a clamp, a beaker containing a few drops of ether is brought up from below until the free surface of the water is in contact with ether vapour. The lowering of tension, which follows the condensation of the vapour, is then strikingly shown by the sudden precipitation of the water.]

Effect of Surface-tension on the Velocity of Waves.—When a series of waves is propagated on the surface of a liquid, the surface-tension has the effect of increasing the pressure at the crests of the waves and diminishing it in the troughs. If the wave-length is λ, the equation of the surface is
$$y = b \sin 2\pi \ \underline{\quad}$$

The pressure due to the surface tension T is
$$p = -T \frac{^2 y}{x^2} \quad \frac{\pi^2}{2} \ y.$$

This pressure must be added to the pressure due to gravity $g\rho y$. Hence the waves will be propagated as if the intensity of gravity had been
$$= g + \frac{f}{} \frac{\pi^2}{2}$$

instead of g. Now it is shown in hydrodynamics that the velocity of propagation of waves in deep water is that acquired by a heavy body falling through half the radius of the circle whose circumference is the wave-length, or
$$^2 = \frac{\lambda}{\pi} \quad \frac{\lambda}{\pi} \quad \frac{\pi T}{\lambda} \qquad (1)$$

This velocity is a minimum when
$$= 2\pi \ \sqrt{\ \frac{\lambda}{\rho}}$$

and the minimum value is
$$= 4\sqrt{\ \frac{g}{}}$$

For waves whose length from crest to crest is greater than λ, the principal force concerned in the motion is that of gravitation. 274For waves whose length is less than λ the

52

principal force concerned is that of surface-tension. Lord Kelvin proposed to distinguish the latter kind of waves by the name of ripples.

When a small body is partly immersed in a liquid originally at rest, and moves horizontally with constant velocity V, waves are propagated through the liquid with various velocities according to their respective wave-lengths. In front of the body the relative velocity of the fluid and the body varies from V where the fluid is at rest, to zero at the cutwater on the front surface of the body. The waves produced by the body will travel forwards faster than the body till they reach a distance from it at which the relative velocity of the body and the fluid is equal to the velocity of propagation corresponding to the wave-length. The waves then travel along with the body at a constant distance in front of it. Hence at a certain distance in front of the body there is a series of waves which are stationary with respect to the body. Of these, the waves of minimum velocity form a stationary wave nearest to the front of the body. Between the body and this first wave the surface is comparatively smooth. Then comes the stationary wave of minimum velocity, which is the most marked of the series. In front of this is a double series of stationary waves, the gravitation waves forming a series increasing in wave-length with their distance in front of the body, and the surface-tension waves or ripples diminishing in wave-length with their distance from the body, and both sets of waves rapidly diminishing in amplitude with their distance from the body.

If the current-function of the water referred to the body considered as origin is ψ, then the equation of the form of the crest of a wave of velocity w, the crest of which travels along with the body, is

$$d\psi = w \, ds$$

where ds is an element of the length of the crest. To integrate this equation for a solid of given form is probably difficult, but it is easy to see that at some distance on either side of the body, where the liquid is sensibly at rest, the crest of the wave will approximate to an asymptote inclined to the path of the body at an angle whose sine is w/V, where w is the velocity of the wave and V is that of the body.

The crests of the different kinds of waves will therefore appear to diverge as they get farther from the body, and the waves themselves will be less and less perceptible. But those whose wave-length is near to that of the wave of minimum velocity will diverge less than any of the others, so that the most marked feature at a distance from the body will be the two long lines of ripples of minimum velocity. If the angle between these is 2θ, the velocity of the body is w sec θ, where w for water is about 23 centimetres per second.

[Lord Kelvin's formula (1) may be applied to find the surface-tension of a clean or contaminated liquid from observations upon the length of waves of known periodic time, travelling over the surface. If $v = \lambda/\tau$ we have

$$= \frac{\lambda^3}{\pi\tau^2} \quad \text{oth} \quad \frac{\pi h}{} \quad \frac{\lambda^2 \rho}{\pi^2} \qquad (2)$$

h denoting the depth of the liquid. In observations upon ripples the factor involving h may usually be omitted, and thus in the case of water ($\rho = 1$)

$$= \frac{3}{\pi\tau^2} \quad \frac{\lambda^2}{\pi^2} \qquad (3)$$

simply. The method has the advantage of independence of what may occur at places where the liquid is in contact with solid bodies.

The waves may be generated by electrically maintained tuning-forks from which dippers touch the surface; but special arrangements are needed for rendering them visible. The obstacles are (1) the smallness of the waves, and (2) the changes which occur at speeds too rapid for the eye to follow. The second obstacle is surmounted by the aid of the stroboscopic method of observation, the light being intermittent in the period of vibration, so that practically only one phase is seen. In order to render visible the small waves employed, and which we may regard as deviations of a plane surface from its true figure, the method by which Foucault tested reflectors is suitable. The following results have been obtained

Clean

4.0

Greasy to the point where camphor motions
nearly cease   3.0

Saturated with olive oil

1.0

Saturated with sodium oleate

5.0

(*Phil. Mag.* November 1890) for the tensions of various water-surfaces at 18° C., reckoned in C.G.S. measure.

The tension for clean water thus found is considerably lower than that (81) adopted by Quincke, but it seems to be entitled to confidence, and at any rate the deficiency is not due to contamination of the surface.

A calculation analogous to that of Lord Kelvin may be applied to find the frequency of small transverse vibrations of a cylinder of liquid under the action of the capillary force. Taking the case where the motion is strictly in two dimensions, we may write as the polar equation of the surface at time t

$$r = a + \alpha_n \cos n\theta \cos pt, \qquad (4)$$

where p is given by

$$p^2 = \frac{(n^3 - n)}{a^3} \qquad (5)$$

If n = 1, the section remains circular, there is no force of restitution, and p = 0. The principal vibration, in which the section becomes elliptical, corresponds to n = 2.

Vibrations of this kind are observed whenever liquid issues from an elliptical or other non-circular hole, or even when it is poured from the lip of an ordinary jug; and they are superposed upon the general progressive motion. Since the phase of vibration depends upon the time elapsed, it is always the same at the same point in space, and thus the motion is *steady* in the hydrodynamical sense, and the boundary of the jet is a fixed surface. In so far as the vibrations may be regarded as isochronous, the distance between consecutive corresponding points of the recurrent figure, or, as it may be called, the *wave-length* of the figure, is directly proportional to the velocity of the jet, *i.e.* to the square root of the head. But as the head increases, so do the *lateral* velocities which go to form the transverse vibrations. A departure from the law of isochronism may then be expected to develop itself.

The transverse vibrations of non-circular jets allow us to solve a problem which at first sight would appear to be of great difficulty. According to Marangoni the diminished surface-tension of soapy water is due to the formation of a film. The formation cannot be instantaneous, and if we could measure the tension of a surface not more than 1/100 of a second old, we might expect to find it undisturbed, or nearly so, from that proper to pure water. In order to carry out the experiment the jet is caused to issue from an elliptical orifice in a thin plate, about 2 mm. by 1 mm., under a head of 15 cm. A comparison under similar circumstances shows that there is hardly any difference in the wave-lengths of the patterns obtained with pure and with soapy water, from which we conclude that at this initial stage, the surface-tensions are the same. As early as 1869 Dupré had arrived at a similar conclusion from experiments upon the vertical rise of fine jets.

A formula, similar to (5), may be given for the frequencies of vibration of a spherical mass of liquid under capillary force. If, as before, the frequency be p/2Π, and a the radius of the sphere, we have

$$p^2 = n(n - 1) \frac{}{(n + 2)}, \qquad (6)$$

$$\frac{}{a^3}$$

n denoting the order of the spherical harmonic by which the deviation from a spherical figure is expressed. To find the radius of the sphere of water which vibrates seconds, put p = 2Π, T = 81, ρ = 1, n = 2. Thus a = 2.54 cms., or one inch very nearly.]

TABLES OF SURFACE-TENSION

In the following tables the units of length, mass and time are the centimetre, the gramme and the second, and the unit of force is that which if it acted on one gramme for one second would communicate to it a velocity of one centimetre per second:—

275

Table of Surface-Tension at 20° C. (Quincke).

Liquid.	Specific Gravity.	Tension of surface separating the liquid from			Angle of contact with glass in presence of		
		ir.	ater.	ercury	ir.	ater.	ercury
Water	1	81	.	418	5° 32'	.	25° 6'
Mercury	13.5432	40	18	.	1° 8'	6° 8'	.
Bisulfuride of Carbon	1.2687	32.1	41.75	372.5	2° 16'	5° 8'	.
Chloroform	1.4878	30.6	29.5	399	.	.	.
Alcohol	0.7906	25.5	.	399	5° 12'	.	.
Olive Oil	0.9136	36.9	20.56	335	1° 50'	7°	47° 2'
Turpentine	0.8867	29.7	11.55	250.5	7° 44'	7° 44'	47° 2'
Petroleum	0.7977	31.7	27.8	284	6° 20'	2° 46'	.
Hydrochloric Acid	1.1	70.1	.	377	.	2° 46'	.
Solution of Hyposulphite of Soda	1.1248	77.5	.	442.5	3° 20'	.	10° 42'

Olive Oil and Alcohol, 12.2.

Olive oil and aqueous alcohol (sp. g. .9231, tension of free surface 25.5), 6.8, angle 87° 48'.

Quincke has determined the surface-tension of a great many substances near their point of fusion or solidification. His method was that of observing the form of a large drop

55

standing on a plane surface. If K is the height of the flat surface of the drop, and k that of the point where its tangent plane is vertical, then

$$T = \tfrac{1}{2}(K - k)^2 g\rho$$

Quincke finds that for several series of substances the surface-tension is nearly proportional to the density, so that if we call $(K - k)^2 = 2T/g\rho$ the specific cohesion, we may state the general results of his experiments as follows:—

Surface-Tensions of Liquids at their Point of Solidification. From Quincke.

Substance.	Temperature of Solidification.	Surface-Tension.
Platinum	2000° C.	1658
Gold	1200°	983
Zinc	360°	860
Tin	230°	587
Mercury	−40°	577
Lead	330°	448
Silver	1000°	419
Bismuth	265°	382
Potassium	58°	364
Sodium	90°	253
Antimony	432°	244
Borax	1000°	212
Carbonate of Soda	1000°	206
Chloride of Sodium	. .	114
Water	0°	86.2
Selenium	217°	70.4
Sulphur	111°	41.3
Phosphorus	43°	41.1
Wax	68°	33.4

The bromides and iodides have a specific cohesion about half that of mercury. The nitrates, chlorides, sugars and fats, as also the metals lead, bismuth and antimony, have a specific cohesion nearly equal to that of mercury. Water, the carbonates and sulphates, and probably phosphates, and the metals platinum, gold, silver, cadmium, tin and copper have a specific cohesion double that of mercury. Zinc, iron and palladium, three times that of mercury, and sodium, six times that of mercury.

RELATION OF SURFACE-TENSION TO TEMPERATURE

It appears from the experiments of Brunner and of Wolf on the ascent of water in tubes that at the temperature t° centigrade

$$= 75.20 \ (1 - 0.00187 \ t) \ (Brunner);$$

$$= 76.08 \ (1 - 0.002 \ t + 0.00000415 \ t^2), \text{ for a tube } .02346 \text{ cm. diameter}$$
(Wolf);

$$= 77.34 \ (1 - 0.00181 \ t), \text{ for a tube } .03098 \text{ cm. diameter (Wolf)}.$$

Lord Kelvin has applied the principles of Thermodynamics to determine the thermal effects of increasing or diminishing the area of the free surface of a liquid, and has shown that in order to keep the temperature constant while the area of the surface increases by unity, an amount of heat must be supplied to the liquid which is dynamically equivalent to the product of the absolute temperature into the decrement of the surface-tension per degree of temperature. We may call this the *latent heat of surface-extension*.

It appears from the experiments of C. Brunner and C.J.E. Wolf that at ordinary temperatures the latent heat of extension of the surface of water is dynamically equivalent to about half the mechanical work done in producing the surface-extension.

REFERENCES.—Further information on some of the matters discussed above will be found in Lord Rayleigh's *Collected Scientific Papers* (1901). In its full extension the subject of capillarity is very wide. Reference may be made to A.W. Reinold and Sir A.W. Rücker (*Phil. Trans.* 1886, p. 627); Sir W. Ramsay and J. Shields (*Zeitschr. physik. Chem.* 1893, 12, p. 433); and on the theoretical side, see papers by Josiah Willard Gibbs; R. Eötvös (*Wied. Ann.*, 1886, 27, p. 452); J.D. Van der Waals, G. Bakker and other writers of the Dutch school.

(J. C. M.; R.)

1In this revision of James Clerk Maxwell's classical article in the ninth edition of the *Encyclopaedia Britannica*, additions are marked by square brackets.

2See Enrico Betti, *Teoria della Capillarità: Nuovo Cimento* (1867); a memoir by M. Stahl, "Ueber einige Punckte in der Theorie der Capillarerscheinungen,"*Pogg. Ann.* cxxxix. p. 239 (1870); and J.D. Van der Waal's *Over de Continuiteit van den Gasen Vloeistoftoestand*. A good account of the subject from a mathematical point of view will be found in James Challis's "Report on the Theory of Capillary Attraction," *Brit. Ass. Report*, iv. p. 235 (1834).

3*Nouvelle théorie de l'action capillaire* (1831).

4*Determinatio superficiei minimae rotatione curvae data duo puncta jungentis circa datum axem ortae* (Göttingen, 1831).

5*Leçons de calcul des variations* (Paris, 1861).

6"Sur la surface de révolution dont la courbure moyenne est constante,"*Liouville's Journal*, vi.

7"Théorie géometrique des rayons et centres de courbure," *Bullet, de l'Acad. de Belgique*, 1857.

8*Tractatus de Theoria Mathematica Phaenomenorum in Liquidis actioni gravitatis detractis observatorum* (Bonn, 1857).

9*Journal de l'Institut*, No. 1260.

10*Statique expérimental et théorique des liquides*, 1873.

CAPISTRANO, GIOVANNI DI (1386-1456), Italian friar, theologian and inquisitor, was born in the little village of Capistrano in the Abruzzi, of a family which had come to Italy with the Angevins. He lived at first a wholly secular life, married, and became a successful magistrate; he took part in the continual struggles of the small Italian states in such a way as to compromise himself. During his captivity he was practically ruined and lost his young wife. He then in despair entered the Franciscan order and at once gave himself up to the most rigorous asceticism, violently defending the ideal of strict observance. He was charged with various missions by the popes Eugenius IV. and Nicholas V., in which he acquitted himself with implacable violence. As legate or inquisitor he persecuted the last

Fraticelli of Ferrara, the Jesuati of Venice, the Jews of Sicily, Moldavia and Poland, and, above all, the Hussites of Germany, Hungary and Bohemia; his aim in the last case was to make conferences impossible between the representatives of Rome and the Bohemians, for every attempt at conciliation seemed to him to be conniving at heresy. Finally, after the taking of Constantinople, he succeeded in gathering troops together for a crusade against the Turks (1455), which at least helped to raise the siege of Belgrade, which was being blockaded by Mahommed II. He died shortly afterwards (October 23, 1456), and was canonized in 1690. Capistrano, in spite of this restless life, found time to work both in the lifetime of his master St Bernardino of Siena and after, at the reform of the order of the minor Franciscans, and to uphold both in his writings and his speeches the most advanced theories upon the papal supremacy as opposed to that of the councils.

See E. Jacob, *Johannes von Capistrano*, vol. i.: "Das Leben und Wirken Capistrans;" vol. ii.: "Die handschriftlichen Aufzeichnungen von Reden und Tractaten Capistrans," (1st series, Breslau, 1903-1905).

(P. A.)

CAPITAL (Lat. *caput*, head), in architecture, the crowning member of the column, which projects on each side as it rises, in order to support the abacus and unite the square form of the latter with the circular shaft. The bulk of the capital may either be convex, as in the Doric capital; concave, as in the bell of the Corinthian capital; or bracketed out, as in the Ionic capital. These are the three principal types on which all capitals are based. The capitals of Greek, Doric, Ionic and Corinthian orders are given in the article ORDER.

From the prominent position it occupies in all monumental buildings, it has always been the favourite feature selected for ornamentation, and consequently it has become the clearest indicator of any style.

FIG. 1.—Lotus Capital from   FIG. 2.—Papyrus Capital from
Karnak.   Karnak.

The two earliest capitals of importance are those which are based on the lotus (fig. 1) and papyrus (fig. 2) plants respectively, and these, with the palm tree capital, were the chief types employed by the Egyptians down to the 3rd centuryB.C., when, 276under the Ptolemaic dynasties, various river plants were employed decoratively and the lotus capital goes through various modifications (fig 3) Some kind of volute capital is shown in the Assyrian bas-reliefs, but no Assyrian capital has ever been found, those exhibited as such in the British Museum are bases.

FIG. 3.—   FIG. 4.—Persian
Modified Lotus   Capital
Capital from Philae.   from Persepolis.

The Persian capital belongs to the third class above mentioned, the brackets are carved with the lion (fig. 4) or the griffin projecting right and left to support and lessen the bearing of the architrave, and on their backs carry other brackets at right angles to support the cross timbers. The profuse decoration underneath the bracket capital in the palace of Xerxes and elsewhere, serves no structural function, but gives some variety to the extenuated shaft.

FIG. 5.—Early Greek Capital from the Tomb of Agamemnon,
Mycenae.

The earliest Greek capital is that shown in the Temple-fresco at Cnossus in Crete (1600 B.C.); it was of the first type—convex, and was probably moulded in stucco: the second is represented by the richly carved example of the columns (fig 5) flanking the tomb of Agamemnon in Mycenae (c. 1100 B.C.), also convex, carved with the chevron device, and with an apophyge on which the buds of some flowers are sculptured. The Doric capital of the temple of Apollo at Syracuse (c. 700 B.C.) follows, in which the echinus moulding has become a more definite form: this in the Parthenon reaches its culmination, where the convexity is at the top and bottom with a delicate uniting curve The sloping side of the echinus becomes flatter in the later examples, and in the Colosseum at Rome forms a quarter round.

FIG. 6.—Corinthian Capital from the Tholos of
Epidaurus.

FIG. 7.—Roman Capital from the Temple of Mars Ultor,
Rome.

In the Ionic capital of the Archaic temple of Diana at Ephesus (560 B.C.) the width of the abacus is twice that of its depth, consequently the earliest Ionic capital known was virtually a bracket capital. A century later, in the temple on the Ilissus, published in Stuart and Revett, the abacus has become square. One of the most beautiful Corinthian capitals is that from the Tholos of Epidaurus (400 B.C.) (fig. 6); it illustrates the transition between the earlier Greek capital of Bassae and the Roman version of the temple of Mars Ultor (fig. 7).

The foliage of the Greek Corinthian capital was based on the Acanthus spinosus, that of the Roman on the Acanthus mollis; the capital of the temple of Vesta and other examples at Pompeii are carved with foliage of a different type.

FIG. 8.—Byzantine Capitals from the central portal of St Mark's,
Venice.

FIG. 9.—Byzantine Capital from
the Church of S. Vitale, Ravenna.

FIG. 10.—Byzantine Capital
from the Church of S. Vitale, Ravenna.

FIG. 11.—
Cushion Capital.

FIG. 12.—Romanesque Capitals from the
Cloister of Monreale,
near Palermo, Sicily.

FIG. 13.—Gothic Capitals from Wells
Cathedral.

FIG. 14.—Gothic Capitals from Amiens Cathedral.

FIG. 15.—Italian Renaissance Capital from S. Maria dei Miracoli,
Venice.

Byzantine capitals are of endless variety; the Roman composite capital would seem to
have been the favourite type they followed at first: subsequently, the block of stone was left
rough as it came from the quarry, and the sculptor, set to carve it, evolved 277new types of
design to his own fancy, so that one rarely meets with many repetitions of the same design.
One of the most remarkable is the capital in which the leaves are carved as if blown by the
wind; the finest example being in Sta Sophia, Thessalonica; those in St Mark's, Venice (fig. 8)
specially attracted Ruskin's fancy. Others are found in St Apollinare-in-classe, Ravenna. The
Thistle and Pine capital is found in St Mark's, Venice; St Luke's, Delphi; the mosques of
Kairawan and of Ibn Tūlūn, Cairo, in the two latter cases being taken from Byzantine
churches. The illustration of the capital in S. Vitale, Ravenna (figs. 9 and 10) shows above it
the dosseret required to carry the arch, the springing of which was much wider than the
abacus of the capital.

The Romanesque and Gothic capitals throughout Europe present the same variety as
in the Byzantine and for the same reason, that the artist evolved his conception of the design
from the block he was carving, but in these styles it goes further on account of the clustering
of columns and piers.

The earliest type of capital in Lombardy and Germany is that which is known as the
cushion-cap, in which the lower portion of the cube block has been cut away to meet the
circular shaft (fig. 11). These early types were generally painted at first with various
geometrical designs, afterwards carved.

In Byzantine capitals, the eagle, the lion and the lamb are occasionally carved, but
treated conventionally.

In the Romanesque and Gothic styles, in addition to birds and beasts, figures are
frequently introduced into capitals, those in the Lombard work being rudely carved and
verging on the grotesque; later, the sculpture reaches a higher standard; in the cloisters of
Monreale (fig. 12) the birds being wonderfully true to nature. In England and France (figs.
13 and 14), the figures introduced into the capitals are sometimes full of character. These
capitals, however, are not equal to those of the Early English school, in which the foliage is
conventionally treated as if it had been copied from metal work, and is of infinite variety,
being found in small village churches as well as in cathedrals.

Reference has only been made to the leading examples of the Roman capitals; in the
Renaissance period (fig. 15) the feature became of the greatest importance and its variety
almost as great as in the Byzantine and Gothic styles. The pilaster, which 278was employed
so extensively in the Revival, called for new combinations in the designs for its capitals. Most
of the ornament can be traced to Roman sources, and although less vigorous, shows much
more delicacy and refinement in its carving.

(R. P. S.)

60

CAPITAL (*i.e.* capital stock or fund), in economics, generally, the accumulated wealth either of a man or a community, that is available for earning interest and producing fresh wealth. In social discussion it is sometimes treated as antithetical to labour, but it is in reality the accumulated savings of labour and of the profits accruing from the savings of labour. It is that portion of the annual produce reserved from consumption to supply future wants, to extend the sphere of production, to improve industrial instruments and processes, to carry out works of public utility, and, in short, to secure and enlarge the various means of progress necessary to an increasing community. It is the increment of wealth or means of subsistence analogous to the increment of population and of the wants of civilized man. Hence J.S. Mill and other economists, when seeking a graphic expression of the service of capital, have called it "abstinence." The labourer serves by giving physical and mental effort in order to supply his means of consumption. The capitalist, or labourer-capitalist, serves by abstaining from consumption, by denying himself the present enjoyment of more or less of his means of consumption, in the prospect of a future profit. This quality, apparent enough in the beginnings of capital, applies equally to all its forms and stages; because whether a capitalist stocks his warehouse with goods and produce, improves land, lends on mortgage or other security, builds a factory, opens a mine, or orders the construction of machines or ships, there is the element of self-deprival for the present, with the risk of ultimate loss of what is his own, and what, instead of saving and embodying income productive form, he might choose to consume. On this ground rests the justification of the claims of capital to its industrial rewards, whether in the form of rent, interest or profits of trade and investment.

To any advance in the arts of industry or the comforts of life, a rate of production exceeding the rate of consumption, with consequent accumulation of resources, or in other words, the formation of capital, is indispensable. The primitive cultivators of the soil, whether those of ancient times or the pioneers who formed settlements in the forests of the New World, soon discovered that their labour would be rendered more effective by implements and auxiliary powers of various kinds, and that until the produce from existing means of cultivation exceeded what was necessary for their subsistence, there could be neither labour on their part to produce such implements and auxiliaries, nor means to purchase them. Every branch of industry has thus had a demand for capital within its own circles from the earliest times. The flint arrow-heads, the stone and bronze utensils of fossiliferous origin, and the rude implements of agriculture, war and navigation, of which we read in Homer, were the forerunners of that rich and wonderful display of tools, machines, engines, furnaces and countless ingenious and costly appliances, which represent so large a portion of the capital of civilized countries, and without which the pre-existing capital could not have been developed. Nor in the cultivation of land, or the production simply of food, is the need of implements, and of other auxiliary power, whether animal or mechanical, the only need immediately experienced. The demands on the surplus of produce over consumption are various and incessant. Near the space of reclaimed ground, from which the cultivator derives but a bare livelihood, are some marshy acres that, if drained and enclosed, would add considerably in two or three years to the produce; the forest and other natural obstructions might also be driven farther back with the result, in a few more years, of profit; fences are necessary to allow of pasture and field crops, roads have to be made and farm buildings to be erected; as the work proceeds more artificial investments follow, and by these successive outlays of past savings in improvements, renewed and enhanced from generation to generation, the land, of little value in its natural state either to the owner and cultivator or the community, is at length brought into a highly productive condition. The history of capital in the soil is substantially the history of capital in all other spheres. No progress can be made in any sphere, small or large, without reserved funds possessed by few or more persons, in small or large amounts, and the progress in all cases is adventured under self-deprival in the meanwhile of acquired value, and more or less risk as to the final result.

Capital is necessarily to be distinguished from money, with which in ordinary nomenclature it is almost identical. Wealth may be in other things than money; oxen, wives, tools, have at different stages of civilization represented the recognized form of capital; and modern usage only treats capital as meaning the command of money because money is the ordinary form of it nowadays. The capital of a country can scarce be said to be less than the whole sum of its investments in a productive form, and possessing a recognized productive value.

Adam Smith's distinction of "fixed" and "circulating" capital in the *Wealth of Nations* (book ii. c. i.) cannot fail to be always useful in exhibiting the various forms and conditions under which capital is employed. Yet the principal phenomena of capital are found to be the same, whether the form of investment be more or less permanent or circulable. The machinery in which capital is "fixed," and which yields a profit without apparently changing hands, is in reality passing away day by day, until it is worn out, and has to be replaced. So also of drainage and other land improvements. When the natural forests have been consumed and the landowners begin to plant trees on the bare places, the plantations while growing are a source of health, shelter and embellishment—they are not without a material profit throughout their various stages to maturity—and when, at the lapse of twenty or more years, they are ready to be cut down, and the timber is sold for useful purposes, there is a harvest of the original capital expended as essentially as in the case of the more rapid yearly crops of wheat or oats. The chief distinction would appear to rest in the element of time elapsing between the outlay of capital and its return. Capital may be employed in short loans or bills of exchange at two or three months, in paying wages of labour for which there may be return in a day or not in less than a year or more, or in operations involving within themselves every form of capital expenditure, and requiring a few years or ninety-nine years for the promised fructification on which they proceed. But the common characteristic of capital is that of a fund yielding a return and reproducing itself whether the time to this end be long or short. The division of expenditure or labour (all expenditure having a destination to labour of one kind or another) into "productive" and "unproductive" by the same authority (book ii. c. 3) is also apposite both for purposes of political economy and practical guidance, though economists have found it difficult to define where "productive expenditure" ends and "unproductive expenditure" begins. Adam Smith includes in his enumeration of the "fixed capital" of a country "the acquired and useful abilities of all the inhabitants"; and in this sense expenditure on education, arts and sciences might be deemed expenditure of the most productive value, and yet be wanting in strict commercial account of the profit and loss. It must be admitted that there is a personal expenditure among all ranks of society, which, though not in any sense a capital expenditure, may become capital and receive a productive application, always to be preferred to the grossly unproductive form, in the interest both of the possessors and of the community.

The subject in its details is full of controversies, and a discussion of it at any length would embrace the whole field of economics. The subject will be found fully dealt with in every important economic work, but the following may be specially consulted:—J.S. Mill, *Principles of Political Economy*; J.E. Cairns, *Some Leading Principles of Political Economy*; F.A. Walker,*Political Economy*; A. Marshall, *Principles of Economics*; E. Bohm v. Bawerk, *Capital and Interest*; K. Marx, *Capital*; J.B. Clark, *Capital and its Earnings*; see also the economic works of W.H. Mallock (*Critical Examination of Socialism*, 1908, &c.) for an insistence on the importance of "ability," or brain-work, as against much of modern socialist theorizing against "capitalism."

279

CAPITAL PUNISHMENT. By this term is now meant the infliction of the penalty of death for crime under the sentence of some properly constituted authority, as distinguished from killing the offender as a matter of self-defence or private vengeance, or under the order of some self-constituted or irregular tribunal unknown to the law, such as that of the Vigilantes of California, or of lynch law (*q.v.*). In the early stages of society a man-slayer was killed by the "avenger of blood" on behalf of the family of the man killed, and not as representing the authority of the state (Pollock and Maitland, *Hist. Eng. Law*, ii. 447.) This mode of dealing with homicide survives in the vendetta of Corsica and of the Mainotes in Greece, and in certain of the southern states of North America. The obligation or inclination to take vengeance depends on the fact of homicide, and not on the circumstances in which it was committed, *i.e.* it is a part of the *lex talionis*. The mischief of this system was alleviated under the Levitical law by the creation of cities of refuge, and in Greece and Italy, both in Pagan and Christian times, by the recognition of the right of sanctuary in temples and churches. A second mode of dealing with homicide was that known to early Teutonic and early Celtic law, where the relatives of the deceased, instead of the life of the slayer, received the wer of the deceased, *i.e.* a payment in proportion to the rank of the slain, and the king received the blood-wite for the loss of his man. But even under this system certain crimes were in Anglo-Saxon law bot-less, *i.e.* no compensation could be paid, and the offender must suffer the penalty of death. In the laws of Khammurabi, king of Babylon (2285-2242 B.C.), the death penalty is imposed for many offences. The modes for executing it specially named are burning, drowning and impalement (*Oldest Code of Laws*, by C.H.W. Johns, 1903). Under the Roman law, "capital" punishment also included punishments which deprived the offender of the status of Roman citizen (*capitis deminutio, capitis amissio*), *e.g.* condemnation to servitude in the mines or to deportation to an island (*Dig.* 48. 19).

United Kingdom.—The modes of capital punishment in England under the Saxon and Danish kings were various: hanging, beheading, burning, drowning, stoning, and precipitation from rocks. The principle on which this **British and foreign laws and methods.** variety depended was that where an offence was such as to entitle the king to outlaw the offender, he forfeited all, life and limb, lands and goods, and that the king might take his life and choose the mode of death. William the Conqueror would not allow judgment of death to be executed by hanging and substituted mutilation; but his successors varied somewhat in their policy as to capital punishment, and by the 13th century the penalty of death became by usage (without legislation) the usual punishment for high and petty treason and for all felonies (except mayhem and petty larceny, *i.e.* theft of property worth less than 1s.); see Stephen, *Hist. Cr. Law*, vol. i. 458; Pollock and Maitland, *Hist. Eng. Law*, vol. ii. 459. It therefore included all the more serious forms of crime against person or property, such as murder, manslaughter, arson, highway robbery, burglary (or hamesucken) and larceny; and when statutory felonies were created they were also punishable by death unless the statute otherwise provided. The death penalty was also extended to heretics under the writ *de heretico comburendo*, which was lawfully issuable under statute from 1382 (5 Ric. II. stat. 5) until 1677 (29 Chas. II. c. 9). For this purpose the legislature had adopted the civil law of the Roman Empire, which was not a part of the English common law (Stephen, *Hist. Cr. Law*, vol. ii. 438-469).

The methods of execution by crucifixion (as under the Roman law), or breaking on the wheel (as under the Roman Dutch law and the Holy Roman Empire), were never recognized by the common law, and would fall within the term "cruel and unusual punishments" in the English Bill of Rights, and in the United States would seem to be unconstitutional (see *Wilkinson v. Utah*, 1889, 136 U.S. 436, 446).

The severity of barbarian and feudal laws was mitigated, so far as common-law offences were concerned, by the influence of the Church as the inheritor of Christian traditions and Roman jurisprudence. The Roman law under the empire did not allow the execution of citizens except under the *Lex Porcia*. But the right of the emperors to legislate *per rescriptum principis* enabled them to disregard the ordinary law when so disposed. The 83rd novel of Justinian provided that criminal causes against clerics should be tried by the judges, and that the convicted cleric should be degraded by his bishop before his condemnation by the secular power, and other novels gave the bishops considerable influence, if not authority, over the lay judiciary. In western Europe the right given by imperial legislation in the Eastern Empire was utilized by the Papacy to claim privilege of clergy, *i.e.* that clerks must be remitted to the bishop for canonical punishment, and not subjected to civil condemnation at all. The history of benefit of clergy is given in Pollock and Maitland, *Hist. English Law*, vol. i. pp. 424-440, and Stephen, *Hist. Cr. Law*, vol. iii. 459, 463. By degrees the privilege was extended not only to persons who could prove ordination or show a genuine tonsure, but all persons who had sufficient learning to be able to read the neck-verse (Ps. li. v. 1). Before the Reformation the ecclesiastical courts had ceased to take any effective action with respect to clerks accused of offences against the king's laws; and by the time of Henry VII. burning on the hand under the order of the king's judges was substituted for the old process of compurgation in use in the spiritual courts.

The effect of the claim of benefit of clergy is said to have been to increase the number of convictions, though it mitigated the punishment; and it became, in fact, a means of showing mercy to certain classes of individuals convicted of crime as a kind of privilege to the educated, *i.e.* to all clerks whether secular or religious (25 Edw. III. stat. 3); and it was allowed only in case of a first conviction, except in the case of clerks who could produce their letters of orders or a certificate of ordination. To prevent a second claim it was the practice to brand murderers with the letter M, and other felons with the Tyburn T, and Ben Jonson was in 1598 so marked for manslaughter.

The reign of Henry VIII. was marked by extreme severity in the execution of criminals—as during this time 72,000 persons are said to have been hanged. After the formation of English settlements in America the severity of the law was mitigated by the practice of reprieving persons sentenced to death on condition of their consenting to be transported to the American colonies, and to enter into bond service there. The practice seems to have been borrowed from Spain, and to have been begun in 1597 (39 Eliz. c. 4). It was applied by Cromwell after his campaign in Ireland, and was in full force immediately after the Restoration, and is recognized in the Habeas Corpus Act 1677, and was used for the Cameronians during Claverhouse's campaign in south-west Scotland. In the 18th century the courts were empowered to sentence felons to transportation (see DEPORTATION) instead of to execution, and this state of the law continued until 1857 (6 *Law Quarterly Review*, p. 388). This power to sentence to transportation at first applied only to felonies with benefit of clergy; but in 1705, on the abolition of the necessity of proving capacity to read, all criminals alike became entitled to the benefit previously reserved to clerks. Benefit of clergy was finally abolished in 1827 as to all persons not having privilege of peerage, and in 1841 as to peers and peeresses. Its beneficial effect had now been exhausted, since no clergyable offences remained capital crimes.

At the end of the 18th century the criminal law of all Europe was ferocious and indiscriminate in its administration of capital punishment for almost all forms of grave crime; and yet owing to poverty, social conditions, and the inefficiency of the police, such forms of crime were far more numerous than they now are. The policy and righteousness of the English law were questioned as early as 1766 by Goldsmith through the mouth of the vicar of Wakefield: "Nor can I avoid even questioning the validity of that right which social combinations have assumed of capitally punishing offences of a slight nature. In cases of murder their right is obvious, as it is the duty of us all from the law of self-defence to cut off that man who has shown a disregard for the 280 life of another. Against such all nature rises in arms; but it is not so against him who steals my property." He adds later: "When by indiscriminate penal laws the nation beholds the same punishment affixed to dissimilar degrees of guilt, the people are led to lose all sense of distinction in the crime, and this distinction is the bulwark of all morality."

The opinion expressed by Goldsmith was strongly supported by Bentham, Romilly, Basil Montaguand Mackintosh in England, and resulted in considerable mitigation of the severity of the law. In 1800 over 200 and in 1819 about 180 crimes were capital. As the result of the labour of these eminent men and their disciples, and of Sir Robert Peel, there are now only four crimes (other than offences against military law or naval discipline) capitally punishable in England—high treason, murder, piracy with violence, and destruction of public arsenals and dockyards (The Dockyards, &c., Protection Act 1772). An attempt to abolish the death penalty for this last offence was made in 1837, but failed, and has not since been renewed. In the case of the last two offences sentence of death need not be pronounced, but may be recorded (4 Geo. IV. c. 48). Since 1838 it has in practice been executed only for murder; the method being by hanging.

The change in the severity of the law is best illustrated by the following statistics:—

Yea rs.	Death Sentences.		Sentences Executed.	
	For all Crimes.	For Murder.	For all Crimes.	For Murder.
183	16	14	52	12

1 3 *	183	01 93 1	9	33	6
8 *	183	11 6	25	6	5
2 *	186	29	28	15	15

* Each of these years followed upon legislation mitigating severity of punishment.

During the twelve years from 1893 to 1904, 788 persons were committed for trial for murder, being an average of 65. The highest number was in 1893 (82) and the lowest in 1900 (51). Of those tried in 1904, 28 (26 males and 2 females) were convicted of murder, 16 (all males) were executed; 9 males and 2 females had their sentences commuted to penal servitude for life.

In Scotland capital punishment can be imposed only for treason, murder and offences against 10 Geo. IV. c. 38, *i.e.*, wilful shooting, stabbing, strangling or throwing corrosives with intent to murder, maim, disfigure, disable, or do grievous bodily harm, in all cases where if death had ensued the offence would have been murder. Prior to 1887 rape, robbery, wilful fire-raising and incest, and many other crimes, were also capital offences; but in practice the pains of law were restricted at the instance of the prosecution. The method is by hanging.

In Ireland capital punishment may be inflicted for the same offences as in England, except offences under the Dockyards Protection Act 1772, and it is carried out in the same manner.

Offences under Military Law.—Thus far only crimes against the ordinary law of the land have been dealt with. But both the Naval Discipline Act of 1866 and the Army Act empower courts-martial to pass sentence for a number of offences against military and naval laws. Such sentences are rarely if ever passed where an ordinary court is within reach, or except in time of war. The offences extend from traitorous communication with the enemy and cowardice on the field to falling asleep while acting as a sentinel on active service. It is for the authority confirming a sentence of death by court-martial to direct the mode of execution, which both in the British and United States armies is usually by shooting or hanging. During the Indian Mutiny some mutineers were executed by being blown from the mouth of cannon. As to the history of military punishments see Clode, *Military and Martial Law.*

British Colonies and Possessions.—Under the Indian Penal Code sentence of death may be passed for waging war against the king (s. 121) and for murder (s. 302). If the murder is committed by a man under sentence of transportation for life the death penalty must be imposed (s. 303). In other cases it is alternative. This code has been in substance adopted in Ceylon, in Straits Settlements and Hong-Kong, and in the Sudan. In most of the British colonies and possessions the death penalty may be imposed only in the case of high treason, wilful murder and piracy with violence. But in New South Wales and Victoria sentence of death may be passed for rape and criminal abuse of girls under ten. In Queensland the law was the same until the passing of the Criminal Code of 1899.

Under the Canadian Criminal Code of 1892 the death sentence may be imposed for treason (s. 657), murder (s. 231), rape (s. 267), piracy with violence (s. 127), and upon subjects of a friendly power who levy war on the king in Canada (s. 68). But the judge is bound by statute to report on all death sentences, and the date of execution is fixed so as to give time for considering the report. The sentence is executed by hanging. In South Africa the criminal law is based on the Roman-Dutch law, under which capital punishment is liable for treason (*crimen perduellionis* or *laesae majestatis*), murder and rape (van Lecuwen, c. 36). In the Cape Colony rape is still capital (R. *v. Nonosi*, 1885; 1 Buchanan, 1898). In Natal rape may be punished by hanging (act no. 22, 1898). Though the Roman-Dutch modes of executing the sentence by decapitation or breaking on the wheel have not been formally abolished, in practice the sentence in the Cape Colony is executed by hanging. In the Transvaal hanging is now the sole mode of executing capital punishment (Criminal Procedure Code, 1903, s. 244). The Roman-Dutch law as to crime and punishments has been superseded in Ceylon and British Guiana by ordinance.

Austria-Hungary.—In Austria capital punishment was in 1787 for a time abolished, but was reintroduced in 1795 for high treason, and in 1803 for certain other crimes. Under the penal code still in force in 1906 it might be inflicted for the offences in the table given below, but not on offenders who were under twenty when they committed the offence. The annexed table indicates that the full sentence was sparingly executed. Under a Penal Code drafted in 1906, however, only two offences were made capital, viz. high treason against the person of the emperor and the graver cases of murder. The sentence is executed by hanging.

Crimes Punishable by Death.	1853 to 1873.		1875 to 1900.		1901 to 1903.	
	Condemned.	Executed.	Condemned.	Executed.	Condemned.	Executed.
High treason	4	0	1	0	0	0
Murder s. 136	8 80	1 02	2 085	8 1	1 80	9
Killing by robbers, s. 141	1 2	3	3 5	1	3	0
Public violence, ss. 85, 87	. .	.	1	0	0	0
Incendiarism, s. 167	5	0	0	0	0	0
Criminal use of explosives (explosives law, s. 4)	. .	.	. .	.	. .	.

Belgium.—Under the Belgian Penal Code of 1867 the death penalty is retained for certain forms of high treason, and for assassination and parricide by poisoning. It may not be pronounced on a person under eighteen. The sentence is executed publicly by the guillotine. No execution seems to have taken place since 1863.

Denmark.—Sentence of death may be imposed for most forms of high treason, aggravated cases of murder, rape and piracy. It is executed publicly by the axe. Offenders under eighteen are not liable.

Finland.—In Finland the death penalty is alleged not to have been inflicted since 1824. It may be imposed for the assassination of the grand duke or grand duchess or the head of a friendly state, and wilful murder of other persons.

France.—Under the *ancien régime* in France, 115 crimes had become capital in 1789. The mode of execution varied, but in some cases it was effected by breaking on the wheel or burning, 281and was coupled with mutilation. Under the Penal Code of 1810, as amended in or after 1832, even so late as 1871, thirty offences were capital, one being perjury against a prisoner resulting in his condemnation to death (art. 361). At present it may be imposed for wounding a public official with intent to murder (art. 233), assassination, parricide, poisoning, killing to commit a crime or escape from justice (arts. 302, 304). But juries freely exercise the power of acquitting in capital cases, or of defeating the capital sentence by finding extenuating circumstances in more than seven-eighths of the cases, which compels the court to reduce the punishment by one or more degrees, *i.e.* below the penalty of death. And in recent times the prerogative of mercy has been continually exercised by the president, even in gross cases where public opinion demanded the extreme penalty. The sentence is executed in public by the guillotine.

Germany.—In many of the states of Germany capital punishment had been abolished (Brunswick, Coburg, Nassau, Oldenburg in 1849; Saxe-Meiningen, Saxe-Weimar, 1862; Baden, 1863; Saxony, 1868). But it has been restored by the Imperial Criminal Code of 1872, in the case of attempts on the life of the emperor, or of the sovereign of any federal state in which the offender happens to be (s. 80), and for deliberate homicide (s. 211)—as opposed to intentional homicide without deliberation—and for certain treasonable acts committed when a state of siege has been proclaimed. The sentence is executed by beheading (s. 13).

Holland.—In Holland there have been no executions since 1860. Capital punishment (by hanging) was abolished in 1870, and was not reintroduced in the Penal Code of 1886.

Italy.—Capital punishment was abolished in Tuscany as far back as 1786, and from Italy has come the chief opposition to the death penalty, originated by Beccaria, and supported by many eminent jurists. Under the Penal Code of 1888 the death penalty was abrogated for all crimes, even for regicide. The cases of homicide in Italy are very numerous compared with those in England, amounting in 1905 to 105 per million as compared with 27 per million in the United Kingdom.

Japan.—The penalty of death is executed by hanging within a prison. It may be imposed for executing or contriving acts of violence against the mikado or certain of his family, and for seditious violence with the object of seizing the territory or subverting the government or laws of Japan, or conspiring with foreign powers to commence hostilities against Japan. It is inflicted for certain forms of homicide, substantially wilful murder in the first degree.

Norway.—Under Norwegian law, up to 1905, sentence of death might be passed for murder with premeditation, but the court might as an alternative decree penal servitude for life. Sentence of death had also to be passed in cases where a person under sentence of penal servitude for life committed murder or culpable homicide, or caused bodily injuries in circumstances warranting a sentence of penal servitude for life, or committed robbery or the graver forms of wilful fire-raising. The sentence was carried out by decapitation (see BEHEADING); but there had been no execution since 1876. The new Norwegian Code, which came into force on the 6th of January 1905, abolished capital punishment.

Portugal.—There has been considerable objection in Portugal to capital punishment, and it was abolished in 1867.

Rumania.—Capital punishment was abolished in 1864.

Russia.—In 1750, under the empress Elizabeth, capital punishment was abolished; but it was restored later and was freely inflicted, the sentence being executed by shooting, beheading or hanging. According to a Home Office Return in England in 1907 the death penalty is abolished, except in cases where the lives of the emperor, empress or heir to the throne are concerned.

Spain.—Under the Spanish Penal Code of 1870 the following crimes are capital:— inducing a foreign power to declare war against Spain, killing the sovereign, parricide and assassination. The method employed is execution in public by the garrote. But the death sentence is rarely imposed, the customary penalty for murder being penal servitude in chains for life, while a parricide is imprisoned in chains "in perpetuity until death."

Sweden.—The severity of the law in Sweden was greatly mitigated so far back as 1777. Under the Penal Code of 1864 the penalty of death may be imposed for certain forms of treason, including attempts on the life of the sovereign or on the independence of Sweden, and for premeditated homicide (*assassinat*), and in certain cases for offences committed by persons under sentence of imprisonment for life. In 1901 a bill to abolish capital punishment was rejected by both houses of the Swedish parliament.

Switzerland.—Capital punishment was abolished in Switzerland in 1874 by Federal legislation; but in 1879, in consequence of a plebiscite, each canton was empowered to restore the death penalty for offences in its territory. The Federal government was unwilling to take this course, but was impelled to it by the fact that, between 1874 and 1879, cases of premeditated murder had considerably increased. Seven of the cantons out of twenty-two have exercised the power given to restore capital punishment. But there do not seem to have been any cases in which the death penalty has been inflicted; and on the assassination of the empress of Austria at Geneva in 1898 it was found that the laws of the canton did not permit the execution of the assassin. The canton of Zug imposes the lowest minimum penalty known, *i.e.* three years' imprisonment for wilful homicide, the maximum being imprisonment for life.

United States of America.—Under the Federal laws sentence of death may be passed for treason against the United States and for piracy and for murder within the Federal jurisdiction. But for the most part the punishment of crime is regulated by the laws of the constituent states of the Union.

The death penalty was abolished in Michigan in 1846 except for treason, and wholly in Wisconsin in 1853. In Maine it was abolished in 1876, re-enacted in 1883, and again abolished in 1887. In Rhode Island it was abolished in 1852, but restored in 1882, only in case of murder committed by a person under sentence of imprisonment for life (Laws, 1896, c. 277, s. 2). In all the other states the death penalty may still be inflicted: in Alabama, Delaware, Georgia, Maryland, and West Virginia, for treason, murder, arson and rape; in Alaska, Arizona, Kansas, New Jersey, Mississippi, Montana, New York, North Dakota, Oregon, and South Dakota, for treason and murder; in Colorado, Idaho, Illinois, Iowa, Massachusetts, Minnesota, Nebraska, New Hampshire, New Mexico, Nevada, Ohio, Oklahoma, Pennsylvania, Utah and Wyoming, for murder only; in Kentucky and Virginia, for treason, murder and rape; in Vermont, for treason, murder and arson; in Indiana, for treason, murder, and for arson if death result; in California, for treason, murder and train-wrecking; in North Carolina, for murder, rape, arson and burglary; in Florida, Missouri, South Carolina, Tennessee and Texas, for murder and rape; in Arkansas and Louisiana, for treason, murder, rape, and administering poison or use of dangerous weapons with intent to murder. Louisiana is cited by Girardin (*le droit de punir*) as a state in which the death penalty was abolished in 1830. Under the influence of the eminent jurist, E. Livingston, who framed the state codes, the legislature certainly passed a resolution against capital punishment. But since as early as 1846 it has been there lawful, subject to a power given to the jury, to bring in a verdict of guilty, "but no capital punishment," which had the effect of imposing a sentence of hard labour for life. In certain states the jury has, under local legislation, the right to award the sentence. The constitutionality of such legislation has been doubted, but has been recognized by the courts of Illinois and Iowa. Sentence of death is executed by hanging, except in seven of the states, where it is carried out by "electrocution" (*q.v.*).

With the mitigation of the law as to punishment, agitation against the theory of capital punishment has lost much of its force. But many European and American writers, and some English writers and associations, advocate the **The question of abolition.** total abolition of the death punishment. The ultimate argument of the opponents of capital punishment is that society has no right to take the life of any one of its members on 282 any ground. But they also object to capital punishment: (1) on religious grounds, because it may deprive the sinner of his full time for repentance; (2) on medical grounds, because homicide is usually if not always evidence of mental disease or irresponsibility; (3) on utilitarian grounds, because capital punishment is not really deterrent, and is actually inflicted in so few instances that criminals discount the risks of undergoing it; (4) on legal grounds, *i.e.* that the sentence being irrevocable and the evidence often circumstantial only, there is great risk of gross injustice in executing a person convicted of murder; (5) on moral grounds, that the punishment does not fit the case nor effect the reformation of the offender. It is to be noted that the English Children Act 1908 expressly forbids the pronouncing or recording the sentence of death against any person under the age of sixteen (s. 103).

The punishment is probably retained, partly from ingrained habit, partly from a sense of its appropriateness for certain crimes, but also that the *ultima ratio* may be available in cases of sufficient gravity to the commonweal. The apparent discrepancy between the number of trials and convictions for murder is not in England any evidence of hostility on the part of juries to capital punishment, which has on the whole lessened rather than increased since the middle of the 19th century. It is rarely if ever necessary in England, though common in America, to question the jurors as to their views on capital punishment. The reasons for the comparatively small number of convictions for murder seem to be: (1) that court and jury in a capital case lean *in favorem vitae*, and if the offence falls short of the full gravity of murder, conviction for manslaughter only results; (2) that in the absence of a statutory classification of the degrees of murder, the prerogative of mercy is exercised in cases falling short of the highest degree of gravity recognized by lawyers and by public opinion; (3) that where the conviction rests on circumstantial evidence the sentence is not executed unless the circumstantial evidence is conclusive; (4) that charges of infanticide against the mothers of illegitimate children are treated mercifully by judge and jury, and usually terminate in acquittal, or in a conviction of concealment of birth; (5) that many persons tried as murderers are obviously insane; (6) that coroners' juries are somewhat recklessly free in returning inquisitions of murder without any evidence which would warrant the conviction of the person accused.

The medical doctrine, and that of Lombroso with respect to criminal atavism and irresponsibility, have probably tended to incline the public mind in favour of capital punishment, and Sir James Stephen and other eminent jurists have even been thereby tempted to advocate the execution of habitual criminals. It certainly seems strange that the community should feel bound carefully to preserve and tend a class of dangerous lunatics, and to give them, as Charles Kingsley says, "the finest air in England and the right to kill two gaolers a week."

The whole question of capital punishment in the United Kingdom was considered by a royal commission appointed in 1864, which reported in 1866 (Parl. Pap., 1866, 10,438). The commission took the opinions of all the judges of the supreme courts in the United Kingdom and of many other eminent persons, and collected the laws of other countries so far as this was ascertainable. The commissioners differed on the question of the expediency of abolishing or retaining capital punishment, and did not report thereon. But they recommended: (1) that it should be restricted throughout the United Kingdom to high treason and murder; (2) alteration of the law of homicide so as to classify homicides according to their gravity, and to confine capital punishment to murder in the first degree; (3) modification of the law as to child murder so as to punish certain cases of infanticide as misdemeanours; (4) authorizing judges to direct sentence of death to be recorded; (5) the abolition—since carried out—of public executions.

AUTHORITIES.—Beccaria, *Dei Delitte e delle Pene* (1790); Bentham,*Rationale of Punishment*; Lammasch, *Grundris des Strafrechts* (Leipzig, 1902); Olivecrona, *De la peine de mort*; Mittermaier, *Capital Punishment*; *Report of the Royal Commission on Capital Punishment* (Parl. Pap., 1866, No. 10,438); Oldfield, *The Penalty of Death* (1901); Pollock and Maitland,*History of English Law*; Pike, *History of Crime*; Sir J.F. Stephen, *History of Crime in England*; S. Walpole, *History of England*, vol. i. p. 191; vol. iv. p. 74; Andrews' *Old Time Punishments; A Century of Law Reform* (London, 1901); Lecture ii. by Sir H.B. Poland; Howard Association Publications.

(W. F. C.)

CAPITO (or KÖPFEL), **WOLFGANG** [FABRICIUS] (1478-1541), German reformer, was born of humble parentage at Hagenau in Alsace. He was educated for the medical profession, but also studied law, and applied himself so earnestly to theology that he received the doctorate in that faculty also, and, having joined the Benedictines, taught for some time at Freiburg. He acted for three years as pastor in Bruchsal, and was then called to the cathedral church of Basel (1515). Here he made the acquaintance of Zwingli and began to correspond with Luther. In 1519 he removed to Mainz at the request of Albrecht, archbishop of that city, who soon made him his chancellor. In 1523 he settled at Strassburg, where he remained till his death in November 1541. He had found it increasingly difficult to reconcile the new religion with the old, and from 1524 was one of the leaders of the reformed faith in Strassburg. He took a prominent part in the earlier ecclesiastical transactions of the 16th century, was present at the second conference of Zurich and at the conference of Marburg, and along with Martin Bucer drew up the *Confessio Tetrapolitana*. Capito was always more concerned for the "unity of the spirit" than for dogmatic formularies, and from his endeavours to conciliate the Lutheran and Zwinglian parties in regard to the sacraments, he seems to have incurred the suspicions of his own friends; while from his intimacy with Martin Cellarius and other divines of the Socinian school he drew on himself the charge of Arianism. His principal works were:—*Institutionum Hebraicarum libri duo;*

Enarrationes in Habacuc et Hoseam Prophetas; a life of Oecolampadius and an account of the synod of Berne (1532).

CAPITULARY (Med. Lat. *capitularium*), a series of legislative or administrative acts emanating from the Merovingian and Carolingian kings, so called as being divided into sections or chapters (*capitula*). With regard to these capitularies two questions arise: (1) as to the means by which they have been handed down to us; (2) as to their true character and scope.

(1) As soon as the capitulary was composed, it was sent to the various functionaries of the Frankish empire, archbishops, bishops, *missi* and counts, a copy being kept by the chancellor in the archives of the palace. At the present day we do not possess a single capitulary in its original form: but very frequently copies of these isolated capitularies were included in various scattered manuscripts, among pieces of a very different nature, ecclesiastical or secular. We find, therefore, a fair number of them in books which go back as far as the 9th or 10th centuries. In recent editions in the case of each capitulary it is carefully indicated from what manuscripts it has been collated.

These capitularies make provisions of a most varied nature; it was therefore found necessary at quite an early date to classify them into chapters according to the subject. In 827 Ansegisus, abbot of St Wandrille at Fontenelle, made such a collection. He embodied them in four books: one of the ecclesiastical capitularies of Charlemagne, one of the ecclesiastical capitularies of Louis the Pious, one of the secular capitularies of Charlemagne, and one of the secular capitularies of Louis, bringing together similar provisions and suppressing duplicates. This collection soon gained an official authority, and after 829 Louis the Pious refers to it, citing book and section.

After 827 new capitularies were naturally promulgated, and before 858 there appeared a second collection in three books, by an author calling himself Benedictus Levita. His aim was, he said, to complete the work of Ansegisus, and bring it up to date by continuing it from 827 to his own day; but the author has not only borrowed prescriptions from the capitularies; he has introduced other documents into his collection, fragments of Roman laws, canons of the councils and especially spurious provisions very similar in character to those of the same date found in the *False Decretals*. His contemporaries did not notice these spurious documents, but accepted the whole collection as 283authentic, and incorporated the four books of Ansegisus and the three of Benedictus Levita into a single collection in seven books. The serious historian of to-day, however, is careful not to use books v., vi. and vii. for purposes of reference.

Early editors chose to republish this collection of Ansegisus and Benedictus as they found it. It was a distinguished French scholar, Étienne Baluze, who led the way to a fresh classification. In 1677 he brought out the *Capitularia regum francorum*, in two folio volumes, in which he published first the capitularies of the Merovingian kings, then those of Pippin, of Charles and of Louis the Pious, which he had found complete in various manuscripts. After the date of 840, he published as supplements the unreliable collection of Ansegisus and Benedictus Levita, with the warning that the latter was quite untrustworthy. He then gave the capitularies of Charles the Bald, and of other Carolingian kings, either contemporaries or successors of Charles, which he had discovered in various places. A second edition of Baluze was published in 1780 in 2 volumes folio by Pierre de Chiniac.

The edition of the Capitularies made in 1835 by George Pertz, in the *Monumenta Germaniae* (folio edition, vol. i., of the *Leges*) was not much advance on that of Baluze. A fresh revision was required, and the editors of the *Monumenta* decided to reissue it in their quarto series, entrusting the work to Dr Alfred Boretius. In 1883 Boretius published his first volume, containing all the detached capitularies up to 827, together with various appendices bearing on them, and the collection of Ansegisus. Boretius, whose health had been ruined by overwork, was unable to finish his work; it was continued by Victor Krause, who collected in vol. ii. the scattered capitularies of a date posterior to 828. Karl Zeumer and Albrecht Werminghoff drew up a detailed index of both volumes, in which all the essential words are noted. A third volume, prepared by Emil Seckel, was to include the collection of Benedictus Levita.

(2) Among the capitularies are to be found documents of a very varied kind. Boretius has divided them into several classes:—

(a) The *Capitula legibus addenda.*—These are additions made by the king of the Franks to the barbarian laws promulgated under the Merovingians, the Salic law, the Ripuarian or the Bavarian. These capitularies have the same weight as the law which they complete; they are particular in their application, applying, that is to say, only to the men subject to that law. Like the laws, they consist chiefly of scales of compensation, rules of procedure and points of civil law. They were solemnly promulgated in the local assemblies where the consent of the people was asked. Charlemagne and Louis the Pious seem to have made efforts to bring the other laws into harmony with the Salic law. It is also to be noted that by certain of the capitularies of this class, the king adds provisions affecting, not only a single law, but all the laws in use throughout the kingdom.

(b) The *Capitula ecclesiastica.*—These capitularies were elaborated in the councils of the bishops; the kings of the Franks sanctioned the canon of the councils, and made them obligatory on all the Christians in the kingdom.

(c) The *Capitula per se scribenda.*—These embodied political decrees which all subjects of the kingdom were bound to observe. They often bore the name of *edictum* or of *constitutio*, and the provisions made in them were permanent. These capitularies were generally elaborated by the king of the Franks in the autumn assemblies or in the committees of the spring assemblies. Frequently we have only the proposition made by the king to the committee, *capitula tractanda cum comitibus, episcopis, et abbatibus*, and not the final form which was adopted.

(d) The *Capitula missorum*, which are the instructions given by Charlemagne and his successors to the *missi* sent into the various parts of the empire. They are sometimes drawn up in common for all the *missi* of a certain year—*capitula missorum generalia*; sometimes for the *missi* sent only on a given circuit—*capitula missorum specialia*. These instructions sometimes hold good only for the circuit of the *missus*; they have no general application and are merely temporary.

(e) With the capitularies have been incorporated various documents; for instance, the rules to be observed in administering the king's private domain (the celebrated capitulary *de villis*, which is doubtless a collection of the instructions sent at various times to the agents of these domains); the partitions of the kingdom among the king's sons, as, the *Divisio regnorum* of 806, or the *Ordinatio imperii* of 817; the oaths of peace and brotherhood which were taken on various occasions by the sons of Louis the Pious, &c.

The merit of clearly establishing these distinctions belongs to Boretius. He has doubtless exaggerated the difference between the *Capitula missorum* and the *Capitula per se scribenda;* among the first are to be found provisions of a general and permanent nature, and among the second temporary measures are often included. But the idea of Boretius is none the less fruitful. In the capitularies there are usually permanent provisions and temporary provisions intermingled; and the observation of this fact has made it possible more clearly to understand certain institutions of Charlemagne, *e.g.* military service.

After the reign of Louis the Pious the capitularies became long and diffuse. Soon, from the 10th century onwards, no provision of general application emanates from the kings. Henceforth the kings only regulated private interests by charters; it was not until the reign of Philip Augustus that general provisions again appeared; but when they did so, they bore the name of ordinances (*ordonnances*).

There were also capitularies of the Lombards. These capitularies formed a continuation of the Lombard laws, and are printed as an appendix to these laws by Boretius in the folio edition of the *Monumenta Germaniae, Leges*, vol. iv.

AUTHORITIES.—Boretius, *Die Capitularien im Longobardenreich* (Halle, 1864); and *Beitrage zur Capitularienkritik* (Leipzig, 1874); G. Seeliger, *Die Kapitularien der Karolinger* (Munich, 1893). See also the histories of institutions or of law by Waitz, Brunner, Fustel de Coulanges, Viollet, Esmein.

(C. Pf.)

CAPITULATION (Lat. *capitulum*, a little head or division; *capitulare*, to treat upon terms), an agreement in time of war for the surrender to a hostile armed force of a particular body of troops, a town or a territory. It is an ordinary incident of war, and therefore no previous instructions from the captor's government are required before finally settling the conditions of capitulation. The most usual of such conditions are freedom of religion and security of private property on the one hand, and a promise not to bear arms within a certain period on the other. Such agreements may be rashly concluded with an inferior officer, on whose authority the enemy are not in the actual position of the war entitled to place reliance. When an agreement is made by an officer who has not the proper authority or who has exceeded the limits of his authority, it is termed a *sponsion*, and, to be binding, must be confirmed by express or tacit ratification. Article 35 of the Hague Convention (1899) on the laws and the customs of war lays down that "capitulations agreed on between the contracting parties must be in accordance with the rules of military honour. When once settled they must be observed by both the parties."

In another sense, capitulation is the name given to an arrangement by which foreigners are withdrawn, for most civil and criminal purposes, from the jurisdiction of the state making the capitulation. Thus in Turkey arrangements termed capitulations (*q.v.*), and treaties confirmatory of them, have been made between the Porte and other states by which foreigners resident in Turkey are subject to the laws of their respective countries. The term is also applied by French writers to the oath which on his election the Holy Roman emperor used to make to the college of electors; this related chiefly to such matters as regalian rights, appeals from local jurisdictions, the rights of the pope, &c.

CAPITULATIONS (from Lat. *caput*, or its Low-Latin diminutive *capitulum*, as indicating the form in which these acts were set down in "chapters"; the Gr. equivalent *cephaleosis*, kephalaiosis, is occasionally used in works of the 17th century), treaties granted by a state and conferring the privilege of extra-territorial jurisdiction within its boundaries on the subjects of another state. Thus, in the 9th century, the caliph Harun-al-Rashid engaged to grant guarantees and commercial facilities to such 284Franks, subjects of the emperor Charlemagne, as should visit the East with the authorization of their emperor. After the break-up of the Frank empire, similar concessions were made to some of the practically independent Italian city states that grew up on its ruins. Thus, in 1098, the prince of Antioch granted a charter of this nature to the city of Genoa; the king of Jerusalem extended the same privilege to Venice in 1123 and to Marseilles in 1136. Salah-ud-din (Saladin), sultan of Babylon (Cairo), granted a charter to the town of Pisa in 1173. The Byzantine emperors followed this example, and Genoa, Pisa and Venice all obtained capitulations. The explanation of the practice is to be found in the fact that the sovereignty of the state was held in those ages to apply only to its subjects; foreigners were excluded from its rights and obligations. The privilege of citizenship was considered too precious to be extended to the alien, who was long practically an outlaw. But when the numbers, wealth and power of foreigners residing within the state became too great, it was found to be politic to subject them to some law, and it was held that this law should be their own. When the Turkish rule was substituted for that of the Byzantine emperors, the system already in existence was continued; the various non-Moslem peoples were allowed their semi-autonomy in matters affecting their personal status, and the Genoese of Galata were confirmed in their privileges. But the first capitulation concluded with a foreign state was that of 1535 granted to the French. Lest it should be imagined that this was a concession wrested by the victorious Christian monarch from the decadent Turk, it should be borne in mind that Turkey was then at the height of her power, and that Francis I. had shortly before sustained a disastrous defeat at Pavia. His only hope of assistance lay in Suleiman I., whose attack on Vienna had been checked by the victorious Charles V. The appeal to Suleiman on the ground of the common interest of France and Turkey in overcoming Charles V.'s overweening power was successful; the secret mission of Frangipani, an unofficial envoy who could be disowned in case of failure, paved the way for De la Forest's embassy in 1534, and in 1536 the capitulations were signed.1They amounted to a treaty of commerce and a treaty allowing the establishment of Frenchmen in Turkey and fixing the jurisdiction to be

72

exercised over them: individual and religious liberty is guaranteed to them, the king of France is empowered to appoint consuls in Turkey, the consuls are recognized as competent to judge the civil and criminal affairs of French subjects in Turkey according to French law, and the consuls may appeal to the officers of the sultan for their aid in the execution of their sentences. This, the first of the capitulations, is practically the prototype of its successors. Five years later, similar capitulations were concluded with Venice. The capitulations were at first held to be in force only during the lifetime of the sultan by whom they were granted; thus in 1569 Sultan Selim II. renewed the French capitulations granted by his predecessor. In 1583 England obtained her first capitulation, until which time France had been the official protector of all Europeans established in Turkey. Later on, England claimed to protect the subjects of other nations, a claim which is rejected in the French capitulations of 1597, 1604 and 1607, the last-named of which explicitly lays down that the subjects of all nations not represented at Constantinople by an ambassador shall be under French protection. In 1613 Holland obtained her first capitulation, with the assistance of the French ambassador, anxious to help a commercial rival of England. In 1673 the French, represented by the marquis de Nointel, succeeded in obtaining the renewal of the capitulations which, for various reasons, had remained unconfirmed since 1607. Louis XIV. had been anxious to secure the protectorate of all Catholics in Turkey, but was obliged to content himself with the recognition of his right to protect all Latins of non-Turkish nationality; his claims for the restoration to the Catholics of the Holy Places usurped by the Greeks was also rejected, the sultan only undertaking to promise to restore their churches to the Jesuit Capuchins. An important commercial gain was the reduction of the import duties from 5 to 3%; and all suits the value of which exceeded 4000 *aspres* in which French subjects sued, or were sued by, an Ottoman subject, were to be heard not by the ordinary tribunals but at the Porte itself. Later, France's friendship secured for Turkey a successful negotiation of the peace of Belgrade in 1739, and the result was the capitulation of 1740; this is no longer limited in duration to the sultan's lifetime but is made perpetual, and, moreover, declares that it cannot be modified without the assent of the French. It conferred on the French ambassador precedence over his colleagues. Austria had obtained capitulations in 1718, modified in 1784; Russia secured similar privileges in 1784. In the course of the 18th century nearly every European power had obtained these, and such newly-established countries as the United States of America, Belgium and Greece followed in the 19th century.

The chief privileges granted under the capitulations to foreigners resident in Turkey are the following: liberty of residence, inviolability of domicile, liberty to travel by land and sea, freedom of commerce, freedom of religion, immunity from local jurisdiction save under certain safeguards, exclusive extra-territorial jurisdiction over foreigners of the same nationality, and competence of the forum of the defendant in cases in which two foreigners are concerned (though the Sublime Porte has long claimed to exercise jurisdiction in criminal cases in which two foreigners of different nationality are concerned—the capitulations are silent on the point and the claim is resisted by the powers).

The same system has been followed by such countries as Persia, China, Japan and Siam.

The practical result of the capitulations in Turkey is to form each separate foreign colony into a sort of *imperium in imperio,* and to hamper the local jurisdiction very considerably. As the state granting the capitulations progresses in civilization it chafes under these restraints in its sovereignty. Turkey's former vassals, Rumania and Servia, though theoretically bound to respect the capitulations so long as they formed part of Turkey, had practically abrogated them long before securing their independence through the treaty of Berlin in 1878. The same may be said of Bulgaria. Japan was liberated from the burden of the capitulations some years ago.

The extra-territorial jurisdiction exercised by the foreign powers over their subjects in Turkey and other countries where capitulations exist is regulated by special legislative enactments; in the case of the United Kingdom by orders in council.

In Turkey the capitulations are practically the only treaties in force with the powers, since the expiration about 1889 of the commercial treaties concluded in 1861-1862. As they all contain the "most-favoured nation" clause, the privileges in any one apply to all the powers, though not always claimed. Thus America and Belgium claim under their treaties with Turkey the right to try all their subjects, even if accused of offences against Ottoman subjects—a claim recently made by Belgium in the case of the Belgian subject Joris, accused of participation in the bomb outrage of 1905 at Yildiz. One peculiar privilege granted in the capitulations of 1675 (Art. 74) authorizes the king of England to buy in Turkey with his own money two cargoes of figs and raisins, in fertile and abundant years and not in times of dearth or scarcity, and provides that after a duty of 3% has been paid thereon no obstacle or hindrance shall be given thereto.

1La Forest, a knight of St John of Jerusalem, was the first resident ambassador of France at Constantinople. He died in 1537.

CAPIZ, a town and the capital of the province of Capiz, Panay, Philippine Islands, on the Capiz or Panay river, about 4 m. from its mouth on the N. coast. Pop. (1903) 18,525. Capiz has a large and beautiful Roman Catholic church (of stone), a Protestant church (with a hospital) and good government buildings, and is the seat of the provincial high school. Alcohol of a superior quality is manufactured in large quantities from the fermented juice of the nipa palm, which grows plentifully in the neighbouring swamps. Fishing and the weaving of fabrics of cotton, hemp and pineapple fibre are important industries. Rice and sugar are raised in abundance. Tobacco, Indian corn 285and cacao are produced to a limited extent; and rice, alcohol, sugar and copra are exported. Coasting vessels ascend the river to the town. The language is Visayan.

CAPMANY Y MONTPALAU, ANTONIO DE (1742-1813), Spanish polygraph, was born at Barcelona on the 24th of November 1742. He retired from the army in 1770, and was subsequently elected secretary of the Royal Academy of History at Madrid. His principal works are—*Memorias históricas sobre la marina, commercio, y artes de la antigua ciudad de Barcelona* (4 vols. 1779-1792); *Teatro histórico-crítico de la elocuencia Española* (1786);*Filiosofía de la elocuencia* (1776), and *Cuestiones críticas sobre varias puntos de historia ecónomica, política, y militar* (1807). Capmany died at Barcelona on the 14th of November 1813. His monograph on the history of his birthplace still preserves much of its original value.

CAPO D'ISTRIA, GIOVANNI ANTONIO [JOANNES],1 COUNT (1776-1831), Russian statesman and president of the Greek republic, was born at Corfu on the 11th of February 1776. He belonged to an ancient Corfiot family which had immigrated from Istria in 1373, the title of count being granted to it by Charles Emmanuel, duke of Savoy, in 1689. The father of Giovanni, Antonio Maria Capo d'Istria, was a man of considerable importance in the island, a stiff aristocrat of the old school, who in 1798, after the treaty of Campo Formio had placed the Ionian Islands under French rule, was imprisoned for his opposition to the new regime, his release next year being the earliest triumph of his son's diplomacy. On the establishment in 1800, under Turkish suzerainty, of the septinsular republic—a settlement negotiated at Constantinople by the elder Capo d'Istria—Giovanni, who had meanwhile studied medicine at Padua, entered the government service as secretary to the legislative council, and in one capacity or another exercised for the next seven years a determining voice in the affairs of the republic. At the beginning of 1807 he was appointed "extraordinary military governor" to organize the defence of Santa Maura against Ali Pasha of Iannina, an enterprise which brought him into contact with Theodores Kolokotrones and other future chiefs of the war of Greek independence, and awoke in him that wider Hellenic patriotism which was so largely to influence his career.

Throughout the period of his official connexion with the Ionian government, Capo d'Istria had been a consistent upholder of Russian influence in the islands; and when the treaty of Tilsit (1807) dashed his hopes by handing over the Ionian republic to Napoleon, he did not relinquish his belief in Russia as the most reliable ally of the Greek cause. He accordingly refused the offers made to him by the French government, and accepted the invitation of the Russian chancellor Romanzov to enter the tsar's service. He went to St Petersburg in 1809, and was appointed to the honorary post of attaché to the foreign office, but it was not till two years after, in 1811, that he was actually employed in diplomatic work as attaché to Baron Stackelberg, the Russian ambassador at Vienna. His knowledge of the near East was here of great service, and in the following year he was attached, as chief of his diplomatic bureau, to Admiral Chichagov, on his mission to the Danubian principalities to stir up trouble in the Balkan peninsula as a diversion on the flank of Austria, and to attempt to supplement the treaty of Bucharest by an offensive and defensive alliance with the Ottoman empire. The Moscow campaign of 1812 intervened; Chichagov was disgraced in consequence of his failure to destroy Napoleon at the passage of the Beresina; but Capo d'Istria was not involved, was made a councillor of state and continued in his diplomatic functions. During the campaign of 1813 he was attached to the staff of Barclay de Tolly and was present at the battles of Lützen, Bautzen, Dresden and Leipzig. With the advance of the allies he was sent to Switzerland to secure the withdrawal of the republic from the French alliance. Here, in spite of his instructions to guarantee the neutrality of Switzerland, he signed on his own responsibility the proclamation issued by Prince Schwarzenberg, stating the intention of the allied troops to march through the country. His motive was to prevent any appearance of disagreement among the allies. The emperor Alexander, to whom he hastened to make an explanation in person, endorsed his action.

Capo d'Istria was present with the allies in Paris, and after the signing of the first peace of Paris he was rewarded by the tsar with the order of St Vladimir and his full confidence. At the congress of Vienna his influence was conspicuous; he represented the tsar on the Swiss committee, was associated with Rasumovsky in negotiating the tangled Polish and Saxon questions, and was the Russian plenipotentiary in the discussions with the Baron vom Stein on the affairs of Germany. His *Mémoire sur l'empire germanique*, of the 9th of February 1815, presented to the tsar, was based on the policy of keeping Germany weak in order to secure Russian preponderance in its councils. It was perhaps from a similar motive that, after the Waterloo campaign, he strenuously opposed the proposals for the dismemberment of France. It was on his advice that the duc de Richelieu persuaded Louis XVIII. to write the autograph letter in which he declared his intention of resigning rather than submit to any diminution of the territories handed down to him by his ancestors.2 The treaty of the 20th of November 1815, which formed for years the basis of the effective concert of Europe, was also largely his work.

On the 26th of September 1815, after the proclamation of the Holy Alliance at the great review on the plain of Vertus, Capo d'Istria was named a secretary of state. On his return to St Petersburg, he shared the ministry of foreign affairs with Count Nesselrode, though the latter as senior signed all documents. Capo d'Istria, however, had sole charge of the newly acquired province of Bessarabia, which he governed conspicuously well. In 1818 he attended the emperor Alexander at the congress of Aix-la-Chapelle, and in the following year obtained leave to visit his home. He travelled by way of Venice, Rome and Naples, his progress exciting the liveliest apprehensions of the powers, notably of Austria. The "Jacobin" pose of the tsar was notorious, his all-embracing ambition hardly less so; and Russian travellers in Italy, notably the emperor's former tutor, César de Laharpe, were little careful in the expression of their sympathy for the ideals of the Carbonari. In Metternich's eyes Capo d'Istria, "the coryphaeus of liberalism," was responsible for the tsar's vagaries, the fount of all the ills of which the times were sick; and, for all the count's diplomatic reticence, the Austrian spies who dogged his footsteps earned their salaries by reporting sayings that set the reactionary courts in a flutter. For Metternich the overthrow of Capo d'Istria's influence became a necessity of political salvation. At Corfu Capo d'Istria became the repository of all the grievances of his countrymen against the robust administration of Sir Thomas Maitland. At the congress of Vienna the count had supported the British protectorate over the Ionian Islands, the advantages of which from the point of view of trade and security were obvious; but the drastic methods of "King Tom's" government, symbolized by a gallows for pirates and other evil-doers in every popular gathering place, offended his local patriotism. He submitted a memorandum on the subject to the tsar, and before returning to Russia travelled via Paris to England to lay the grievances of the Ionians before the British government. His reception was a cold one, mainly due to his own disingenuousness, for he refused to show British ministers the memorandum which he had already submitted to the Russian emperor, on the ground that it was intended only for his own private use. The whole thing seemed, rightly or wrongly, an excuse for the intervention of Russia in affairs which were by treaty wholly British.

On his return to St Petersburg in the autumn of 1819, Capo d'Istria resumed his influence in the intimate counsels of the tsar. The murder of the Russian agent, Kotzebue, in March, had shaken but not destroyed Alexander's liberalism, and it was Capo d'Istria who drew up the emperor's protest against the Carlsbad decrees and the declaration of his adherence to constitutional views (see ALEXANDER I.). In October 1820 Capo 286d'Istria accompanied the tsar to the congress at Troppau. The events of the year—the murder of the due de Berry in March, the Revolutions in Spain and in Naples—had produced their effect. Alexander was, in Metternich's exultant language, "a changed man," and Capo d'Istria apparently shared his conversion to reactionary principles. The Austrian chancellor now put forth all his powers to bring Alexander under his own influence, and to overthrow Capo d'Istria, whom he despised, distrusted and feared. In 1821 Alexander Ypsilanti's misguided raid into the Danubian principalities gave him his opportunity. The news reached the tsar at the congress of Laibach, and to Capo d'Istria was entrusted the task of writing the letter to Ypsilanti in which the tsar repudiated his claim, publicly proclaimed that he had the sympathy and support of Russia. For a while the position of Capo d'Istria was saved; but it was known that he had been approached by the agent of the Greek *Hetairia* before Ypsilanti, and that he had encouraged Ypsilanti to take up the ill-fated adventure which he himself had refused; he was hated at the Russian court as an upstart Greek, and Metternich was never weary of impressing on all and sundry that he was "using Russian policy for Greek ends." At last nothing but long habit and native loyalty to those who had served him well, prevented Alexander from parting with a minister who had ceased to possess his confidence. Capo d'Istria, anticipating his dismissal, resigned on the eve of the tsar's departure for the congress of Verona (1822), and retired into private life at Geneva.

On the 11th of April 1827, the Greek national assembly at Troezene elected Capo d'Istria president of the republic. The vote was a triumph for the Russian faction, for the count, even after his fall, had not lost the personal regard of the emperor Alexander, nor ceased to consider himself a Russian official. He accepted the offer, but was in no hurry to take up the thankless task. In July he visited the emperor Nicholas I. at Tsarskoye Selo, receiving permission to proceed and instructions as to the policy he should adopt, and he next made a tour of the courts of Europe in search of moral and material support. The news of the battle of Navarino (20th of October 1827) hastened his arrival; the British frigate "Warspite" was placed at his disposal to carry him to Greece, and on the 19th of January 1828 he landed at Nauplia.

Capo d'Istria's rule in Greece had to contend against immense difficulties—the utter poverty of the treasury, the barbarism of the people but recently emancipated, the continued presence of Ibrahim Pasha, with an unbroken army, in the south of the Morea. His strength lay in his experience of affairs and in the support of Russia; but he was by inheritance an aristocrat and by training an official, lacking in broad human sympathy, and therefore little fitted to deal with the wild and democratic elements of the society it was his task to control. The Greeks could understand the international status given to them by his presidency, and for a while the enthusiasm evoked by his arrival made him master of the situation. He thoroughly represented Greek sentiment, too, in his refusal to accept the narrow limits which the powers, in successive protocols, sought to impose on the new state (see GREECE). But the Russian administrative system by which he sought to restrain the native turbulence was bound in the end to be fatal to him. The wild chiefs of the revolution won over at first by their inclusion in his government, were offended by his European airs and Russian uniform, and alienated by his preference for the educated Greeks of the Phanar and of Corfu, his promotion of his brothers Viaro and Agostino to high commands causing special offence. Dissatisfaction ended in open rebellion; the islands revolted; Capo d'Istria called in the aid of the Russian admiral; and Miaoulis, the hero of the Greek war at sea, blew up the warships under his command to prevent their falling into the hands of the government. On land, so far as the president was concerned, the climax was reached with the attempt to coerce the Mavromichales of the Maina, the bravest and most turbulent of the mountain clans, whose chief Petros Mavromichales, commonly known as Petrobey, had played a leading part in the War of Independence. The result was an insurrection in the Maina (Easter, 1830), and the imprisonment of those of the Mavromichales, including Petrobey, who happened to be in the power of the government. At the news of their chieftain's imprisonment the Mainots, who had for a while been pacified, once more flew to arms and threatened to march on Nauplia; but negotiations were opened, and on the advice of the Russian minister Petrobey consented to make his submission to the president. Unhappily, when he was brought under guard to the appointed interview, Capo d'Istria, in a moment of irritation and weariness, refused to see him. Maddened with rage at this insult from a man who had not struck a blow for Greece, the proud old chief, on his way back to prison, called out to two of his kinsmen, his son George and his brother Constantino, "You see how I fare," and passed on. According to the code of the Maina this was a command to take revenge. Next day, the 9th of October 1831, the two placed themselves at the door of the church where Capo d'Istria was accustomed to worship. As he passed in Constantine shot him down, and as he fell George thrust a dagger into his heart.

AUTHORITIES.—Carl W.P. Mendelssohn-Bartholdy's *Graf Johann Kapodistrias* (Berlin, 1864) is based on all the sources, printed and unprinted, available at the time of publication, and contains an excellent guide to these. This may be supplemented by the historical sections of F. de Marten's *Recueil des traites condus par la Russie, &c.* (1874, &c.). A sketch of Capo d'Istria's activity as president will be found in W. Alison Phillips's *The War of Greek Independence* (London, 1897). Many of Capo d'Istria's despatches, &c., are published in the collections of diplomatic correspondence mentioned in the bibliography of the article EUROPE:*History*. Under the Russian title "Zapiska grapha Joanna Capodistrias" is published in the series of the Imperial Russian Historical Society, vol. iii. p. 163 (St Petersburg, 1868)the *Aperçu de ma carrière publique*, written by Capo d'Istria for presentation to the emperor Alexander, and dated at Geneva 12/24 December 1826. Of unpublished materials may be mentioned the letters of Capo d'Istria to Sir Richard Church, vol. xvi. of the Church Papers in the British Museum (*Add. MSS.* 36453-36571). See further bibliography to chapter vi. of vol. x. of the *Cambridge Modern History*(1907).

(W. A. P.)

1After his election to the Greek presidency in 1827, Capo d'Istria, whose baptismal names were Giovanni Antonio, signed himself Joannes Capodistrias, the form by which he is very commonly known.

2The letter was written by Michael Stourdza and *copied* by Louis.

CAPODISTRIA, a town and seaport of Austria, in Istria, 15 m. S.W. of Trieste by rail. Pop. (1900) 10,711, mostly Italians. It is situated on a small island, which occupies the end of a large bay in the Gulf of Trieste, and which is connected with the mainland by a causeway half a mile in length. Capodistria is an old town with small streets, and has preserved remarkably well its Italian, almost its Venetian character. The most noteworthy buildings are the cathedral, the town-hall and the *Loggia* or the old law-court, all situated in the principal square. In addition to the extraction of salt from the sea in the extensive salt works near the town, fishing and shipbuilding are the other principal occupations of the population. Trade is chiefly in sea-salt, wine and oil. Capodistria is usually identified with the town of Aegida, mentioned by Pliny, which appears by an inscription to have afterwards received (in the 6th century) the name of Justinopolis from Justin II. When at the beginning of the 13th century Istria fell into the hands of the patriarchs of Aquileia, they made this town the capital of the whole province. Thence it acquired its actual name, which means the capital of Istria. It was captured by the Venetians in 1279, and passed into Austrian possession in 1797.

CAPONIER (from the Fr. *caponnière*, properly a capon-cote or house), in fortification, a work constructed in the ditch of a fort. Its fire (musketry, machine-guns, case shot, &c.) sweeps the bottom of the ditch and prevents an enemy from establishing himself in it. The term is used in a military sense as early as in the late 17th century. In various bastioned systems of fortification a caponier served merely as a covered means of access to outworks, the bastion trace providing for the defence of the ditch by fire from the main parapet.

CAPPADOCIA, in ancient geography, an extensive inland district of Asia Minor. In the time of Herodotus the Cappadocians occupied the whole region from Mount Taurus to the Euxine. That author tells us that the name of the Cappadocians (Katpatouka) was applied to them by the Persians, while they were termed by the Greeks "Syrians," or "White Syrians" (*Leucosyri*). Under the later kings of the Persian empire the 287were divided into two satrapies or governments, the one comprising the central and inland portion, to which the name of Cappadocia continued to be applied by Greek geographers, while the other was called Cappadocia κατὰ Πόντον, or simply Pontus (*q.v.*). This division had already come about before the time of Xenophon. As after the fall of the Persian government the two provinces continued to be separate, the distinction was perpetuated, and the name Cappadocia came to be restricted to the inland province (sometimes called Great Cappadocia), which alone will be considered in the present article.

Cappadocia, in this sense, was bounded S. by the chain of Mount Taurus, E. by the Euphrates, N. by Pontus, and W. vaguely by the great central salt "Desert" (*Axylon*). But it is impossible to define its limits with accuracy. Strabo, the only ancient author who gives any circumstantial account of the country, greatly exaggerated its dimensions; it was in reality about 250 m. in length by less than 150 in breadth. With the exception of a narrow strip of the district called Melitene, on the east, which forms part of the valley of the Euphrates, the whole of this region is a high upland tract, attaining to more than 3000 ft., and constituting the most elevated portion of the great tableland of Asia Minor (*q.v.*). The western parts of the province, where it adjoins Lycaonia, extending thence to the foot of Mount Taurus, are open treeless plains, affording pasture in modern as in ancient times to numerous flocks of sheep, but almost wholly desolate. But out of the midst of this great upland level rise detached groups or masses of mountains, mostly of volcanic origin, of which the loftiest are Mount Argaeus (still called by the Turks Erjish Dagh), (13,100 ft.), and Hassan Dagh to the south-west (8000 ft.).

The eastern portion of the province is of a more varied and broken character, being traversed by the mountain system called by the Greeks Anti-Taurus. Between these mountains and the southern chain of Taurus, properly so called, lies the region called in ancient times Cataonia, occupying an upland plain surrounded by mountains. This district in the time of Strabo formed a portion of Cappadocia and was completely assimilated; but earlier writers and the Persian military system regarded the Cataonians as a distinct people.

Cappadocia contained the sources of the Sarus and Pyramus rivers with their higher affluents, and also the middle course of the Halys (see ASIA MINOR), and the whole course of the tributary of Euphrates now called Tokhma Su. But as no one of these rivers was navigable or served to fertilize the lands along its torrential course, none has much importance in the history of the province.

The kingdom of Cappadocia, which was still in existence in the time of Strabo, as a nominally independent state, was divided, according to that geographer, into ten districts. Of these *Cataonia* has been described; the adjoining district of *Melitene*, which did not originally form part of Cappadocia at all, but was annexed to it by Ariarathes I., was a fertile tract adjoining the Euphrates; its chief town retains the name of Malatia. *Cilicia* was the name given to the district in which Caesarea, the capital of the whole country was situated, and in which rose the conspicuous Mount Argaeus. *Tyanitis*, the region of which Tyana was the capital, was a level tract in the extreme south, extending to the foot of Mount Taurus. *Garsauritis* appears to have comprised the western or south-western districts adjoining Lycaonia; its chief town was Archelais.*Laviansene* or *Laviniane* was the country south and south-east of Sivas, through which ran the road from Sebastea to Caesarea: *Sargarausene* lay south of the above, and included Uzun Yaila and the upper basin of the Tokhma Su;*Saravene* lay west of Laviansene and included the modern district of Ak Dagh;*Chamanene* lay west again of the above along the middle course of the

78

Halys:*Morimene* was the north-western district extending along the edge of the central desert as far south as Melegob.

The only two cities of Cappadocia considered by Strabo to deserve that appellation were Mazaca, the capital of the kingdom under its native monarchs (see CAESAREA-MAZACA); and Tyana, not far from the foot of the Taurus, the site of which is marked by a great mound at a place called Kiz (or Ekuz) Hissar, about 12 m. south-west of Nigdeh. Archelais, founded by Archelaus, the last king of the country, subsequently became a Roman colony, and a place of some importance. It is now Akserai.

Several localities in the Cappadocian country were the sites of famous temples. Among these the most celebrated were those of Comana (*q.v.*) and Venasa in Morimene, where a male god was served by over 3000 *hieroduli*. The local sanctity of Venasa has been perpetuated by the Moslem veneration for Haji Bektash, the founder of the order of dervishes to which the Janissaries used in great part to belong. Cappadocia was remarkable for the number of its slaves, which constituted the principal wealth of its monarchs. Large numbers were sent to Rome but did not enjoy a good reputation. The Cappadocian peasants are still in the habit of taking service in the West of the peninsula and only returning to their homes after long absences; their labour is now much valued by employers, as they are a strong sober folk. The province was celebrated for its horses, as well as for its vast flocks of sheep; but from its elevation above the sea, and the coldness of its climate, it could never have been rich and fertile.

History.—Nothing is known of the history of Cappadocia before it became subject to the Persian empire, except that the country was the home of a great "Hittite" power centred at Boghaz-Keui (see PTERIA), which has left monuments at many places, *e.g.* Nevsheher, Fraktin, Gorun, Malatia, various points about Albistan and Derendeh, Bulgur Maden, Andaval and Tyana. Possibly the princes of the last named city were independent. With the decline of the Syro-Cappadocians after their defeat by Croesus, Cappadocia was left in the power of a sort of feudal aristocracy, dwelling in strong castles and keeping the peasants in a servile condition, which later made them apt for foreign slavery. It was included in the third Persian satrapy in the division established by Darius, but long continued to be governed by rulers of its own, none apparently supreme over the whole country and all more or less tributary to the Great King. Thoroughly subdued at last by the satrap Datames, Cappadocia recovered independence under a single ruler, Ariarathes (hence called Ariarathes I.), who was a contemporary of Alexander the Great, and maintained himself on the throne of Cappadocia after the fall of the Persian monarchy.

The province was not visited by Alexander, who contented himself with the tributary acknowledgment of his sovereignty made by Ariarathes before the conqueror's departure from Asia Minor; and the continuity of the native dynasty was only interrupted for a short time after Alexander's death, when the kingdom fell, in the general partition of the empire, to Eumenes. His claims were made good in 322 by the regent Perdiccas, who crucified Ariarathes; but in the dissensions following Eumenes's death, the son of Ariarathes recovered his inheritance and left it to a line of successors, who mostly bore the name of the founder of the dynasty, Under the fourth of the name Cappadocia came into relations with Rome, first as a foe espousing the cause of Antiochus the Great, then as an ally against Perseus of Macedon. The kings henceforward threw in their lot with the Republic as against the Seleucids, to whom they had been from time to time tributary. Ariarathes V. marched with the Roman proconsul Crassus against Aristonicus, a claimant to the throne of Pergammum, and their forces were annihilated (130 B.C.). The imbroglio which followed his death ultimately led to interference by the rising power of Pontus and the intrigues and wars which ended in the failure of the dynasty. The Cappadocians, supported by Rome against Mithradates, elected a native lord, Ariobarzanes, to succeed (93B.C.); but it was not till Rome had disposed at once of the Pontic and Armenian kings that his rule was established (63 B.C.). In the civil wars Cappadocia was now for Pompey, now for Caesar, now for Antony, now against him. The Ariobarzanes dynasty came to an end and a certain Archelaus reigned in its stead, by favour first of Antony, then of Octavian, and maintained tributary independence till A.D. 17, when the emperor Tiberius, on Archelaus's death in disgrace, reduced Cappadocia at last to a province. Vespasian in A.D. 70 288joined Armenia Minor to it and made the combined province a frontier bulwark. It remained, under various provincial redistributions, part of the Eastern Empire till late in the 11th century, though often ravaged both by Persians and Arabs. But before it passed into Seljuk hands (1074), and from them ultimately to the Osmanlis, it had already become largely Armenian in religion and speech; and thus we find the southern part referred to as "Hermeniorum terra" by crusading chroniclers. At this day the north-east and east parts of the province are largely inhabited by Armenians. The native kings had done much to Hellenize Cappadocia, which had previously received a strong Iranian colour; but it was left to Christianity to complete their work. Though pre-Hellenic usages long survived in the local cults and habits, a part of the people has remained more or less Hellenic to this day, in spite of its envelopment by Moslem conquerors and converts. The tradition of its early church, illuminated by the names of the two Gregories and Basil of Caesarea, has been perpetuated by the survival of a native Orthodox element throughout the west and north-west of the province; and in the remoter valleys Greek speech has never wholly died out. Its use has once more become general under Greek propagandist influence, and the Cappadocian "Greeks" are now a flourishing community.

BIBLIOGRAPHY.—W. Wright, *Empire of the Hittites* (1884); G. Perrot and C. Chipiez, *Hist. de l'art dans l'antiquité*, vol. iv. (1886); A.H. Sayce, *Hittites*(1892) (see also PTERIA); J.G. Droysen, *Gesch. des Hellenismus* (3rd ed., 1878); A. Holm, *Gesch. Griech.* (Eng. trans., 1886); Th. Reinach, *Mithridate Eupator* (1890); E.R. Bevan, *House of Seleucus* (1902); Th. Mommsen,*Provinces of the Roman Empire* (Eng. trans., 1886); J. Marquardt, *Röm. Staatsverwaltung*, i. (1874); W.M. Ramsey, *Hist. Geog. of Asia Minor*(1890); C. Ritter, *Erdkunde*, xviii. xix. (1858-1859); D.G. Hogarth and J.A.R. Munro, *Mod. and Anc. Roads in E. Asia Minor* (R.G.S. Supp. Papers, iii. 1893); G. Perrot, *Souvenirs d'un voyage dans l'A. Mineure* (1864); H.J. v. Lennep, *Travels in Asia Minor* (1870); E. Chantre, *Mission en Cappadocie* (1898); H.F. Tozer, *Turkish Armenia* (1881); H.C. Barkley,*Ride Through A.M. and Armenia* (1891); Lord Warkworth, *Notes of a Diary in As. Turkey* (1898); M. Sykes, *Dar ul-Islam* (1904).

(E. H. B.; D. G. H.)

CAPPEL, a French family which produced some distinguished jurists and theologians in the 15th and 16th centuries. In 1491, Guillaume Cappel, as rector of the university of Paris, protested against a tithe which Innocent VIII. claimed from that body. His nephew, Jacques Cappel (d. 1541), the real founder of the family, was himself advocate-general at the parlement of Paris, and in a celebrated address delivered before the court in 1537, against the emperor Charles V., claimed for Francis I. the counties of Artois, Flanders and Charolais. He left nine children, of whom three became Protestants. The eldest, Jacques (1529-1586), sieur du Tilloy, wrote several treatises on jurisprudence. Louis (1534-1586), sieur de Moriambert, the fifth son, was a most ardent Protestant. In 1570 he presented a confession of faith to Charles IX. in the name of his co-religionists. He disputed at Sedan before the duc de Bouillon with the Jesuit, Jean Maldouat (1534-1583), and wrote in defence of Protestantism. The seventh son, Ange (1537-1623), seigneur du Luat, was secretary to Henry IV., and enjoyed the esteem of Sully. Among those who remained Catholic should be mentioned Guillaume, the translator of Machiavelli. The eldest son Jacques also left two sons, famous in the history of Protestantism:—Jacques (1570-1624), pastor of the church founded by himself on his fief of le Tilloy and afterwards at Sedan, where he became professor of Hebrew, distinguished as historian, philologist and exegetical scholar; and Louis (see below).

On the protest of Guillaume Cappel, see Du Bellay, *Historia Universitatis Parisiensis*, vol. v. On the family, see the sketch by another Jacques Cappel, "De Capellorum gente," in the *Commentarii et notae criticae in Vetus Testamentum* of Louis Cappel, his father (Amsterdam, 1689). Consult Eugène and Emile Haag, *La France protestante*, vol. iii. (new edition, 1881).

CAPPEL, LOUIS (1585-1658), French Protestant divine and scholar, a Huguenot whose descent is traced above, was born at St Elier, near Sedan, in 1585. He studied theology at Sedan and Saumur; and Arabic at Oxford, where he spent two years. At the age of twenty-eight he accepted the chair of Hebrew at Saumur, and twenty years afterwards was appointed professor of theology. Amongst his fellow lecturers were Moses Amyraut and Josué de la Place. As a Hebrew scholar he made a special study of the history of the Hebrew text, which led him to the conclusion that the vowel points and accents are not an original part of the Hebrew language, but were inserted by the Massorete Jews of Tiberias, not earlier than the 5th century A.D., and that the primitive Hebrew characters are those now known as the Samaritan, while the square characters are Aramaic and were substituted for the more ancient at the time of the captivity. These conclusions were hotly contested by Johannes Buxtorf, being in conflict with the views of his father, Johannes Buxtorf senior, notwithstanding the fact that Elias Levita had already disputed the antiquity of the vowel points and that neither Jerome nor the Talmud shows any acquaintance with them. His second important work, *Critica Sacra,* was distasteful from a theological point of view. He had completed it in 1634; but owing to the fierce opposition with which he had to contend, he was only able to print it at Paris in 1650, by aid of a son, who had turned Catholic. The various readings in the Old Testament text and the differences between the ancient versions and the Massoretic text convinced him that the idea of the integrity of the Hebrew text, as commonly held by Protestants, was untenable. This amounted to an attack on the verbal inspiration of Scripture. Bitter, however, as was the opposition to his views, it was not long before his results were accepted by scholars.

Cappel was also the author of *Annotationes et Commentarii in Vetus Testamentum, Chronologia Sacra,* and other biblical works, as well as of several other treatises on Hebrew, among which are the *Arcanum Punctuationis revelatum* (1624) and the *Diatriba de veris et antiquis Ebraeorum literis* (1645). His *Commentarius de Capellorum gente,* giving an account of the family to which he belonged, was published by his nephew James Cappel (1639-1722), who, at the age of eighteen, became professor of Hebrew at Saumur, but, on the revocation of the edict of Nantes, fled to England, where he died in 1722. See Herzog-Hauck,*Realencyklopädie.*

CAPPELLO, BIANCA (1548-1587), grand duchess of Tuscany, was the daughter of Bartolommeo Cappello, a member of one of the richest and noblest Venetian families, and was famed for her great beauty. At the age of fifteen she fell in love with Pietro Bonaventuri, a young Florentine clerk in the firm of Salviati, and on the 28th of November 1563 escaped with him to Florence, where they were married and she had a daughter named Pellegrina. The Venetian government made every effort to have Bianca arrested and brought back, but the grand duke Cosimo de' Medici intervened in her favour and she was left unmolested. However she did not get on well with her husband's family, who were very poor and made her do menial work, until at last her beauty attracted Francesco, the grand duke's son, a vicious and unprincipled rake. Although already married to the virtuous and charming Archduchess Giovanna of Austria, he seduced the fair Venetian and loaded her with jewels, money and other presents. Bianca's accommodating husband was given court employment, and consoled himself with other ladies; in 1572 he was murdered in the streets of Florence in consequence of some amorous intrigue, though possibly Bianca and Francesco were privy to the deed. On the death of Cosimo in 1574 Francesco succeeded to the grand duchy; he now installed Bianca in a fine palace close to his own and outraged his wife by flaunting his mistress before her. As Giovanna had borne Francesco no sons, Bianca was very anxious to present him with an heir, for otherwise her position would remain very insecure. But although she resorted to all sorts of expedients, even to that of trying to pass off a changeling as the grand duke's child, she was not successful. In 1578 Giovanna died; a few days later Francesco secretly married Bianca, and on the 10th of June, 1579, the marriage was publicly announced. The Venetian government now put aside its resentment and was officially represented at the magnificent wedding festivities, for it saw in Bianca Cappello an instrument for cementing good relations with Tuscany. But the long expected heir failed to come, and Bianca realized that if her husband were to die before her she was lost, for his family, especially his brother Cardinal 289Ferdinand, hated her bitterly, as an adventuress and interloper. In October 1587 both the grand duke and his wife died of colic within a couple of days of each other. At the time poison was suspected, but documentary evidence has proved the suspicion to be unfounded.

See S. Romanin, *Lezioni di storia Veneta,* vol. ii. (Florence, 1875); G.E. Saltini, *Tragedie Medicee domestiche* (Florence, 1898).

(L. V.*)

CAPPERONNIER, CLAUDE (1671-1744), French classical scholar, the son of a tanner, was born at Montdidier on the 1st of May 1671. He studied at Amiens and Paris, and took orders in the Church of Rome, but devoted himself almost entirely to classical studies. He declined a professorship in the university of Bâle, and was afterwards appointed (1722) to the Greek chair in the Collège de France. He published an edition of Quintilian (1725) and left behind him at his death an edition of the ancient Latin Rhetoricians, which was published in 1756. He furnished much material for Robert Estienne's *Thesaurus Linguae Latinae.* His nephew, Jean Capperonnier (1716-1775), his successor in the chair of Greek at the Collège de France, was also a distinguished scholar, and published valuable editions of classical authors—Caesar, Anacreon, Plautus, Sophocles.

CAPPONI, GINO, MARQUIS (1792-1876), Italian statesman and historian, was born on the 13th of September 1792. The Capponi family is one of the most illustrious Florentine houses, and is mentioned as early as 1250; it acquired great wealth as a mercantile and banking firm, and many of its members distinguished themselves in the service of the republic and the Medicis (see CAPPONI, PIERO), and later in that of the house of Lorraine. Gino was the son of the Marquis Pier Roberto Capponi, a nobleman greatly attached to the reigning grand duke of Tuscany, Ferdinand III. When that prince was deposed by the French in 1799 the Capponi family followed him into exile at Vienna, where they remained until he exchanged his rights to the grand duchy for a German principality (1803). The Capponi then returned to Florence, and in 1811 Gino married the marchesina Giulia Riccardi. Although the family were very anti-French Gino was chosen with other notables to pay homage to Napoleon in Paris in 1813. On the fall of Napoleon Ferdinand returned to Tuscany (September 1814), but the restoration proved less reactionary there than in any other part of Italy. Young Capponi was well received at court, but not being satisfied with the life of a mere man of fashion, he devoted himself to serious study and foreign travel. After sundry journeys in Italy he again visited Paris in 1818, and then went to England. He became deeply interested in English institutions, and carefully studied the constitution, the electoral system, university life, industrial organization, &c. At Edinburgh he met Francis Jeffrey, the editor of the*Edinburgh Review,* and conceived a desire to found a similar review in Italy. Besides knowing Jeffrey he made the acquaintance of many prominent statesmen and men of letters, including Lord John Russell, the duke of Bedford, Dugald Stewart, Ugo Foscolo, &c. This visit had a great effect in forming his character, and while it made him an ardent Anglophil, he realized more and more the distressing conditions of his own country. He returned to Italy in 1820, and on reaching Florence he set to work to found a review on the lines of the*Edinburgh,* which should attract the best literary talent. This he achieved with the help of the Swiss G.P. Vieusseux, and the result was the *Antologia.* He contributed largely to its columns, as well as to those of the *Archivio Storico,*another of Vieusseux's ventures. Capponi began to take a more active interest in politics, and entered into communication with the Liberals of all parts of Italy. He had discussed the possibility of liberating Italy with Prince Charles Albert of Savoy-Carignano, to whom he had introduced the Milanese revolutionist Count Confalonieri (*q.v.*). But the collapse of the rising of 1821 and the imprisonment of Confalonieri made Capponi despair of achieving anything by revolution, and he devoted himself to the economic development of Tuscany and to study. At his beautiful villa of Varramista he collected materials for a history of the Church; his work was interrupted by family troubles and by increasing blindness, but although by 1844 he had completely lost his sight he continued to work by means of amanuenses. In 1847 he again plunged into politics and discussed plans for an Italian alliance against Austria. When the grand duke Leopold II. decided in 1848 to grant his people a constitution, Capponi was made a member of the commission to draw it up, and he eventually became prime minister. During his short tenure of office he conducted foreign affairs with great skill, and made every effort to save the Italian situation after the defeat of Charles Albert on the Mincio. In

October 1848 he resigned; soon afterwards the grand duke fled, anarchy followed, and then in 1849 he returned, but with an escort of Austrian soldiery. The blind statesman thanked God that he could not see the hated white uniforms in Florence. He returned to his studies and commenced his great *Storia della Repubblica di Firenze*; but he followed political affairs with great interest, and helped to convince Lord John Russell, who stayed with him in 1859, of the hopelessness of the grand duke's position. On Leopold's second flight (27th of April 1859) a Tuscan assembly was summoned, and Capponi elected member of it. He voted for the grand duke's deposition and for the union of Tuscany with Piedmont. King Victor Emmanuel made him senator in 1860. His last years were devoted almost exclusively to his Florentine history, which was published in 1875 and achieved an immediate success. This was Capponi's swan song, for on the 3rd of February 1876 he died at the age of eighty-four.

Capponi was one of the best specimens of the Tuscan landlord class. "He represents," wrote his biographer Tabarrini, "one of the most striking personalities of a generation, now wholly passed away, which did not resign itself to the beatitudes of 1815, but wished to raise Italy from the humble state to which the European peace of that year had condemned her; and he succeeded by first raising the character of the Italians in the opinion of foreigners, so as to deserve their esteem and respect." He knew nearly all the most interesting people in Italy, besides many distinguished foreigners: Giuseppe Giusti, the poet, A. Manzoni, the novelist, Niccolò Tommaseo, Richard Cobden, A. von Reumont, the historian, were among those whom he entertained at his palace or his villas, and many were the struggling students and revolutionists to whom he gave assistance. As a historian his reputation rests on his *Storia della Repubblica di Firenze* (Florence, 1875); it was the first comprehensive Italian book on the subject based on documents and written in a modern critical spirit, and if the chapters on the early history of the city are now obsolete in view of recent discoveries, yet, as a whole, it remains a standard work. Besides his history a large number of essays and pamphlets have been published in his *Scritti Inediti*.

See M. Tabarrini, *Gino Capponi* (Florence, 1879); and A. von Reumont,*Gino Capponi* (Gotha, 1880).

(L. V.*)

CAPPONI, PIERO (1447-1496), Florentine statesman and warrior. He was at first intended for a business career, but Lorenzo de' Medici, appreciating his ability, sent him as ambassador to various courts, where he acquitted himself with distinction. On the death of Lorenzo (1492), who was succeeded by his son, the weak and incapable Piero, Capponi became one of the leaders of the anti-Medicean faction which two years later expelled him from Florence. Capponi was then made chief of the republic and conducted public affairs with great skill, notably in the difficult negotiations with Charles VIII. of France, who had invaded Italy in 1494 and in whose camp the exiled Medici had taken refuge. In November Charles, on his way to Naples, entered Florence with his army, and immediately began to behave as though he were the conqueror of the city, because he had entered it lance in rest. The signory was anxious to be on good terms with him, but when he spoke in favour of the Medici their temper changed at once, and the citizens were ordered to arm and be prepared for all emergencies. Tumults broke out between French soldiers and Florentine citizens, barricades were erected and stones began to fly from the windows. This alarmed Charles, who lowered his tone and said nothing more about conquered cities or the Medici. The Florentines were willing to pay him a large sum of money, but in settling the amount further disagreements arose. Charles, who was full of the Medici's promises, made exorbitant demands, and finally presented an ultimatum to the signory, who rejected it. "Then we shall sound our trumpets," said the king, to which Capponi replied "And we shall toll our bells," and tore up the ultimatum in the king's face. Charles, who did not relish the idea of house-to-house fighting, was forced to moderate his claims, and concluded a more equitable treaty with the republic. On the 28th of November he departed, and Capponi was appointed to reform the government of Florence. But being more at home in the camp than in the council chamber, he was glad of the opportunity of leading the armies of the republic against the Pisan rebels. He proved a most capable general, but while besieging the castle of Soiana, he was killed on the 25th of September 1496. His death was greatly regretted, for the Florentines recognized in him their ablest statesman and warrior.

See under SAVONAROLA, FLORENCE, MEDICI, CHARLES VIII. The "Vita di Piero di Gino Capponi," by V. Acciaiuoli (published in the *Archivio Storico Italiano*, series 1, vol. iv. part 2a, 1853), is the chief contemporary authority; see also P. Villari, *Savonarola*, vol. i. (Florence, 1887), and Gino Capponi,*Storia delta Repubblica di Firenze*, vol. ii. (Florence, 1875).

(L. V.*)

CAPRAIA (anc. *Capraria*, from Lat. *capra*, wild-goat), an island of Italy, off the N.W. coast (the highest point 1466 ft. above sea-level), belonging to the province of Genoa, 42 m. S.S.E. of Leghorn by sea. Pop. (1901) 547. It is of volcanic origin, and is partly occupied by a penal agricultural colony. It produces wine, and is a centre of the anchovy fishery. It became Genoese in 1527 and was strongly fortified. In 1796 it was occupied for a short time by Nelson. About 20 m. to the north is the island of Gorgona (highest point 836 ft.), also famous for its anchovies.

CAPRERA, an island off the N.E. coast of Sardinia, about 1 m. in length. It is connected by a bridge with La Maddalena. Its chief interest lies in its connexion with Garibaldi, who first established himself there in 1854, and died there on the 2nd of June 1882. His tomb is visited on this anniversary by Italians from all parts. Roman remains, including a bust of Maximian, have been found upon the island.

CAPRI (anc. *Capreae*), an island on the S. side of the Bay of Naples, of which it commands a fine view; it forms part of the province of Naples, and is distant about 20 m. S. of the town of Naples. Pop. (1901) of the commune of Capri, 3890, of Anacapri, 2316. It divides the exits from the bay into two, the Bocca Grande, about 16 m. wide, between Capri and Ischia, and the Bocca Piccola, 3 m. wide between Capri and the extreme south-west point of the peninsula of Sorrento. It is 4 m. in length and the greatest width is 1½ m., the total area being 5½ sq. m. The highest point is the Monte Solaro (1920 ft.) on the west, while at the east end the cliffs rise to a height of 900 ft. sheer from the sea. The only safe landing-place is on the north side. There are two small towns, Capri (450 ft.) and Anacapri (980 ft.), which until the construction of a carriage road in 1874 were connected only by a flight of 784 steps (the substructures of which at least are ancient). The island lacks water, and is dusty during drought, but is fertile, producing fruit, wine and olive oil; the indigenous flora comprises 800 species. The fishing industry also is important. But the prosperity of the island depends mainly upon foreign visitors (some 30,000 annually), who are attracted by the remarkable beauty of the scenery (that of the coast being especially fine), the views of the sea and of the Bay of Naples, and the purity of the air. The famous Blue Grotto, the most celebrated of the many caves in the rocky shores of the island, was known in Roman times, but lost until 1826, when it was rediscovered. Another beautiful grotto has green instead of blue refractions; the effect in both cases is due to the light entering by a small entrance.

The high land in the west of the island and the somewhat less elevated region in the east are formed of Upper Tithonian and Lower Cretaceous limestones, the latter containing Rudistes. The intervening depression, which seems to be bounded on the west by a fault, is filled to a large extent by sandstones and marls of Eocene age. A superficial layer of recent volcanic tuffs occurs in several parts of the island. The Blue Grotto is in the Tithonian limestones; it shows indications of recent changes of level.

The earliest mythical inhabitants (though some have localized the Sirens here) are the Teleboi from Acarnania under their king Telon. Neolithic remains were found in 1882 in the Grotta delle Felci, a cave on the south coast. In historical times we find the island occupied by Greeks. It subsequently fell into the hands of Neapolis, and remained so until the time of Augustus, who took it in exchange for Aenaria (Ischia) and often resided there. Tiberius, who spent the last ten years of his life at Capri, built no fewer than twelve villas there; to these the great majority of the numerous and considerable ancient remains on the island belong. All these villas can be identified with more or less certainty, the best preserved being those on the east extremity, consisting of a large number of vaulted substructures and the foundations perhaps of a *pharos* (lighthouse). One was known as Villa Jovis, and the other eleven were probably named after other deities. The existence of numerous ancient cisterns shows that in Roman as in modern times rain-water was largely used for lack of springs. After Tiberius's death the island seems to have been little visited by the emperors, and we hear of it only as a place of banishment for the wife and sister of Commodus. The island, having been at first the property of Neapolis, and later of the emperors, never had upon it any community with civic rights. Even in imperial times Greek was largely spoken there, for about as many Greek as Latin inscriptions have been found. The medieval town was on the north side at the chief landing-place (Marina Grande), and to it belonged the church of S. Costanzo, an early Christian building. It was abandoned in the 15th century on account of the inroads of pirates, and the inhabitants took refuge higher up at the two towns of Capri and Anacapri.

In 1806 the island was taken by the English fleet under Sir Sidney Smith, and strongly fortified, but in 1808 it was retaken by the French under Lamarque. In 1813 it was restored to Ferdinand I. of the Two Sicilies.

See J. Beloch, *Campanien* (Breslau, 1890), 278 seq.; G. Feola, *Rapporto sullo stato dei ruderi Augusto-Tiberiani*—MS. inedito, publicato dal Dott. Ignazio Cerio (Naples, 1894); F. Furchheim, *Bibliografia dell' Isola di Capri e della provincia Sorrentina* (Naples, 1899); C. Weichhardt, *Das Schloss des Tiberius und andere Römerbauten auf Capri* (Leipzig, 1900).

(T. As.)

CAPRICCIO, or CAPRICE (Ital. for a sudden motion or fancy), a musical term for a lively composition of an original and fantastic nature, not following a set musical form, although the first known, written for the harpsichord, partook of the nature of a fugue. The word is also used for pieces of a fanciful type, in the nature of transcriptions and variations.

CAPRICORNUS ("THE GOAT"), in astronomy, the tenth sign of the zodiac (*q.v.*), represented by the symbol   intended to denote the crooked horns of this animal. The word is derived from Lat. *caper*, a goat, and *cornu*, a horn. It is also a constellation of the southern hemisphere, mentioned by Eudoxus (4th century B.C.) and Aratus (3rd century B.C.); Ptolemy and Tycho Brahe catalogued 28 stars, Hevelius gave 29. It was represented by the ancients as a creature having the forepart a goat, and the hindpart a fish, or sometimes simply as a goat. An interesting member of this constellation is α-*Capricorni*, a pair of stars of 3rd and 4th magnitudes, each of which has a companion of the 9th magnitude.

CAPRIFOLIACEAE, a natural order of plants belonging to the sympetalous or higher division of Dicotyledons, that namely which is characterized by having the petals of the flower united. The plants are mainly shrubs and trees; British representatives are *Sambucus* (elder), *Viburnum* (guelder-rose and wayfaring tree), *Lonicera* (honeysuckle) (see fig.); *Adoxa* (moschatel), a small herb with a creeping stem and small yellowish-green flowers, is occasionally found on damp hedge-banks; *Linnaea*, a slender creeping evergreen with a thread-like stem and pink bell-shaped 291 flower, a northern plant, occurs in fir-forests and plantations in the north of England and Scotland. The leaves are opposite, simple as in honeysuckle, or compound as in elder; they have usually no stipules. The flowers are regular as in *Viburnum*

Flowering shoot of *Lonicera Caprifolium*, slightly reduced. 1, Fruit slightly reduced; 2, horizontal plan of arrangement of flower.

and *Sambucus*, more rarely two-lipped as in *Lonicera*; the sepals and petals are usually five in number and placed above the ovary, the five stamens are attached to the corolla-tube, there are three to five carpels, and the fruit is a berry as in honeysuckle or snowberry (*Symphoricarpus*), or a stone fruit, with several, usually three, stones, as in *Sambucus*.

In *Sambucus* and *Viburnum* the small white flowers are massed in heads; honey is secreted at the base of the styles and, the tube of the flower being very short, is exposed to the visits of flies and insects with short probosces. The flowers of *Lonicera*, which have a long tube, open in the evening, when they are sweet-scented and are visited by hawk-moths. The order contains about 250 species, chiefly natives of the north temperate zone and the mountains of the tropics. Several genera afford ornamental plants; such are *Lonicera*, erect shrubs or twiners with long-tubed white, yellow or red flowers; *Symphoricarpus*, a North American shrub, with small whitish pendulous flowers and white berries;*Diervilla* (also known as *Weigelia*), and *Viburnum*, including *V. Opulus*, guelder rose, in the cultivated forms of which the corolla has become enlarged at the expense of the essential organs and the flowers are neuter.

CAPRIVI DE CAPRERA DE MONTECUCCOLI, GEORG LEO VON, COUNT (1831-1899), German soldier and statesman, was born on the 24th of February 1831 at Charlottenburg. The family springs from Carniola, and the name was originally written Kopriva; in the 18th century one branch settled in Wernigerode, and several members entered the Prussian service; the father of the chancellor held a high judicial post, and was made a life member of the Prussian House of Lords. Caprivi was educated in Berlin, and entered the army in 1849; he took part in the campaign of 1866, being attached to the staff of the ist army. In 1870 he served as chief of the staff to the 10th army corps, which formed part of the 2nd army, and took part in the battles before Metz as well as in those round Orleans, in which he highly distinguished himself. One of the most delicate strategical problems of the whole war was the question of whether to change the direction of the 10th corps on the morning of the 16th of August before Vionville, and in this, as well as in the actual manoeuvres of the corps on that day, Caprivi, as representative of, and counsellor to, his chief, General v. Voigts-Rhetz, took a leading part. At the battle of Beaune-la-Rolande, the turning-point of the Orleans campaign, the 10th corps bore the brunt of the fighting. After the peace he held several important military offices, and in 1883 was made chief of the admiralty, in which post he had to command the fleet and to organize and represent the department in the Reichstag. He resigned in 1888, when the command was separated from the representation in parliament, and was appointed commander of the 10th army corps. Bismarck had already referred to him as a possible successor to himself, for Caprivi had shown great administrative ability, and was unconnected with any political party; and in March 1890 he was appointed chancellor, Prussian minister president and foreign minister. He was quite unknown to the public, and the choice caused some surprise, but it was fully justified. The chief events of his administration, which lasted for four years, are narrated elsewhere, in the article on Germany. He showed great ability in quickly mastering the business, with which he was hitherto quite unacquainted, as he himself acknowledged; his speeches in the Reichstag were admirably clear, dignified and to the point. His first achievement was the conclusion in July 1890 of a general agreement with Great Britain regarding the spheres of influence of the two countries in Africa. Bismarck had supported the colonial parties in Germany in pretensions to which it was impossible for Great Britain to give her consent, and the relations between the two powers were in consequence somewhat strained. Caprivi adopted a conciliatory attitude, and succeeded in negotiating terms with Lord Salisbury which gave to Germany all she could reasonably expect. But the abandonment of an aggressive policy in East Africa and in Nigeria, and in the withdrawal of German claims to Zanzibar (in exchange for Heligoland) aroused the hostility of the colonial parties, who bitterly attacked the new chancellor. Caprivi had, however, by making the frontiers of the Congo Free State and German East Africa meet, "cut" the Cape to Cairo connexion of the British, an achievement which caused much dismay in British colonial circles, regular treaties having been obtained from native chiefs over large areas which the chancellor secured for Germany. In Nigeria also Caprivi by the 1890 agreement, and by another concluded in 1893, made an excellent bargain for his country, while in South-West Africa he obtained a long but narrow extension eastward to the Zambezi of the German protectorate (this strip of territory being known as "Caprivi's Finger"). In his African policy the chancellor proved far-sighted, and gained for the new protectorates a period for internal development and consolidation. The Anglo-German agreement of 1890 was followed by commercial treaties with Austria, Rumania, &c.; by concluding them he earned the express commendation of the emperor and the title of count, but he was from this time relentlessly attacked by the Agrarians, who made it a ground for their distrust that he was not himself a landed proprietor; and from this time he had to depend much on the support of the Liberals and other parties who had been formerly in opposition. The reorganization of the army caused a parliamentary crisis, but he carried it through successfully, only, however, to earn the enmity of the more old-fashioned soldiers, who would not forgive him for shortening the period of service. His position was seriously compromised by the failure in 1892 to carry an education bill which he had defended by saying that the question at issue was Christianity or Atheism, and he resigned the presidency of the Prussian ministry, which was then given to Count Eulenburg. In 1894, a difference arose between Eulenburg and Caprivi concerning the bill for an amendment of the criminal code (the *Umsturz Vorlage*), and in October the emperor dismissed both. Caprivi's fall was probably the work of the Agrarians, but it was also due to the fact that, while he showed very high ability in conducting the business of the country, he made no attempt to secure his personal position by forming a party either in parliament or at court. He interpreted his position rather as a soldier; he did his duty, but did not think of defending himself. He 292suffered much from the attacks made on him by the followers of Bismarck, and he was closely associated with the social ostracism of that statesman; we do not know, however, in regard either to this or to the other events of his administration, to what extent Caprivi was really the author of the policy he carried out, and to what extent he was obeying the orders of the emperor. With a loyalty which cannot be too highly praised, he always refused, even after his abrupt dismissal, to justify himself, and he could not be persuaded even to write memoirs for later publication. The last years of his life were spent in absolute retirement, for he could not return even to the military duties which he had left with great reluctance at the orders of the emperor. He died unmarried on the 6th of February 1899, at the age of sixty-eight.

See R. Arndt, *Die Reden des Grafen v. Caprivi* (Berlin, 1894), with a biography.

(J. W. HE.)

CAPRONNIER, JEAN BAPTISTE (1814-1891), Belgian stained-glass painter, was born in Brussels in 1814, and died there in 1891. He had much to do with the modern revival of glass-painting, and first made his reputation by his study of the old methods of workmanship, and his clever restorations of old examples, and copies made for the Brussels archaeological museum. He carried out windows for various churches in Brussels, Bruges, Amsterdam and elsewhere, and his work was commissioned also for France, Italy and England. At the Paris Exhibition of 1855 he won the only medal given for glass-painting.

CAPSICUM, a genus of plants, the fruits of which are used as peppers (seeCAYENNE PEPPER for botany, &c.). As used in medicine, the ripe fruit of the*capsicum mimum* (or *frutescans*), containing the active principle capsaicin (capsacutin), first isolated by Thresh in 1876, has remarkable physiological properties. Applied locally to the skin or mucous membrane, it causes redness and later vesication. Internally in small doses it stimulates gastric secretions and causes dilatation of the vessels; but if used internally in excess for a long period it will cause subacute gastritis. In single doses in excess it causes renal irritation and inflammation and strangury. The administration of capsicum is valuable in atony of the stomach due to chronic alcoholism, its hot stimulating effect not only increasing the appetite but to a certain degree satisfying the craving for alcohol. It is also useful in the flatulency of the aged, where it prevents the development of gas, and has a marked effect on anorexia. It has been used in functional torpidity of the kidney. Externally capsicum plaster placed over the affected muscles is useful in rheumatism and lumbago. Capsicum wool, known as calorific wool, made by dissolving the oleoresin of capsicum in ether and pouring it on to absorbent cotton-wool, is useful in rheumatic affections.

CAPSTAN (also spelt in other forms, or as "capstock" and "cable stock," connected with the O. Fr. *capestan* or *cabestan*, from Lat. *capistrum*, a halter,*capere*, to take hold of; the conjecture that it came from the Span. *cabra*, goat, and *estanto*, standing, is untenable), an appliance used on board ship and on dock walls, for heaving-in or veering cables and hawsers, whether of iron, steel or hemp. It differs from a windlass, which is used for the same purposes, in having the axis on which the rope is wound vertical instead of horizontal. The word seems to have come into English (14th century) from French or Spanish shipmen at the time of the Crusades. The earlier forms were of a comparatively simple character, made of wood with an iron spindle and worked by manual labour with wooden capstan bars. As heavier cables were supplied to ships, difficulty was found, when riding at anchor, in holding, checking and veering cable. A cable-holder (W.H. Harfield's) was tested in H.M.S. "Newcastle" (wooden frigate) in 1870 and proved effective; its first development in 1876 was the application in the form of a windlass secured to the deck, driven by a messenger chain from the capstan, fitted in H.M.S. "Inflexible" (fig. 1).

FIG. 1.

The capstans and engine are shown at A, A, A, and the windlass B is driven by messenger chains C, C. The four cables (dotted line D, D) lead to their respective cable-holders, fitted with a brake, and by these means each cable-holder can be connected to the main driving shaft, and any cable hove-in or veered independently of the other; by using steam power instead of manual, the previous slow motion was obviated. In H.M.S. "Collingwood" steam power was used to work the windlass directly by means of worm gearing; the windlass was divided into two parts, so that the one on the port side could be worked independently of that on the starboard, and vice versa. An independent capstan in both ships, arranged to take either of the cables, could be worked by hand or steam. In the "Collingwood's" windlass the cables remained on their holders, and could be hove-in or veered without being touched.

Napier's patent windlass for merchant ships (1906) resembles an appliance fitted in the earlier second-class cruisers of the British navy (1890 to 1900). Two cable wheels or cable-holders are mounted loose on a horizontal axle, one on each side of a worm wheel which is tightly keyed on the middle part of the axle. A vertical steam engine with two cylinders, placed one on each side of the framing, drives a second horizontal axle which is connected by a set of bevel gears to an upright worm shaft, which works the worm wheel. This worm wheel can be connected by means of sliding bolts to one or both of the cable wheels, enabling one or both cables to be hove-in or veered as necessary. A brake, of Napier's self-holding differential type, is fitted to each cable wheel, and is controlled by hand wheels on the aft side of the windlass. For warping purposes, warping drums are fitted (made portable if required). A third central capstan, fitted forward of the windlass, is connected to the upright worm shaft by a horizontal shaft and bevel wheels. It can also be worked by manual labour with capstan bars. Fig. 2 represents the arrangement of the capstans on the forecastle of a battleship, fitted by Napier Brothers. Deep-bodied capstans have been superseded by low drum-headed ones, over which the guns may be fired. The three capstans or cable-holders of cast steel, capable of taking 211/16 in. cables, are fitted on vertical spindles, which pass down through the main and armoured decks to the platform one, where the steam engine and gearing are placed. The gearing consists of worm and wheel gears, so arranged that the three capstans can be worked singly or in conjunction, when heaving-in or veering, and the brakes (of the type previously mentioned) are controlled by a portable hand wheel fitted on the aft side of each. The cable-holders can be used for riding at anchor (see CABLE). The middle line capstan E is keyed to vertical spindles and can be coupled up to the capstan engine, by clutch and drop bolts in the capstan engine room; it is fitted with a cable-holder, to take either the port or starboard cables, and in addition is provided with portable whelps, enabling it to be used for warping. It can also be worked by manual labour with capstan bars, a drum-head E', fitted on the spindle on the main deck, enabling additional capstan bars to be used if required.

88

FIG. 2.—Elevation
looking aft.

FIG. 3.— Napier Brothers' capstan.

To avoid carrying steam pipes aft, the after capstan is worked 293by an electric motor
which is kept below the water-line. Napier Brothers' capstan (fig. 3) is for warping purposes,
for working the stern anchor with wire hawser and for coaling. It is placed on the upper
deck, and is fitted with a drum-head for capstan bars, with pawls and pawl rim on the deck
plate, the pawls A being lifted and placed on their rests B when working with the motor. The
upper portion of the capstan, together with its drum-head, is portable, being fixed to the
centre boss with keys and gun-metal screws. The centre boss is keyed to the spindle, which
passes through the deck and carries at its lower end a coupling for connecting to the worm
wheel gear. For working by motor, the additional security of two drop bolts is provided. The
gearing consists of a single worm and worm wheel, working in an oil-bath, the worm shaft
being coupled direct to the motor spindle. The motor is of the semi-enclosed type, the
working and live parts being protected by a perforated metallic covering; it is worked off a
100-volt circuit, at a speed under full load conditions of 300 revolutions per minute. The
motor is of a 4-pole type and compound wound, the shunt winding limiting the speed on
light load to not more than 1000 revolutions per minute. A frictional break is provided,
pulled off by means of a shunt-excited magnet. The controller is of the reversing drum type,
with not less than four steps in either direction, and is fitted with a magnetic blow-out. The
control is effected by a removable hand wheel on a portable pedestal, fitted on top with a
circular dial plate and indicating pointer; the hand wheel reverses the current as well as
graduates the speed in either direction. All capstans of the British navy, after being fitted on
board ship, are tested for lifting power and speed; with foremost (steam) capstans, the steam
being at 150 ℔ pressure, the anchor is usually let go in 16 to 25 fathoms water, and the
speed ascertained by observing the time taken to heave-in not less than a length of cable, 75
ft.; the length must be hove-in in three minutes, or at the rate of 25 ft. per minute. With the
after capstan (motor) of first-class battleships and cruisers, a weight is used instead of an
anchor, the test being to lift 9 tons at the rate of 25 ft. per minute. Capstans on dock walls in
British government dockyards are usually driven by hydraulic or air pressure, conveyed
through pipes to small engines underneath the capstans.

(J. W. D.)

CAPSULE (from the Lat. *capsula*, a small box), a term in botany for a dry seed vessel,
as in the poppy, iris, foxglove, &c., containing one or more cells. When ripe the capsule
opens and scatters the seed (see BOTANY). The word is used also for a small gelatinous case
enclosing a dose of medicine, and for a metal cap or cover on bottles and jars. In anatomy
the term is used to denote a cover or envelope partly or wholly surrounding a structure.
Every diarthrodial joint possesses a fibrous or ligamentous capsule, lined with synovial
membrane, attached to the adjacent ends of the articulating bones. The term is particularly
applied to the sac which encloses the crystalline lens of the eye; to Glisson's capsule, a thin
areolar coat of fibrous tissue lying inside the tunica serosa of the liver; to the glomerular
capsules in the kidney substance; to the suprarenal capsules, two small flattened organs in
the epigastric region; and to the internal and external capsules of the brain (see BRAIN, fig.
14 and explanation).

CAPTAIN (derived from Lat. *caput*, head, through the Low Lat. *capitanus*), a chief or leader, in various connexions, but particularly a grade officer in the army or navy.

At sea the name of captain is given to all who command ships whether they belong to the military navy of their country or not, or whether they hold the substantive rank or not. Thus a lieutenant when in command of a vessel is addressed as captain. In France a naval lieutenant is addressed as *mon capitaine* because he has that comparative rank in the army. The master of a merchant ship is known as her captain. But the name is also used in the strict sense of foreman, or head man, to describe many of the minor or "petty" officers of a British or American man-of-war—the captain of a top, of the forecastle, or of a gun. The title "post captain" in the British navy means simply full captain, and is the equivalent of the French *capitaine de vaisseau*. It had its origin in the fact that captains appointed to a ship of twenty guns and upwards were included in, or "posted" on, the permanent list of captains from among whom the admirals were chosen. The captain of the fleet is an officer who acts as chief of the staff to an admiral commanding a large force. The position is equivalent to flag rank, but is held by a captain. Staff captain is the highest grade of the officers entrusted with the navigation of a ship or fleet.

The military rank of captain (Fr. *capitaine*, Ger. *Hauptmann*, or in the cavalry, *Rittmeister*), which was formerly the title of an officer of high rank corresponding to the modern general officer or colonel, has with the gradual subdivision and articulation of armies, come to be applied to the commanders of companies or squadrons, and in general to officers of the grade equivalent to this command (see OFFICERS).

The title of "captain-general" was formerly used in the general sense of a military commander-in-chief, and is still similarly used in Spain. In the Spanish army there are eight captains-general, each of whom has command of a "region" corresponding to an army corps district. The same title was formerly given to the Spanish governors of the colonial provinces in the New World. The official title of the governor of Jamaica is "captain-general and governor-in-chief."

CAPTAL (Lat. *capitalis*, "first," "chief"), a medieval feudal title in Gascony. According to Du Cange the designation captal (*capital, captau, capitau*) was applied loosely to the more illustrious nobles of Aquitaine, counts, viscounts, &c., probably as *capitales domini*, "principal lords," though he quotes more fanciful explanations. As an actual title the word was used only by the lords of Trene, Puychagut, Epernon and Buch. It is best known in connexion with the famous soldier, Jean de Grailly, captal of Bush (d. 1376), the "captal de Buch" *par excellence*, immortalized by Froissart as the confidant of the Black Prince and the champion of the English cause against France. His active part in the war began in 1364, when he ravaged the country between Paris and Rouen, but was beaten by Bertrand du Guesclin at Cocherel and taken prisoner. Released next year, he received the seigniory of Nemours and took the oath of fealty to the French king, Charles V., but soon resigned his new fief and returned to his allegiance to the English king. In 1367 he took part in the battle of Navarette, in which Du Guesclin was taken prisoner, the captal being entrusted with his safe-keeping. In 1371 Jean de Grailly was appointed constable of Aquitaine, but was taken prisoner next year and interned in the Temple at Paris where, resisting all the tempting offers of the French king, he remained till his death five years later.

CAPTION (Lat. *captio*, a taking or catching), a term still used in law, especially Scots, for arrest or apprehension. From the obsolete sense of a catching at any possible plea or objection comes the adjective "captious," *i.e.* sophistical or fault-finding. The term also has an old legal use, to signify the part of an indictment, &c., which shows where, when and by what authority it is taken, found or executed; so its opening or heading. From this is derived the modern sense of the heading of an article in a book or newspaper.

CAPTIVE (from Lat. *capere*, to take), one who is captured in warfare. As a term of International Law, it has been displaced by that of "prisoner of war." The position and treatment of captives or prisoners of war is now dealt with fully in chapter ii. of the regulations annexed to the Hague Convention respecting the Laws and Customs of War on Land, of the 18th of October 1907.

See PEACE CONFERENCE and WAR; also Sir T. Barclay, supplement to *Problems of International Practice and Diplomacy*, for comparison of texts of 1899 and 1907.

294

CAPTURE (from Lat. *capere*, to take; Fr. *prise maritime*; Ger. *Wegnahme*), in international law, the taking possession by a belligerent vessel of an enemy or neutral merchant or non-fighting ship. If an enemy ship is captured she becomes forthwith lawful prize (*q.v.*); when a neutral ship, the belligerent commander, in case her papers are not conclusive, has a right to search her. If he finds contraband on board or the papers or cargo or circumstances excite any serious suspicion in his mind, which the master of the ship has been unable to dispel, he places an officer and a few of his crew on board and sends her to the nearest port where there is a prize court for trial. The word is also used for the vessel thus captured (see BLOCKADE, CONTRABAND).

(T. BA.)

CAPUA (anc. *Casilinum*), a town and archiepiscopal see of Campania, Italy, in the province of Caserta, 7 m. W. by rail from the town of Caserta. Pop. (1901) 14,285. It was erected in 856 by Bishop Landulf on the site of Casilinum (*q.v.*) after the destruction of the ancient Capua by the Saracens in 840, but it only occupies the site of the original pre-Roman town on the left (south) bank of the river.

The cathedral of S. Stefano, erected in 856, has a handsome atrium and a lofty Lombard campanile, and a (modernized) interior with three aisles; both it and the atrium have ancient granite columns. The Romanesque crypt, with ancient columns, has also been restored. It has a fine paschal candlestick, and the fragments of a pulpit with marble mosaic of the 13th century. There are also preserved in the cathedral a fine Exultet roll and an *evangelarium* of the end of the 12th century, bound in bronze decorated with gold filigree and enamels. The mosaics of the beginning of the 12th century in the apses of the cathedral and of S. Benedetto, were destroyed about 1720 and 1620 respectively. The small church of S. Marcello was also built in 856. In 1232-1240 Frederick II. erected a castle to guard the Roman bridge over the Volturno, composed of a triumphal arch with two towers. This was demolished in 1557. The statues with which it was decorated were contemporary imitations of classical sculptures. Some of them are still preserved in the Museo Campano (E. Bertaux, *L'Art dans l'Italie méridionale*, Paris, 1904, i. 707). The Museo Campano also contains a considerable collection of antiquities from the ancient Capua.

Capua changed hands frequently during the middle ages. One of the most memorable facts in its history is the terrible attack made on it in 1501 by Caesar Borgia, who had entered the town by treachery, in which 5000 lives were sacrificed. It remained a part of the kingdom of Naples until the 2nd of November 1860, when, a month after the battle of the Volturno, it surrendered to the Italian troops.

(T. AS.)

CAPUA (mod. *S. Maria di Capua Vetere*), the chief ancient city of Campania, and one of the most important towns of ancient Italy, situated 16 m. N. of Neapolis, on the N.E. edge of the Campanian plain. Its site in a position not naturally defensible, together with the regularity of its plan, indicates that it is not a very ancient town, though it very likely occupies the site of an early Oscan settlement. Its foundation is attributed by Cato to the Etruscans, and the date given as about 260 years before it was "taken" by Rome (Vell. i. 7). If this be referred, not to its capture in the second Punic War (211 B.C.) but to its submission to Rome in 338 B.C., we get about 600 B.C. as the date of its foundation, a period at which the Etruscan power was at its highest, and which may perhaps, therefore, be accepted.1 The origin of the name is probably *Campus*, a plain,2 as the adjective *Campanus* shows, *Capuanus* being a later form stigmatized as incorrect by Varro (*De LL* x. 16). The derivation from κάπυς (a vulture, Latinized into *Volturnum* by some

91

authorities who tell us that this was the original name), and that from *caput* (as though the name had been given it as the "head" of the twelve Etruscan cities of Campania), must be rejected. The Etruscan supremacy in Campania came to an end with the Samnite invasion in the latter half of the 5th century B.C. (see CAMPANIA); these conquerors, however, entered into alliance with Rome for protection against the Samnite mountain tribes, and with Capua came the dependent communities Casilinum, Calatia, Atella, so that the greater part of Campania now fell under Roman supremacy. The citizens received the *civitas sine suffragio*. In the second Samnite War they proved untrustworthy, so that the Ager Falernus on the right bank of the Volturnus was taken from them and distributed among citizens of Rome, the *tribus Falerna* being thus formed; and in 318 the powers of the native officials (*meddices*) were limited by the appointment of officials with the title *praefecti Capuam Cumas* (taking their name from the most important towns of Campania); these were at first mere deputies of the *praetor urbanus*, but after 123 B.C. were elected Roman magistrates, four in number; they governed the whole of Campania until the time of Augustus, when they were abolished. In 312 B.C. Capua was connected with Rome by the construction of the Via Appia, the most important of the military highways of Italy. The gate by which it left the Servian walls of Rome bore the name Porta Capena—perhaps the only case in which a gate in this enceinte bears the name of the place to which it led. At what time the Via Latina was prolonged to Casilinum is doubtful (it is quite possible that it was done when Capua fell under Roman supremacy, *i.e.* before the construction of the Via Appia); it afforded a route only 6 m. longer, and the difficulties in connexion with its construction were much less; it also avoided the troublesome journey through the Pomptine Marshes (see T. Ashby in *Papers of the British School at Rome*, i. 217, London, 1902). The importance of Capua increased steadily during the 3rd century, and at the beginning of the second Punic War it was considered to be only slightly behind Rome and Carthage themselves, and was able to furnish 30,000 infantry and 4000 cavalry. Until after the defeat of Cannae it remained faithful to Rome, but, after a vain demand that one of the consuls should always be selected from it, it transferred its allegiance to Hannibal, who made it his winter-quarters, with bad results to the *morale* of his troops (see PUNIC WARS). After a long siege it was taken by the Romans in 211 B.C. and severely punished; its magistrates and communal organization were abolished, the inhabitants losing their civic rights, and its territory became Roman state domain. Parts of it were sold in 205 and 199 B.C., another part was divided among the citizens of the new colonies of Volturnum and Liternum established near the coast in 194 B.C., but the greater portion of it was reserved to be let by the state. Considerable difficulties occurred in preventing illegal encroachments by private persons, and it became necessary to buy a number of them out in 162 B.C. It was, after that period, let, not to large but to small proprietors. Frequent attempts were made by the democratic leaders to divide the land among new settlers. Brutus in 83 B.C. actually succeeded in establishing a colony, but it was soon dissolved; and Cicero's speeches *De Lege Agraria* were directed against a similar attempt by Servilius Rullus in 63 B.C. In the meantime the necessary organization of the inhabitants of this thickly-populated district was in a measure supplied by grouping them round important shrines, especially that of Diana Tifatina, in connexion with which a *pagus Dianae* existed, as we learn from many inscriptions; a *pagus Herculaneus* is also known. The town of Capua belonged to none of these organizations, and was entirely dependent on the *praefecti*. It enjoyed great prosperity, however, owing to its spelt, which was worked into groats, wine, roses, spices, unguents, &c., and also owing to its manufactures, especially of bronze objects, of which both the elder Cato and the elder Pliny speak in the highest terms (*De agr.* 135; *Hist. Nat.* xxiv. 95). Its luxury remained proverbial; and Campania is especially spoken of as the home of gladiatorial combats. From the gladiatorial schools of Campania came Spartacus and his followers in 73 B.C. Julius Caesar as consul in 59 B.C. succeeded in carrying out the establishment of a colony in connexion with his agrarian law, and 20,000 Roman citizens were settled in this territory. The number of colonists was increased by Mark 295Antony, Augustus (who constructed an aqueduct from the Mons Tifata, and gave the town of Capua estates in the district of Cnossus in Crete to the value of 12 million sesterces—£120,000), and Nero. In the war of A.D. 69 it took the side of Vitellius. Under the later empire it is not often mentioned; but in the 4th century it was the seat of the *consularis Campaniae* and its chief town, though Ausonius puts it behind Mediolanum (Milan) and Aquileia in his *ordo nobilium urbium*. Under Constantine we hear of the foundation of a Christian church in Capua. In A.D. 456 it was taken and destroyed by Genseric, but must have been soon rebuilt: it was, however, finally destroyed by the Saracens in 840 and the church of S. Maria Maggiore, founded about 497, alone remained. It contains 52 ancient marble columns, but was modernized in 1766. The site was only occupied in the late middle ages by a village which has, however, outgrown the medieval Capua in modern days.

Remains.—No pre-Roman remains have been found within the town of Capua itself, but important cemeteries have been discovered on all sides of it, the earliest of which go back to the 7th or 6th century B.C. The tombs are of various forms, partly chambers with frescoes on the walls, partly cubical blocks of peperino, hollowed out, with grooved lids. The objects found within them consist mainly of vases of bronze (many of them without feet, and with incised designs of Etruscan style) and of clay, some of Greek, some of local manufacture, and of paintings. On the east of the town, in the Patturelli property, a temple has been discovered with Oscan votive inscriptions, some of them inscribed upon terra-cotta tablets, others on *cippi*, while of a group of 150 tufa statuettes (representing a matron holding one or more children in her lap) three bore Latin inscriptions of the early imperial period. The site of the town being in a perfectly flat plain, without natural defences, it was possible to lay it out regularly. Its length from east to west is accurately determined by the fact that the Via Appia, which runs from north-west to south-east from Casilinum to Calatia, turns due east very soon after passing the so-called Arco Campano (a triumphal arch of good brickwork, once faced with marble, with three openings, erected in honour of some emperor unknown), and continues to run in this direction for 5413½ English feet (= 6000 ancient Oscan feet). The west gate was the Porta Romana; remains of the east gate (the name of which we do not know) have been found. This fact shows that the main street of the town was perfectly orientated, and that before the Via Appia was constructed, *i.e.* in all probability in pre-Roman times. The width of the town from north to south cannot be so accurately determined as the line of the north and south walls is not known, though it can be approximately fixed by the absence of tombs (Beloch fixes it at 4000 Oscan feet = 3609 English feet), nor is it absolutely certain (though it is in the highest degree probable, for Cicero praises its regular arrangement and fine streets) that the plan of the town was rectangular. Within the town are remains of thermae on the north of the Via Appia and of a theatre opposite, on the south. The former consisted of a large crypto-porticus round three sides of a court, the south side being open to the road; it now lies under the prisons. Beloch (see below) attributes this to the Oscan period; but the construction as shown in Labruzzi's drawing (v. 17)3 is partly of brick-work and *opus reticulatum*, which may, of course, belong to a restoration. The stage of the theatre had its back to the road; Labruzzi (v. 18) gives an interesting view of the *cavea*. It appears from inscriptions that it was erected after the time of Augustus. Other inscriptions, however, prove the existence of a theatre as early as 94 B.C., so that the existence of another elsewhere must be assumed. We know that the Roman colony was divided into regions and possessed a capitolium, with a temple of Jupiter, within the town, and that the market-place, for unguents especially, was called Seplasia; we also hear of an *aedes alba*, probably the original senate house, which stood in an open space known as *albana*. But the sites of all these are quite uncertain. Outside the town on the north is the amphitheatre, built in the time of Augustus, restored by Hadrian and dedicated by Antoninus Pius, as the inscription over the main entrance recorded. The exterior was formed by 80 Doric arcades of four storeys each, but only two arches now remain. The keystones were adorned with heads of divinities. The interior is better preserved; beneath the arena are subterranean passages like those in the amphitheatre at Puteoli. It is one of the largest in existence; the longer diameter is 185 yds., the shorter 152, and the arena measures 83 by 49 yds., the corresponding dimensions in the colosseum at Rome being 205, 170, 93 and 58 yds. To the east are considerable remains of baths—a large octagonal building, an apse against which the church of S. Maria delle Grazie is built, and several heaps of debris. On the Via Appia, to the south-east of the east gate of the town, are two large and well-preserved tombs of the Roman period, known as *le Carceri vecchie* and *la Conocchia*. To the east of the amphitheatre an ancient road, the Via Dianae, leads north to the Pagus Dianae, on the west slopes of the Mons Tifata, a community which sprang up round the famous and ancient temple of Diana, and probably received an independent organization after the abolition of that of Capua in 211 B.C. The place often served as a base for attacks on the latter, and Sulla, after his defeat of C. Norbanus, gave the whole of the mountain to the temple. Within the territory of the *pagus* were several other temples with their *magistri*. After the restoration of the community of Capua, we find *magistri* of the temple of Diana still existing, but they were probably officials of Capua itself. The site is occupied by the Benedictine church of S. Angelo in Formis4 which dates from 944, and was reconstructed by the abbot Desiderius (afterwards Pope Victor III.) of Monte Cassino in 1073, with interesting paintings, dating from the end of the 11th century to the middle of the 12th, in which five different styles may be distinguished. They form a complete representation of all the chief episodes of the New Testament (see F.X. Kraus, *Jahrbuch d. k. preuss. Kunstsammlungen*, xiv.). Deposits of votive objects (*favissae*), removed from the ancient temple from time to time as new ones came in and occupied all the available space, have been found, and considerable remains of buildings belonging to the Vicus Dianae (among them a triumphal arch and some baths, also a hall with frescoes, representing the goddess herself ready for the chase) still exist.

The ancient road from Capua went on beyond the Vicus Dianae to the Volturnus (remains of the bridge still exist) and then turned east along the river valley to Caiatia and Telesia. Other roads ran to Puteoli and Cumae (the so-called Via Campana) and to Neapolis, and as we have seen the Via Appia passed through Capua, which was thus the most important road centre of Campania (*q.v.*).

See Th. Mommsen in *Corpus Inscrip. Lat.* x. (Berlin, 1883), p. 365 seq.; J. Beloch, *Campanien* (Breslau, 1890), 295 seq.; Ch. Hülsen in Pauly-Wissowa, *Realencyclopädie* (Stuttgart, 1899), iii. 1555.

(T. AS.)

1G. Patroni, in *Atti del Congresso Internazionale di Scienze Storiche* (Rome, 1904), v. 217, is inclined to place it considerably earlier.

2Livy iv. 37, "Vulturnum Etruscorum urbem quae nunc Capua est, ab Samnitibus captam (425 B.C.) Capuamque ab duce eorum Capye, vel, quod propius vero est, a campestri agro appellatam."

3For these drawings see T. Ashby, "Dessins inédits de Carlo Labruzzi," in*Mélanges de l'École française*, 1903, 414.

4The name comes from the aqueduct (*forma*) erected by Augustus for the supply of Capua, remains of which still exist.

CAPUCHIN MONKEY, the English name of a tropical American monkey scientifically known as *Cebus capucinus*; the plural, capuchins, is extended to embrace all the numerous species of the same genus, whose range extends from Nicaragua to Paraguay. These monkeys, whose native name is sapajou, are the typical representatives of the family *Cebidae*, and belong to a sub-family in which the tail is generally prehensile. From the other genera of that group (*Cebinae*) with prehensile tails capuchins are distinguished by the comparative shortness of that appendage, and the absence of a naked area on the under surface of its extremity. The hair is not woolly, the general build is rather stout, and the limbs are of moderate length and slenderness. The name capuchin is derived from the somewhat cowl-like form assumed by the thick hair on the crown of the head of the sapajous. In their native haunts these monkeys go about in troops of considerable size, frequenting the summits of the tall forest-trees, from which they seldom, if ever, descend. In addition to fruits of various kinds, they consume tender shoots and buds, insects, eggs and young birds. Many of the 296species are difficult to distinguish, and very little is known of their habits in a wild state, although several members of the group are common in captivity (seePRIMATES).

(R. L.*)

CAPUCHINS, an order of friars in the Roman Catholic Church, the chief and only permanent offshoot from the Franciscans. It arose about the year 1520, when Matteo di Bassi, an "Observant" Franciscan, became possessed of the idea that the habit worn by the

94

Franciscans was not the one that St Francis had worn; accordingly he made himself a pointed or pyramidal hood and also allowed his beard to grow and went about bare-footed. His superiors tried to suppress these innovations, but in 1528 he obtained the sanction of Clement VII. and also the permission to live as a hermit and to go about everywhere preaching to the poor; and these permissions were not only for himself, but for all such as might join him in the attempt to restore the most literal observance possible of St Francis's rule. Matteo was soon joined by others. The Observants opposed the movement, but the Conventuals supported it, and so Matteo and his companions were formed into a congregation, called the Hermit Friars Minor, as a branch of the Conventual Franciscans, but with a vicar of their own, subject to the jurisdiction of the general of the Conventuals. From their hood (*capuche*) they received the popular name of Capuchins. In 1529 they had four houses and held their first general chapter, at which their special rules were drawn up. The eremitical idea was abandoned, but the life was to be one of extreme austerity, simplicity and poverty—in all things as near an approach to St Francis's idea as was practicable. Neither the monasteries nor the congregation should possess anything, nor were any devices to be resorted to for evading this law; no large provision against temporal wants should be made, and the supplies in the house should never exceed what was necessary for a few days. Everything was to be obtained by begging, and the friars were not allowed even to touch money. The communities were to be small, eight being fixed as the normal number and twelve as the limit. In furniture and clothing extreme simplicity was enjoined and the friars were to go bare-footed without even sandals. Besides the choral canonical office, a portion of which was recited at midnight, there were two hours of private prayer daily. The fasts and disciplines were rigorous and frequent. The great external work was preaching and spiritual ministrations among the poor. In theology the Capuchins abandoned the later Franciscan school of Scotus, and returned to the earlier school of Bonaventura (*q.v.*). The new congregation at the outset of its history underwent a series of severe blows. The two founders left it, Matteo di Bassi to return to the Observants, while his first companion, on being superseded in the office of vicar, became so insubordinate that he had to be expelled. The case of the third vicar, Bernardino Ochino (*q.v.*), who became a Calvinist, 1543, and married, was even more disastrous. This mishap brought the whole congregation under the suspicion of heretical tendencies and the pope resolved to suppress it; he was with difficulty induced to allow it to continue, but the Capuchins were forbidden to preach. In a couple of years the authorities were satisfied as to the soundness of the general body of Capuchin friars, and the permission to preach was restored. The congregation at once began to multiply with extraordinary rapidity, and by the end of the 16th century the Capuchins had spread all over the Catholic parts of Europe, so that in 1619 they were freed from their dependence on the Conventual Franciscans and became an independent order, with a general of their own. They are said to have had at that time 1500 houses divided into fifty provinces. They were one of the chief factors in the Catholic Counter-reformation, working assiduously among the poor, preaching, catechizing, confessing in all parts, and impressing the minds of the common people by the great poverty and austerity of their life. By these means they were also extraordinarily successful in making converts from Protestantism to Catholicism. Nor were the activities of the Capuchins confined to Europe. From an early date they undertook missions to the heathen in America, Asia and Africa, and at the middle of the 17th century a Capuchin missionary college was founded in Rome for the purpose of preparing their subjects for foreign missions. A large number of Capuchins have suffered martyrdom for the Gospel. This activity in Europe and elsewhere continued until the close of the 18th century, when the number of Capuchin friars was estimated at 31,000.

Like all other orders, the Capuchins suffered severely from the secularizations and revolutions of the end of the 18th century and the first half of the 19th; but they survived the strain, and during the latter part of the 19th century rapidly recovered ground. At the beginning of the present century there were fifty provinces with some 500 monasteries and 300 hospices or lesser houses; and the number of Capuchin friars, including lay-brothers, was reckoned at 9500. In England there are ten or twelve Capuchin monasteries, and in Ireland three. The Capuchins now possess the church of the Portiuncula at Assisi. The Capuchins still keep up their missionary work and have some 200 missionary stations in all parts of the world—notably India, Abyssinia and the Turkish empire. Though "the poorest of all orders," it has attracted into its ranks an extraordinary number of the highest nobility and even of royalty. The celebrated Father Mathew, the apostle of Temperance in Ireland, was a Capuchin friar. Like the Franciscans the Capuchins wear a brown habit.

The Capuchines are Capuchin nuns. They were founded in 1538 in Naples. They lived according to the rules and regulations of the Capuchin friars, and so austere was the life that they were called "Sisters of Suffering." The order spread to France and Spain, and a few convents still exist.

In order fully to grasp the meaning of the Capuchin reform, it is necessary to know the outlines of Franciscan history (see FRANCISCANS). There does not appear to be any modern general history of the Capuchin order as a whole, though there are histories of various provinces and of the foreign missions. The references to all this literature will be found in the article "Kapuzinerorden" in Wetzer und Welte, *Kirchenlexicon* (2nd ed.), which is the best general sketch on the subject. Shorter sketches, with the needful references, are given in Max Heimbucher, *Orden und Kongregationen*(1896), i. § 44, and in Herzog-Hauck, *Realencyklopädie* (3rd ed.), art. "Kapuziner." Helyot's *Hist. des ordres religieux* (1792), vii. c. 24 and c. 27, gives an account of the Capuchins up to the end of the 17th century.

(E. C. B.)

CAPUS, ALFRED (1858-   ), French author, was born at Aix, in Provence, on the 25th of November 1858. In 1878 he published, in collaboration with L. Vonoven, a volume of short stories, and in the next year the two produced a one-act piece, *Le Mari malgré lui*, at the Théâtre Cluny. He had been educated as an engineer, but became a journalist, and joined the staff of the *Figaro* in 1894. His novels, *Qui perd gagne* (1890), *Faux Départ* (1891),*Années d'aventures* (1895), which belong to this period, describe the struggles of three young men at the beginning of their career. From the first of these he took his first comedy, *Brignol et sa file* (Vaudeville, 23rd November 1894). Among his later plays are *Innocent* (1896), written with Alphonse Allais; *Petites folles* (1897); *Rosine* (1897); *Mariage bourgeois* (1898); *Les Maris de Léontine*(1900); *La Bourse ou la vie* (1900), *La Veine* (1901); *La Petite Fonctionnaire*(1901); *Les Deux Écoles* (1902); *La Châtelaine (1902); L' Adversaire* (1903), with Emmanuel Arène, which was produced in London by Mr George Alexander as *The Man of the Moment*, and *Notre Jeunesse* (1904), the first of his plays to be represented at the Théâtre Français; *Monsieur Piégois* (1905); and, in collaboration with Lucien Descaves, *L' Attentat* (1906).

See Édouard Quet, *Alfred Capus* (1904), with appreciations by various authors, in the series of *Célébrités d' aujourd'hui*.

CAPYBARA, or CARPINCHO (*Hydrochaerus capybara*), the largest living rodent mammal, characterized by its moderately long limbs, partially-webbed toes, of which there are four in front and three behind, hoof-like nails, sparse hair, short ears, cleft upper lip and the absence of a tail. The dentition is peculiar on account of the great size and complexity of the last upper molar, which is composed of about twelve plates, and exceeds in length the three teeth in front. The front surface of the incisors has a broad, shallow groove. Capybaras are aquatic rodents, frequenting the banks of lakes and rivers, and 297being sometimes found where the water is brackish. They generally associate in herds, and spend most of the day in covert on the banks, feeding in the evening and morning. When disturbed they make for the water, in which they swim and dive with expertness, often remaining below the surface for several minutes. Their usual food consists of water-plants and bark, but in cultivated districts they do much harm to crops. Their cry is a low, abrupt grunt. From five to eight is the usual number in a litter, of which there appears to be only one in the year; and the young are carried on their parent's back when in the water. Extinct species of capybara occur in the tertiary deposits of Argentina, some of which were considerably larger than the living form. Capybaras belong to the family*Caviidae*, the leading characteristics of which are given in RODENTIA. When full-grown the entire length of the animal is about 4 ft., and the girth 3 ft. Their geographical range extends from Guiana to the river Plate. Capybaras can be easily tamed; numbers are killed on land by jaguars and in the water by caimans—the alligators of South America.

CAR (Late Lat. *carra*), a term originally applied to a small two-wheeled vehicle for transport (see CARRIAGE), but also to almost anything in the nature of a carriage, chariot, &c., and to the carrying-part of a balloon. With some specific qualification (tram-car, street-car, railway-car, sleeping-car, motor-car, &c.) it is combined to serve as a general word instead of carriage or vehicle. From Ireland comes the "jaunting-car," which is in general use, both in the towns, where it is the commonest public carriage for hire, and in the country districts, where it is employed to carry the mails and for the use of tourists. The gentry and more well-to-do farmers also use it as a private carriage in all parts of Ireland. The genuine Irish jaunting-car is a two-wheeled vehicle constructed to carry four persons besides the driver. In the centre, at right angles to the axle, is a "well" about 18 in. deep, used for carrying parcels or small luggage, and covered with a lid which is usually furnished with a cushion. The "well" provides a low back to each of the two seats, which are in the form of wings placed over each wheel, with foot boards hanging outside the wheel on hinges, so that when not in use they can be turned up over the wheel, thus reducing the width of the car (sometimes very necessary in the narrow country roads) and protecting the seats from the weather. The passengers on each side sit with their backs to each other, with the "well" between them. The driver sits on a movable box-seat, or "dicky," a few inches high, placed across the head of the "well," with a footboard to which there is usually no splash-board attached. A more modern form of jaunting-car, known as a "long car," chiefly used for tourists, is a four-wheeled vehicle constructed on the same plan, which accommodates as many as eight or ten passengers on each side, and two in addition on a high box-seat beside the driver. In the city of Cork a carriage known as an "inside car" is in common use. It is a two-wheeled covered carriage in which the passengers sit face to face as in a wagonette. In remote country districts the poorer peasants still sometimes use a primitive form of vehicle, called a "low-backed car," a simple square shallow box or shelf of wood fastened to an axle without springs. The two wheels are solid wooden disks of the rudest construction, generally without the protection of metal tires, and so small in diameter that the body of the car is raised only a few inches from the ground.

CARABINIERS, originally mounted troops of the French army, armed with the carabine (carbine). In 1690 one company of carabiniers was maintained in each regiment of cavalry. Their duties were analogous to those of grenadiers in infantry regiments—scouting, detached work, and, in general, all duties requiring special activity and address. They fought mounted and dismounted alike, and even took part in siege warfare in the trenches. At the battle of Neerwinden in 1693 all the carabinier companies present were united in one body, and after the action Louis XIV. consolidated them into a permanent regiment with the name Royal Carabiniers. This was one of the old regiments which survived the French Revolution, at which time the title was changed to "horse grenadiers"; it is represented in the French army of to-day by the 11th Cuirassiers. The carabiniers (6th Dragoon Guards) of the British army date from 1685, and received the title from being armed with the carabine in 1692. Regimentally therefore they were one year senior to the French regiment of Royal Carabiniers, and as a matter of fact they took part as a regiment in the battle of Neerwinden. Up to 1745 their title was "The King's Carabiniers"; from 1745 to 1788 they were called the 3rd Irish Horse, and from 1788 they have borne their present title. In the German army, one carabinier regiment alone (2nd Saxon Reiter regiment) remains of the cavalry corps which formerly in various states bore the title. In Italy the gendarmerie are called *carabinieri*.

CARABOBO, the smallest of the thirteen states of Venezuela, bounded N. by the Caribbean Sea, E. by the state of Aragua, S. by Zamora and W. by Lara. Its area is 2985 sq. m., and its population, according to an official estimate of 1905, is 221,891. The greater part of its surface is mountainous with moderately elevated valleys of great fertility and productiveness, but south of the Cordillera there are extensive grassy plains conterminous with those of Guárico and Zamora, on which large herds of cattle are pastured. The principal products of the state are cattle, hides and cheese from the southern plains, coffee and cereals from the higher valleys, sugar and aguardiente from the lower valleys about Lake

Valencia, and cacao, coco-nuts and coco-nut fibre from the coast. Various minerals are also found in its south-west districts, about Nirgua. The capital is Valencia, and its principal towns are Puerto Cabello, Montalbán (estimated pop. in 1904 7500), 30 m. W.S.W. of Valencia; Nirgua (pop. in 1891 8394), an important commercial and mining town 36½ m. S.W. of Valencia, 2500 ft. above sea level; and Ocumare (pop. in 1891 7493), near the coast 18½ m. E. of Puerto Cabello, celebrated for the fine quality of its cacao. Carabobo is best known for the battle fought on the 24th of June 1821 on a plain at the southern exit from the passes through the Cordillera in this state, between the revolutionists under Bolívar and the Spanish forces under La Torre. It was one of the four decisive battles of the war, though the forces engaged were only a part of the two armies and numbered 2400 revolutionists (composed of 1500 mounted *llaneros* known as the "Apure legion," and 900 British), and 3000 Spaniards. The day was won by the British, who drove the Spaniards from the field at the point of the bayonet, although at a terrible loss of life. The British legion was afterwards acclaimed by Bolívar as "Salvadores de mi Patria." The Spanish forces continued the war until near the end of 1823, but their operations were restricted to the districts on the coast.

CARACAL, the capital of the department of Romanatzi, Rumania; situated in the plains between the lower reaches of the Jiu and Olt rivers, and on the railway from Corabia, beside the Danube, to Hermannstadt in Transylvania. Pop. (1900) 12,055. Caracal has little trade, except in grain. Its chief buildings are the prefecture, school of arts and crafts and several churches. There are some ruins of a tower, built in A.D. 217 by the Roman emperor Caracalla, after whom the place is named. In 1596 Michael the Brave of Walachia defeated the Turks near Caracal.

CARACAL (*Lynx caracal*), sometimes called Persian lynx, an animal widely distributed throughout south-western Asia, and over a large portion of Africa. It is somewhat larger than a fox, of a uniform reddish brown colour above, and whitish beneath, with two white spots above each of the eyes, and a tuft of long black hair at the tip of the ears; to these it owes its name, which is derived from Turkish words signifying "black-ear." There is little information as to the habits of this animal in a wild state. Dr W.T. Blanford considers that it dwells among grass and bushes rather than in forests. Its prey is said to consist largely of gazelles, small deer, hares and peafowl and other birds. The caracal is easily tamed, and in some parts of India is trained to capture the smaller antelopes and deer and such birds as the crane and pelican. According to Blyth, it is a favourite amusement among the natives to let loose a couple of tame caracals among a flock of pigeons feeding on the ground, when each will strike down a number of birds before the flock can escape. Frequent reference is made in Greek and Roman literature to the lynx, and from such descriptions as are given of it there is little doubt that the caracal, and not the European lynx, was referred to. In South Africa, where the caracal abounds, its hide is made by the Zulus into skin-cloaks, known as karosses. According to W.L. Sclater, these when used as blankets are said to be beneficial in cases of rheumatism; an ointment prepared from the fat of the animal being employed for the same purpose. The North African caracal has been separated as *Lynx*, or *Caracal, berberorum*, but it is best regarded as a local race.

CARACALLA (or CARACALLUS), **MARCUS AURELIUS ANTONINUS**(186-217), Roman emperor, eldest son of the emperor Septimius Severus, was born at Lugdunum (Lyons) on the 4th of April 186. His original name was Bassianus; his nickname Caracalla was derived from the long Gallic tunic which he wore and introduced into the army. He further received the imperial title of Marcus Aurelius Antoninus at the time when his father declared himself the adopted son of M. Aurelius. After the death of Severus (211) at Eboracum (York) in Britain, Caracalla and his brother Geta, who had accompanied their father, returned to Rome as colleagues in the supreme power. In order to secure the sole authority, Caracalla barbarously murdered his brother in his mother's arms, and at the same time put to death some 20,000 persons, who were suspected of favouring him, amongst them the jurist Papinianus. An important act of his reign (212) was the bestowal of the rights of Roman citizenship upon all free inhabitants of the empire, although the main object of

98

Caracalla was doubtless to increase the amount of revenue derived from the tax on inheritances or legacies to which only Roman citizens were liable. His own extravagances and the demands of the soldiery were a perpetual drain upon his resources, to meet which he resorted to taxes and extortion of every description. He spent the remainder of his reign wandering from place to place, a mode of life to which he was said to have been driven by the pangs of remorse. Handing over the reins of government to his mother, he set out in 213 for Raetia, where he carried on war against the Alamanni; in 214 he attacked the Goths in Dacia, whence he proceeded by way of Thrace to Asia Minor, and in 215 crossed to Alexandria. Here he took vengeance for the bitter sarcasms of the inhabitants against himself and his mother by ordering a general massacre of the youths capable of bearing arms. In 216 he ravaged Mesopotamia because Artabanus, the Parthian king, refused to give him his daughter in marriage. He spent the winter at Edessa, and in 217, when he recommenced his campaign, he was murdered between Edessa and Carrhae on the 8th of April at the instigation of Opellius (Opilius) Macrinus, praefect of the praetorian guard, who succeeded him. Amongst the numerous buildings with which Caracalla adorned the city, the most famous are the*thermae*, and the triumphal arch of Septimius Severus in the forum.

AUTHORITIES.—Dio Cassius lxxvii., lxxviii.; Herodian iii. 10, iv. 14; lives of Caracalla, Severus and Geta, in *Scriptores Historiae Augustae*; Eutropius viii. 19-22; Aurelius Victor, *De Caesaribus*, 20-23; *Epit.* 20-23; Zosimus i. 9-10; H. Schiller, *Geschichte der römischen Kaiserzeit* (1883), 738 ff.; Pauly-Wissowa, *Realencyclopädie*, ii. 2434 ff. (von Rohden).

CARÁCAS, the principal city and the capital of the United States of Venezuela, situated at the western extremity of an elevated valley of the Venezuelan Coast Range known as the plain of Chacao, 6½ m. S.S.E. of La Guaira, its port on the Caribbean coast, in lat. 10° 30′ N., long. 67° 4′ W. The plain is about 11 m. long by 3 m. wide, and is separated from the coast by a part of the mountain chain which extends along almost the entire water front of the republic. It is covered with well-cultivated plantations. The Guaira river, a branch of the Tuy, traverses the plain from west to east, and flows past the city on the south. Among its many small tributaries are the Catuche, Caroata and Anauco, which flow down through the city from the north and give it a natural surface drainage. The city is built at the narrow end of the valley and at the foot of the Cerro de Avila, and stands from 2887 to 3442 ft. above sea level, the elevation of the Plaza de Bolívar, its topographical centre, being 3025 ft. Two miles north-east is the famous Silla de Carácas, whose twin summits, like a gigantic old-fashioned saddle (*silla*), rise to an elevation of 8622 ft.; and the Naigueté, still farther eastward, overlooks the valley from a height of 9186 ft. The climate of Carácas is often described as that of perpetual spring. It is subject, however, to extreme and rapid variations in temperature, to alternations of dry and humid winds (the latter, called *catias*, being irritating and oppressive), to chilling night mists brought up from the coast by the westerly winds, and to other influences productive of malaria, catarrh, fevers, bilious disorders and rheumatism. The maximum and minimum temperatures range from 84° to 48° F., the annual mean being about 66°, and the daily variation is often as much as 15°. The city is built with its streets running between the cardinal points of the compass and crossing each other at right angles. Two intersecting central streets also divide the city into four sections, in each of which the streets are methodically named and numbered, as North 3rd, 5th, 7th, &c., or West 2nd, 4th, 6th, &c., according to direction and location. This method of numeration dates from the time of Guzman Blanco, but the common people adhere to the names bestowed upon the city squares in earlier times. The streets are narrow, but are clean and well-paved, and are lighted by electricity and gas. There are several handsome squares and public gardens, adorned with statues, trees and shrubbery. The principal square is the Plaza de Bolívar, the conventional centre of the city, in which stands a bronze equestrian statue of Bolívar, and on which face the cathedral, archbishop's residence, Casa Amarilla, national library, general post office and other public offices. The Independencia Park, formerly called Calvario Park, which occupies a hill on the west side of the city, is the largest and most attractive of the public gardens. Among the public edifices are the capitol, which occupies a whole square, the university, of nearly equal size, the cathedral, pantheon, masonic temple (built by the state in the spendthrift days of Guzman Blanco), national library, opera-house, and a number of large churches. The city is generously provided with all the modern public services, including two street car lines, local and long distance telephone lines, electric power and light, and waterworks. The principal water supply is derived from the Macarao river, 15 m. distant. Railway connexion with the port of La Guaira was opened in 1883 by means of a line 23 m. long. Another line (the Gran Ferrocarril de Venezuela) passes through the mountains to Valencia, 111 m. distant, and two short lines run to neighbouring villages, one to Petare and Santa Lucia, and the other to El Valle. The archbishop of Venezuela resides in Carácas and has ecclesiastical jurisdiction over the dioceses of Ciudad Bolívar, Calabozo, Barquisimeto, Mérida and Maracaibo. There are no manufactures of note.

Carácas was founded in 1567 by Diego de Losada under the pious title of Santiago de León de Carácas, and has been successively capital of the province of Carácas, of the captaincy-general of Carácas and Venezuela, and of the republic of Venezuela. It is also one of the two chief cities, or capitals, of the Federal district. It was the birthplace of Simón Bolívar, and claims the distinction of being the first colony in South America to overthrow Spanish colonial authority. The city was almost totally destroyed by the great earthquake of 1812. In the war of independence it was repeatedly subjected to pillage and slaughter by both parties in the strife, and did not recover its losses for many years. In 1810 its population was estimated at 50,000; seventy-one years later the census of 1881 gave it only 55,638. In 1891 its urban population was computed to be 72,429, which in 1904 was estimated to have increased to about 90,000.

CARACCI, LODOVICO, AGOSTINO, and **ANNIBALE,** three celebrated Italian painters, were born at Bologna in 1555, 1557, and 1560 respectively. Lodovico, the eldest, son of a butcher, was uncle to the two younger, Agostino and Annibale, sons of a tailor, and had nearly finished his professional studies before the 299others had begun their education. From being a reputed dunce, while studying under Tintoretto in Venice, he gradually rose, by an attentive observation of nature and a careful examination of the works of the great masters preserved at Bologna, Venice, Florence and Parma, to measure himself with the teachers of his day, and ultimately projected the opening of a rival school in his native place. Finding himself unable to accomplish his design without assistance, he sent for his two nephews, and induced them to abandon their handicrafts (Agostino being a goldsmith, and Annibale a tailor) for the profession of painting. Agostino he first placed under the care of Fontana, retaining Annibale in his own studio; but he afterwards sent both to Venice and Parma to copy the works of Titian, Tintoretto and Correggio, on which his own taste had been formed. On their return, the three relatives, assisted by an eminent anatomist, Anthony de la Tour, opened, in 1589, an academy of painting under the name of the Incamminati (or, as we might paraphrase it, the Right Road), provided with numerous casts, books and bassi-rilievi, which Lodovico had collected in his travels. From the affability and kindness of the Caracci, and their zeal for the scientific education of the students, their academy rose rapidly in popular estimation, and soon every other school of art in Bologna was deserted and closed. They continued together till, at the invitation of Cardinal Farnese, Annibale and Agostino went to Rome in 1600 to paint the gallery of the cardinal's palace. The superior praises awarded to Agostino inflamed the jealousy of Annibale, already kindled by the brilliant reception given by the pupils of the Incamminati to Agostino's still highly celebrated picture of the "Communion of St Jerome," and the latter was dismissed to Parma to paint the great saloon of the Casino. Here he died in 1602, when on the eve of finishing his renowned painting of "Celestial, Terrestrial and Venal Love." Annibale continued to work alone at the Farnese gallery till the designs were completed; but, disappointed at the miserable remuneration offered by the cardinal, he retired to Naples, where an unsuccessful contest for a great work in the church of the Jesuits threw him into a fever, of which he died in 1609. Lodovico always remained at his academy in Bologna (excepting for a short visit to his cousin at Rome), though invited to execute paintings in all parts of the country. He died in 1619, and was interred in the church of Santa Maria Maddalena. The works of Lodovico are numerous in the chapels of Bologna. The most famous are—The "Madonna standing on the moon, with St Francis and St Jerome beside her, attended by a retinue of angels"; "John the Baptist," "St Jerome," "St Benedict" and "St Cecilia"; and the "Limbo of the Fathers." He was by far the most amiable of the three painters, rising superior to all feelings of jealousy towards his rivals, and though he received large sums for his productions, yet, from his almost unparalleled liberality to the students of the academy, he died poor. With skill in painting Agostino combined the greatest proficiency in engraving (which he had studied under Cornelius de Cort) and high accomplishments as a scholar. He died not untroubled by remorse for the indecencies which, in accordance with the corruption of the time, he had introduced into some of his engravings. The works of Annibale are more diversified in style than those of the others, and comprise specimens of painting after the manner of Correggio, Titian, Paolo Veronese, Raphael and Michelangelo. The most distinguished are the "Dead Christ in the lap of the Madonna"; the "Infant and St John"; "St Catherine"; "St Roch distributing alms" (now in the Dresden gallery); and the "Saviour wailed over by the Maries," at present in possession of the earl of Carlisle. He frequently gave great importance to the landscape in his compositions. The reputation of Annibale is tarnished by his jealousy and vindictiveness towards his brother, and the licentiousness of his disposition, which contributed to bring him to a comparatively early grave.

The three Caracci were the founders of the so-called Eclectic school of painting,—the principle of which was to study in the works of the great masters the several excellences for which they had been respectively pre-eminent, and to combine these in the productions of the school itself; for instance, there was to be the design of Raphael, the power of Michelangelo, the colour of Titian, and so on.

See A. Venturi, *I Caracci e la loro scuola*, 1895.

(W. M. R.)

CARACCIOLO, FRANCESCO, PRINCE (1732-1799), Neapolitan admiral and revolutionist, was born on the 18th of January 1732, of a noble Neapolitan family. He entered the navy and learned his seamanship under Rodney. He fought with distinction in the British service in the American War of Independence, against the Barbary pirates, and against the French at Toulon under Lord Hotham. The Bourbons placed the greatest confidence in his skill. When on the approach of the French to Naples King Ferdinand IV. and Queen Mary Caroline fled to Sicily on board Nelson's ship the "Vanguard" (December 1798), Caracciolo escorted them on the frigate "Sannita." He was the only prominent Neapolitan trusted by the king, but even the admiral's loyalty was shaken by Ferdinand's cowardly flight. On reaching Palermo Caracciolo asked permission to return to Naples to look after his own private affairs (January 1799). This was granted, but when he arrived at Naples he found all the aristocracy and educated middle classes infatuated with the French revolutionary ideas, and he himself was received with great enthusiasm. He seems at first to have intended to live a retired life; but, finding that he must either join the Republican party or escape to Procida, then in the hands of the English, in which case even his intimates would regard him as a traitor and his property would have been confiscated, he was induced to adhere to the new order of things and took command of the republic's naval forces. Once at sea, he fought actively against the British and Neapolitan squadrons and prevented the landing of some Royalist bands. A few days later all the French troops in Naples, except 500 men, were recalled to the north of Italy.

Caracciolo then attacked Admiral Thurn, who from the "Minerva" commanded the Royalist fleet, and did some damage to that vessel. But the British fleet on the one hand and Cardinal Fabrizio Ruffo's army on the other made resistance impossible. The Republicans and the 500 French had retired to the castles, and Caracciolo landed and tried to escape in disguise. But he was betrayed and arrested by a Royalist officer, who on the 29th of June brought him in chains on board Nelson's flagship the "Foudroyant." It is doubtful whether Caracciolo should have been included in the capitulation concluded with the Republicans in the castles, as that document promised life and liberty to those who surrendered before the blockade of the forts, whereas he was arrested afterwards, but as the whole capitulation was violated the point is immaterial. Moreover, the admiral's fate was decided even before his capture, because on the 27th of June the British minister, Sir W. Hamilton, had communicated to Nelson Queen Mary Caroline's wish that Caracciolo should be hanged. As soon as he was brought on board, Nelson ordered Thurn to summon a court martial composed of Caracciolo's former officers, Thurn himself being a personal enemy of the accused. The court was held on board the "Foudroyant," which was British territory—a most indefensible proceeding. Caracciolo was charged with high treason; he had asked to be judged by British officers, which was refused, nor was he allowed to summon witnesses in his defence. He was condemned to death by three votes to two, and as soon as the sentence was communicated to Nelson the latter ordered that he should be hanged at the yard-arm of the "Minerva" the next morning, and his body thrown into the sea at sundown. Even the customary twenty-four hours' respite for confession was denied him, and his request to be shot instead of hanged refused. The sentence was duly carried out on the 30th of June 1799.

Caracciolo was technically a traitor to the king whose uniform he had worn, but apart from the wave of revolutionary enthusiasm which had spread all over the educated classes of Italy, and the fact that treason to a government like that of the Neapolitan Bourbons could hardly be regarded as a crime, there was no necessity for Nelson to make himself the executor of the revenge of Ferdinand and Mary Caroline. His greatest offence, as Captain Mahan remarks (*Life of Nelson*, i. 440), was 300committed against his own country by sacrificing his inalienable character as the representative of the king of Great Britain to his secondary and artificial character as delegate of the king of Naples. The only explanation of Nelson's conduct is to be found in his infatuation for Lady Hamilton, whose low ambition made her use her influence over him in the interest of Queen Mary Caroline's malignant spite.

AUTHORITIES.—Besides the general works on Nelson and Naples, such as P. Colletta's *Storia del Reame di Napoli* (Florence, 1848), there is a large amount of special literature on the subject. *Nelson and the Neapolitan Jacobins* (Navy Records Society, 1903), contains all the documents on the episode, including those incorrectly transcribed by A. Dumas in his *Borboni di Napoli* (Naples, 1862-1863), with an introduction defending Nelson by H.C. Gutteridge; the work contains a bibliography. The case against Nelson is set forth by Professor P. Villari in his article "Nelson, Caracciolo, e la Repubblica Napolitana" (*Nuova Antologia*, 16th February 1899); Captain A.T. Mahan has replied in "The Neapolitan Republic and Nelson's Accusers" (*English Historical Review*, July 1899), "Nelson at Naples" (*ibid.*, October 1900), and "Nelson at Naples" (*Athenaeum*, 8th July 1899); see also F. Lemmi, *Nelson e Caracciolo* (Florence, 1898); C. Giglioli, *Naples in 1799* (London, 1903); Freiherr von Helfert, *Fabrizio Ruffo* (Vienna, 1882); H. Hüffer, *Die neapolitanische Republik des Jahres 1799* (Leipzig, 1884).

(L. V.*)

CARACOLE (a Fr. word, the origin of which is doubtful, meaning the wheeling about of a horse; in Spanish and Portuguese *caracol* means a snail with a spiral shell), a turn or wheeling in horsemanship to the left or right, or to both alternately, so that the movements of the horse describe a zig-zag course. The term has been used loosely and erroneously to describe any display of fancy riding. It is also used for a spiral staircase in a tower.

CARACTACUS, strictly CARATĀCUS, the Latin form of a Celtic name, which survives in Caradoc and other proper names. The most famous bearer of the name was the British chieftain who led the native resistance to the Roman invaders in A.D. 48-51, and was finally captured and sent to Rome (Tac. *Ann.* xii. 33, Dio. lx.). Two old camps on the Welsh border are now called Caer Caradoc, but the names seem to be the invention of antiquaries and not genuinely ancient memorials of the Celtic hero.

CARADOC SERIES, in geology, the name introduced by R.I. Murchison in 1839 for the sandstone series of Caer Caradoc in Shropshire, England. The limits of Murchison's Caradoc series have since been somewhat modified, and through the labours of C. Lapworth the several members of the series have been precisely defined by means of graptolitic zones. These zones are identical with those found in the rocks of the same age in North Wales, the Bala series (*q.v.*), and the terms Bala or Caradoc series are used indifferently by geologists when referring to the uppermost substage of the Ordovician System. The Ordovician rocks of the Caradoc district have been subdivided into the following beds, in descending order: the *Trinucleus* shales, Acton Scott beds, Longville flags, Chatwell and Soudley sandstones, Harnage shales and Hoar Edge grits and limestone. In the Corndon district in the same county the Caradoc series is represented by the Harrington group of ashes and shales and the Spy Wood group beneath them; these two groups of strata are sometimes spoken of as the Chirbury series. In the Breidden district are the barren Criggeon shales with ashes and flows of andesite.

In the Lake district the Coniston limestone series represents the Upper Caradocian, the lower portion being taken up by part of the great Borrowdale volcanic series of rocks. The Coniston limestone series contains the following subdivisions:—

Ashgill group (Ashgill shales and *Staurocephalus* limestone).

Kiesley limestone.

Sleddale group (Applethwaite beds = Upper Coniston limestone conglomerate; Yarlside rhyolite; stye end beds = Lower Coniston limestone).

Roman Fell group (Corona beds).

The Dufton shales and Drygill shales are equivalents of the Sleddale group.

Rocks of Caradoc age are well developed in southern Scotland; in the Girvan district they have been described as the Ardmillan series with the Drummock group and Barren Flagstone group in the upper portion, and the Whitehouse, Ardwell and Balclatchie groups in the lower part. Similarly, two divisions, known as the Upper and Lower Hartfell series, are recognized in the southern and central area, in Peeblesshire, Ayrshire and Dumfriesshire.

In Ireland the Caradoc or Bala series is represented by the limestones of Portraine near Dublin and of the Chair of Kildare; by the Ballymoney series of Wexford and Carnalea shales of Co. Down. In the Lough Mask district beds of this age are found, as in Wales, interstratified with volcanic lavas and tuffs. Other localities are known in counties Tyrone, Meath and Louth, also in Lambay Island.

See ORDOVICIAN SYSTEM; also C. Lapworth, *Ann. and Mag. Nat. Hist.*, 5th series, vol. vi., 1880; *Geol. Mag.*, 1889; C. Lapworth and W.W. Watts, *Proc. Geol. Assoc.*, xiii., 1894; J.E. Marr, *Geol. Mag.*, 1892; J.E. Marr and T. Roberts, *Q.J.G.S.*, 1885; B.N. Peach and J. Home, "Silurian Rocks of Great Britain," vol. I., 1899 (*Mem. Geol. Survey*).

(J. A. H.)

CARALES (Gr. Κάραλις, mod. *Cagliari, q.v.*), the most important ancient city of Sardinia, situated on the south coast of the island. Its foundation is generally attributed to the Carthaginians, and Punic tombs exist in considerable numbers near the present cemetery on the east and still more on the rocky plateau to the north-west of the town. It first appears in Roman history in the Second Punic War, and probably obtained full Roman civic rights from Julius Caesar. In imperial times it was the most important town in the island, mainly owing to its fine sheltered harbour, where a detachment of the *classis Misenas* was stationed. In the 4th and 5th centuries it was probably the seat of the *praeses Sardiniae*. It is mentioned as an important harbour in the Gothic and Gildonic wars. It was also the chief point of the road system of Sardinia. Roads ran hence to Olbia by the east coast, and through the centre of the island, to Othoca (Oristano) direct, and thence to Olbia (probably the most frequented route), through the mining district to Sulci and along the south and west coasts to Othoca. The hill occupied by the Pisan fortifications and the medieval town within them must have been the acropolis of the Carthaginian settlement; it is impossible to suppose that a citadel presenting such natural advantages was not occupied. The Romans, too, probably made use of it, though the lower quarters were mainly occupied in imperial times. A. Taramelli (*Notizie degli Scavi*, 1905, 41 seq.) rightly points out that the nucleus of the Roman *municipium* is probably represented by the present quarter of the Marina, in which the streets intersect at right angles and Roman remains are frequently found in the subsoil. An inscription found some way to the north towards the amphitheatre speaks of paving in the squares and streets, and of drains constructed under Domitian in A.D. 83 (F. Vivanet in *Notizie degli Scavi*, 1897, 279). The amphitheatre occupies a natural depression in the rock just below the acropolis, and open towards the sea with a fine view. Its axes are 95½ and 79 yds., and it is in the main cut in the rock, though some parts of it are built with concrete. Below it, to the south, are considerable remains of ancient reservoirs for rain-water, upon which the city entirely depended. This nucleus extended both to the east and to the west; in the former direction it ran some way inland, on the east of the castle hill. Here were the *ambulationes* or public promenades constructed by the pro-consul Q. Caecilius Metellus before A.D. 6 (*Corp. Inscrip. Lat.* x., Berlin, 1883, No. 7581). Here also, not far from the shore, the remains of Roman baths, with a fine coloured mosaic pavement, representing deities riding on marine monsters, were found in 1907. To the east was the necropolis of Bonaria, where both Punic and Roman tombs exist, and where, on the site of the present cemetery, Christian catacombs have been discovered (F. Vivanet in *Notizie degli Scavi*, 1892, 183 seq.; G. Pinza in *Nuovo Bullettino di Archeologia Cristiana*, 1901, 61 seq.). But the western quarter seems to have been far more important; it extended along the lagoon of S. Gilla (which lies to the north-west of the town, and which until the middle ages was an open bay) and on the lower slopes of the hill which rises above it. The chief discoveries which have been made are noted by Taramelli (loc. cit.) and include some important buildings, of which a large Roman house (or group of houses) is the only one now visible (G. Spano in*Notizie degli Scavi*, 1876, 148, 173; 1877, 285; 1880, 105, 405). Beyond this quarter begins an extensive Roman necropolis extending along the edge of the hill north-east of the high road leading to the north-west; the most 301important tomb is the so-called Grotta delle Vipere, the rock-hewn tomb of Cassius Philippus and Atilia Pomptilla, the sides of which are covered with inscriptions (*Corpus Inscr. Lat.* x., Berlin, 1883, Nos. 7563-7578). Other tombs are also to be found on the high ground near the Punic tombs already mentioned. The latter are hewn perpendicularly in the rock, while the Roman tombs are chambers excavated horizontally. In the lagoon itself were found a large number of terra cottas, made of local clay, some being masks of both divinities and men (among them grotesques) others representing hands and feet, others various animals, and of *amphorae* of various sizes and other vases. Some of the *amphorae* contained animals' bones, possibly the remains of sacrifices. These objects are of the Punic period; they were all found in groups, and had apparently been arranged on a platform of piles in what was then a bay, in readiness for shipment (F. Vivanet in*Notizie degli Scavi*, 1893, 255). It is probable that the acropolis of Carales was occupied even in prehistoric times; but more abundant traces of prehistoric settlements (pottery and fragments of obsidian, also kitchen middens, containing bones of animals and shells of molluscs used for human food) have been found on the Capo S. Elia to the south-east of the modern town (see A. Taramelli in*Notizie degli Scavi*, 1904, 19 seq.). An inscription records the existence of a temple of Venus Erycina on this promontory in Roman times. The museum contains an interesting collection of objects from many of the sites mentioned, and also from other parts of the island; it is in fact the most important in Sardinia, and is especially strong in prehistoric bronzes (see <u>SARDINIA</u>).

For the Roman inscriptions see *C.I.L.* cit., Nos. 7552-7807.

(T. AS.)

CARAN D'ACHE, the pseudonym (meaning "lead-pencil") of Emmanuel Poiré (1858-1909), French artist and illustrator, who was born and educated at Moscow, being the grandson of one of Napoleon's officers who had settled in Russia. He determined to be a military painter, and when he arrived in Paris from Russia he found an artistic adviser in Detaille. He served five years in the army, where the principal work allotted to him was the drawing of uniforms for the ministry of war. He embellished a short-lived journal, *La Vie militaire*, with a series of illustrations, among them being some good-tempered caricatures of the German army, which showed how accurately he was acquainted with military detail. His special gift lay in pictorial anecdote, the story being represented at its different stages with irresistible effect, in the artist's own mannered simplicity. Much of his work was contributed to *La Vie parisienne, Le Figaro illustré, La Caricature, Le Chat noir*, and he also issued various albums of sketches, the*Carnet de chèques*, illustrating the Panama scandals, *Album de croquis militaires et d'histoire sans légendes, Histoire de Marlborough*, &c., besides illustrating a good many books, notably the *Prince Kozakokoff* of Bemadaky. He died on the 26th of February 1909.

A collection of his work was exhibited at the Fine Art Society's rooms in London in 1898. The catalogue contained a prefatory note by M.H. Spielmann.

CARAPACE (a Fr. word, from the Span, *carapacho*, a shield or armour), the upper shell of a crustacean, tortoise or turtle. The covering of the armadillo is called a carapace, as is also the hard case in which certain of the Infusoria are enclosed.

CARAPEGUA, an interior town of Paraguay, 37 m. S.E. of Asunción on the old route between that city and the missions. Pop. (est.) 13,000 (probably the population of the large rural district about the town is included in this estimate). The town (founded in 1725) is situated in a fertile country producing cotton, tobacco, Indian corn, sugar-cane and mandioca. It has two schools, a church and modern public buildings.

CARAT (Arab. *Qīrāt*, weight of four grains; Gr. κεράτιον, little horn, the fruit of the carob or locust tree), a small weight (originally in the form of a seed) used for diamonds and precious stones, and a measure for determining the fineness of gold. The exact weight of the carat, in practice, now varies slightly in different places. In 1877 a syndicate of London, Paris and Amsterdam jewellers fixed the weight at 205 milligrammes (3.163 troy grains). The South African carat, according to Gardner Williams (general manager of the De Beers mines), is equal to 3.174 grains (*The Diamond Mines of South Africa*, 1902). The fineness of gold is measured by a ratio with 24 carats as a standard; thus 2 parts of alloy make it 22-carat gold, and so on.

CARAUSIUS, MARCUS AURELIUS, tyrant or usurper in Britain, A.D.286-293, was a Menapian from Belgic Gaul, a man of humble origin, who in his early days had been a pilot. Having entered the Roman army, he rapidly obtained promotion, and was stationed by the emperor Maximian at Gessoriacum (Bononia, *Boulogne*) to protect the coasts and channel from Frankish and Saxon pirates. He at first acted energetically, but was subsequently accused of having entered into partnership with the barbarians and was sentenced to death by the emperor. Carausius thereupon crossed over to Britain and proclaimed himself an independent ruler. The legions at once joined him; numbers of Franks enlisted in his service; an increased and well-equipped fleet secured him the command of the neighbouring seas. In 289 Maximian attempted to recover the island, but his fleet was damaged by a storm and he was defeated. Maximian and Diocletian were compelled to acknowledge the rule of Carausius in Britain; numerous coins are extant with the heads of Carausius, Diocletian and Maximian, bearing the legend "Carausius et fratres sui." In 292 Constantius Chlorus besieged and captured Gessoriacum (hitherto in possession of Carausius), together with part of his fleet and naval stores. Constantius then made extensive preparations to ensure the reconquest of Britain, but before they were completed Carausius was murdered by Allectus, his praefect of the guards (Aurelius Victor, *Caesares*, 39; Eutropius ix. 21, 22; Eumenius, *Panegyrici* ii. 12, v. 12). A Roman mile-stone found near Carlisle (1895) bears the inscription IMP. C[aes] M. AUR[elius] MAUS. The meaning of MAUS is doubtful, but it may be an anticipation of ARAUS (see F.J. Haverfield in *Cumberland and Westmoreland Antiquarian Soc. Transactions*, 1895, p. 437).

A copper coin found at Richborough, inscribed *Domino Carausio Ces.*, must be ascribed to a Carausius of later date, since the type of the reverse is not found until the middle of the 4th century at the earliest. Nothing is known of this Carausius (A.J. Evans in *Numismatic Chronicle*, 1887, "On a coin of a second Carausius Caesar in Britain in the Fifth Century").

See J. Watts de Peyster, *The History of Carausius, the Dutch Augustus*(1858); P.H. Webb, *The Reign and Coinage of Carausius* (1908).

CARAVACA, a town of south-eastern Spain, in the province of Murcia; near the left bank of the river Caravaca, a tributary of the Segura. Pop. (1900) 15,846. Caravaca is dominated by the medieval castle of Santa Cruz, and contains several convents and a fine parish church, with a miraculous cross celebrated for its healing power, in honour of which a yearly festival is held on the 3rd of May. The hills which extend to the north are rich in marble and iron. Despite the lack of railway communication, the town is a considerable industrial centre, with large iron-works, tanneries and manufactories of paper, chocolate and oil.

CARAVAGGIO, MICHELANGELO AMERIGHI (or MERIGI) **DA**(1569-1609), Italian painter, was born in the village of Caravaggio, in Lombardy, from which he received his name. He was originally a mason's labourer, but his powerful genius directed him to painting, at which he worked with immitigable energy and amazing force. He despised every sort of idealism whether noble or emasculate, became the head of the Naturalisti (unmodified imitators of ordinary nature) in painting, and adopted a style of potent contrasts of light and shadow, laid on with a sort of fury, indicative of that fierce temper which led the artist to commit a homicide in a gambling quarrel at Rome. To avoid the consequences of his crime he fled to Naples and to Malta, where he was imprisoned for another attempt to avenge a quarrel. Escaping to Sicily, he was attacked by a party sent in pursuit of him, and severely wounded. Being pardoned, he set out for Rome; but having been arrested by mistake before his arrival, and afterwards released, and left to shift for himself in excessive heat, and still suffering from wounds and hardships, 302he died of fever on the beach at Pontercole in 1609. His best pictures are the "Entombment of Christ," now in the Vatican; "St Sebastian," in the Roman Capitol; a magnificent whole-length portrait of a grand-master of the Knights of Malta, Alof de Vignacourt, and his page, in the Louvre; and the Borghese "Supper at Emmaus."

CARAVAGGIO, POLIDORO CALDARA DA (1495 or 1492-1543), a celebrated painter of frieze and other decorations in the Vatican. His merits were such that, while a mere mortar-carrier to the artists engaged in that work, he attracted the admiration of Raphael, then employed on his great pictures in the Loggie of the palace. Polidoro's works, as well as those of his master, Maturino of Florence, have mostly perished, but are well known by the fine etchings of P.S. Bartoli, C. Alberti, &c. On the sack of Rome by the army of the Constable de Bourbon in 1527, Polidoro fled to Naples. Thence he went to Messina, where he was much employed, and gained a considerable fortune, with which he was about to return to the mainland of Italy when he was robbed and murdered by an assistant, Tonno Calabrese, in 1543. Two of his principal paintings are a Crucifixion, painted in Messina, and "Christ bearing the Cross" in the Naples gallery.

CARAVAN (more correctly *Karwan*), a Persian word, adopted into the later Arabic vocabulary, and denoting, throughout Asiatic Turkey and Persia,1 a body of traders travelling together for greater security against robbers (and in particular against Bedouins, Kurds, Tatars and the like, whose grazing-grounds the proposed route may traverse) and for mutual assistance in the matter of provisions, water and so forth. These precautions are due to the absence of settled government, inns and roads. These conditions having existed from time immemorial in the major part of western Asia, and still existing, caravans always have been the principal means for the transfer of merchandise. In these companies camels are generally employed for the transport of heavy goods, especially where the track, like that between Damascus and Bagdad, for example, lies across level, sandy and arid districts. The camels are harnessed in strings of fifty or more at a time, a hair-rope connecting the rear of one beast with the head of another; the leader is gaily decorated with parti-coloured trappings, tassels and bells; an unladen ass precedes the file, for luck, say some, for guidance, say others. Where the route is rocky and steep, as that between Damascus and Aleppo, mules, or even asses, are used for burdens. The wealthier members ride, where possible, on horseback. Every man carries arms; but these are in truth more for show than for use, and are commonly flung away in the presence of any serious robber attack. Should greater peril than ordinary be anticipated, the protection of a company of soldiers is habitually pre-engaged,— an expensive, and ordinarily a useless adjunct. A leader or director, called*Karawan-Bashi* (headman), or, out of compliment, *Karawan-Seraskier*(general), but most often simply

106

designated *Raïs* (chief), is before starting appointed by common consent. His duties are those of general manager, spokesman, arbitrator and so forth; his remuneration is indefinite. But in the matter of sales or purchases, either on the way or at the destination, each member of the caravan acts for himself.

The number of camels or mules in a single caravan varies from forty or so up to six hundred and more; sometimes, as on the reopening of a long-closed route, it reaches a thousand. The ordinary caravan seasons are the months of spring, early summer and later autumn. Friday, in accordance with a recommendation made in the Koran itself, is the favourite day for setting out, the most auspicious hour being that immediately following noonday prayer. The first day's march never does more than just clear the starting-point. Subsequently each day's route is divided into two stages,—from 3 or 4 A.M. to about 10 in the forenoon, and from between 2 and 3 P.M. till 6 or even 8 in the evening. Thus the time passed daily on the road averages from ten to twelve hours, and, as the ordinary pace of a laden camel does not exceed 2 m. an hour, that of a mule being 2¾, a distance varying from 23 to 28 m. is gone over every marching day. But prolonged halts of two, three, four and even more days often occur. The hours of halt, start and movement, the precise lines of route, and the selection or avoidance of particular localities are determined by common consent. But if, as sometimes happens, the services of a professional guide, or those of a military officer have been engaged, his decisions are final. While the caravan is on its way, the five stated daily prayers are, within certain limits, anticipated, deferred or curtailed, so as the better to coincide with the regular and necessary halts,—a practice authorized by orthodox Mahommedan custom and tradition.

Two caravans are mentioned in Genesis xxxvii.; the route on which they were passing seems to have coincided with that nowadays travelled by Syrian caravans on their way to Egypt. Other allusions to caravans may be found in Job, in Isaiah and in the Psalms. Eastern literature is full of such references.

The yearly pilgrim-bands, bound from various quarters of the Mahommedan world to their common destination, Mecca, are sometimes, but inaccurately, styled by European writers caravans; their proper designation is *Hajj*, a collective word for pilgrimages and pilgrims. The two principal pilgrim-caravans start yearly, the one from Damascus, or, to speak more exactly, from Mozarib, a village station three days' journey to the south of the Syrian capital, the other from Cairo in Egypt.2 This latter was formerly joined on its route, near Akaba of the Red Sea, by the North African Hajj, which, however, now goes from Egypt by sea from Suez; the former gathers up bands from Anatolia, Kurdistan, Mesopotamia and Syria. Besides these a third, but smaller Hajj of Persians, chiefly sets out from Suk-esh-Sheiukh, in the neighbourhood of Meshed Ali, on the lower Euphrates; a fourth of negroes, Nubians, etc., unites at Yambu on the Hejaz coast, whither they have crossed from Kosseir in Upper Egypt; a fifth of Indians and Malays, centres at Jidda; a sixth and seventh, of southern or eastern Arabs arrive, the former from Yemen, the latter from Nejd.

The Syrian Hajj is headed by the pasha of Damascus, either in person or by a vicarious official of high rank, and is further accompanied by the *Sorrah Amir* or "Guardian of the Purse," a Turkish officer from Constantinople. The Egyptian company is commanded by an amir or ruler, appointed by the Cairene government, and is accompanied by the famous "Maḥmal," or sacred pavilion. The other bands above mentioned have each their own amir, besides their*mekowwams* or agents, whose business it is to see after provisions, water and the like, and are not seldom encumbered with a numerous retinue of servants and other attendants. Lastly, a considerable force of soldiery accompanies both the Syrian and the Egyptian Hajj.

No guides properly so-called attend these pilgrim-caravans, the routes followed being invariably the same, and well known. But Bedouin bands generally offer themselves by way of escort, and not seldom designedly lead their clients into the dangers from which they bargain to keep them safe. This they are the readier to do because, in addition to the personal luxuries with which many of the pilgrims provide themselves for the journey, a large amount of wealth, both in merchandise and coins, is habitually to be found among the travellers, who, in accordance with Mahommedan tradition, consider it not merely lawful but praiseworthy to unite mercantile speculation with religious duty. Nor has any one, the pasha himself or the amir and the military, when present, excepted, any acknowledged authority or general control in the pilgrim-caravans; nor is there any orderly subdivision of management or service. The pilgrims do, indeed, often coalesce in companies among themselves for mutual help, but necessity, circumstance or caprice governs all details, and thus it happens that numbers, sometimes as many as a third of the entire Hajj, yearly perish by their own negligence or by misfortune,—dying, some of thirst, others of fatigue and sickness, others at the hand of robbers on the way. In fact the principal 303routes are in many places lined for miles together with the bones of camels and men.

The numbers which compose these pilgrim caravans are much exaggerated by popular rumour; yet it is certain that the Syrian and Egyptian sometimes amount to 5000 each, with 25,000 or 30,000 camels in train. Large supplies of food and water have to be carried, the more so at times that the pilgrim season, following as it does the Mahommedan calendar, which is lunar, falls for years together in the very hottest season. Hence, too, the journey is usually accomplished by night marches, the hours being from 3 to 4 P.M. to 6 or 7 A.M. of the following day. Torches are lighted on the road, the pace is slower than that of an ordinary caravan, and does not exceed 2 m. an hour.

See MECCA and MAHOMMEDAN RELIGION.

1In Arabia proper it is rarely employed in speech and never in writing, strictly Arabic words such as *Rikb* ("assembled riders") or *Qāfila* ("wayfaring band") being in ordinary use.

2The Syrian and Egyptian haj; have been able, since 1908, to travel by the railway from Damascus to the Hejaz.

CARAVANSERAI, a public building, for the shelter of a caravan (*q.v.*) and of wayfarers generally in Asiatic Turkey. It is commonly constructed in the neighbourhood, but not within the walls, of a town or village. It is quadrangular in form, with a dead wall outside; this wall has small windows high up, but in the lower parts merely a few narrow air-holes. Inside a cloister-like arcade, surrounded by cellular store-rooms, forms the ground floor, and a somewhat lighter arcade, giving access to little dwelling-rooms, runs round it above. Broad open flights of stone steps connect the storeys. The central court is open to the sky, and generally has in its centre a well with a fountain-basin beside it. A spacious gateway, high and wide enough to admit the passage of a loaded camel, forms the sole entrance, which is furnished with heavy doors, and is further guarded within by massive iron chains, drawn across at night. The entry is paved with flagstones, and there are stone seats on each side. The court itself is generally paved, and large enough to admit of three or four hundred crouching camels or tethered mules; the bales of merchandise are piled away under the lower arcade, or stored up in the cellars behind it. The upstairs apartments are for human lodging; cooking is usually carried on in one or more corners of the quadrangle below. Should the caravanserai be a small one, the merchants and their goods alone find place within, the beasts of burden being left outside. A porter, appointed by the municipal authority of the place, is always present, lodged just within the gate, and sometimes one or more assistants. These form a guard of the building and of the goods and persons in it, and have the right to maintain order and, within certain limits, decorum; but they have no further control over the temporary occupants of the place, which is always kept open for all arrivals from prayer-time at early dawn till late in the evening. A small gratuity is expected by the porter, but he has no legal claim for payment, his maintenance being provided for out of the funds of the institution. Neither food nor provender is supplied.

Many caravanserais in Syria, Mesopotamia and Anatolia have considerable architectural merit; their style of construction is in general that known as Saracenic; their massive walls are of hewn stone; their proportions apt and grand. The portals especially are often decorated with intricate carving; so also is the prayer-niche within. These buildings, with their belongings, are works of charity, and are supported, repaired and so forth out of funds derived from pious legacies, most often of land or rentals. Sometimes a municipality

108

takes on itself to construct and maintain a caravanserai; but in any case the institution is tax-free, and its revenues are inalienable. When, as sometimes happens, those revenues have been dissipated by peculation, neglect or change of times, the caravanserai passes through downward stages of dilapidation to total ruin (of which only too many examples may be seen) unless some new charity intervene to repair and renew it.

Khans, i.e. places analogous to inns and hotels, where not lodging only, but often food and other necessaries or comforts may be had for payment, are sometimes by inaccurate writers confounded with caravanserais. They are generally to be found within the town or village precincts, and are of much smaller dimensions than caravanserais. The khan of Asad Pasha at Damascus is a model of constructive skill and architectural beauty.

CARAVEL, or CARVEL (from the Gr. κάραβος, a light ship, through the Ital. *carabella* and the Span. *carabas*), a name applied at different times and in different countries to ships of very varying appearance and build, as in Turkey to a ship of war, and in France to a small boat used in the herring fishery. In the 15th and 16th centuries, caravels were much used by the Portuguese and Spanish for long voyages. They were roundish ships, with a double tower at the stern, and a single one in the bows, and were galley rigged. Two out of the three vessels in which Columbus sailed on his voyage of discovery to America were "caravels." Carvel, the older English form, is now used only in the term "carvel-built," for a boat in which the planking is flush with the edges laid side to side, in distinction from "clinker-built," where the edges overlap.

CARAVELLAS, a small seaport of southern Bahia, Brazil, on the Caravellas river a few miles above its mouth, which is dangerously obstructed by sandbars. Pop. (1890) of the municipality 5482, about one-half of whom lived in the town. Caravellas was once the centre of a flourishing whale fishery, but has since fallen into decay. It is the port of the Bahia & Minas railway, whose traffic is comparatively unimportant.

CARAWAY, the fruit, or so-called seed, of *Carum Carui,* an umbelliferous plant growing throughout the northern and central parts of Europe and Asia, and naturalized in waste places in England. The plant has finely-cut leaves and compound umbels of small white flowers. The fruits are laterally compressed and ovate, the mericarps (the two portions into which the ripe fruit splits) being subcylindrical, slightly arched, and marked with five distinct pale ridges. Caraways evolve a pleasant aromatic odour when bruised, and they have an agreeable spicy taste. They yield from 3 to 6% of a volatile oil, the chief constituent of which is cymene aldehyde. Cymene itself is present, having the formula $CH_3C_6H_4CH(CH_3)_2$; also carvone $C_{10}H_{14}O$, and limonene, a terpene. The dose of the oil is ½-3 minims. The plant is cultivated in north and central Europe, and Morocco, as well as in the south of England, the produce of more northerly latitudes being richer in essential oil than that grown in southern regions. The essential oil is largely obtained by distillation for use in medicine as an aromatic stimulant and carminative, and as a flavouring material in cookery and in liqueurs for drinking. Caraways are, however, more extensively consumed entire in certain kinds of cheese, cakes and bread, and they form the basis of a popular article of confectionery known as caraway comfits.

CARBALLO, a town of north-western Spain, in the province of Corunna; on the right bank of the river Allones, 20 m. S.W. of the city of Corunna. Pop. (1900) 13,032. Carballo is the central market of a thriving agricultural district. At San Juan de Carballo, on the opposite bank of the Allones, there are hot sulphurous springs.

CARBAZOL, $C_{12}H_9N$, a chemical constituent of coal-tar and crude anthracene. From the latter it may be obtained by fusion with caustic potash when it is converted into carbazol-potassium, which can be easily separated by distilling off the anthracene. It may be prepared synthetically by passing the vapours of diphenylamine or aniline through a red-hot tube; by heating diorthodiaminodiphenyl with 25% sulphuric acid to 200° C. for 15 hours;

by heating orthoaminodiphenyl with lime; or by heating thiodiphenylamine with copper powder. It is also obtained as a decomposition product of brucine or strychnine, when these alkaloids are distilled with zinc dust. It is easily soluble in the common organic solvents, and crystallizes in plates or tables melting at 238° C. It is a very stable compound, possessing feebly basic properties and characterized by its ready sublimation. It distils unchanged, even when the operation is carried out in the presence of zinc dust. On being heated with caustic potash in a current of carbonic acid, it gives carbazol carbonic acid $C_{12}H_8N \cdot COOH$; melted with oxalic acid it gives carbazol blue. It dissolves in concentrated sulphuric acid to a clear yellow solution. The potassium salt reacts with the alkyl iodides to give N-substituted alkyl derivatives. It gives the pine-shaving reaction, in this respect resembling pyrrol (*q.v.*).

304

CARBIDE, in chemistry, a compound of carbon with another element. The introduction of the electric furnace into practical chemistry was followed by the preparation of many metallic carbides previously unknown, some of which, especially calcium carbide, are now of great commercial importance. Carbides of the following general formulae have been obtained by H. Moissan (M denotes an atom of metal and C of carbon):—

M3C = manganese, iron; M2C = molybdenum; M3C2 = chromium; MC = zirconium; M4C3 = beryllium, aluminium; M2C3 = uranium; MC2 = barium, calcium, strontium, lithium, thorium, &c.; MC4 = chromium.

The principal methods for the preparation of carbides may be classified as follows:— (1) direct union at a high temperature, *e.g.* lithium, iron, chromium, tungsten, &c.; (2) by the reduction of oxides with carbon at high temperatures,*e.g.* calcium, barium, strontium, manganese, chromium, &c.; (3) by the reduction of carbonates with magnesium in the presence of carbon, *e.g.* calcium, lithium; (4) by the action of metals on acetylene or metallic derivatives of acetylene, *e.g.*, sodium, potassium. The metallic carbides are crystalline solids, the greater number being decomposed by water into a metallic hydrate and a hydrocarbon; sometimes hydrogen is also evolved. Calcium carbide owes its industrial importance to its decomposition into acetylene; lithium carbide behaves similarly. Methane is yielded by aluminium and beryllium carbides, and, mixed with hydrogen, by manganese carbide. The important carbides are mentioned in the separate articles on the various metals. The commercial aspect of calcium carbide is treated in the article ACETYLENE.

CARBINE (Fr. *carabine*, Ger. *Karabiner*), a word which came into use towards the end of the 16th century to denote a form of small fire-arm, shorter than the musket and chiefly used by mounted men. It has retained this significance, through all subsequent modifications of small-arm design, to the present day, and is now as a rule a shortened and otherwise slightly modified form of the ordinary rifle (*q.v.*).

CARBO, the name of a Roman plebeian family of the gens Papiria. The following are the most important members in Roman history:—

1. GAIUS PAPIRIUS CARBO, statesman and orator. He was associated with C. Gracchus in carrying out the provisions of the agrarian law of Tiberius Gracchus (see GRACCHUS). When tribune of the people (131 B.C.) he carried a law extending voting by ballot to the enactment and repeal of laws; another proposal, that the tribunes should be allowed to become candidates for the same office in the year immediately following, was defeated by the younger Scipio Africanus. Carbo was suspected of having been concerned in the sudden death of Scipio (129), if not his actual murderer. He subsequently went over to the optimates, and (when consul in 120) successfully defended Lucius Opimius, the murderer of Gaius Gracchus, when he was impeached for the murder of citizens without a trial, and even went so far as to say that Gracchus had been justly slain. But the optimates did not trust Carbo. He was impeached by Licinius Crassus on a similar charge, and, feeling that he had nothing to hope for from the optimates and that his condemnation was certain, he committed suicide.

See Livy, *Epit.* 59; Appian, *Bell. Civ.* i. 18: Vell. Pat. ii. 4; Val. Max. iii. 7. 6; A.H.J. Greenidge, *History of Rome* (1904).

2. His son, GAIUS PAPIRIUS CARBO, surnamed Arvina, was a staunch supporter of the aristocracy, and was put to death by the Marian party in 82. He is known chiefly for the law (Plautia Papiria) carried by him and M. Plautius Silvanus when tribunes of the people in 90 (or 89), whereby the Roman franchise was offered to every Italian ally domiciled in Italy at the time when the law was enacted, provided he made application personally within sixty days to the praetor at Rome (see ROME: History, II. "The Republic," Period C.). The object of the law was to conciliate the states at war with Rome and to secure the loyalty of the federate states. Like his father, Carbo was an orator of distinction.

See Cicero, Pro Archia, 4; Vell. Pat. ii. 26; Appian, Bell. Civ. i. 88.

3. GNAEUS PAPIRIUS CARBO (c. 130-82 B.C.), nephew of (1). He was a strong supporter of the Marian party, and took part in the blockade of Rome (87). In 85 he was chosen by Cinna as his colleague in the consulship, and extensive preparations were made for carrying on war in Greece against Sulla, who had announced his intention of returning to Italy. Cinna and Carbo declared themselves consuls for the following year, and large bodies of troops were transported across the Adriatic; but when Cinna was murdered by his own soldiers, who refused to engage in civil war, Carbo was obliged to bring them back. In 82 Carbo, then consul for the third time with the younger Marius, fought an indecisive engagement with Sulla near Clusium, but was defeated with great loss in an attack on the camp of Sulla's general, Q. Caecilius Metellus Pius [see under METELLUS (6)] near Faventia. Although he still had a large army and the Samnites remained faithful to him, Carbo was so disheartened by his failure to relieve Praeneste, where the younger Marius had taken refuge, that he decided to leave Italy. He first fled to Africa, thence to the island of Cossyra (Pentellaria), where he was arrested, taken in chains before Pompey at Lilybaeum and put to death.

See Appian, Bell. Civ. i. 67-98; Livy, Epit. 79, 84, 88, 89; Plutarch, Pompey, 5, 6, 10, and Sulla, 28; Cicero, ad Fam. ix. 21; Eutropius, v. 8, 9; Orosius, v. 20; Valerius Maximus, v. 3. 5, ix. 13. 2; art. SULLA, L. CORNELIUS.

CARBOHYDRATE, in chemistry, the generic name for compounds empirically represented by the formula $Cx(H2O)y$. They are essentially vegetable products, and include the sugars, starches, gums and celluloses (q.v.).

CARBOLIC ACID or PHENOL (hydroxy-benzene), $C6H5OH$, an acid found in the urine of the herbivorae, and in small quantity in castoreum (F. Wöhler, Ann., 1848, 67, p. 360). Its principal commercial source is the fraction of coal-tar which distils between 150 and 200° C., in which it was discovered in 1834 by F. Runge. In order to obtain the phenol from this distillate, it is treated with caustic soda, which dissolves the phenol and its homologues together with a certain quantity of naphthalene and other hydrocarbons. The solution is diluted with water, and the hydrocarbons are thereby precipitated and separated. The solution is then acidified, and the phenols are liberated and form an oily layer on the surface of the acid. This layer is separated, and the phenol recovered by a process of fractional distillation. It may be synthetically prepared by fusing potassium benzene sulphonate with caustic alkalis (A. Kekulé, A. Wurtz); by the action of nitrous acid on aniline; by passing oxygen into boiling benzene containing aluminium chloride (C. Friedel and J.M. Crafts, Ann. Chim. Phys., 1888 (6) 14, p. 435); by heating phenol carboxylic acids with baryta; and, in small quantities by the oxidation of benzene with hydrogen peroxide or nascent ozone (A.R. Leeds, Ber., 1881, 14, p. 976).

It crystallizes in rhombic needles, which melt at 42.5-43° C., and boil at 182-183° C.; its specific gravity is 1.0906 (0° C.). It has a characteristic smell, and a biting taste; it is poisonous, and acts as a powerful antiseptic. It dissolves in water, 15 parts of water dissolving about one part of phenol at 16-17° C., but it is miscible in all proportions at about 70° C.; it is volatile in steam, and is readily soluble in alcohol, ether, benzene, carbon bisulphide, chloroform and glacial acetic acid. It is also readily soluble in solutions of the caustic alkalis, slightly soluble in aqueous ammonia solution, and almost insoluble in sodium carbonate solution. When exposed in the moist condition to the air it gradually acquires a red colour. With ferric chloride it gives a violet coloration, and with bromine water a white precipitate of tribrom-phenol.

When phenol is passed through a red-hot tube a complex decomposition takes place, resulting in the formation of benzene, toluene, naphthalene, &c. (J.G. Kramers, *Ann.*, 1877, 189, p. 129). Chromium oxychloride reacts violently on phenol, producing hydroquinone ether, $O(C_6H_4OH)_2$; chromic acid gives phenoquinone, and potassium permanganate gives paradiphenol, oxalic acid, and some salicylic acid (R. Henriques, *Ber.*, 1888, 21, p. 1620). In alkaline solution, potassium permanganate oxidizes it to inactive tartaric acid and carbon dioxide (O. Doebner, *Ber.*, 1891, 24, p. 1755). When distilled over lead oxide, it forms diphenylene oxide, $(C_6H_4)_2O$; and 305when heated with oxalic acid and concentrated sulphuric acid, it forms aurin, $C_{19}H_{14}O_3$. It condenses with aceto-acetic ester, in the presence of sulphuric acid, to β-methyl coumarin (H. v. Pechmann and J.B. Cohen, *Ber.*, 1884, 17, p. 2188).

The hydrogen of the hydroxyl group in phenol can be replaced by metals, by alkyl groups and by acid radicals. The metallic derivatives (phenolates, phenates or carbolates) of the alkali metals are obtained by dissolving phenol in a solution of a caustic alkali, in the absence of air. Potassium phenolate, C_6H_5OK, crystallizes in fine needles, is very hygroscopic and oxidizes rapidly on exposure. Other phenolates may be obtained from potassium phenolate by precipitation. The alkyl derivatives may be obtained by heating phenol with one molecular proportion of a caustic alkali and of an alkyl iodide. They are compounds which greatly resemble the mixed ethers of the aliphatic series. They are not decomposed by boiling alkalis, but on heating with hydriodic acid they split into their components. *Anisol*, phenyl methyl ether, $C_6H_5 \cdot O \cdot CH_3$, is prepared either by the above method or by the action of diazo-methane on phenol, $C_6H_5OH + CH_2N_2 = N_2 + C_6H_5 \cdot O \cdot CH_3$ (H. v. Pechmann, *Ber.*, 1895, 28, p. 857); by distilling anisic acid (para-methoxy benzoic acid) with baryta or by boiling phenyl diazonium chloride with methyl alcohol. It is a colourless pleasant-smelling liquid which boils at 154.3° C. *Phenetol*, phenyl ethyl ether, $C_6H_5 \cdot O \cdot C_2H_5$, a liquid boiling at 172° C., may be obtained by similar methods. A. Hantzsch (*Ber.*, 1901, 34, p. 3337) has shown that in the action of alcohols on diazonium salts an increase in the molecular weight of the alcohol and an accumulation of negative groups in the aromatic nucleus lead to a diminution in the yield of the ether produced and to the production of a secondary reaction, resulting in the formation of a certain amount of an aromatic hydrocarbon.

The acid esters of phenol are best obtained by the action of acid chlorides or anhydrides on phenol or its sodium or potassium salt, or by digesting phenol with an acid in the presence of phosphorus oxychloride (F. Rasinski, *Jour. f. prak. Chem.*, 1882 [2], 26, p. 62). Phenyl acetate, $C_6H_5 \cdot O \cdot COCH_3$, a colourless liquid of boiling point 193° C., may be prepared by heating phenol with acetamide. When heated with aniline it yields phenol and acetanilide. Phenyl benzoate, $C_6H_5 \cdot O \cdot COC_6H_5$, prepared from phenol and benzoyl chloride, crystallizes in monoclinic prisms, which melt at 68-69° C. and boil at 314° C.

Phenol is characterized by the readiness with which it forms substitution products; chlorine and bromine, for example, react readily with phenol, forming ortho- and para-chlor- and -bromphenol, and, by further action, trichlor- and tribrom-phenol. Iodphenol is obtained by the action of iodine and iodic acid on phenol dissolved in a dilute solution of caustic potash. Nitro-phenols are readily obtained by the action of nitric acid on phenol. By the action of dilute nitric acid, ortho- and para-nitrophenols are obtained, the ortho-compound being separated from the para-compound by distillation in a current of steam. Ortho-nitrophenol, $C_6H_4 \cdot OH \cdot NO_2(1 \cdot 2)$, crystallizes in yellow needles which melt at 45° C. and boil at 214°C. Para-nitrophenol, $C_6H_4 \cdot OH \cdot NO_2(1 \cdot 4)$, crystallizes in long colourless needles which melt at 114°C. Meta-nitrophenol, $C_6H_4 \cdot OH \cdot NO_2 \cdot (1 \cdot 3)$, is prepared from meta-nitraniline by diazotizing the base and boiling the resulting diazonium salt with water. By nitrating phenol with concentrated nitric acid, no care being taken to keep the temperature of reaction down, trinitrophenol (picric acid) is obtained (see PICRIC ACID). By the reduction of nitro-phenols, the corresponding aminophenols are obtained, and of these, the meta- and para-derivatives are the most important. Para-aminophenol,

C6H4·OH·NH2(1·4) melts at 148° C., with decomposition. Its most important derivative is phenacetin. Meta-aminophenol, C6H4·OH·NH2(1·3), and dimethyl meta-aminophenol, C6H4·OH·N(CH3)2(1·3), are extensively employed in the manufacture of the important dyestuffs known as the rhodamines. The aminophenols also find application as developers in photography, the more important of these developers being amidol, the hydrochloride of diaminophenol, ortol, the hydrochloride of para-methylaminophenol, C6H4·OH·NHCH3·HCl(1·4), rodinal, para-aminophenol, and metol, the sulphate of a methylaminophenol sulphonic acid. Meta-aminophenol is prepared by reducing meta-nitrophenol, or by heating resorcin with ammonium chloride and ammonia to 200° C. Dimethyl-meta-aminophenol is prepared by heating meta-aminophenol with methyl alcohol and hydrochloric acid in an autoclave; by sulphonation of dimethylaniline, the sulphonic acid formed being finally fused with potash; or by nitrating dimethylaniline, in the presence of sulphuric, acid at 0° C. In the latter case a mixture of nitro-compounds is obtained which can be separated by the addition of sodium carbonate. The meta-nitro-compound, which is precipitated last, is then reduced, and the amino group so formed is replaced by the hydroxyl group by means of the Sandmeyer reaction. Dimethyl-meta-aminophenol crystallizes in small prisms which melt at 87° C. It condenses with phthalic anhydride to form rhodamine, and with succinic anhydride to rhodamine S.

Phenol dissolves readily in concentrated sulphuric acid, a mixture of phenol-ortho- and -para-sulphonic acids being formed. These acids may be separated by conversion into their potassium salts, which are then fractionally crystallized, the potassium salt of the para-acid separating first. The ortho-acid, in the form of its aqueous solution, is sometimes used as an antiseptic, under the name of aseptol. A *thiophenol*, C6H5SH, is known, and is prepared by the action of phosphorus pentasulphide on phenol, or by distilling a mixture of sodium benzene sulphonate and potassium sulphydrate. It is a colourless liquid, which possesses a very disagreeable smell, and boils at 168° C.

Various methods have been devised for the quantitative determination of phenol. J. Messinger and G. Vortmann (*Ber.*, 1890, 23, p. 2753) dissolve phenol in caustic alkali, make the solution up to known volume, take an aliquot part, warm it to 60° C., and add decinormal iodine solution until the liquid is of a deep yellow colour. The mixture is then cooled, acidified by means of sulphuric acid, and titrated with decinormal sodium thiosulphate solution. S.B. Schryver (*Jour, of Soc. Chem. Industry*, 1899, 18, p. 553) adds excess of sodamide to a solution of the phenol in a suitable solvent, absorbs the liberated ammonia in an excess of acid, and titrates the excess of acid. See also C.E. Smith, *Amer. Jour. Pharm.*, 1898, 369.

Pharmacology and Therapeutics.—Carbolic acid is an efficient parasiticide, and is largely used in destroying the fungus of ringworm and of the skin disease known as *pityriasis versicolor*. When a solution of the strength of about 1 in 20 is applied to the skin it produces a local anaesthesia which lasts for many hours. If concentrated, however, it acts as a caustic. It never produces vesication. The drug is absorbed through the unbroken skin—a very valuable property in the treatment of such conditions as an incipient whitlow. A piece of cotton wool soaked in strong carbolic acid will relieve the pain of dental caries, but is useless in other forms of toothache. Taken internally, in doses of from one to three grains, carbolic acid will often relieve obstinate cases of vomiting and has some value as a gastric antiseptic.

Toxicology.—Carbolic acid is distinguished from all other acids so-called—except oxalic acid and hydrocyanic acid—in that it is a neurotic poison, having a marked action directly upon the nervous system. In all cases of carbolic acid poisoning the nervous influence is seen. If it be absorbed from a surgical dressing there are no irritant symptoms, but when the acid is swallowed in concentrated form, symptoms of gastro-intestinal irritation occur. The patient becomes collapsed, and the skin is cold and clammy. The breathing becomes shallow, the drug killing, like nearly all neurotic poisons (alcohol, morphia, prussic acid, &c.), by paralysis of the respiratory centre, and the patient dying in a state of coma. The condition of the urine is of the utmost importance, as it is often a clue to the diagnosis, and in surgical cases may be the first warning that absorption is occurring to an undue degree. The urine becomes dark green in colour owing to the formation of various oxidation products such as pyrocatechin. Fifteen grains constitute an exceedingly dangerous dose for an adult male of average weight. Other symptoms of undue absorption are vertigo, deafness, sounds in the ears, stupefaction, a subnormal temperature, nausea, vomiting and a weak pulse (Sir Thomas Fraser).

The antidote in cases of carbolic acid poisoning is any soluble sulphate. Carbolic acid and sulphates combine in the blood to form sulpho-carbolates, which are innocuous. The symptoms of nerve-poisoning are due to the carbolic acid (or its salts) which circulate in the blood after all the sulphates in the blood have been used up in the formation of sulpho-carbolates (hence, during administration of carbolic acid, the urine should frequently be tested for the presence of free sulphates; as long as these occur in the urine, they are present in the blood and there is no danger). The treatment is therefore to administer an ounce of sodium sulphate in water by the mouth, or to inject a similar quantity of the salt in solution directly into a vein or into the subcutaneous tissues. Magnesium sulphate may be given by the mouth, but is poisonous if injected intravenously. If the acid has been swallowed, wash out the stomach and give chalk, the carbolate of calcium being insoluble. Alkalis which form soluble carbolates are useless. Give ether and brandy subcutaneously and apply hot water-bottles and blankets if there are signs of collapse.

CARBON (symbol C, atomic weight 12), one of the chemical non-metallic elements. It is found native as the diamond (*q.v.*), graphite (*q.v.*), as a constituent of all animal and vegetable tissues and of coal and petroleum. It also enters (as carbonates) into the composition of many minerals, such as chalk, dolomite, 306calcite, witherite, calamine and spathic iron ore. In combination with oxygen (as carbon dioxide) it is also found to a small extent in the atmosphere. It is a solid substance which occurs in several modifications, differing very much in their physical properties. *Amorphous carbon* is obtained by the destructive distillation of many carbon compounds, the various kinds differing very greatly as regards physical characters and purity, according to the substance used for their preparation. The most common varieties met with are lampblack, gas carbon, wood charcoal, animal charcoal and coke. *Lampblack* is prepared by burning tar, resin, turpentine and other substances rich in carbon, with a limited supply of air; the products of combustion being conducted into condensing chambers in which cloths are suspended, on which the carbon collects. It is further purified by heating in closed vessels, but even then it still contains a certain amount of mineral matter and more or less hydrocarbons. It is used in the manufacture of printer's ink, in the preparation of black paint and in calico printing. *Gas carbon* is produced by the destructive distillation of coal in the manufacture of illuminating gas (see GAS: *Manufacture*), being probably formed by the decomposition of gaseous hydrocarbons. It is a very dense form of carbon, and is a good conductor of heat and electricity. It is used in the manufacture of carbon rods for arc lights, and for the negative element in the Bunsen battery.

Charcoal is a porous form of carbon; several varieties exist. *Sugar charcoal* is obtained by the carbonization of sugar. It is purified by boiling with acids, to remove any mineral matter, and is then ignited for a long time in a current of chlorine in order to remove the last traces of hydrogen. *Animal charcoal* (bone black) is prepared by charring bones in iron retorts. It is a very impure form of carbon, containing on the average about 80% of calcium phosphate. It possesses a much greater decolorizing and absorbing power than wood charcoal. A variety of animal charcoal is sometimes prepared by calcining fresh blood with potassium carbonate in large cylinders, the mass being purified by boiling out with dilute hydrochloric acid and subsequent reheating. *Wood charcoal* is a hard and brittle black substance, which retains the external structure of the wood from which it is made. It is prepared (where wood is plentiful) by stacking the wood in heaps, which are covered with earth or with brushwood and turf, and then burning the heap slowly in a limited supply of air. The combustion of the wood is conducted from the top downwards, and from the exterior towards the centre; great care has to be taken that the process is carried out slowly. The disadvantage in this process is that the by-products, such as pyroligneous acid, acetone, wood spirit, &c., are lost; as an alternative method, wood is frequently carbonized in ovens or retorts and the volatile products are condensed and utilized.

114

Charcoal varies considerably in its properties, depending upon the particular variety of wood from which it is prepared, and also upon the process used in its manufacture. It can be made at a temperature as low as 300° C., and is then a soft, very friable material possessing a low ignition point. When made at higher temperatures it is much more dense, and its ignition point is considerably higher. Charcoal burns when heated in air, usually without the formation of flame, although a flame is apparent if the temperature be raised. It is characterized by its power of absorbing gases; thus, according to J. Hunter [*Phil. Mag.*, 1863 (4), 25, p. 363], one volume of charcoal absorbs (at 0° C. and 760 mm. pressure) 171.7 ccs. of ammonia, 86.3 ccs. of nitrous oxide, 67.7 ccs. of carbon monoxide, 21.2 ccs. of carbon dioxide, 17.9 ccs. of oxygen, 15.2 ccs. of nitrogen, and 4.4 ccs. of hydrogen [see also J. Dewar, *Ann. Chim. Phys.*, 1904 (8), 3, p. 5]. It also has the power of absorbing colouring matters from solution. Charcoal is used as a fuel and as a reducing agent in metallurgical processes.

The element carbon unites directly with hydrogen to form acetylene when an electric arc is passed between carbon poles in an atmosphere of hydrogen (M. Berthelot); it also unites directly with fluorine, producing, chiefly, carbon tetrafluoride CF_4. It burns when heated in an atmosphere of oxygen, forming carbon dioxide, and when heated in sulphur vapour it forms carbon bisulphide (*q.v.*). When heated with nitrogenous substances, in the presence of carbonated or caustic alkali, it forms cyanides. It combines directly with silicon, at the temperature of the electric furnace, yielding *carborundum*, SiC; and H. Moissan has also shown that it will combine with many metals at the temperature of the electric furnace, to form carbides (*q.v.*).

The specific heat of carbon varies with the temperature the following values having been obtained by H.F. Weber (*Jahresberichte*, 1874, p. 63):—

Diamond		Graphite.		Porous wood carbon.	
t°.	S p. Ht.	t°.	S p. Ht.	t°.	S p. Ht.
50.5	0.0635	50.3	0.1138	−23	0.1653
10.6	0.0955	10.7	0.1437	−99	0.1935
10.7	0.1128	10.8	0.1604	−223	0.2385
5.5	0.1765	1.3	0.1990		
06.1	0.2733	01.6	0.2966		
06.7	0.4408	41.9	0.4454		
85.0	0.4589	77.0	0.4670		

The atomic weight of carbon has been determined by J.B.A. Dumas and by J.S. Stas [*Ann. Chim. Phys.*, 1841 (3), 1, p. 1: *Jahresb.*, 1849, 223] by estimating the amount of carbon dioxide formed on burning graphite or diamond in a current of oxygen, the value obtained being 12.0 (O = 16). Confirmatory evidence has also been obtained by O.L. Erdmann and R.F. Marchand (*Jour. Prak. Chem.*, 1841, 23, p. 159; see also F.W. Clarke, *Jahresb.*, 1881, p. 7).

Compounds.—Three oxides of carbon are known, namely, carbon suboxide, C_3O_2, carbon monoxide, CO, and carbon dioxide, CO_2. *Carbon suboxide*, C_3O_2, is formed by the action of phosphorus pentoxide on ethyl malonate (O. Diels and B. Wolf, *Ber.*, 1906, 39, p. 689), $CH_2(COOC_2H_5)_2 = 2C_2H_4 + 2H_2O + C_3O_2$. At ordinary temperatures it is a colourless gas, possessing a penetrating and suffocating smell. It liquefies at 7° C. It is an exceedingly reactive compound, combining with water to form malonic acid, with hydrogen chloride to form malonyl chloride, and with ammonia to form malonamide. When kept for some time in sealed tubes it changes to a yellowish liquid, from which a yellow flocculent substance gradually separates, and finally it suddenly solidifies to a dark red mass, which appears to be a polymeric form. Its vapour density agrees with the molecular formula C_3O_2, and this formula is also confirmed by exploding the gas with oxygen and measuring the amount of carbon dioxide produced (see KETENES).

Carbon monoxide, CO, is found to some extent in volcanic gases. It was first prepared in 1776 by J.M.F. Lassone (*Mem. Acad. Paris*) by heating zinc oxide with carbon, and was for some time considered to be identical with hydrogen. Cruikshank concluded that it was an oxide of carbon, a fact which was confirmed by Clement and J.B. Désormes (*Ann. Chim. Phys.*, 1801, 38, p. 285). It may be prepared by passing carbon dioxide over red-hot carbon, or red-hot iron; by heating carbonates (magnesite, chalk, &c.) with zinc dust or iron; or by heating many metallic oxides with carbon. It may also be prepared by heating formic and oxalic acids (or their salts) with concentrated sulphuric acid (in the case of oxalic acid, an equal volume of carbon dioxide is produced); and by heating potassium ferrocyanide with a large excess of concentrated sulphuric acid, $K_4Fe(CN)_6 + 6H_2SO_4 + 6H_2O = 2K_2SO_4 + FeSO_4 + 3(NH_4)_2SO_4 + 6CO$. It is a colourless, odourless gas of specific gravity 0.967 (air = 1). It is one of the most difficultly liquefiable gases, its critical temperature being $-139.5°$ C., and its critical pressure 35.5 atmos. The liquid boils at $-190°$ C., and solidifies at $-211°$C. (L.P. Cailletet,*Comptes rendus*, 1884, 99, p. 706). It is only very slightly soluble in water. It burns with a characteristic pale blue flame to form carbon dioxide. It is very poisonous, uniting with the haemoglobin of the blood to form carbonyl-haemoglobin. It is a powerful reducing agent, especially at high temperatures. It is rapidly absorbed by an ammoniacal or acid (hydrochloric acid) solution of cuprous chloride. It unites directly with chlorine, forming carbonyl chloride or phosgene (see below), and with nickel and iron to form nickel and iron carbonyls (see NICKEL and IRON). It also combines directly with potassium hydride to form potassium formate (see FORMIC ACID). The volume composition of carbon monoxide is established by exploding a mixture of the gas with oxygen, two volumes of the gas combining with one volume of oxygen to form two volumes of carbon dioxide. This fact, coupled with the determination of the vapour density of the gas, establishes the molecular formula CO.

Carbon dioxide, CO_2, is a gas first distinguished from air by van Helmont (1577-1644), who observed that it was formed in fermentation processes and during combustion, and gave to it the name *gas sylvestre*. J. Black (*Edin. Phys. and Lit. Essays*, 1755) showed that it was a constituent of the carbonated alkalis and called it "fixed air." T.O. Bergman, in 1774, pointed out its acid character, and A.L. Lavoisier (1781-1788) first proved it to be an oxide of carbon by burning carbon in the oxygen obtained from the decomposition of mercuric oxide. It is a regular constituent of the atmosphere, and is found in many spring waters and in volcanic gases; it also occurs in the uncombined condition at the Grotto del Cane (Naples) and in the Poison Valley (Java). It is a constituent of the minerals cerussite, malachite, azurite, spathic iron ore, calamine, strontianite, witherite, calcite aragonite, limestone, &c. It may be prepared by burning carbon in excess of air or oxygen, by the direct decomposition of many carbonates by heat, and by the decomposition of carbonates 307 with mineral acids, $M_2CO_8 + 2HCl = 2MCl + H_2O + CO_2$. It is also formed in ordinary fermentation processes, in the combustion of all carbon compounds (oil, gas, candles, coal, &c.), and in the process of respiration.

It is a colourless gas, possessing a faint pungent smell and a slightly acid taste. It does not burn, and does not support ordinary combustion, but the alkali metals and magnesium, if strongly heated, will continue to burn in the gas with formation of oxides and liberation of carbon. Its specific gravity is 1.529 (air = 1). It is readily condensed, passing into the liquid condition at $0°$ C. under a pressure of 35 atmospheres. Its critical temperature is $31.35°$ C., and its critical pressure is 72.9 atmos. The liquid boils at $-78.2°$ C. (1 atmo.), and by rapid evaporation can be made to solidify to a snow-white solid which melts at $-65°$ C.(see LIQUID GASES). Carbon dioxide is moderately soluble in water, its coefficient of solubility at $0°$ C. being 1.7977 (R. Bunsen). It is still more soluble in alcohol. The solution of the gas in water shows a faintly acid reaction and is supposed to contain*carbonic acid*,

H_2CO_3. The gas is rapidly absorbed by solutions of the caustic alkalis, with the production of alkaline carbonates ($q.v.$), and it combines readily with potassium hydride to form potassium formate. It unites directly with ammonia gas to form ammonium carbamate, NH_2COONH_4. It may be readily recognized by the white precipitate which it forms when passed through lime or baryta water. Carbon dioxide dissociates, when strongly heated, into carbon monoxide and oxygen, the reaction being a balanced action; the extent of dissociation for varying temperatures and pressures has been calculated by H. Le Chatelier (*Zeit. Phys. Chem.*, 1888, 2, p. 782; see H. Sainte-Claire Deville, *Comptes rendus*, 1863, 56, p. 195 et seq.). The volume composition of carbon dioxide is determined by burning carbon in oxygen, when it is found that the volume of carbon dioxide formed is the same as that of the oxygen required for its production, hence carbon dioxide contains its own volume of oxygen. Carbon dioxide finds industrial application in the preparation of soda by the Solvay process, in the sugar industry, in the manufacture of mineral waters, and in the artificial production of ice.

Carbonyl chloride (phosgene), $COCl_2$, was first obtained by John Davy (*Phil. Trans.*, 1812, 40, p. 220). It may be prepared by the direct union of carbon monoxide and chlorine in sunlight (Th. Wilm and G. Wischin, *Ann.*, 1868, 14, p. 150); by the action of phosphorus pentoxide on carbon tetrachloride at 200-210° C. (G. Gustavson, *Ber.*, 1872, 5, p. 30), $4CCl_4 + P_4O_{10} = 2CO_2 + 4POCl_3 + 2COCl_2$; by the oxidation of chloroform with chromic acid mixture (A. Emmerling and B. Lengyel, *Ber.*, 1869, 2, p. 54), $4CHCl_3 + 3O_2 = 4COCl_2 + 2H_2O + 2Cl_2$; or most conveniently by heating carbon tetrachloride with fuming sulphuric acid (H. Erdmann, *Ber.*, 1893, 26, p. 1993), $2SO_3 + CCl_4 = S_2O_5Cl_2 + COCl_2$.

It is a colourless gas, possessing an unpleasant pungent smell. Its vapour density is 3.46 (air = 1). It may be condensed to a liquid, which boils at 8° C. It is readily soluble in benzene, glacial acetic acid, and in many hydrocarbons. Water decomposes it violently, with formation of carbon dioxide and hydrochloric acid. It reacts with alcohol to form chlorcarbonic ester and ultimately diethyl carbonate (see CARBONATES), and with ammonia it yields urea ($q.v.$). It is employed commercially in the production of colouring matters (see BENZOPHENONE), and for various synthetic processes.

Carbon oxysulphide, COS, was first prepared by C. Than in 1867 (*Ann. Suppl.*, 5, p. 236) by passing carbon monoxide and sulphur vapour through a tube at a moderate heat. It is also formed by the action of sulphuretted hydrogen on the isocyanic esters, $2CONC_2H_5 + H_2S = COS + CO(NHC_2H_5)_2$, by the action of concentrated sulphuric acid on the isothiocyanic esters, $RNCS + H_2O = COS + RNH_2$, or of dilute sulphuric acid on the thiocyanates. In the latter reaction various other compounds, such as carbon dioxide, carbon bisulphide and hydrocyanic acid, are produced. They are removed by passing the vapours in succession through concentrated solutions of the caustic alkalis, concentrated sulphuric acid, and triethyl phosphine; the residual gas is then purified by liquefaction (W. Hempel, *Zeit. angew. Chemie*, 1901, 14, p. 865). It is also formed when sulphur trioxide reacts with carbon bisulphide at 100° C., $CS_2 + 3SO_3 = COS + 4SO_2$, and by the decomposition of ethyl potassium thiocarbonate with hydrochloric acid, $CO(OC_2H_5)SK + HCl = COS + KCl + C_2H_5OH$. It is a colourless, odourless gas, which burns with a blue flame and is decomposed by heat. Its vapour density is 2.1046 (air = 1). The liquefied gas boils at −47° C. under atmospheric pressure. It is soluble in water; the aqueous solution gradually decomposes on standing, forming carbon dioxide and sulphuretted hydrogen. It is easily soluble in solutions of the caustic alkalis, provided they are not too concentrated, forming solutions of alkaline carbonates and sulphides, $COS + 4KHO = K_2CO_3 + K_2S + 2H_2O$.

CARBONADO, a name given in Brazil to a dark massive form of impure diamond, known also as "carbonate" and in trade simply as carbon. It is sometimes called black diamond. Generally it is found in small masses of irregular polyhedral form, black, brown or dark-grey in colour, with a dull resinoid lustre; and breaking with a granular fracture, paler in colour, and in some cases much resembling that of fine-grained steel. Being slightly cellular, its specific gravity is rather less than that of crystallized diamond. It is found almost exclusively in the state of Bahia in Brazil, where it occurs in the *cascalho* or diamond-bearing gravel. Borneo also yields it in small quantity. Formerly of little or no value, it came into use on the introduction of Leschot's diamond-drills, and is now extremely valuable for mounting in the steel crowns used for diamond-boring. Having no cleavage, the carbon is less liable to fracture on the rotation of the drill than is crystallized diamond. The largest piece of carbonado ever recorded was found in Bahia in 1895, and weighed 3150 carats. Pieces of large size are, however, relatively less valuable than those of moderate dimensions, since they require the expenditure of much labour in reducing them to fragments of a suitable size for mounting in the drill-heads. Ilmenite has sometimes been mistaken in the South African mines for carbonado.

(F. W. R.*)

CARBONARI (an Italian word meaning "charcoal-burners"), the name of certain secret societies of a revolutionary tendency which played an active part in the history of Italy and France early in the 19th century. Societies of a similar nature had existed in other countries and epochs, but the stories of the derivation of the Carbonari from mysterious brotherhoods of the middle ages are purely fantastic. The Carbonari were probably an offshoot of the Freemasons, from whom they differed in important particulars, and first began to assume importance in southern Italy during the Napoleonic wars. In the reign (1808-1815) of Joachim Murat a number of secret societies arose in various parts of the country with the object of freeing it from foreign rule and obtaining constitutional liberties; they were ready to support the Neapolitan Bourbons or Murat, if either had fulfilled these aspirations. Their watch-words were freedom and independence, but they were not agreed as to any particular form of government to be afterwards established. Murat's minister of police was a certain Malghella (a Genoese), who favoured the Carbonari movement, and was indeed the instigator of all that was Italian in the king's policy. Murat himself had at first protected the sectarians, especially when he was quarrelling with Napoleon, but later, Lord William Bentinck entered into negotiations with them from Sicily, where he represented Great Britain, through their leader Vincenzo Federici (known as Capobianco), holding out promises of a constitution for Naples similar to that which had been established in Sicily under British auspices in 1812. Some Carbonarist disorders having broken out in Calabria, Murat sent General Manhès against the rebels; the movement was ruthlessly quelled and Capobianco hanged in September 1813 (see Greco, *Intorno al tentativo dei Carbonari di Citeriore Calabria nel 1813*). But Malghella continued secretly to protect the Carbonari and even to organize them, so that on the return of the Bourbons in 1815 King Ferdinand IV. found his kingdom swarming with them. The society comprised nobles, officers of the army, small landlords, government officials, peasants and even priests. Its organization was both curious and mysterious, and had a fantastic ritual full of symbols taken from the Christian religion, as well as from the trade of charcoal-burning, which was extensively practised in the mountains of the Abruzzi and Calabria. A lodge was called a *vendita* (sale), members saluted each other as *buoni cugini* (good cousins), God was the "Grand Master of the Universe," Christ the "Honorary Grand Master," also known as "the Lamb," and every Carbonaro was pledged to deliver the Lamb from the Wolf, *i.e.* tyranny. Its red, blue and black flag was the standard of revolution in Italy until substituted by the red, white and green in 1831.

When King Ferdinand felt himself securely re-established at Naples he determined to exterminate the Carbonari, and to this end his minister of police, the prince of Canosa, set up another secret society called the *Calderai del Contrappeso* (braziers of the counterpoise), recruited from the brigands and the dregs of the people, who committed hideous excesses against supposed Liberals, but failed to exterminate the movement. On the contrary, Carbonarism flourished and spread to other parts of Italy, and countless lodges sprang up, their adherents comprising persons in all ranks of society, including, it is said, some of royal blood, who had patriotic sentiments and desired to see Italy free from foreigners. In Romagna the movement was taken up with enthusiasm, but it also led to a certain number of murders owing to the fiery character of the Romagnols, although its criminal record is on the whole a very small one. Among the foreigners who joined it for love of Italy was Lord Byron. The first rising actively promoted by the Carbonari was the Neapolitan revolution of 1820. Several regiments were composed entirely of persons affiliated to the society, and on the 1st of July a military mutiny broke out at Monteforte, led by two officers named Morelli and Silvati, to the cry of "God, the King and the Constitution." The troops sent against them, under General Pepe, himself a Carbonaro, sympathized with the mutineers, and the king, being powerless to resist, granted the constitution (13th of July), which he swore on the altar to observe. But the Carbonari were unable to carry on the government, and after the separatist revolt of Sicily had broken out the king went to the congress of Laibach, and obtained from the emperor of Austria the loan of an army with which to restore the autocracy. He returned to Naples early in 1821 with 50,000 Austrians, defeated the constitutionalists under Pepe, dismissed parliament, and set to work to persecute all who had been in any way connected with the movement.

A similar movement broke out in Piedmont in March 1821. Here as in Naples the Carbonari comprised many men of rank, such as Santorre di Santarosa, Count San Marzano, Giacinto di Collegno, and Count Moffa di Lisio, all officers in the army, and they were more or less encouraged by Charles Albert, the heir-presumptive to the throne. The rising was crushed, and a number of the leaders were condemned to death or long terms of imprisonment, but most of them escaped. At Milan there was only the vaguest attempt at conspiracy; but Silvio Pellico, Maroncelli and Count Confalonieri were implicated as having invited the Piedmontese to invade Lombardy, and were condemned to pass many years in the dungeons of the Spielberg.

The French revolution of 1830 had its echo in Italy, and Carbonarism raised its head in Parma, Modena and Romagna the following year. In the papal states a society called the Sanfedisti or Bande della Santa Fede had been formed to checkmate the Carbonari, and their behaviour and character resembled those of the Calderai of Naples. In 1831 Romagna and the Marches rose in rebellion and shook off the papal yoke with astonishing ease. At Parma the duchess, having rejected the demand for a constitution, left the city and returned under Austrian protection. At Modena, Duke Francis IV., the worst of all Italian tyrants, was expelled by a Carbonarist rising, and a dictatorship was established under Biagio Nardi on the 5th of February. Francis returned with an Austrian force and hanged the conspirators, including Ciro Menotti. The Austrians occupied Romagna and restored the province to the pope, but though many arrests of Carbonari were made there were no executions. Among those implicated in the Carbonarist movement was Louis Napoleon, who even in after years, when he was ruling France as Napoleon III., never quite forgot that he had once been a conspirator, a fact which influenced his Italian policy. The Austrians retired from Romagna and the Marches in July 1831, but Carbonarism and anarchy having broken out again, they returned, while the French occupied Ancona. The Carbonari after these events ceased to have much importance, their place being taken by the more energetic Giovane Italia Society presided over by Mazzini.

In France, Carbonarism began to take root about 1820, and was more thoroughly organized than in Italy. The example of the Spanish and Italian revolutions incited the French Carbonari, and risings occurred at Belfort, Thouars, La Rochelle and other towns in 1821, which though easily quelled revealed the nature and organization of the movement. The Carbonarist lodges proved active centres of discontent until 1830, when, after contributing to the July revolution of that year, most of their members adhered to Louis Philippe's government.

The Carbonarist movement undoubtedly played an important part in the Italian Risorgimento, and if it did not actively contribute to the wars and revolutions of 1848-49, 1859-60 and 1866, it prepared the way for those events. One of its chief merits was that it brought Italians of different classes and provinces together, and taught them to work in harmony for the overthrow of tyranny and foreign rule.

BIBLIOGRAPHY.—Much information on the Carbonari will be found in R.M. Johnston's *Napoleonic Empire in Southern Italy* (2 vols., London, 1904), which contains a full bibliography; D. Spadoni's *Sette, cospirazioni, e cospiratori* (Turin, 1904) is an excellent monograph; *Memoirs of the Secret Societies of Southern Italy*, said to be by one Bertoldi or Bartholdy (London, 1821, Ital. transl. by A.M. Cavallotti, Rome, 1904); Saint-Edme,*Constitution et organisation des Carbonari*, P. Colletta, *Storia del Reame di Napoli* (Florence, 1848); B. King, *A History of Italian Unity* (London, 1899), with bibliography.

CARBONATES. (1) The metallic carbonates are the salts of carbonic acid, H2CO3. Many are found as minerals, the more important of such naturally occurring carbonates being cerussite (lead carbonate, PbCO3), malachite and azurite (both basic copper carbonates), calamine (zinc carbonate, ZnCO3), witherite (barium carbonate, BaCO3), strontianite (strontium carbonate, SrCO3), calcite (calcium carbonate, CaCO3), dolomite (calcium magnesium carbonate, CaCO3·MgCO3), and sodium carbonate, Na2CO3. Most metals form carbonates (aluminium and chromium are exceptions), the alkali metals yielding both acid and normal carbonates of the types MHCO3 and M2CO3 (M = one atom of a monovalent metal); whilst bismuth, copper and magnesium appear only to form basic carbonates. The acid carbonates of the alkali metals can be prepared by saturating an aqueous solution of the alkaline hydroxide with carbon dioxide, M·OH + CO2 = MHCO3, and from these acid salts the normal salts may be obtained by gentle heating, carbon dioxide and water being produced at the same time, 2MHCO3 = M2CO3 + HO2 + CO2. Most other carbonates are formed by precipitation of salts of the metals by means of alkaline carbonates. All carbonates, except those of the alkali metals and of thallium, are insoluble in water; and the majority decompose when heated strongly, carbon dioxide being liberated and a residue of an oxide of the metal left. The alkaline carbonates undergo only a very slight decomposition, even at a very bright red heat. The carbonates are decomposed by mineral acids, with formation of the corresponding salt of the acid, and liberation of carbon dioxide. Many carbonates which are insoluble in water dissolve in water containing carbon dioxide. The individual carbonates are described under the various metals.

(2) The organic carbonates are the esters of carbonic acid, H2CO3, and of the unknown ortho-carbonic acid, C(OH)4. The acid esters of carbonic acid of the type HO·CO·OR are not known in the free state, but J.B. Dumas obtained barium methyl carbonate by the action of carbon dioxide on baryta dissolved in methyl alcohol (*Ann.*, 1840, 35, p. 283).

Potassium ethyl carbonate, KO·CO·OC2H5, is obtained in the form of pearly scales when carbon dioxide is passed into an alcoholic solution of potassium ethylate, CO2 + KOC2H5 = KO·CO·OC2H5. It is not very stable, water decomposing it into alcohol and the alkaline carbonate. The normal esters may be prepared by the action of silver carbonate on the alkyl iodides, or by the action of alcohols on the chlorcarbonic esters. These normal esters are colourless, pleasant-smelling liquids, which are readily soluble in water. They show all the reactions of esters, being readily hydrolysed by caustic alkalis, and reacting with ammonia to produce carbamic esters and urea. By heating with phosphorus pentachloride an alkyl group is eliminated and a chlorcarbonic ester formed. Dimethylcarbonate, CO(OCH3)2, is a colourless liquid, which boils at 90.6° C., and is prepared by heating the methyl ester of chlorcarbonic acid with lead oxide. Diethylcarbonate, CO(OC2H5)2, is a colourless liquid, which boils at 125.8° C.; its specific gravity is 0.978 (20°) [H. Kopp]. When it is heated to 120° C. with sodium ethylate it decomposes into ethyl ether and sodium ethyl carbonate (A. Geuther, *Zeit. f. Chemie*, 1868).

Ortho-carbonic ester, C(OC2H5)4 is formed by the action of sodium ethylate on chlorpicrin (H. Bassett, *Ann.*, 1864, 132, p. 54), CCl3NO2 + 4C2H5ONa = C(OC2H5)4 + NaNO2 + 3NaCl. It is an ethereal-smelling liquid, which boils at 158-159° C., and has a specific 309gravity of 0.925. When heated with ammonia it yields guanidine, and on boiling with alcoholic potash it yields potassium carbonate.

Chlorcarbonic ester, Cl·CO·OC2H5, is formed by the addition of well-cooled absolute alcohol to phosgene (carbonyl chloride). It is a pungent-smelling liquid, which fumes strongly on exposure to air. It boils at 93.1°C., and has a specific gravity of 1.144 (15°C.). When heated with ammonia it yields urethane. Sodium amalgam converts it into formic acid; whilst with alcohol it yields the normal carbonic ester. It is easily broken down by many substances (aluminium chloride, zinc chloride, &c.) into ethyl chloride and carbon dioxide.

Percarbonates.—Barium percarbonate, BaCO4, is obtained by passing an excess of carbon dioxide into water containing barium peroxide in suspension; it is fairly stable, and yields hydrogen peroxide when treated with acids (E. Merck, *Abs. J.C.S.*, 1907, ii. p. 859). Sodium percarbonates of the formulae Na2CO4, Na2C2O6, Na2CO5, NaHCO4 (two isomers) are obtained by the action of gaseous or solid carbon dioxide on the peroxides Na2O2, Na2O3, NaHO2 (two isomers) in the presence of water at a low temperature (R. Wolffenstein and E. Peltner, *Ber.*, 1908, 41, pp. 275, 280). Potassium percarbonate, K2C2O6, is obtained in the electrolysis of potassium carbonate at −10 to −15°.

CARBON BISULPHIDE, CS2, a chemical product first discovered in 1796 by W.A. Lampadius, who obtained it by heating a mixture of charcoal and pyrites. It may be more conveniently prepared by passing the vapour of sulphur over red hot charcoal, the uncondensed gases so produced being led into a tower containing plates over which a vegetable oil is allowed to flow in order to absorb any carbon bisulphide vapour, and then into a second tower containing lime, which absorbs any sulphuretted hydrogen. The crude product is very impure and possesses an offensive smell; it may be purified by forcing a fine spray of lime water through the liquid until the escaping water is quite clear, the washed bisulphide being then mixed with a little colourless oil and distilled at a low temperature. For further methods of purification see J. Singer (*Journ. of Soc. Chem. Ind.*, 1889, p. 93), Th. Sidot (*Jahresb.*, 1869, p. 243), E. Allary (*Bull. de la Soc. Chim.*, 1881, 35, p. 491), E. Obach (*Jour. prak. Chem.*, 1882 (2), 26, p. 282).

When perfectly pure, carbon bisulphide is a colourless, somewhat pleasant smelling, highly refractive liquid, of specific gravity 1.2661 (18°/4°) (J.W. Brühl) or 1.29215 (0°/4°) (T.E. Thorpe). It boils at 46.04° C. (T.E. Thorpe, *Journ. Chem. Soc.*, 1880, 37, p. 364). Its critical temperature is 277.7° C., and its critical pressure is 78.1 atmos. (J. Dewar, *Chem. News*, 1885, 51, p. 27). It solidifies at about −116°C., and liquefies again at about −110°C. (K. Olszewski, *Jahresb.*, 1883, p. 75). It is a mono-molecular liquid (W. Ramsay and J. Shields, *Jour. Chem. Soc.*, 1893, 63, p. 1089). It is very volatile, the vapour being heavy and very inflammable. It burns with a pale blue flame to form carbon dioxide and sulphur dioxide. It is almost insoluble in water, but mixes in all proportions with absolute alcohol, ether, benzene and various oils. It is a good solvent for sulphur, phosphorus, wax, iodine, &c. It dissociates when heated to a sufficiently high temperature. A mixture of carbon bisulphide vapour and nitric oxide burns with a very intense blue-coloured flame, which is very rich in the violet or actinic rays. When heated with water in a sealed tube to 150° C. it yields carbon dioxide and sulphuretted hydrogen. Zinc and hydrochloric acid reduce it to tri-thioformaldehyde (CH2S)3 (A. Girard, *Comptes rendus*, 1856, 43, p. 396). When passed through a red-hot tube with chlorine it yields carbon tetrachloride and sulphur chloride (H. Kolbe). Potassium, when heated, burns in the vapour of carbon bisulphide, forming potassium sulphide and liberating carbon. In contact with chlorine monoxide it forms carbonyl chloride and thionyl chloride (P. Schützenberger, *Ber.*, 1869, 2, p. 219). When passed with carbon dioxide through a red-hot tube it yields carbon oxysulphide, COS (C. Winkler), and when passed over sodamide it yields ammonium thiocyanate. A mixture of carbon bisulphide vapour and sulphuretted hydrogen, when passed over heated copper, gives, amongst other products, some methane.

Carbon bisulphide slowly oxidizes on exposure to air, but by the action of potassium permanganate or chromic acid it is readily oxidized to carbon dioxide and sulphuric acid. By the action of aqueous alkalis, carbon bisulphide is converted into a mixture of an alkaline carbonate and an alkaline thiocarbonate (J. Berzelius, *Pogg. Ann.*, 1825, 6, p. 444), 6KHO + 3CS2 = K2CO3 + 2K2CS3 + 3H2O; on the other hand, an alcoholic solution of a caustic alkali converts it into a xanthate (A. Vogel, *Jahresb.*, 1853, p. 643),

$$CS2 + KHO + R \cdot OH = H2O + RO \cdot CS \cdot SK.$$

Aqueous and alcoholic solutions of ammonia convert carbon bisulphide into ammonium dithiocarbamate, which readily breaks down into ammonium thiocyanate and sulphuretted hydrogen (A.W. Hofmann),

$$CS2 + 2NH3 \rightarrow NH2 \cdot CSS \cdot NH4 \rightarrow H2S + NH4CNS.$$

Carbon bisulphide combines with primary amines to form alkyl dithiocarbamates, which when heated lose sulphuretted hydrogen and leave a residue of a dialkyl thio-urea,

121

$$CS2 + 2R \cdot NH2 \rightarrow R \cdot NH \cdot CSS \cdot NH3R \rightarrow CS(NHR)2 + H2S;$$

or if the aqueous solution of the dithiocarbamate be boiled with mercuric chloride or silver nitrate solution, a mustard oil (*q.v.*) is formed,

$$R \cdot NH \cdot CSS \cdot NH3R + HgCl2 \rightarrow Hg(R \cdot NH \cdot CSS)2 \rightarrow 2RNCS + HgS + H2S.$$

Carbon bisulphide is used as a solvent for caoutchouc, for extracting essential oils, as a germicide, and as an insecticide.

Carbon monosulphide, CS, is formed when a silent electric discharge is passed through a mixture of carbon bisulphide vapour and hydrogen or carbon monoxide (S.M. Losanitsch and M.Z. Jovitschitsch, *Ber.*, 1897, 30. p. 135).

CARBONDALE, a city of Lackawanna county, Pennsylvania, U.S.A., on the Lackawanna river, 16 m. N.E. of Scranton. Pop. (1890) 10,833; (1900) 13,536, of whom 2553 were foreign-born; (1910 census) 17,040. Carbondale is served by the Erie, the Delaware & Hudson (which has machine shops here), and the New York, Ontario & Western railways. The city lies near the upper end of the Lackawanna valley, and the scenery of the surrounding mountains makes it a summer resort of some importance. It has a public library, a small park, an emergency hospital and the Carbondale city private hospital. Carbondale is situated in one of the richest anthracite coal regions of the state, and its principal interest is in coal. Among its manufactures are foundry and machine shop products, sheet-iron, silk, glass, thermometers and hydrometers, bobbins and refrigerating machines. The value of the city's factory products increased from $1,146,181 in 1900 to $2,315,695 in 1905, or 102%. The settlement of the place began in 1824 with the opening of the coal mines, and Carbondale was chartered as a city in 1851.

CARBONIC ACID, in chemistry, properly H2CO3, the acid assumed to be formed when carbon dioxide is dissolved in water; its salts are termed carbonates. The name is also given to the neutral carbon dioxide from its power of forming salts with oxides, and on account of the acid nature of its solution; and, although not systematic, this use is very common.

CARBONIFEROUS SYSTEM, in geology, the whole of the great series of stratified rocks and associated volcanic rocks which occur above the Devonian or Old Red Sandstone and below the Permian or Triassic systems, belonging to the Carboniferous period. The name was first applied by W.D. Conybeare in 1821 to the coal-bearing strata of England and Wales, including the related grits and limestones immediately beneath them. The term is a relic of that early period in the history of stratigraphy when each group of strata was supposed to be distinguished by some peculiar lithological character. In this case the carbonaceous beds—coal-seams—naturally appealed most strongly to the imagination, and the name is a good one, notwithstanding the fact that coal-seams occupy but a small fraction of the total thickness of the Carboniferous system; and although subsequent investigations have demonstrated the existence of coal in other geological formations, in none of these does it play so prominent a part. The stratified rocks of this system include marine limestones, shales and sandstones; estuarine, lagoonal and fresh-water shales, sandstones and marls with beds of coal, oil-bearing rocks, gypsum and salt.

In many parts of the world there is no sharp line of demarcation between the Devonian and the Carboniferous rocks; neither can the fossil faunas and floras be clearly separated at any well-defined line; this is true in Britain, Belgium, Russia, Westphalia and parts of North America. Again, at the summit of the Carboniferous series, both the rocks and their fossil contents merge gradually into those of the succeeding Permian 310system, as in Russia, Bohemia, the Saar region and Texas. This has led certain geologists to classify the Devonian, Carboniferous and Permian into one grand system; E. Renevier in 1874 proposed to include these three into a single "Carbonique" system, later he retained only the two latter groups. There seems to be sufficient reason, however, to maintain each of these groups as a separate system and limit the term Carboniferous (*carbonifèrien*) in the manner indicated above. At the same time it must be remembered that there is in India, South Africa, the

Urals, in Australasia and parts of North America an important series of rocks, with a "Permo-Carboniferous" fauna, which constitutes a passage formation between the Carboniferous, *sensu stricto*, and Jurassic rocks.

Stratigraphy.—No assemblage of stratified rocks has received such careful and detailed examination as the Carboniferous system; consequently our knowledge of the stratigraphical sequence in isolated local areas, where the coals have been exploited, is very full.

In Europe, the system is very completely developed in the British Isles, where was made the first successful attempt at a classification of its various members, although at a somewhat earlier date Omalius d'Halloy had recognized a *terrain bituminifère* or coal-bearing series in the Belgian region.

The area within which the Carboniferous rocks of Britain occur is sufficiently extensive to contain more than one type of the system, and thus to cast much light on the varied geographical conditions under which these rocks were accumulated. In prosecuting the study of this part of British geology it is soon discovered, and it is essential to bear in mind, that, during the Carboniferous period, the land whence the chief supplies of sediment were derived rose mainly to the north and north-west, as it seems to have done from very early geological time. While therefore the centre and south of England lay under clear water of moderate depth, the north of the country and the south of Scotland were covered by shallow water, which was continually receiving sand and mud from the adjacent northern land. Hence vertical sections of the Carboniferous formations of Britain differ greatly according to the districts in which they are taken.

The Coal-Measures and Millstone Grit are usually grouped together in the *Upper Carboniferous*, the Carboniferous Limestone series constituting the *Lower Carboniferous*.

In addition to the above broad subdivisions, Murchison and Sedgwick, when working upon the rocks of Devonshire and Cornwall, recognized, with the assistance of W. Lonsdale, another phase of sedimentation. This comprised dark shales, with grits and thin limestones and thin, impure coals, locally called "culm" (*q.v.*). These geologists appropriated the term "culm" for the whole of this facies in the west of England, and subsequently traced the same type on the European continent, where it is widely developed in the western centre.

Besides the considerable exposed area of Carboniferous rocks in Great Britain, there is as much or more that is covered by younger formations; this is true particularly of the eastern side of England and the south-eastern counties, where the coal-measures have already been found at Dover.

From England, Carboniferous rocks can be followed across northern and central France, into Germany, Bohemia, the Alps, Italy and Spain. In Russia this system occupies some 30,000 sq. m., and it extends northward at least as far as Spitsbergen. Carboniferous rocks are present in North and South Africa, and in India and Australasia; in China they cover thousands of square miles, and in the United States and British North America they occupy no less than 200,000 sq. m.; they are known also in South America.

The subjoined table expresses the typical subdivisions which can be recognized, with modifications, in the United Kingdom.

oal Me asu res.	Upper: Red and grey sandstones, marls and clays with occasional breccias, thin coals and limestones with *Spirorbis*, workable coals in the South Wales, Bristol, Somerset and Forest of Dean coalfields.
	Middle: Sandstones, marls, shales and the most important of the British coals.
	Lower: Flaggy hard sandstones (ganister), shales and thin coal seams.
illst one Gri t.	Grits (coarse and fine), shales, thin coal seams and occasional thin limestones. The fossil plants connect this group with the coal-measures; the marine fossils have, to some extent, a Carboniferous limestone aspect.
arb	*Upper black shales* with thin limestones (Pendleside group) connecting this series with the Millstone grit above.

onif ero us Lim esto ne Seri es.	The *thick, main or scaur limestone* (mountain limestone) of the centre and south of England, Wales and Ireland, which splits up in the Yorkshire dales (Yoredale group) into a succession of stout limestone beds between beds of sandstone and shale, and becomes increasingly detrital in character as it is traced northwards. *Lower limestone shales* of the south and centre of England with marine fossils, and the Calciferous Sandstone group of Scotland with marine, estuarine and terrestrial fossils.

(See BERNICIAN, TUEDIAN and AVONIAN.)

At an early period, owing to the immense commercial importance of the coal seams, it became the practice to distinguish a "productive" (*flotzfuhrend, terrain houiller*) and an "unproductive," barren (*flotzleerer*) Lower Carboniferous; these two groups correspond in North America to the "Carboniferous" and "Sub-Carboniferous" respectively, or, as they are now sometimes styled, the "Pennsylvanian" and "Mississippian." But it was soon discovered that the "productive" beds were not regularly restricted to the upper or younger division, and, as E. Kayser points out, the real state of the matter is more accurately represented by the subjoined tabular scheme.

	Continental Type of Deposit.	Marine Type of Formation.	
Upper Carboniferous	Upper*Productive*Carbo niferous	Younger Carboniferous limestone and the*Fusulina* limestone of Russia and Western North America	
Lower Carboniferous	Lower*Productive*Carbo niferous	C ulm (in part)	Lower Carboniferous limestone series

While the continental type of deposit, with its coal beds, was the earliest to be formed in certain areas, and the marine series came on later, in other regions this order was reversed. It should be observed, however, that the repeated intercalation of marine deposits within the continental series and the frequent occurrence of thin coaly layers in the marine series makes any hard and fast distinction of this kind impossible.

The so-called "unproductive" or barren strata, that is, those without workable coals, are not always limestones; quite as often they are shales, red sandstones and red marls.

In subdividing the strata of the Carboniferous system and correlating the major divisions in different areas, just as in other great systems, use has to be made of the fossil contents of the rocks; stratigraphical units, based on lithology, are useless for this purpose. The groups of organisms utilized for zoning and correlation by different workers include brachiopods, pelecypods, cephalopods, corals, fishes and plants; and the results of the comparison of the faunas and floras of different areas where Carboniferous rocks occur are generalized in the table below.

The relative value of any group of animals or plants for the correlation of distant areas must vary greatly with the varying conditions of sedimentation and with the precise definition of the zonal species and with many other factors. It is found that the subdivisions in this system demanded by palaeobotanists do not always coincide with those acknowledged by palaeozoologists; nevertheless there is general agreement as to the main divisional lines.

Breaks in the Stratigraphic Sequence.—The sequence of Carboniferous strata is not everywhere one of unbroken continuity. From central France eastward towards the Carpathians only later portions of the system are found. These generally rest upon crystalline rocks, but in places they contain evidence of the denuded surfaces of Lower Carboniferous, as in the basin of Charleroi, where the equivalent of 311the Millstone Grit contains fragments of chert which can only have come from the waste of the earlier limestones. This unconformity is generally found about the same horizon in the continental Culm areas, and it occurs again in the western part of the English Culm.

Tabular Statement of the Principal Subdivisions of the Carboniferous System.

		European Development.	America.	Predominant Plant Types.
Upper Carboniferous.	Coal Measures = Terrain Houiller.	Ouralien = (marine type) and Stephanien = (continental type)	Pennsylvanian	Ferns and Annularias
		Moscovien = (marine type) and Westphalien = (continental type)		Sigillarias and Calamites
Lower Carboniferous.	Carboniferous Limestone Series.	Dinantien = (marine pelagic, including continental deposits in some areas) and Culm = (marine littoral)	Mississippian	Lycopods

In the eastern border of the Rhenish Schiefergebirge the Permian rests unconformably upon Lower Carboniferous rocks. In the United States, in Missouri, Pennsylvania, West Virginia, Kentucky, Ohio and elsewhere, there is an unconformable junction between the Lower and Upper Carboniferous, representing an interval of time during which the lower member was strongly eroded; it has even been proposed to regard the Mississippian (Lower Carboniferous) as a distinct geological period, mainly on account of this break in the succession.

Thickness of Carboniferous Rocks.—The great variety of conditions under which the sediments and limestones were formed naturally produced corresponding inequalities in the thickness. In the Eurasian land area the greatest thickness of Carboniferous rocks is in the west; in North America it is in the east. In Britain the Carboniferous limestone series is 2000-3500 ft. thick; in the Ural mountains it is over 4500 ft.; the Culm in Moravia is credited with the enormous thickness of over 42,000 ft. The Upper Carboniferous in Lancashire is from 12,000 to 13,000 ft.; elsewhere in Britain it is thinner. In western Germany this portion attains a thickness of 10,000 ft. In Pennsylvania the sandstone and shale, at its maximum, reaches 4400 ft., but even within the limits of the state this formation has thinned out to no more than 300 ft. in places. In Colorado the Lower Carboniferous is only 400-500 ft. thick; while the limestones of the Mississippi basin amount to 1500 ft. and in Virginia are 2000 ft. thick.

Life of the Carboniferous Period.—We have seen that in the Carboniferous rocks there are two phases of sedimentation, the one marine, the other continental; corresponding with these there are two distinct faunal facies.

(1) *Fauna of the Marine Strata.*—Numerically, the most important inhabitants of the clear Carboniferous seas were the crinoids, corals, Foraminifera and brachiopods. Each of these groups contributed at one place or another towards the upbuilding of great masses of limestone. For the first time in the earth's history we find Foraminifera taking a prominent part in the marine faunas; the genus *Fusulina* was abundant in what is now Russia, China, Japan, North America; *Valvulina* had a wide range, as also had *Endothyra* and *Archaediscus; Saccammina* is a form well known in Britain and Belgium, and many others have been described; some Carboniferous genera are still extant. Radiolaria are found in cherts in the Culm of Devonshire and Cornwall, in Russia, Germany and elsewhere. Sponges are represented by spicules and anchor ropes. Corals, both reef-builders and others, flourished in the clearer waters; rugose forms are represented by Amplexoid, Zaphrentid and Cyathophyllid types, and by*Lithostrotion* and *Phillipsastraea;* common tabulate forms

125

are *Chaetetes, Chladochonus, Michelinia,* &c. Amongst the echinoderms crinoids were the most numerous individually, dense submarine thickets of the long-stemmed kinds appear to have flourished in many places where their remains consolidated into thick beds of rock; prominent genera are *Cyathocrinus, Woodocrinus, Actinocrinus;* sea-urchins, *Archaeocidaris, Palaeechinus,*&c., were present; while the curious extinct Blastoids, which included the groups of *Pentremitidae* and *Codasteridae,* attained their maximum development.

Annelids (*Spirorbis, Serpulites,* &c.) are common fossils on certain horizons. The Bryozoa were also abundant in some regions (*Polypora, Fenestella*), including the remarkable form known as *Archimedes.*

Brachiopods occupied an important place; most typical were the Productids, some of which reached a great size and had very thick shells. Other common genera are *Spirifer, Chonetes, Athyris,* Rhynchonellids and Terebratulids, *Discina* and *Crania.* Some species had an almost world-wide range with only minor variations; such are *Productus semireticulatus, P. cora, P. pustulosus; Orthotetes (Streptorbynchus) crenistria, Dielasma hastata,* and many others.

Pelecypods among the true mollusca were increasing in numbers and importance (*Aviculopecten, Posidonomya*); *Nucula, Carbonicola, Edmondia, Conocardium, Modiola.* Gasteropods also were numerous (*Murchisonia, Euomphalus, Naticopsis*). The Pteropods were well represented by *Conularia* and *Bellerophon.* Amongst the Cephalopods, the most striking feature is the rise and development of the Goniatites (*Glyphioceras, Gastrioceras,* &c.); straight-shelled forms still lived on in some variety (*Orthoceras, Actinoceras*), along with numerous nautiloids.

Trilobites during this period sank to a very subordinate position, but Ostracods (*Cythere, Kirkbya, Beyrichia*) were abundant.

Many fish inhabited the Carboniferous seas and most of these were Elasmobranchs, sharks with crushing pavement teeth (*Psammodus*), adapted for grinding the shells of brachiopods, crustaceans, &c. Other sharks had piercing teeth (*Cladoselache* and *Cladodus*); some, the petalodonts, had peculiar cycloid cutting teeth. The Arthrodirans, so prominent during the Devonian period, disappeared before the close of the Carboniferous. Most of the sharks lived in the sea continuously, but the ganoids frequenting the coastal waters appear to have migrated inland. About 700 species of Carboniferous fish have been described largely from teeth, spines and dermal ossicles.

(2) *Flora and Fauna of the Lagoonal or Continental Facies.*—The strata deposited during this period are the earliest in which the remains of plants take a prominent place. The fossil plants which are found in the upper beds of the preceding Devonian system are so closely related to those in the Lower Carboniferous, that from a palaeobotanical standpoint the two form one indivisible period.

In the Lower Carboniferous the flora was composed of six great groups of plants, viz. the Equisetales (Horse-tails), the Lycopodiales (Club mosses), the Filicales (Ferns) and Cycadofilices, the Sphenophyllales and Cordaitales. These six groups were the dominant types throughout the period, but during Upper Carboniferous time three other groups arose, the Coniferales, the Cycadophyta, and the Ginkgoales (of which *Ginkgo biloba* is the only modern representative). Algae and fungi also were present, but there were no flowering plants. The true ferns, including tree ferns with a height of upwards of 60 ft., were associated with many plants possessing a fern-like habit (Cycadofilices) and others whose affinities have not yet been definitely determined. The fronds of some of these Carboniferous ferns are almost identical with those of living species. Probably many of the ferns were epiphytic. *Pecopteris, Cyclopteris, Neuropteris, Alethopteris, Sphenopteris*are common genera; *Megaphyton* and *Caulopteris* were tree ferns. Our modern diminutive "horse-tails" with scaly leaves were represented in the Carboniferous period by gigantic calamites, often with a diameter of 1 to 2 ft. and a height of 50 to 90 ft. The Carboniferous forerunners of the tiny club-moss were then great trees with dichotomously branching stems and crowded linear leaves, such as *Lepidodendron* (with its fruit cone called*Lepidostrobus*), *Halonia, Lepidophloios* and *Sigillaria,* the largest plants of the period, with trunks sometimes 5 ft. in diameter and 100 ft. high. The roots of several of these forms are known as *Stigmaria. Sphenophyllum* was a slender climbing plant with whorls of leaves, which was probably related both to the calamites and the lycopods. *Cordaites,* a tall plant (20-30 ft.) with yucca-like leaves, was related to the cycads and conifers; the catkin-like inflorescence, which bore yew-like

126

berries, is called *Cardiocarpus*. Many large trees which have been looked upon as conifers on account of their wood structure may perhaps belong more properly to the Cordaitales. True coniferous trees (*Walchia*) do appear at the top of the coal measures.

The animals preserved in the continental type of Carboniferous deposit naturally differ markedly from the fossil remains of the purely marine portions of the system. The inhabitants of the waters of this geographical phase include mollusca, which are supposed to have lived in brackish or fresh water, such as *Anthracomya, Naiadites, Carbonicola*, and many forms of Crustacea, *e.g.* (*Bairdia Carbonia*), phyllopods (*Estheria*), phyllocarids (*Acanthocaris, Dithyrocaris*), schizopods (*Anthrapalaemon*), Eurypterids (*Eurypterus, Glyptoscorpius*). Fishes were abundant, many of the smaller ganoids are beautifully preserved in an entire condition, other larger forms are represented by fin spines, teeth and bones; *Ctenodus, Uronemus, Acanthodes, Cheirodus, Gyracanthus* are characteristic genera.

Frequently a temporary return of marine conditions permitted the entombment of such salt water genera as *Lingula, Orbiculoidea, Productus* in the thin beds known as "marine bands."

Remains of air-breathing insects, myriapods and arachnids show that these forms of life were both well developed and individually numerous. Among the insects we find the Orthoptera, Neuroptera, Hemiptera and Coleoptera represented; cockroaches were particularly abundant; crickets, beetles, locusts, walking-stick insects, mayflies and bugs are found, but there were neither flies, moths, butterflies nor bees, which is no more than we should expect from the conditions of plant life. Many insects, &c., have been obtained from the coalfields of Saarbrück and Commentry, and from the hollow trunks of fossil trees in Nova Scotia. Certain British coalfields have yielded good specimens: *Archaeoptilus*, from the Derbyshire coalfield, had a spread of wing extending to more than 14 in.; some specimens (*Brodia*) still exhibit traces of brilliant wing colours. In the Nova Scotian tree trunks land snails (*Archaeozonites, Dendropupa*) have been found.

In the later Carboniferous rocks the earliest amphibians make their appearance in considerable numbers; they were all Stegocephalians (Labyrinthodonts) with long bodies, a head covered with bony plates and weak or undeveloped limbs. The largest were about 7 or 8 ft. long, the smallest only a few inches. Some were probably fluviatile in habit (*Loxomma, Anthracosaurus, Ophiderpeton*); others may have been terrestrial (*Dendrerpeton, Hylerpeton*). Certain footprints in the coal measures of Kansas have been supposed to belong to lacertilian or dinosaurian forms.

The Physical Conditions during the Period.—In western Europe the advent of the Carboniferous period was accompanied by the production of a series of synclines which permitted the formation of organic limestones, free from the sediments which generally characterized the concluding phases of the preceding Devonian deposition. The old land area still existed to the north, but doubtless much reduced in height; against this land, detrital deposits still continued to be formed, as in Scotland; while over central Ireland and central and northern England the clearer waters of the sea furnished a suitable home for countless corals, brachiopods and foraminifera and great beds of sea lilies; sponges flourished in many parts of the sea, and their remains contributed largely to the formation of the beds of chert. This clearer water extended from Ireland across north-central England and through South Wales and Somerset into Belgium and Westphalia; but a narrow ridge of elevated older rocks ran across the centre of England towards Belgium at this time.

Traced eastward into north Germany, Thuringia and Silesia, the limestones pass into the detrital culm formations, which owe their existence to a southern uplifted massif, the complement of the synclines already mentioned. Sediments approaching to the culm type, with similar flora and fauna, were deposited in synclinal hollows in parts of France and Spain.

Thus western Europe in early Carboniferous time was occupied by a series of constricted, gulf-like seas; and on account of the steady progress of intermittent warping movements of the crust, we find that the areas of clearer water, in which the limestone-building organisms could exist, were repeatedly able to spread, thus forming those thin limestones found interbedded with shale and sandstone which occur typically in the Yoredale district of Yorkshire and in the region to the north, and also in the culm deposits of central Europe. The spread of these limestones was repeatedly checked by the steady influx of detritus from the land during the pauses in movements of depression. Looking eastward, towards central and northern Russia, we find a wider and much more open sea; but the continental type of deposit prevailed in the northern portion, and here, as in Scotland, we find coal-beds amongst the sediments (Moscow basin). Farther south in the Donetz basin the coals only appear at the close of the Lower Carboniferous.

In North America, the crustal movements at the beginning of the period are less evident than in Europe, but a marked parallelism exists; for in the east, in the Appalachian tract, we find detrital sediments prevailing, while the open sea, with great deposits of limestone, lay out towards the west in the direction of that similar open sea which lay towards the east of Europe and extended through Asia.

The close of the early Carboniferous period was marked by an augmentation of the orogenic movements. The gentler synclines and anticlines of the earlier part of the period became accentuated, giving rise to pronounced mountain ridges, right across Europe.

This movement commenced in the central and western part of the continent and continued throughout the whole Carboniferous period. The mountains then formed have been called the "Palaeozoic Alps" by E. Kayser, the "Hercynian Mountains" by M. Bertrand. The most western range extended from Ireland through Wales and the south of England to the central plateau of France; this was the "Armorican range" of E. Suess. The eastern part of the chain passed from South France through the Vosges, the Black Forest, Thuringia, Harz, the Fichtelgebirge, Bohemia, the Sudetes, and possibly farther east; this constitutes the "Varischen Alps" of Suess.

The sea had gained somewhat at the beginning of the Carboniferous period in western Europe, but the effect of these movements, combined with the rapid formation of detrital deposits from the rising land areas, was to drive the sea steadily from the north towards the south, until the open sea (with limestones) was relegated to what is now the Mediterranean and to Russia and thence eastward. Similar events were meanwhile happening in North America, for the seas were steadily filled with sediments which drove them from the north-east towards the south-west, and doubtless those movements which at the close of this period uplifted the Appalachian mountains were already operative in the same direction.

The folding of the Ural mountains began in the earlier part of this period and was continued, after its close, into the Permian; and there are traces of uplifts in central Asia and Armenia.

None of these movements appears to have affected the southern hemisphere.

The net result of the erogenic movements was, that at the close of the period there existed a great northern continental mass, embracing Europe, North Asia and North America; and a great southern continental mass, including South America, Africa, Australia and India. Between these land masses lay a great Mediterranean sea—the "Tethys" of Suess.

The conditions under which the beds of coal were formed will be found described under that head; it will be sufficient to notice here that some coal seams were undoubtedly formed by jungle or swamp-like growths on the site of the deposit, and it is equally true that others were formed by the transport and deposition of vegetable detritus. The main point to observe in this connexion is that large tracts of land in many parts of the world were at a critical level as regards the sea, a condition highly favourable to frequent extensive incursions of marine waters over the low-lying areas in a period of extreme crustal instability.

Vulcanicity.—In intimate relationship with the mountain-building orogenic crustal movements was the prevalence of volcanic activity during the earlier part of this period. In the Lower Carboniferous rocks of Scotland intercalated volcanic rocks are strikingly abundant, and now form an important feature in the geology of the southern portion of that country. Of these rocks Sir Archibald Geikie says: "Two great phases or types of volcanic action during Carboniferous time may be recognized—(1) Plateaus, where the volcanic materials discharged copiously from many scattered openings now form broad tablelands or ranges of hills, sometimes many hundreds of square miles in extent and 1500 ft. or more in thickness; (2) Puys, where the ejections were often confined to the discharge of a small amount of fragmentary materials from a single independent vent." The plateau type was most extensively developed during the formation of the Calciferous Sandstone; the puy type was of somewhat later date. Basic lavas, with andesites, trachytes, tuffs and agglomerates are the most common Scottish rocks of this period. Similar eruptions, but on a much smaller scale, took place in other parts of Great Britain.

Granites, porphyries and porphyrites belonging to this period occur in the Saxon Erzgebirge, the Harz, Thüringerwald, Vosges, Brittany, Cornwall and Christiania. Porphyrites and tuffs are known in the French Carboniferous. In China, at the close of the period, there were enormous eruptions of melaphyre, porphyrite and quartz-porphyry. In North America, the principal region of volcanic activity lay in the west; great thicknesses of igneous rocks occur in the Lower Carboniferous rocks of British Columbia, and from the middle of the period until near its close volcanoes were active from Alaska to California. Igneous rocks of this period are found also in Australasia.

Climate.—That the vegetation during this period was unusually exuberant there can be no doubt, and that a general uniformity of climatic conditions prevailed is shown not only by the wide distribution of coal measures, but by the uniformity of plant types over the whole earth. It is well, however, to guard against an over-estimation of this exuberance; it must be borne in mind that the physiographic conditions were peculiarly favourable to the preservation of plant remains, conditions that do not appear to have obtained so completely in any other period. The climate, we may assume from the distribution of land and water, was generally moist, and it was probably mild if not warm; conditions favourable to the growth of certain types of plants. But there is no good evidence for an excess of carbon dioxide in the atmosphere—an assumption founded on the luxuriance of the vegetation, coupled with the fact that vulcanicity was active and wide-ranging. Carbon dioxide may have been present in the air in greater abundance in earlier periods than it is at present, but there is no reason to suppose that the percentage was appreciably higher in the Carboniferous period than it is now.

The occurrence of *red deposits* in western Australia, Scotland, the Ural mountains, in Michigan, Montana and Nova Scotia, &c., associated in some instances with the formation of gypsum and salt, clearly points to the existence of areas of excessive evaporation, such as are found in land-locked waters in regions where something like desert conditions prevail. The xerophytic structures found in some of the plants might seem to corroborate this view; but similar structures are assumed by many plants when dwelling in brackish marshes and morasses.

The abundance of corals in some of the Carboniferous seas and possibly also the large size of some of the Productids and foraminifera may be taken as evidence of warm or temperate waters.

In spite of the bulk of the evidence being in favour of geniality of climate, it is necessary to observe that certain deposits have been recognized as glacial; in the culm of the Frankenwald, in the coal basins of central France, and in central England, certain conglomeratic beds have been assigned, somewhat doubtfully, to this origin. They have also been regarded as the result of torrential action. Glacial deposits certainly do exist in the Permo-carboniferous formations, which are described under that head, but in the true Carboniferous system glaciation may be taken as not proven. The foreign boulders of granite, gneiss, &c., found in the coal-measures of some districts, are quite as likely to have been dropped by rafts of vegetation as to have been carried by floating icebergs.

313

Economic Products.—Foremost among the useful products of the Carboniferous rocks is the coal (*q.v.*) itself; but associated with the coal seams in Great Britain, North America and elsewhere, are very important beds of ironstone, fire-clay, terra-cotta clay, and occasionally oil shale and alum shale. Oil and gas are of importance in the Lower Carboniferous Pocono sandstone of West Virginia and in the Berea grit of Ohio, where brine also occurs.

In the Carboniferous Limestone series, the purer kinds of limestone are used for the manufacture of lime, bleaching powder and similar products, also as a flux in the smelting of iron; some of the less pure varieties are used in making cement. The beds of chert are utilized in the pottery industry, and some of the harder and more crystalline limestones are beautiful marbles, capable of taking a high polish.

129

The sandstones are used for building, and for millstones and grindstones. Within the Carboniferous rocks, but due to the action of various agencies long after their deposition, are important ore formations; such are the Rio Tinto ores of Spain, the lead and zinc ores and some haematite of the Pennine and Mendip hills and other British localities, and many ore regions in the United States.

REFERENCES.—For a good general account of the Carboniferous system, see A. Geikie, *Text Book of Geology*, vol. ii. (4th ed., 1903); and for the American development see T.C. Chamberlin and R.D. Salisbury, *Geology*, vol. ii. (1906). These two works give abundant references to the literature of the subject. See also, *Recent Additions to Geological Literature*, published annually by the Geological Society of London since 1893; and *Neues Jahrbuch fur Mineralogie* (Stuttgart).

(J. A. H.)

CARBORUNDUM, a silicide of carbon formed by the action of carbon on sand (silica) at high temperatures, which on account of its great hardness is an important abrasive, and also has possible applications in the metallurgy of iron and steel. Its name was derived from *carbon* and *corundum* (a form of alumina), from a mistaken view as to its composition. It was first obtained accidentally in 1891 by Acheson in America, when he was experimenting with the electric furnace in the hope of producing artificial diamonds. The experiments were followed up in an incandescence furnace, which on a larger scale is now employed for the industrial manufacture of the product. A full description of the process has been given in the *Journ. Soc. Chem. Industry*, 1897, vol. xvi. p. 863. The furnace is rectangular, about 16 ft. long and 5 ft. wide by 5 ft. high, with massive brick end walls 2 ft. thick, through which are built the carbon poles, consisting of bundles of 60 parallel 3-in. carbon rods, each 3 ft. in length, with a copper rod let into the outer end to connect it with a copper cap, which in turn is connected with one of the terminals of the generating dynamo. The spaces between the carbons of the electrode are packed tightly with graphite. In preparing the furnace for use, transverse iron screens are placed temporarily across each end, the space between these and the end walls being rammed with fine coke, and that in the interior is filled to the level of the centre of the carbon poles with the charge, consisting of 34 parts of coke, with 54 of sand, 10 of sawdust and 2 of salt. A longitudinal trench is then formed in the middle, and in this is arranged a cylindrical pile of fragments of coke about ½ in. or more in diameter, so that they form a core, about 21 in. in diameter, connecting the carbon poles in the end walls. Temporary side walls are then built up, the iron screens are removed, and a further quantity of charge is heaped up about 3 ft. above the top of the furnace. An alternating current of about 1700 amperes at 190 volts is now switched on; as the mass becomes heated by the passage of the current the resistance diminishes, and the current is regulated until after about 2 hours or less from starting it is maintained constant at about 6000 amperes and 125 volts. Carbon monoxide is given off and burns freely around the sides and top of the furnace, tinged yellow after a time by the sodium in the salt mixed with the charge. Meanwhile a shrinkage takes place, which is made good by the addition of a further quantity of charge until the operation is complete, usually in about 36 hours from the commencement. The current is then switched off, and the side walls, after cooling for a day, are taken down, the comparatively unaltered charge from the top is removed, and the products are carefully extracted. These consist of the inner carbon core, which at the temperature of the furnace will have been for the most part converted into graphite, then a thin black crust of graphite mixed with carborundum, next a layer of nearly pure crystallized carborundum about a foot in thickness, then grey amorphous carbide of silicon mixed with increasing proportions of unaltered charge, and lastly, on the outside, the portion of the charge which had never reached the temperature necessary for reaction, and which is altered only by the intrusion of salt from the inner part of the furnace. Special precautions are taken in making and breaking the intense current here used (amounting at the end to about 750 kilowatts, or 1000 E.H.P.), a water-regulator consisting of removable iron plates dipped in salt water being used for the purpose. In such a furnace as that above described the charge weighs about 14 tons, the yield of carborundum is about 3 tons, and the expenditure of energy about 3.9 kilowatt-hours (5.2 H.P.-hours) per pound of finished product. The carborundum thus produced is crystalline, greenish, bluish or brownish in colour, sometimes opaque, but often translucent, resisting the action of even the strongest acids, and the action of air or of sulphur at high temperatures. The crude product can therefore be treated with hot sulphuric acid to purify it. In hardness it nearly equals the diamond, and it is used for tool-grinding in the form of vitrified wheels (mixed with powdered porcelain and iron, pressed into shape and fired in a kiln). Carborundum paper, made like emery paper, is now largely used in place of garnet paper in American shoe factories, and finds a market in other directions. The amorphous carbide, which was at first a waste product, has been tried, it is reported, with success as a lining for steel furnaces, as it is said not to be affected by iron or iron oxide at a white heat.

(W. G. M.)

CARBOY (from the Pers. *qarābah*, a flagon), a large globular glass vessel or bottle, encased in wicker or iron-work for protection, used chiefly for holding vitriol, nitric acid and other corrosive liquids.

CARBUNCLE (Lat. *carbunculus*, diminutive of *carbo*, a glowing coal), in mineralogy, a garnet (*q.v.*) cut with a convex surface. In medicine the name given to an acute local inflammation of the deeper layers of the skin, followed by sloughing. It is accompanied by great local tension and by constitutional disturbance, and in the early stages the pain is often extremely acute. A hard flattened swelling of a deep-red colour is noticed on the back, face or extremities. This gradually extends until in some instances it may become as large as a dinner-plate. Towards the centre of the mass numerous small openings form on the surface, from which blood and matter escape. Through these openings a yellow slough or "core" of leathery consistence can be seen. Carbuncle is an intense local inflammation caused by septic germs which have in some manner found their way to the part. It is particularly apt to occur in persons whose health is depressed by mental worries, or by such troubles as chronic disease of the kidneys or blood-vessels, or by diabetes. The attack ends in mortification of the affected tissue, and, after much suffering, the core or mortified part slowly comes away. The modern treatment consists in cutting into the inflamed area, scraping out the germ-laden core at the earliest possible moment, and applying germicides. This method relieves the pain at once, materially diminishes the risk of blood-poisoning, and hastens convalescence.

(E. O.*)

CARCAGÉNTE, or CARCAJÉNTE, a town of eastern Spain, in the province of Valencia; near the right bank of the river Júcar, at the junction between the Valencia-Murcia and Carcagénte-Denia railways. Pop. (1900) 12,262. Carcagénte is a picturesque town, of considerable antiquity. Various Roman remains have been found in its neighbourhood. It is surrounded by groves of orange, palm and mulberry trees, and contains many Moorish houses, whose old-fashioned blue-tiled cupolas contrast with the chimneys of the silk mills and linen factories opened in modern times. An important local industry is the cultivation of rice, for which the moist and warm climate of the low-lying Júcar valley is well suited.

CÁRCAR, a town of the province of Cebú, island of Cebú, Philippine Islands, on the Cárcar river near its mouth at the head of Cárcar Bay, 23 m. S.W. of Cebú, the capital. It is connected with Cebú by a railway, and a branch of this railway extending across the island to Barili and Dumanjug was projected in 1908. Cárcar has some coast trade. The surrounding country is rugged, and produces Indian corn and sugar in considerable quantity. The language is Cebú-Visayan. Cárcar was founded in 1624.

CARCASS, the dead body of an animal. As a butcher's term, the word means the body of an animal without the head, extremities and offal. It is also used of a hollow iron case filled with combustibles, and fired from a howitzer to set fire to buildings, ships, &c., the flames issuing through holes pierced in the sides. The word is common in various forms to Romanic languages, but the ultimate origin is obscure. Possible derivations are from the

Lat. *caro*, flesh, and Ital. *casso* or *cassa*, chest, or from a Med. Gr. ταρκάσιον, a quiver, for which the Fr. is *carquois*, and Port. *carcaz*.

CARCASSONNE, a city of south-western France, capital of the department of Aude, 57 m. S.E. of Toulouse, on the Southern railway between that city and Narbonne. Pop. (1906) 25,346. Carcassonne is divided by the river Aude into two distinct towns, the Ville Basse and the Cité, which are connected by two bridges, one modern, the other dating from the 13th century. The Cité occupies the summit of an abrupt and isolated hill on the right bank of the river. Its dirty and irregular streets are inhabited by a scanty population of workpeople, and its interest lies mainly in its ancient fortifications (see FORTIFICATION AND SIEGECRAFT) which, for completeness and strength, are unique in France and probably in Europe. They consist of a double line of ramparts, of which the outer measures more than 1600 yds. in circumference. These are protected at frequent intervals by towers, and can be entered only by two gates, one to the east, the other to the west, both of which are themselves elaborately fortified (see GATE). In the interior, and to the north of the western gate, a citadel adjoins the fortifications. A portion of the inner line is attributed to the Visigoths of the 6th century; the rest, including the castle, seems to belong to the 11th or 12th century, while the outer circuit has been referred mainly to the end of the 13th. The old cathedral of St Nazaire dates from the 11th to the 14th centuries. The nave was begun in 1096 and is Romanesque in style; the transept and choir, which contain magnificent stained glass of the Renaissance period, are of Gothic architecture. Both the fortifications and the church were restored by Viollet-le-Duc between 1850 and 1880. On the left bank of the Aude, between it and the Canal du Midi, lies the new town, clean, well-built and flourishing, with streets intersecting each other at right angles. It is surrounded by boulevards occupying the site of its ramparts, and is well provided with fountains, public squares and gardens planted with fine plane-trees. The most interesting buildings are the cathedral of St Michel, dating from the 13th century but restored in modern times, and St Vincent, a church of the 14th century, remarkable for the width of its nave.

Carcassonne is the seat of a bishop, a prefect and a court of assizes, and has tribunals of first instance and of commerce, a chamber of commerce and a branch of the Bank of France. It also has a lycée for boys, training-colleges, theological seminaries, a library and a museum rich in paintings. The old cloth industry is almost extinct. The town is, however, an important wine-market, and the vineyards of the vicinity are the chief source of its prosperity, which is enhanced by its port on the Canal du Midi. Tanning and leather-dressing, distilling, the manufacture of agricultural implements, furniture and corks, cooperage and the preparation of preserved fruits, are prominent industries.

Carcassonne occupies the site of *Carcaso*, an ancient city of Gallia Narbonensis, which belonged to the Volcae Tectosages. It was a place of some importance at the time of Caesar's invasion, but makes almost no appearance in Roman history. On the disintegration of the empire, it fell into the hands of the Visigoths, who, in spite of the attacks of the Franks, especially in 585, retained possession till 724, when they were expelled by the Arabs, destined in turn to yield before long to Pippin the Short. From about 819 to 1082 Carcassonne formed a separate countship, and from the latter date till 1247 a viscountship. Towards the end of the 11th century the viscounts of Carcassonne assumed the style of viscounts of Béziers, which town and its lords they had dominated since the fall of the Carolingian empire. The viscounty of Carcassonne, together with that of Béziers, was confiscated to the crown in 1247, as a result of the part played by the viscount Raymond Roger against Simon de Montfort in the Albigensian crusade, during which in 1209 the city was taken by the Crusaders (see ALBIGENSES). A revolt of the city against the royal authority was severely punished in 1262 by the expulsion of its principal inhabitants, who were, however, permitted to take up their quarters on the other side of the river. This was the origin of the new town, which was fortified in 1347. During the religious wars, Carcassonne several times changed hands, and it did not recognize Henry IV. till 1596.

See E.E. Viollet-le-Duc, *La Cité de Carcassonne* (Paris, 1858); L. Fédié, *Histoire de Carcassonne* (Carcassonne, 1887).

CARDAMOM, the fruit of several plants of the genera *Elettaria* and *Amomum*, belonging to the natural order Zingiberaceae, the principal of which is *Elettaria Cardamomum*, from which the true officinal or Malabar cardamom is derived. The Malabar cardamom plant is a large perennial herb with a thick fleshy root-stock, which sends up flowering stems, 6 to 12 ft. high. The large leaves are arranged in two rows, have very long sheaths enveloping the stem and a lanceolate spreading blade 1 to 2½ ft. long. The fruit is an ovate-triangular, three-celled, three-valved capsule (about 1/5 in. long, of a dirty yellow colour) enclosing numerous angular seeds, which form the valuable part of the plant. It is a native of the mountainous parts of the Malabar coast of India, and the fruits are procured either from wild plants or by cultivation throughout Travancore, western Mysore, and along the western Ghauts. A cardamom of much larger size found growing in Ceylon was formerly regarded as belonging to a distinct species, and described as such under the name of *Elettaria major*; but it is now known to be only a variety of the Malabar cardamom. In commerce, several varieties are distinguished according to their size and flavour. The most esteemed are known as "shorts," a name given to such capsules as are from a quarter to half an inch long and about a quarter broad. Following these come "short-longs" and "long-longs," also distinguished by their size, the largest reaching to about an inch in length. The Ceylon cardamom attains a length of an inch and a half and is about a third of an inch broad, with a brownish pericarp and a distinct aromatic odour. Among the other plants, the fruits of which pass in commerce as cardamoms, are the round or cluster cardamom, *Amomum Cardamomum*, a native of Siam and Java; the bastard cardamom of Siam, *A. xanthioides* —the Bengal cardamom, which is the fruit of *A. subulatum*, a native of Nepal; the Java cardamom, produced by *A. maximum*; and the Korarima cardamom of Somaliland. The last-named is the product of a plant which is unknown botanically. Cardamoms generally are possessed of a pleasant aromatic odour, and an agreeable, spicy taste. On account of their flavour they are much used with other medicines, and they form a principal ingredient in curries and compounded spices. In the north of Europe they are much used as a spice and flavouring material for cakes and liqueurs; and they are very extensively employed in the East for chewing with betel, &c.

CARDAN [Ital. CARDANO], GIROLAMO [GERONYMO or HIERONIMO] (1501-1576), Italian mathematician, physician and astrologer, born at Pavia on the 24th of September 1501, was the illegitimate son of Facio Cardano (1444-1524), a learned jurist of Milan, himself distinguished by a taste for mathematics. He was educated at the university of Pavia, and subsequently at that of Padua, where he graduated in medicine. He was, however, excluded from the College of Physicians at Milan on account of his illegitimate birth, and it is not surprising that his first book should have been an exposure of the fallacies of the faculty. A fortunate cure of the child of the Milanese senator Sfondrato now brought him into notice, and the interest of his patron procured him admission into the medical body. About this time (1539) he obtained additional celebrity by the publication of his *Practica arithmeticae generalis*, a work of great merit 315 for the time, and he became engaged in a correspondence with Niccolo Tartaglia, who had discovered a solution of cubic equations. This discovery Tartaglia had kept to himself, but he was ultimately induced to communicate it to Cardan under a solemn promise that it should never be divulged. Cardan, however, published it in his comprehensive treatise on algebra (*Artis magnae sive de regulis Algebrae liber unus*) which appeared at Nuremberg in 1545 (see ALGEBRA: *History*). Two years previously he had published a work even more highly regarded by his contemporaries, his celebrated treatise on astrology. As a believer in astrology Cardan was on a level with the best minds of his age; the distinction consisted in the comparatively cautious spirit of his inquiries and his disposition to confirm his assertions by an appeal to facts, or what he believed to be such. A very considerable part of his treatise is based upon observations carefully collected by himself, and seemingly well calculated to support his theories so far as they extend. Numerous instances of his belief in dreams and omens may be collected from his writings, and he especially valued himself on being one of the five or six celebrated men to whom, as to Socrates, had been vouchsafed the assistance of a guardian daemon.

In 1547 he was appointed professor of medicine at Pavia. The publication of his works on algebra and astrology at this juncture had gained for him a European renown, and procured him flattering offers from Pope Paul III. and the king of Denmark, both of which he declined. In 1551 his reputation was crowned by the publication of his great work, *De Subtilitate Rerum*, which embodied the soundest physical learning of his time and simultaneously represented its most advanced spirit of speculation. It was followed some years later by a similar treatise, *De Varietate Rerum* (1557), the two making in effect but one book. A great portion of this is occupied by endeavours, commonly futile, to explain ordinary natural phenomena, but its chief interest for us consists in the hints and glimpses it affords of principles beyond the full comprehension of the writer himself, and which the world was then by no means ready to entertain. The inorganic realm of Nature he asserts to be animated no less than the organic; all creation is progressive development; all animals were originally worms; the inferior metals must be regarded as *conatus naturae* towards the production of gold. The indefinite variability of species is implied in the remark that Nature is seldom content with a single variation from a customary type. The oviparous habits of birds are explained by their tendency to favour the perpetuation of the species, precisely in the manner of modern naturalists. Animals were not created for the use of man, but exist for their own sakes. The origin of life depends upon cosmic laws, which Cardan naturally connects with his favourite study of astrology. The physical divergencies of mankind arise from the effects of climate and the variety of human circumstances in general. Cardan's views on the dissimilarity of languages are much more philosophical than usual at his time; and his treatise altogether, though weak in particular details, is strong in its pervading sense of the unity and omnipotence of natural law, which renders it in some degree an adumbration of the course of science since the author's day. It was attacked by J.C. Scaliger, whom Cardan refuted without difficulty.

The celebrity which Cardan had acquired led in the same year (1551) to his journey to Scotland as the medical adviser of Archbishop Hamilton of St Andrews. The archbishop was supposed to be suffering from consumption, a complaint which Cardan, under a false impression, as he frankly admits, had represented himself as competent to cure. He was of great service to the archbishop, whose complaint proved to be asthmatical; but the principal interest attaching to his expedition is derived from his account of the disputes of the medical faculty at Paris, and of the court of Edward VI. of England. The Parisian doctors were disturbed by the heresies of Vesalius, who was beginning to introduce anatomical study from the human subject. Cardan's liberality of temper led him to sympathize with the innovator. His account of Edward VI.'s disposition and understanding is extremely favourable, and is entitled to credit as that of a competent observer without bias towards either side of the religious question. He cast the king's nativity, and indulged in a number of predictions which were effectually confuted by the royal youth's death in the following year.

Cardan had now attained the summit of his prosperity, and the rest of his life was little but a series of disasters. His principal misfortunes arose from the crimes and calamities of his sons, one of whom was an utter reprobate, while the tragic fate of the other overwhelmed the father with anguish. This son, Giovanni Battista, also a physician, had contracted an imprudent marriage with a girl of indifferent character, Brandonia Seroni, who subsequently proved unfaithful to him. The injured husband revenged himself with poison; the deed was detected, and the exceptional severity of the punishment seems to justify Cardan in attributing it to the rancour of his medical rivals, with whom he had never at any time been on good terms. The blow all but crushed him; his reputation and his practice waned; he addicted himself to gaming, a vice to which he had always been prone; his mind became unhinged and filled with distempered imaginations. He was ultimately banished from Milan on some accusation not specified, and although the decree was ultimately rescinded, he found it advisable to accept a professorship at Bologna (1562). While residing there in moderate comfort, and mainly occupied with the composition of supplements to his former works, he was suddenly arrested on a charge not stated, but in all probability heresy. Though he had always been careful to keep on terms with the Church, the bent of his mind had been palpably towards free thought, and the circumstance had probably attracted the attention of Pius V., who then ruled the Church in the spirit, as he had formerly exercised the functions,

134

of an inquisitor. Through the intercession, as would appear, of some influential cardinals, Cardan was released, but was deprived of his professorship, prohibited from teaching and publishing any further, and removed to Rome, where he spent his remaining years in receipt of a pension from the pope. It seems to have been urged in his favour that his intellect had been disturbed by grief for the loss of his son—an assertion to which his frequent hallucinations lent some countenance, though the existence of any serious derangement is disproved by the lucidity and coherence of his last writings. He occupied his time at Rome in the composition of his commentaries, *De Vita Propria*, which, along with a companion treatise, *De Libris Propriis*, is our principal authority for his biography. Though he had burned much, he left behind him more than a hundred MSS., not twenty of which have been printed. He died at Rome on the 21st of September 1576.

Alike intellectually and morally, Cardan is one of the most interesting personages connected with the revival of science in Europe. He had no especial bent towards any scientific pursuit, but appears as the man of versatile ability, delighting in research for its own sake. He possessed the true scientific spirit in perfection; nothing, he tells us, among the king of France's treasures appeared to him so worthy of admiration as a certain natural curiosity which he took for the horn of a unicorn. It has been injurious to his fame to have been compelled to labour, partly in fields of research where no important discovery was then attainable, partly in those where his discoveries could only serve as the stepping-stones to others, by which they were inevitably eclipsed. His medical career serves as an illustration of the former case, and his mathematical of the latter. His medical knowledge was wholly empirical; restrained by the authority of Galen, and debarred from the practice of anatomy, nothing more could be expected than that he should stumble on some fortunate nostrums. As a mathematician, on the other hand, he effected important advances in science, but such as merely paved the way for discoveries which have obscured his own. From his astrology no results could be expected; but even here the scientific character of his mind is displayed in his common-sense treatment of what usually passed for a mystical and occult study. His prognostications are as strictly empirical as his prescriptions, and rest quite as much upon the observations which he supposed himself to have made in his practice. As frequently is the case with men incapable of rightly ordering 316their own lives, he is full of wisdom and sound advice for others; his ethical precepts and practical rules are frequently excellent. To complete the catalogue of his accomplishments, he is no contemptible poet.

The work of Cardan's, however, which retains most interest for this generation is his autobiography, *De Vita Propria*. In its clearness and frankness of self-revelation this book stands almost alone among records of its class. It may be compared with the autobiography of another celebrated Italian of the age, Benvenuto Cellini, but is much more free from vanity and self-consciousness, unless the extreme candour with which Cardan reveals his own errors is to be regarded as vanity in a more subtle form. The general impression is highly favourable to the writer, whose impetuosity and fits of reckless dissipation appear as mere exaggerations of the warmth of heart which imparted such strength to his domestic affections, and in the region of science imparted that passionate devotion to research which could alone have enabled him to persevere so resolutely and effect such marked advances in such multifarious fields of inquiry.

Cardan's autobiography has been most ably condensed, and at the same time supplemented by information from the general body of his writings and other sources, by Henry Morley (*Jerome Cardan*, 1854, 2 vols). His capital treatises, *De Subtilitate* and *De Varietate Rerum*, are combined and fully analysed in vol. ii. of Rixner and Siber's *Leben und Lehrmeinungen berühmter Physiker am Ende des xvi. und am Anfange des xvii. Jahrhunderts* (Sulzbach, 1820). Cardan's works were edited in ten volumes by Sponius (Lyons, 1663). A biography was prefixed by Gabriel Naudé, whose unreasonable depreciation has unduly lowered Cardan's character with posterity.

(R. G.)

CÁRDENAS (*San Juan de Dios de Cárdenas*), a maritime town of Cuba, in Matanzas province, about 75 m. E. of Havana, on the level and somewhat marshy shore of a spacious bay of the northern coast of the island, sheltered by a long promontory. Pop. (1907) 24,280.

It has railway communication with the trunk railway of the island, and communicates by regular steamers with all the coast towns. The city lies between the sea and hills. There are broad streets, various squares (including the Plaza de Colón, with a bronze statue of Columbus given to the city by Queen Isabel II. and erected in 1862) and substantial business buildings. Cárdenas is one of the principal sugar-exporting towns of Cuba. The shallowness of the harbour necessitates lighterage and repeated loading of cargoes. The surrounding region is famed for its fertility. A large quantity of asphalt has been taken from the bed of the harbour. A flow of fresh water from the bed of the harbour is another peculiar feature; it comes presumably from the outlets of subterranean rivers. There is a large United States business element, which has been, indeed, prominent in the city ever since its foundation. At El Varadero, on a peninsula at the mouth of the bay, there is fine sea-bathing on a long beach, and El Varadero is a winter resort. Cárdenas was founded in 1828, and in 1861 already had 12,910 inhabitants. In 1850 General Narciso Lopez landed here on a filibustering expedition, and held the town for a few hours, abandoning it when he saw that the people would not rise to support him in his efforts to secure Cuban independence. On the 11th of May 1898 an American torpedo-boat and revenue cutter here attacked three Spanish gun-boats, and Ensign Worth Bagley (1874-1898) was killed—the first American naval officer to lose his life in the Spanish-American War.

CARDIFF, a city, municipal, county and parliamentary borough, seaport and market-town, and the county town of Glamorganshire, South Wales, situated on the Taff, 1 m. above its outflow, 145¼ m. from London by the Great Western railway via Badminton, 40½ m. W. of Bristol and 45½ m. E.S.E. of Swansea. Cardiff is also the terminus of both the Taff Vale and the Rhymney railways, the latter affording the London & North-Western railway access to the town. The Barry line from Barry dock joins the Great Western and Taff Vale railways at Cardiff, and the Cardiff Railway Company (which owns all the docks) has a line from Pontypridd via Llanishen to the docks. The Glamorganshire canal, opened in 1794, runs from Cardiff to Merthyr Tydfil, with a branch to Aberdare. The increase of the population of Cardiff during the 19th century was phenomenal; from 1870 inhabitants in 1801, and 6187 in 1831 it grew to 32,954 in 1861. The borough, which originally comprised only the parishes of St John's and St Mary's, was in 1875 and 1895 extended so as to include Roath and a large part of Llandaff, known as Canton, on the right of the Taff. The whole area was united as one civil parish in 1903, and the population in 1901 was 164,333, of whom only about 8% spoke Welsh.

Probably no town in the kingdom has a nobler group of public buildings than those in Cathays Park, which also commands a view of the castle ramparts and the old keep. On opposite sides of a fine avenue are the assize courts and new town hall (with municipal offices), which are both in the Renaissance style. The Glamorgan county council has also a site of one acre in the park for offices.

The University College of South Wales and Monmouthshire, founded in 1883, under the principalship of J. Viriamu Jones, for some time carried on its work in temporary buildings, pending the erection of the commodious and imposing building from the plans of Mr W.D. Caröe, in Cathays Park, where the registry of the university of Wales (of which the college is a constituent) is also situated. The Drapers' Company has given £15,500 towards building a library, in addition to previous donations to the engineering department and the scholarship fund of the college. The college has departments for arts, pure and applied science and technology, medicine, public health, music, and for the training of men and women teachers for elementary and secondary schools. Its library includes the Salesbury collection of books relating to Wales. Aberdare Hall is a hostel for the women students. The Baptist theological college of Pontypool was removed to Cardiff in 1895.

The public library and museum were founded in 1863, but in 1882 were removed to a new building which was enlarged in 1896. The library is especially rich in books and MSS. relating to Wales and in Celtic literature generally. These comprise the Welsh portion of the MSS. which belonged to Sir Thomas Phillipps of Middlehill (including the Book of Aneurin—one of the "Four ancient books of Wales"), purchased for £3500. A catalogue of the printed books in the Welsh department, which soon became a standard work of reference, was published in 1898, while a calendar of the Welsh MSS. was issued by the Historical MSS. Commission in 1903. There are six branch libraries, while a scheme of school libraries has been in operation since 1899. The chief features of the museum are collections of the fossils, birds and flora of Wales and of obsolete Welsh domestic appliances, casts of the pre-Norman monuments of Wales, and reproductions of metal and ivory work illustrating various periods of art and civilization. There is also a unique collection of Swansea and Nantgarw china. The fine arts department contains twenty-seven oil paintings by modern English and continental artists bequeathed by William Menelaus of Dowlais in 1883, the Pyke-Thompson collection of about 100 water-colour paintings presented in 1899, and some 3000 prints and drawings relating to Wales. In 1905 Cardiff was selected by a privy council committee to be the site of a state-aided national museum for Wales, the whole contents of the museum and art gallery, together with a site in Cathays Park, having been offered by the corporation for the purpose. A charter providing for its government was granted on the 19th of March 1907. In Cathays Park there is also a "gorsedd" or bardic circle of huge monoliths erected in connexion with the eisteddfod of 1899.

The other public buildings of the town include the infirmary founded in 1837, the present buildings being erected in 1883, and subsequently enlarged; the sanatorium, the seamen's hospital, the South Wales Institute of Mining Engineers (which has a library) built in 1894, the exchange, an institute for the blind, a school for the deaf and dumb, and one of the two prisons for the county (the other being at Swansea). There are a technical school, an intermediate school for boys and another for girls, a "higher-grade" and a pupil teachers' school. A musical festival is held triennially.

In the business part the buildings are also for the most part imposing and the thoroughfares spacious, while the chief 317suburban streets are planted with trees. The Taff is spanned by two bridges, one a four-arched bridge rebuilt in 1858-1859 leading to Llandaff, and the other a cantilever with a central swinging span of 190 ft. 8 in.

In virtue of its being the shire-town, Cardiff acquired in 1535 the right to send one representative to parliament, which it did until 1832, from which date Cowbridge and Llantrisant have been joined with it as contributory boroughs returning one member. The great sessions for the county were during their whole existence from 1542 to 1830 held at Cardiff, but the assizes (which replaced them) have since then been held at Swansea and Cardiff alternately, as also are the quarter sessions for Glamorgan. The borough has a separate commission of the peace, having a stipendiary magistrate since 1858. It was granted a separate court of quarter sessions in 1890, it was constituted a county borough in 1888, and, by letters patent dated the 28th of October 1905, it was created a city and the dignity of lord mayor conferred on its chief magistrate. The corporation consists of ten aldermen and thirty councillors, and the area of the municipal borough is 8408 acres.

Under powers secured in 1884, the town obtains its chief water supply from a gathering ground near the sources of the Taff on the old red sandstone beyond the northern out-crop of the mineral basin and on the southern slopes of the Brecknock Beacons. Here two reservoirs of a combined capacity of 668 million gallons have been constructed, and a conduit some 36 m. long laid to Cardiff at a total cost of about £1,250,000. A third reservoir is authorized. A gas company, first incorporated in 1837, supplies the city as well as Llandaff and Penarth with gas, but the corporation also supplies electric power both for lighting and working the tramways, which were purchased from a private company in 1898. The city owned in 1905 about 290 acres of parks and "open spaces," the chief being Roath Park of 100 acres (including a botanical garden of 15 acres), Llandaff fields of 70 acres, and Cathays Park of 60 acres, which was acquired in 1900 mainly with the view of placing in it the chief public buildings of the town.

Commerce and Industries.—Edward II.'s charter of 1324 indicates that Cardiff had become even then a trading and shipping centre of some importance. It enjoyed a brief existence as a staple town from 1327 to 1332. During the reigns of Elizabeth and James I. it was notorious as a resort of pirates, while some of the ironfounders of the district were suspected of secretly supplying Spain with ordnance. It was for centuries a "head port," its limits extending from Chepstow to Llanelly; in the 18th century it sank to the position of "a

137

creek" of the port of Bristol, but about 1840 it was made independent, its limits for customs' purposes being defined as from the Rumney estuary to Nash Point, so that technically the "port of Cardiff" includes Barry and Penarth as well as Cardiff proper. Down to the end of the 18th century there was only a primitive quay on the river side for shipping purposes. Coal was brought down from the hills on the backs of mules, and iron carried in two-ton wagons. In 1798 the first dock (12 acres in extent) was constructed at the terminus of the Glamorgan canal from Merthyr. The commercial greatness of Cardiff is due to the vast coal and iron deposits of the country drained by the Taff and Rhymney, between whose outlets the town is situated. But a great impetus to its development was given by the 2nd marquess of Bute, who has often been described as the second founder of Cardiff. In 1830 he obtained the first act for the construction of a dock which (now known as the West Bute dock) was opened in 1839 and measures (with its basin) 19½ acres. The opening of the Taff Vale railway in 1840 and of the South Wales railway to Cardiff in 1850 necessitated further accommodation, and the trustees of the marquess (who died in 1848) began in 1851 and opened in 1855 the East Bute dock and basin measuring 46¼ acres. The Rhymney railway to Cardiff was completed in 1858 and the trade of the port so vastly increased that the shipment of coal and coke went up from 4562 tons in 1839 to 1,796,000 tons in 1860. In 1864 the Bute trustees unsuccessfully sought powers for constructing three additional docks to cost two millions sterling, but under the more limited powers granted in 1866, the Roath basin (12 acres) was opened in 1874, and (under a substituted act of 1882) the Roath dock (33 acres) was opened in 1887. All these docks were constructed by the Bute family at a cost approaching three millions sterling. Still they fell far short of the requirements of the district for in 1865 the Taff Vale Railway Company opened a dock of 26 acres under the headland at Penarth, while in 1884 a group of colliery owners, dissatisfied with their treatment at Cardiff, obtained powers to construct docks at Barry which are now 114 acres in extent. The Bute trustees in 1885 acquired the Glamorgan canal and its dock, and in the following year obtained an act for vesting their various docks and the canal in a company now known as the Cardiff Railway Company. The South Bute dock of 50½ acres, authorized in 1894 and capable of accommodating the largest vessels afloat, was opened in 1907, bringing the whole dock area of Cardiff (including timber ponds) to about 210 acres. There are also ten private graving and floating docks and one public graving dock. There is ample equipment of fixed and movable staiths and cranes of various sizes up to 70 tons, the Lewis-Hunter patent cranes being largely used for shipping coal owing to their minimizing the breakage of coal and securing its even distribution. The landing of foreign cattle is permitted by the Board of Trade, and there are cattle lairs and abattoirs near the Cardiff wharf. The total exports of the Cardiff docks in 1906 amounted to 8,767,502 tons, of which 8,433,629 tons were coal, coke and patent fuel, 151,912 were iron and steel and their manufactures, and 181,076 tons of general merchandise. What Cardiff lacks is a corresponding import trade, for its imports in 1906 amounted to only 2,108,133 tons, of which the chief items were iron ore (895,610 tons), pit-wood (303,407), grain and flour (298,197). Taking "the port of Cardiff" in its technical sense as including Barry and Penarth, it is the first port in the kingdom for shipping cleared to foreign countries and British possessions, second in the kingdom for its timber imports, and first in the world for shipment of coal.

The east moors, stretching towards the outlet of the Rhymney river, have become an important metallurgical quarter. Copper works were established here in 1866, followed long after by tin-stamping and enamel works. In 1888 the Dowlais Iron Company (now Messrs Guest, Keen & Nettlefold, Ltd.) acquired here some ninety acres on which were built four blast furnaces and six Siemens' smelting furnaces. There are also in the city several large grain mills and breweries, a biscuit factory, wire and hemp roperies, fuel works, general foundries and engineering works. At Ely, 3½ m. out of Cardiff, there are also breweries, a small tin works and large paper works. The newspapers of Cardiff include two weeklies, the *Cardiff Times* and *Weekly Mail*, founded in 1857 and 1870 respectively, two morning dailies, the *South Wales Daily News* and *Western Mail*, established in 1872 and 1869 respectively, and two evening dailies.

History and Historic Buildings.—In documents of the first half of the 12th century the name is variously spelt as *Kairdif, Cairti* and *Kardid*. The Welsh form of the name, Caerdydd (pronounced Caerdeeth, with the accent on the second syllable) suggests that the name means "the fort of (Aulus?) Didius," rather than Caer Dâf ("the fortress on the Taff"), which is nowhere found (except in Leland), though Caer Dyv once existed as a variant. No traces have been found of any pre-Roman settlement at Cardiff. Excavations carried out by the marquess of Bute from 1889 onward furnished for the first time conclusive proof that Cardiff had been a Roman station, and also revealed the sequence of changes which it had subsequently undergone. There was first, on the site occupied by the present castle, a camp of about ten acres, probably constructed after the conquest of the Silures A.D. 75-77, so as to command the passage of the Taff, which was here crossed by the Via Maritima running from Gloucester to St David's. In later Roman times there were added a series of polygonal bastions, of the type found at Caerwent. To this period also belongs the massive rampart, over 10 ft. thick, and the north gateway, one of the most perfect Roman gateways in Great Britain. After the departure of the Romans the walls became ruinous or were partly pulled down, 318perhaps by sea rovers from the north. In this period of anarchy the native princes of Glamorgan had their principal demesne, not at the camp but a mile to the north at Llystalybont, now merely a thatched farmhouse, while some Saxon invaders threw up within the camp a large moated mound on which the Normans about the beginning of the 12th century built the great shell-keep which is practically all that remains of their original castle. Its builder was probably Robert, earl of Gloucester, who also built Bristol castle. Then or possibly even earlier the old rampart was for two-thirds of its circuit buried under enormous earthworks, the remainder being rebuilt. It was in the keep, and not, as tradition says, in the much later "Black Tower" (also called "Duke Robert's Tower"), that Robert, duke of Normandy, was imprisoned by order of his brother Henry I. from 1108 until his death in 1134. Considerable additions of later date, in the Decorated and Perpendicular styles, are due to the Despensers and to Beauchamp, earl of Warwick, while the present residential part is of various dates ranging from the 15th century down to the last half of the 19th, when a thorough restoration, including the addition of a superbly ornamented clock-tower, was carried out. The original ditch, about 20 yds. wide, still exists on three sides, but it is now converted into a "feeder" for the docks and canal. Geoffrey of Monmouth was at one time chaplain of the castle, where he probably wrote some of his works. The scene of the "sparrow-hawk" tournament, described in *Geraint and Enid*, one of the Arthurian romances, is laid at Cardiff.

On the conquest of the district by the Normans under Fitz Hamon, Cardiff became the caput of the seigniory of Glamorgan, and the castle the residence of its lords. The castle and lordship descended by heirship, male and female, through the families of De Clare, Despenser, Beauchamp and Neville to Richard III., on whose fall they escheated to the Crown, and were granted later, first to Jasper Tudor, and finally by Edward VI. in 1550 to Sir William Herbert, afterwards created Baron Herbert of Cardiff and earl of Pembroke. Through the daughter and grand-daughter of the 7th earl the castle and estates became the property of the 1st marquess of Bute (who was created Baron Cardiff in 1776), to whose direct descendant they now belong.

The town received its earliest known grant of municipal privileges sometime before 1147 from Fitz Hamon's successor and son-in-law Robert, earl of Gloucester. In 1284 the inhabitants petitioned the burgesses of Hereford for a certified copy of the customs of the latter town, and these furnished a model for the later demands of the growing community at Cardiff from its lords, while Cardiff in turn furnished the model for the Glamorgan towns such as Neath and Kenfig. In 1324 Edward II. granted a number of exemptions to Cardiff and other towns in South Wales, and this grant was confirmed by Edward III. in 1359, Henry IV. in 1400, Henry VI. in 1452, and Edward IV. in 1465.

Its most important early charter was that granted in 1340 by Hugh le Despenser, whereby the burgesses acquired the right to nominate persons from whom the constable of the castle should select a bailiff and other officers, two ancient fairs, held on the 29th of June and 19th of September, were confirmed, and extensive trading privileges were granted, including the right to form a merchant gild. A charter granted in 1421 by Richard de Beauchamp provided that the town should be governed by twelve elected aldermen, but that the constable of the castle should be mayor. In 1581 Queen Elizabeth granted a confirmatory charter to the mayor and bailiffs direct without reference to the lord of the castle. The town was treated as a borough by prescription until 1608, when James I. confirmed its status by express incorporation, adding also to its rights of self-government, and granting it a third fair (on the 30th of November). In 1687 the town surrendered this charter to James II., who in a substituted one, which, however, was never acted upon, reserved to the Crown the right of removing any member of the corporation from office. The first step towards the modern improvement of the town was taken in 1774, when a special act was obtained for the purpose. Nineteen private acts and provisional orders were obtained during the 19th century.

Among the many early English kings who visited or passed through Cardiff was Henry II., on whom in 1171, outside St Piran's chapel (which has long since disappeared), was urged the duty of Sunday observance. About 1153, Ivor Bâch (or the Little), a neighbouring Welsh chieftain, seized the castle and for a time held William, earl of Gloucester, and the countess prisoners in the hills. In 1404 Owen Glendower burnt the town, except the quarters of the Friars Minors. In 1645, after the battle of Naseby, Charles I. visited the town, which until then had been mainly Royalist, but about a month later was taken by the Parliamentarians. In 1648, a week after the Royalists had been decisively defeated by Colonel Horton at St Fagan's, 4 m. west of Cardiff, Cromwell passed through the town on his way to Pembroke.

Outside the north-west angle of the castle, Richard de Clare in 1256 founded a Dominican priory, which was burnt by Glendower in 1404. Though rebuilt, the building fell into decay after the Dissolution. The site was excavated in 1887. Outside the north-east angle a Franciscan friary was founded in 1280 by Gilbert de Clare, which at the Dissolution became the residence of a branch of the Herbert family. Its site was explored in 1896. The only other building of historic interest is the church of St John the Baptist, which is in the Perpendicular style, its fine tower having been built about 1443 by Hart, who also built the towers of Wrexham and St Stephen's, Bristol. In the Herbert chapel is a fine altar tomb of two brothers of the family. A sculptured stone reredos by W. Goscombe John was erected in 1896. The original church of St Mary's, at the mouth of the river, was swept away by a tidal wave in 1607: Wordsworth took this as a subject for a sonnet.

In 1555 Rawlins White, a fisherman, was burnt at Cardiff for his Protestantism, and in 1679 two Catholic priests were executed for recusancy. Cardiff was the birthplace of Christopher Love (b. 1618), Puritan author, and of William Erbury, sometime vicar of St Mary's in the town, who, with his curate, Walter Cradock, were among the founders of Welsh nonconformity.

As to Roman Cardiff see articles by J. Ward in the *Archaeologia* for 1901 (vol. lvii.), and in *Archaeologia Cambrensis* for 1908. As to the castle and the Black and Gray Friars see *Archaeologia Cambrensis*, 3rd series, viii. 251 (reprinted in Clark's *Medieval Military Architecture*), 5th series, vi. 97; vii. 283; xvii. 55; 6th series, i. 69. The charters of Cardiff and "Materials for a History of the County Borough from the Earliest Times" were published by order of the corporation in *Cardiff Records* (5 vols., 1898, sqq.). See also a *Handbook of Cardiff and District*, prepared for the use of the British Association, 1891; *Cardiff, an Illustrated Handbook*, 1896; the *Annual Report* of the Cardiff Chamber of Commerce; the *Calendar* of the University College.

(D. LL. T.)

CARDIGAN, JAMES THOMAS BRUDENELL, 7TH EARL OF (1797-1868),

English lieutenant-general, son of the 6th earl of Cardigan (the title dating from 1661), was born at Hambleden, Bucks, on the 16th of October 1797. He studied for several terms at Christ Church, Oxford; and in 1818 entered parliament. He entered the army in 1824 as cornet in the 8th Hussars, and was promoted within eight years, by purchase, to be lieutenant-colonel in the 15th Hussars. With this regiment he made himself one of the most unpopular of commanding officers. He gave the reins to his natural overbearing and quarrelsome temper, treating his men with excessive rigour and indulging in unscrupulous licentiousness. Within two years he held 105 courts-martial, and made more than 700 arrests, although the actual strength of his regiment was only 350 men. In consequence of one of his numerous personal quarrels, he left the regiment in 1834; but two years later, at the urgent entreaty of his father, he was appointed to the command of the 11th Hussars. He played the same part as before, and was censured for it; but he was allowed to retain his post, and the discipline and equipment of his regiment, in which he took great pride, and on which he spent large sums of money, received high commendation from the duke of Wellington. He succeeded to the peerage on the death of his father in August 1837. In September 1840 Lord Cardigan fought a duel, on Wimbledon common, with one of his own officers. The latter was wounded, and Lord Cardigan was tried before the House of Lords on a charge of feloniously shooting his adversary. But the trial was a mere sham, and on a trivial technical ground he was acquitted. In 1854, at the outbreak of the Crimean War, he was appointed to the command of the light cavalry brigade, with the rank of major-general, and he spent a very large sum in the purchase of horses and on the equipment of his regiment. He took a prominent part in the early actions of the campaign, and displayed throughout the greatest personal courage and the greatest recklessness in exposing his men. In the charge of the light brigade at Balaklava (*q.v.*) he was the first man to reach the line of the Russian guns; and Cardigan and his men alike have been credited by the bitterest critics of the charge with splendid daring and unquestioning obedience to orders. At the close of the war he was created K.C.B., and was appointed inspector-general of cavalry, and this post he held till 1860. In 1863 he engaged without success in legal proceedings against an officer who had published an account of Balaklava which the earl held to contain a reflection on his military character. He attained the rank of lieutenant-general in 1861. He was twice married, in 1826 and 1858, but had no children. On his death, which took place on the 28th of March 1868, the family titles (including the English barony of Brudenell, cr. 1628) passed to his relative, the second marquess of Ailesbury.

CARDIGAN (*Aberteifi*), a seaport, market-town and municipal borough, and the county town of Cardiganshire, Wales, picturesquely situated on the right bank of the Teifi about 3 m. above its mouth. Pop. (1901) 3511. It is connected by an ancient stone bridge with the suburb of Bridgend on the southern or Pembroke bank of the river. It is the terminal station of the Whitland-Cardigan branch of the Great Western railway. Owing to the bar at the estuary of the Teifi, the shipping trade is inconsiderable, but there are brick-works and foundries in the town; and as the centre of a large agricultural district, Cardigan market is well attended. There is a curious local custom of mixing "culm," a compound of clay and small coal, in the streets. The town has for the most part a modern and prosperous appearance. Two bastions with some of the curtain wall of the ancient castle remain, whilst the dwelling-house known as Castle Green contains part of a drum tower, and some vaulted chambers of the 13th century. The chancel of the Priory church of St Mary is an interesting specimen of early Perpendicular work, and the elaborate tracery of its fine east window contains some fragments of ancient stained glass. It is the only existing portion of a Benedictine house which was originally founded by Prince Rhys ap Griffith in the 12th century.

Although a Celtic settlement doubtless existed near the mouth of the Teifi from an early period, it was not until Norman times that Cardigan became a place of importance. Its castle was first erected by Roger de Montgomery about the year 1091, and throughout the 12th and 13th centuries this stronghold of Cardigan played no small part in the constant warfare between Welsh and English, either side from time to time gaining possession of the castle and the small town dependent on it. In 1136 the English army under Randolf, earl of Chester, was severely defeated by the Welsh at Crûg Mawr, now called Bank-y-Warren, a rounded hill 2 m. north-east of the town. During the latter part of the 12th century the castle became the residence of Rhys ap Griffith, prince and justiciar of South Wales (d. 1196), who kept considerable state within its walls, and entertained here in 1188 Archbishop Baldwin and Giraldus Cambrensis during their preaching of the Third Crusade. In 1284 Edward I. spent a month in the castle, settling the affairs of South Wales. This famous pile was finally taken and destroyed by the Parliamentarian Major-General Laugharne in 1645. The lordship, castle and town of Cardigan formed part of the dower bestowed on Queen Catherine of Aragon by King Henry VII. Henry VIII.'s charter of 1542 confirmed earlier privileges granted by Edward I. and other monarchs, and provided for the government of the town by a duly elected mayor, two bailiffs and a coroner. In the assizes and quarter sessions were removed hence to Lampeter, which has a more central position in the county. Cardigan was declared a parliamentary borough in 1536, but in 1885 its representation was merged in that of the county.

CARDIGANSHIRE (*Ceredigion, Sir Aberteifi*), a county of South Wales, bounded N. by Merioneth, E. by Montgomery, Radnor and Brecon, S. by Carmarthen and Pembroke, and W. by Cardigan Bay of the Irish Sea. It has an area of 688 sq. m., so that it ranks fifth in size of the Welsh countries. The whole of Cardiganshire is hilly or undulating, with the exception of the great bogs of Borth and Tregaron, but the mountains generally have little grandeur in their character; Plinlimmon itself, on the boundary of the county with Montgomeryshire, in spite of its elevation of 2463 ft., being singularly deficient in boldness of outline. Of other hills, only Tregaron Mountain (1778 ft.) exceeds 1500 ft. in height. Of the rivers by far the most important is the Teifi, or Tivy, which rises above Tregaron in Llyn Teifi, one of a group of tiny lakes which are usually termed the Teifi Pools, and flows southward through the county as far as Lampeter, forming from this point onwards its southern boundary. A succession of deep pools and rushing shallows, the Teifi has from the earliest times been celebrated for the quantity and quality of its salmon, which are netted in great numbers on Cardigan Bar. Trout and sewin (a local species of sea-trout) are also plentiful, so that the Teifi is much frequented by anglers. This river is also believed to have been the last British haunt of the beaver (*afangc, lost-llydan*), for the slaying of which a very heavy penalty was exacted by the old royal laws of Wales. Giraldus Cambrensis, Michael Drayton, and other writers allude to this circumstance, though at what date the beaver became extinct in these waters is quite uncertain. On the Teifi may frequently be observed fishermen in coracles. Other rivers worthy of mention are the Dovey (Dyfi), separating Cardigan from Merioneth in the extreme north; the Rheidol and the Ystwyth, which rise in Plinlimmon; and the Aeron, which has its source in Llyn Eiddwen, a pool in the hilly district known as Mynydd Bach. All these streams flow westward into Cardigan Bay.

The valley of the Teifi presents many points of great beauty and interest between Llandyssul and the sea. The rapids of Henllan, the falls of Cenarth and the wooded cliffs of Coedmore constitute some of the finest scenery in South Wales. The valley of the Aeron is well wooded and fertile, while the Rheidol contains amidst striking surroundings the famous cascade spanned by the Devil's Bridge, which is known to the Welsh as Pont-ar-Fynach (the Monks' Bridge).

Geology.—The rocks of Cardiganshire consist of shales, slates and grits which have been folded and uptilted so that nowhere do they retain their original horizontality. They belong entirely to the Ordovician and Silurian periods; they have yielded few fossils, and much work remains to be done upon them before the stratigraphical subdivisions can be clearly defined. Many metalliferous lodes occur in the rocks, and the lead mines have long been famous; it was from the profits of his mining speculations, carried on chiefly in this county, that the celebrated Sir Hugh Myddleton was enabled to carry out his gigantic project for supplying London with water by means of the New River. Copper and zinc ores have also been obtained. Tregaron is the centre of the mining district, and the Lisburne, Goginan and Cwm Ystwyth mines are among the most important.

The slates have been worked at Devil's Bridge, Corris, Strata Florida, Goginan, &c. Glacial drift occupies some of the lower ground, and peaty bogs are common on the mountains. A small tract of blown sand lies at the mouth of the river Dovey.

Industries.—The climate on the coast is mild and salubrious, but that of the hill country is cold, bleak and rainy. The cultivated crops consist of oats, wheat, barley, turnips and potatoes; and in the lower districts on the coast, especially in the neighbourhood of Cardigan, Aberaeron and Llanrhystyd, good crops are raised. The uplands are mostly covered by wild heathy pastures, which afford good grazing for Welsh mountain sheep and ponies. The country has long been celebrated for its breed of "Cardiganshire cobs," for which high prices are often obtained from English dealers, who frequent the local horse fairs, especially Dalis Fair at Lampeter. Cattle, sheep, pigs, butter, oats, wool, flannel and

142

coarse slates form the principal 320 articles of export. Hand-looms are by no means uncommon in the remote parts of the country, and clog-making of alder wood meets a local demand. The North Cardiganshire lead-mines, of which the Lisburne, Goginan and Cwm Ystwyth mines are the most noted, have been famous, and are said to have been worked by the Romans. Some of the lead raised is very rich in silver, and in the 17th century so great was the amount of silver obtained that a mint for coining it was erected by virtue of letters patent at Aberystwyth.

Communications.—The railways within the county are the Cambrian, by means of which access is given to Aberystwyth from all parts of the kingdom; and the former Manchester & Milford line, which runs south from Aberystwyth by Lampeter to Pencader, and has been acquired by the Great Western railway. The lower valley of the Teifi, or Tivyside, is reached by means of two branch lines of the Great Western railway—one from Whitland to Cardigan, and the other from Pencader to Llandyssul and Newcastle-Emlyn.

Population and Administration.—The area of the administrative county is 443,071 acres, with a population in 1891 of 63,467, and in 1901 of 60,237. The municipal boroughs are Aberystwyth (pop. 8013), Cardigan (3511) and Lampeter (1722). Aberaeron and New Quay are urban districts. Other towns are Tregaron (1509), an ancient but decayed market-town in a wild boggy district; Aberaeron (1331), a small seaport, and Llandyssul (2801,) a rising place on the Teifi with woollen factories. In modern times several small watering-places have sprung up on the coast, notably at Borth, New Quay, Tresaith, Aberporth and Gwbert. Quarter sessions are held at Lampeter, and here also are held the assizes for the county, which lies in the South Wales circuit. The county returns one member of parliament, and has no parliamentary borough. Ecclesiastically it lies wholly in the diocese of St David's, and contains sixty-six parishes.

History.—In spite of its poverty and sparse population, Cardiganshire has never ceased to play a prominent part in all Welsh political, literary and educational movements. The early history of the district is obscure, but at the time of the Roman invasion it was tenanted by the Dimetae, a Celtic tribe, within whose limits was comprised the greater portion of the south-west of Wales. After the departure of the Romans, the whole basin of the Teifi eventually fell into the power of Ceredig, son of Cunedda Wledig of North Wales; and the district, peopled with his subjects and nearly co-extensive with the existing shire, obtained the name of Ceredigion, later corrupted into Cardigan. During the 5th and 6th centuries Ceredigion was largely civilized by Celtic missionaries, notably by St David and St Padarn, the latter of whom founded a bishopric at Llanbadarn Fawr, which in the 8th century became merged in the see of St David's. Two important local traditions, evidently based on fact, are associated with this remote era:—the inundation of the Cantref-y-Gwaelod and the synod of Llanddewi Brefi. The Cantref-y-Gwaelod (the lowland Hundred), a large tract of flat pasture-land containing sixteen townships, and protected from the inroad of the sea by sluices, was suddenly submerged at an uncertain date about the year 500. The legend of its destruction declares that Seithenyn, the drunken keeper of the sluices, carelessly let in the waters of the bay, with the result that the land was lost for ever, and Prince Gwyddno and his son Elphin, with all their subjects, were forced to migrate to the wild region of Snowdon. This tale has ever been a favourite theme with Welsh bards, so that "the sigh of Gwyddno when the wave turned over his land" remains a familiar figure of speech throughout Wales. In support of this story it may be mentioned that there are indications of submerged dwellings and roads (*e.g.* the Sarn Cynfelin and Sarn Badrig) between the mouth of the Dovey and Cardigan Head. The famous synod of Brefi, an historical fact clouded by miraculous details, probably took place early in the 6th century, when at a largely attended meeting of the Welsh clergy held at Brefi, near the source of the Teifi, St David's eloquence for ever silenced the champions of the Pelagian heresy. In the 10th and 11th centuries the coast of Ceredigion suffered much from the inroads of the Danes, and in later times of the Normans and Flemings; but on the whole the native inhabitants seem to have maintained a successful resistance. By the close of the 11th century most of Ceredigion had been reduced by the Normans, and during the 12th and 13th centuries it formed a favourite battle ground between the Welsh princes and the English forces. By the Statutes of Rhuddlan (1284) Edward I. constituted Ceredigion out of the former principality of Wales a shire on the

143

English model, dividing the new county into six hundreds and fixing the assizes at Carmarthen. By the act of Union in the reign of Henry VIII., the boundaries of the county were subsequently enlarged to their present size by the addition of certain outlying portions of the Marches round Tregaron and Cardigan, and the assizes were assigned to the county town. During the rebellion of Owen Glendower in the opening years of the 15th century, the county was again disturbed, and Owen for a short time actually held a court in Aberystwyth Castle. In the year 1485, according to local tradition, Henry of Richmond marched through South Cardiganshire on his way to Bosworth Field, and he is stated to have raised recruits round Llanarth, where the old mansion of Wern, still standing, is pointed out as his halting-place on this occasion. Under Henry VIII. Cardiganshire was for the first time empowered to send a representative member to parliament, and under Mary the same privilege was extended to the boroughs. During the Great Rebellion the county—which possessed at least three leading Parliamentarians in the persons of Sir John Vaughan, of Crosswood, afterwards chief justice of the common pleas; Sir Richard Pryse, of Gogerddan; and James Philipps, of Cardigan Priory—seems to have been less Royalist in its sympathies than other parts of Wales. At this time the castles of Cardigan and Aberystwyth, both held in the name of King Charles, were reduced to ruins by the Cromwellian army. In the 18th century the Methodist movement found great support in the county; in fact, Daniel Rowland (1713-1790), curate of Llangeitho, was one of the chief leaders of this important revival. The 19th century witnessed the foundation of two important educational centres in the county:— St David's College at Lampeter (1827), and one of the three colleges of the university of Wales at Aberystwyth (1872). In the years 1842-1843 the county was much disturbed by the Rebecca Riots, during which a large number of turnpike gates were destroyed by local mobs. Forty-five years later it was affected by the Welsh agrarian agitation against payment of tithe, which produced some scenes of violence against the distraining police, especially in the district round Llangranog.

Chief amongst the county families of Cardigan is that of Lloyd, descendants of the powerful Cadifor ap Dinawal, lord of Castle Howell, in the 12th century. Certain branches of this family, such as the Lloyds of Millfield (Maes-y-felin), the Lloyds of Llanlyr and the Lloyds of Peterwell, are extinct, but others are still flourishing. The family of Vaughan of Crosswood, or Trawscoed (now represented by the earl of Lisburne), has held its family estates in the male line for many centuries. A representative in the female line of the ancient house of Pryse, long prominent in the annals of the county, still possesses the old family seat of Gogerddan. Other families worthy of mention are Lloyd of Bronwydd, Powell of Nanteos and Johnes of Hafod and Llanfair-Clydogau.

Antiquities.—Scattered over all parts of the county are numerous British or early medieval tumuli and camps. Traces of the ancient Roman road, the *Via Occidentalis*—called by the Welsh *Sarn Helen*, a corruption of *Sarn Lleon*, Road of the Legion—are to be found in the eastern districts of the county; and at Llanio are to be seen what are perhaps the remains of the Roman military station of Loventium. There are also various inscribed and incised stones, of which good examples exist in the churchyards of Llanbadarn Fawr and Llanddewi Brefi. In buildings of interest Cardiganshire is singularly deficient. Besides the ruins of Aberystwyth and Cardigan Castles, and of Strata Florida Abbey, there is a large cruciform church of the 12th century at Llanbadarn Fawr; whilst the massive parish church of Llanddewi Brefi once formed part of the minster of a prebendal college founded by Bishop Beck of St David's towards the close of the 13th century. Tregaron, Llanwenog, Llandyssul and Llanarth own parish churches with western towers of early date, but for the most part the ecclesiastical structures of Cardiganshire are small in size and mean in appearance, and many of them were entirely rebuilt during the latter half of the 19th century. The little church of Eglwys Newydd, near the Devil's Bridge, contains one of Sir Francis Chantrey's masterpieces, a white marble group in memory of Mariamne Johnes (1818), the daughter of Thomas Johnes, of Hafod (1748-1816), the translator of Froissart.

Customs, etc.—The old Welsh costume, customs and superstitions are fast disappearing, although they linger in remote districts such as the neighbourhood of Llangeitho. The steeple-crowned beaver hat has practically vanished, although it was in general use within living memory; but the short petticoat and overskirt (*pais-a-gŵn-bâch*), the frilled mob-cap, little check shawl and buckled shoes are still worn by many of the older women. Of peculiarly Welsh customs, the bidding (*gwahoddiad*) is not quite extinct in the county. The bidding was a formal invitation sent by a betrothed pair through a bidder (*gwahoddwr*) to request the presence and gifts of all their neighbours at the forthcoming marriage. All presents sent were duly registered in a book with a view to repayment, when a similar occasion should arise in the case of the donors. When printing became cheap and common, the services of the professional bidder were often dispensed with, and instead printed leaflets were circulated. The curious horse wedding (*priodas ceffylau*) at which the man and his friends pursued the future bride to the church porch on horseback, and then returned home at full gallop, became obsolete before the end of the 19th century. Of the practices connected with death, the wake, or watching of the corpse, alone remains; but the habit of attending funerals, even those of strangers, is still popular with both sexes, so that a funeral procession in Cardiganshire is often a very imposing sight. Nearly all the old superstitions, once so prevalent, concerning the fairies (*tylwyth teg*) and fairy rings, goblins (*bwbachod*), and the teulu, or phantom funeral, are rapidly dying out; but in the corpse candle (*canwll corph*), a mysterious light which acts as a death-portent and is traditionally connected with St David, are still found many believers.

AUTHORITIES.—Sir S.R. Meyrick, *History and Antiquities of Cardiganshire*(London, 1806); Rev. G. Eyre Evans, *Cardiganshire and its Antiquities*(Aberystwyth, 1903); E.R. Horsfall-Turner, *Walks and Wanderings in County Cardigan* (Bingley).

CARDINAL (Lat. *cardinalis*), in the Roman Church, the title of the highest dignitaries next to the pope. The cardinals constitute the council or senate of the sovereign pontiff, his auxiliaries in the general government of the Church; it is they who act as administrators of the Church during a vacancy of the Holy See and elect the new pope. Together they constitute a spiritual body called the Sacred College. The dignity of cardinal is not an essential part of the legal constitution of the Church; it is a reflection of and participation in the sovereign dignity of the Head of the Church, by the chief clergy of the Church of Rome. The present position is the result of a long process of evolution, of which there are several interesting survivals.

The name is derived from *cardo*, hinge; like many other words (the word*pope* in particular) it was originally of a more general application, before it was reserved exclusively to the members of the Sacred College, and the word is still used adjectivally in the sense of pre-eminent or that on which everything else "hinges." As early as the 6th century we find mentioned, in the letters of St Gregory, cardinal bishops and priests. This expression signifies clergy who are attached to their particular church in a stable relation, as a door is attached to a building by its hinges (see Thomassin, *Vetus et nova discipl.* vol. 1, lib. ii. cap. 113-115). Moreover, this sense is still preserved in the present day in the expressions *incardinatio, excardinatio*, which signify the act by which a bishop permanently attaches a foreign cleric to his diocese, or allows one of his own clergy to leave his diocese in order to belong to another. For a long time, too, the superior clergy, and especially the canons of cathedrals or the heads of important churches, were *cardinales* (see examples in Du Cange, *Glossarium, s.v.*). Gradually, however, this title was confined by usage to the Roman cardinals, until Pius V., by his constitution of the 15th of February 1568, reserved it to them exclusively.

The grouping of the cardinals into a body called the Sacred College, the College of Cardinals, is connected, in the case at least of cardinal priests, with the ancient *presbyterium*, which existed in each church from the earliest times.***The Sacred College.***The Sacred College as such was not, however, definitively constituted until the uniting of the three orders of cardinals into a single body, the body which was to elect the pope; and this only took place in the 12th century. Up till that time the elements remained distinct, and there were separate classes: the "Roman" bishops, *i.e.* bishops of sees near Rome, presbyters of the "titles" (*tituli*) of Rome, and deacons of the Roman Church. Nowadays, the Sacred College is still composed of three orders or categories: cardinal bishops, cardinal priests, and cardinal deacons. But the process of evolution has not been the same in the case of all these orders.

Cardinal bishops are the bishops of suburbicarian churches, situated in the immediate neighbourhood of Rome. Very early we find them assisting the pope in his ritual functions and in dealing with important business; **Cardinal bishops.** they formed a kind of permanent synod (cf. the σύνοδος ἐνδημοῦσα of Constantinople): and they also took the place of the pope in the ceremonies of the liturgy, excepting the most important ones, and especially in the service of the cathedral at Rome, the Lateran. A passage from the life of Stephen II. (A.D. 769), in the *Liber Pontificalis* (ed. Duchesne, i. p. 478), shows clearly that they were seven in number and served for a week in turn: *Hic constituit ut omni dominico die a septem Episcopis cardinalibus hebdomadariis, qui in ecclesia Salvatoris* (the Lateran) *observant, missarum solemnia super altare Beati Petri celebrarentur.* They were called "cardinal bishops of the Lateran church," as recorded by St Peter Damian in 1058 (Ep. 1, lib. ii.). Their sees are the same to-day as they were then: Ostia, Porto, Santa Rufina (Sylva Candida), Albano, Sabina, Tusculum (Frascati) and Palestrina. From time immemorial the bishop of Ostia has had the privilege of sacring the pope, and on this ground he enjoys the right of wearing the "pallium"; he is *ex officio* dean of the suburbicarian bishops, and consequently dean of the Sacred College. His episcopal see having been in ruins for a long time, that of Velletri has been joined to it. The second rank belongs to the bishop of Porto, who is *ex officio* vice-dean of the Sacred College; his episcopal see being also in ruins Calixtus II. added to it that of Santa Rufina, thus reducing the number of suburbicarian bishoprics and cardinal bishops to six; this number was adhered to by Sixtus V., and has not varied since.

The second order of cardinals is that of the cardinal priests. It represents and is a continuation of the ancient *presbyterium*; but in Rome the process of evolution was different from that in the other episcopal towns. In the latter, **Cardinal priests.** the division into parishes was but slowly accomplished; there is no authority for their existence before the year 1000; the bishop with the higher clergy, now developed into the chapter, were in residence at the cathedral, which formed, as it were, the one parish in the town. At Rome, on the contrary (and doubtless at Alexandria), certain churches, to which were attached certain districts, were at an early date entrusted to one or more priests. These churches, in which the liturgy was celebrated, or certain sacraments administered, were called *tituli* (titles). According to the *Liber Pontificalis* (ed. Duchesne, i. pp. 122, 126, 164), the titles of Rome, numbering twenty-five, were already established as early as the 1st century; this seems hardly probable, but it was certainly the case in the 5th century. The priest serving one of these churches was the priest of that title, and, similarly, the church which he served was that priest's title. When several priests were attached to the same church, only the first, or principal one, had the title; he alone was the *presbyter cardinalis.* This practice explains how it is that the Roman presbyterium did not give rise to a cathedral chapter, but to cardinal priests, each attached to his title. As the higher 322clergy of Rome gradually acquired a more important status, the relations between the cardinal priest and the church of which he bore the title became more and more nominal; but they have never entirely ceased. Even to-day every cardinal priest has his title, a church in Rome of which he is the spiritual head, and the name of which appears in his official signature, *e.g.* "Herbertus tituli sanctorum Andreae et Gregorii sanctae romanae ecclesiae presbyter cardinalis Vaughan." When the attachment of the cardinal priest to his title had become no more than a tradition, the number of cardinal titles, which in the 11th century had reached twenty-eight, was increased according to need, and it was held an honour for a church to be made titulary. The last general rearrangement of the titular churches was begun by Clement VIII. and completed by Paul V.; Leo XIII. made a title of the church of San Vitale. To-day, according to the *Gerarchia Pontificia* the cardinal titles number fifty-three; since the highest possible number of cardinal priests is fifty, and this number is never reached, it follows that there are always a certain number of vacant titles. The first title is that of San Lorenzo in Lucina, and the cardinal priest of the oldest standing takes the name of "first priest,"*protopresbyter.*

The third order of cardinals is that of the cardinal deacons. For a long time the Roman Church, faithful to the example of the primitive church at Jerusalem (Acts vi.), had only seven deacons. Their special function was the administration **Cardinal deacons.** of her temporal property, and particularly works of charity. Between them were divided at an early date the fourteen districts (*regiones*) of Rome, grouped two by two so as to constitute the seven ecclesiastical districts. Now the charitable works were carried on in establishments called *diaconiae*, adjoining churches which were specially appropriated to each *diaconia*. The connexion between the names (*diaconus*) and (*diaconia*) and the presence of a church in connexion with each diaconia gradually established for the deacons a position analogous to that of priests. In the 8th century Pope Adrian found sixteen diaconiae and founded two others (*Lib. Pont.* ed. Duchesne, i. p. 509); in the 12th century the cardinal deacons, who then numbered eighteen, were no longer distinguished by an ecclesiastical district, as they had formerly been, but by the name of the church connected with some diaconia (loc. cit. p. 364). By the time of Sixtus V. the connexion between a cardinal deacon and his diaconia was merely nominal. Sixtus reduced the number of cardinal deacons to fourteen; and this is still the number to-day. Except that his church is called a diaconia, and not a title, the cardinal deacon is in this respect assimilated to the cardinal priest; but he does not mention his diaconia in his official signature: *e.g.* "Joannes Henricus diaconus cardinalis Newman." There are at present sixteen diaconiae, the chief being that of Santa Maria in Via lata; the cardinal deacon of longest standing takes the name of "first deacon," *protodiaconus.*

Cardinals can pass from one order, title or see to another, by a process of "option." When a suburbicarian see falls vacant, the cardinals resident at Rome have the right of "opting" for it in order of rank,—that is to say, of claiming it in consistory and receiving their promotion to it. In the same way cardinal deacons can pass after ten years to the order of priests, while retaining after their passage the rank in the Sacred College given them by the date of their promotion.

With the exception of the classes resulting from the order to which they belong, there are no distinctions between the rights of the various cardinals. As to the ordination obligatory upon them, it is that indicated in their title; cardinal bishops must naturally be bishops; for cardinal priests it is enough to have received the priesthood, though many of them are actually bishops; similarly, it is enough for cardinal deacons to have received the diaconate, though most of them are priests; cases have occurred, however, even in quite recent times, of cardinals who have only received the diaconate, *e.g.* Cardinal Mertel.

There is one cardinal chosen by the pope from among the Sacred College to whom is entrusted the administration of the common property; this is the cardinal camerlengo or chamberlain (*camerarius*). His office is an important one, for during the vacancy of the Holy See it is he who exercises all external authority, especially that connected with the Conclave.

The number of the cardinals reaches a total of 70: six cardinal bishops, fifty cardinal priests and fourteen cardinal deacons. This number was definitively fixed by Sixtus V. (constit. *Postquam*, 5th December 1586); but the Sacred College **Number and distribution.** never reaches its full number, and there are always ten or so "vacant hats," as the saying goes. Though the rule laid down by Sixtus V. has not been modified since, before him the number of cardinals was far from being constant. For a long time it varied in the neighbourhood of twenty; in 1331 John XXII. said that there were twenty cardinals; in 1378 they were reckoned at 23. Their number increased during the Great Schism because there were several rival obediences. The councils of Constance and Basel reduced the number of cardinals to 24; but it did not rest at that for long, and in the 16th century was more than doubled. In 1517 Leo X., in order to introduce strong supporters of himself into the Sacred College, created 31 cardinals at the same time. The highest number was reached under Pius IV., when the cardinals numbered as many as 76.

The composition of the Sacred College is subject to no definite law; but the necessity for giving a first representation to different interests, especially in view of the election of the popes, has for a long time past thrown open the Sacred College to representatives of the episcopate of the Catholic nations. From the 11th century onwards are to be found cases in which the pope summoned to its ranks persons who did not belong to the Roman Church, particularly abbots, who were not even required to give up the direction of their monasteries. In the following century occur a few cases of bishops being created cardinals without having to leave their see, and of cardinals upon whom were conferred foreign bishoprics (cf.

Thomassin, loc. cit. cap. 114, n. 9). Of the cardinals created by the popes of Avignon the majority were French, and in 1331 John XXII. remarks that 17 cardinals were French out of the 20 who then existed. The councils of Constance and Basel forbade that more than a third of the cardinals should belong to the same country. After the return of the popes to Rome and after the Great Schism, the ancient customs were soon resumed; the cardinals were for the most part Italians, the entire number of cardinals' hats conferred on the other Catholic nations only amounting to a minority. The non-Italian cardinals, with rare exceptions, are not resident in Rome; together with the rank of cardinal they receive a dispensation from residing *in curia*; they are none the less, as cardinals, priests or deacons of the Roman Church.

The reform of the College of Cardinals inaugurated by the councils of Constance and Basel, though without much immediate success, was not only concerned with the number and nationality of the cardinals; it also dealt with conditions *Qualifications.* of age, learning and other qualifications: men of the most honourable character, aged not less than thirty, were to be chosen; at least a third were to be chosen from among the graduates of the universities; persons of royal blood and princes were not to be admitted in too great numbers, and lastly, relatives of the pope were to be set aside. Moreover, in order to secure the effectiveness of these reforms, selection of the new cardinals was to be made by the votes of the members of the Sacred College given in writing. This mode of control was perhaps excessive, and the reform consequently remained ineffective. Up to the middle of the 16th century there were still instances of unfortunate and even scandalous appointments to the cardinalate of very young men, of relatives or favourites of the popes and of men whose qualifications were by no means ecclesiastical. In the Sacred College as elsewhere nepotism and an exaggerated estimate of temporal interests were rife. At last a real reform was effected. The council of Trent (sess. xxiv. cap. i. *de reform.*) requires for cardinals all the qualifications prescribed by law for bishops. Sixtus V. defined these still more clearly, and his regulations are still in force: a cardinal must, in the year of his promotion, be of the canonical age required for his reception into the order demanded by his rank.*i.e.* 22 for the diaconate, 23 for the priesthood and 30 for the episcopate, and if not already ordained he must take orders in the year of his appointment. Men of illegitimate birth are 323excluded, as well as near relatives of the pope (with one exception) and of the cardinals; the personal qualities to be most sought for are learning, holiness and an honourable life. All these recommendations have been, on the whole, well observed, and are so better than ever in the present day. We may add that the religious orders have had a certain number of representatives, four, at least, in the Sacred College, since Sixtus V., several of whom, as we know, became popes. As to the cardinals' hats granted at the request of the heads of Catholic states, they are subject to negotiations analogous to those concerning nominations to the episcopate, though entailing no concordatory agreement, strictly speaking, on the part of the popes.

The *creation* of cardinals (to use the official term) is in fact nowadays the function of the pope alone. It is accomplished by the publication of the persons chosen by the pope in secret consistory (*q.v.*). No other formality is *Creation.* essential; and the provision of Eugenius IV., which required the reception of the insignia of the cardinalate for the promotion to be valid, was abrogated before long, and definitely annulled by the declaration of Pius V. of the 26th of January 1571. Similarly neither the consent nor the vote of the Sacred College is required. It is true that a Roman *Ceremoniale* of 1338 (Thomassin, loc. cit. cap. 114, n. 12) still enjoins upon the pope to consult the Sacred College, on the Wednesdays during Ember days, as to whether it is necessary to nominate new cardinals, and if so, how many; but this is only a survival of the ritual of the ancient form of ordination. The injunctions of the councils of Constance and Basel as to the written vote of the cardinals became before very long a dead letter, but there still remains a relic of them. In the consistory, when the pope has nominated those whom he desires to raise to the purple, he puts to the cardinals present the question: "Quid vobis videtur?" The cardinals bend the head as a sign of their consent, and the pope then continues: "Itaque, auctoritate omnipotentis Dei, sanctorum Apostolorum Petri et Pauli, et Nostra, creamus et publicamus sanctae romanae Ecclesiae cardinales N. et N., etc."

The new dignitary, who has been warned of his nomination several weeks in advance by "biglietto" (note) from the office of the secretary of state, is then officially informed of it by a *ceremoniarius* of the pope; he at once waits upon the pope, to whom he is presented by one of the cardinals. The pope first invests him with the rochet and red biretta, but there is no formal ceremony. The conferring of the cardinal's red hat takes place a few days later in a public consistory; while placing the hat on his head the pope pronounces the following words: "Ad laudem omnipotentis Dei et Sanctae Sedis ornamentum, accipe galerum rubrum, insigne singularis dignitatis cardinalatus, per quod designatur quod ad mortem et sanguinis effusionem inclusive pro exaltatione sanctae fidei, pace et quiete populi christiani, augmento et statu sacrosanctae romanae Ecclesiae, te intrepidum exhibere debeas, in nomine Patris et Filii et Spiritus Sancti." While pronouncing the last words the pope makes the sign of the cross three times over the new cardinal. The public consistory is immediately followed by a secret consistory, to accomplish the last ceremonies. The pope begins by closing the mouth of the new cardinal, who is led before him, as a symbol of the discretion he should observe; after this he bestows on him the cardinal's ring, assigns him a title or diaconia; and finally, after going through the formality of consulting the Sacred College, finishes with the symbolic ceremony of the opening of the mouth, signifying the right and duty of the new cardinal to express his opinion and vote in the matters which it will fall to him to consider.

When the cardinals are resident abroad and appointed at the request of the heads of their state, a member of the Noble Guard is sent on the same day that the consistory is held to take the new dignitary the cardinal's "calotte"; after a few days the red biretta is brought to him by a Roman prelate, with the powers of an *ablegatus*; the biretta is conferred on him with great pomp by the head of the state. But the conferring of the red hat always takes place at the hands of the pope in a public consistory.

Sometimes, after nominating the cardinals, the pope adds that he also appoints a certain number of others, whose names he does not divulge, but reserves the right of publishing at a later date. These cardinals, whose names he conceals **Cardinals "in petto."** "in his breast," are for that reason called cardinals *in pectore* (Ital. *in petto*). This practice seems to go back to Martin V., who may have had recourse to this expedient in order to avoid the necessity of soliciting the votes of the cardinals; but for a long time past the popes have only resorted to it for quite other reasons. If the pope dies before making known the cardinals *in petto*, the promotion is not valid; if he publishes them, the cardinals take rank from the day on which they were reserved *in pectore*, the promotion acting retrospectively, even in the matter of emoluments. This method has sometimes been used by the popes to ensure to certain prelates who had merit, but were poor, the means of paying the expenses of their promotion. In March 1875 Pius IX. announced the nomination of several cardinals *in petto*, whose names would be given in his will. It was pointed out to the pope that this posthumous publication would not be a pontifical act, and ran the risk of being contested, or even declared invalid; Pius IX. gave way before this reasoning, and published the names in a subsequent consistory (Sept. 17).

The dignity of the cardinals is a participation in that of the sovereign pontiff, and as such places them above all the other ecclesiastical dignitaries and prelates. This rank, however, has not always been assigned to them; **Dignity.** but was attributed to the cardinal bishops before it was to the rest. Their common prerogative was definitively established when they became the sole electors of the pope, at a period when the papacy, under pontiffs like Innocent III., shone with its most brilliant lustre. For example, at the council of Lyons in 1245 all the cardinals took precedence of the archbishops and bishops. It was in 1245, or perhaps the year before, that Innocent IV. granted the cardinals the privilege of wearing the red hat; as to the scarlet robe which still forms their costume of ceremony, it was already worn by cardinals performing the functions of legate; and the use was soon extended to all. As to their civil relations, cardinals were assimilated by the Catholic kings to the rank of princes of the blood royal, cardinals being the highest in the Church, after the pope, just as princes of the blood royal are the first in the kingdom after the king. Of the many ecclesiastical privileges enjoyed by the cardinals, we will mention only two: the real, though nowadays restricted, jurisdiction which they exercise over the churches forming their title or diaconia; and the official style of address conferred on them by Urban VIII. (10th of June 1630), of Eminence,*Eminentissimo signore.*

The most lofty function of the cardinals is the election of the pope (see CONCLAVE). But this function is necessarily intermittent, and they have many others to fulfil *sede plena.* On those rare occasions on which the pope *Functions.* officiates in person, they carry out, according to their respective orders, their former functions in the ritual. But they are, above all, the assistants of the pope in the administration of the Church; they fill certain permanent offices, such as those of chancellor, penitentiary, &c.; or again, temporary missions, such as that of legate *a latere;* they have seats in the councils and tribunals which deal with the affairs of the Church, and the Roman congregations of cardinals (see CURIA ROMANA).

BIBLIOGRAPHY.—All works on canon law contain a treatise on the cardinals. See particularly, for the history, Thomassin, *Vetus et nova discipl.,* tom. I., lib. ii., cap. 113-115. For history and law, Phillips, *Kirchenrecht,* vol. vi.; Hinschius, *System des kathol. Kirchenrechts,* vol. i. p. 312. For the canonical aspect, Ferraris, *Prompta bibliotheca, s.v.* "Cardinales"; Bouix, *De curia romana* (Paris, 1859), pp. 5-141; Card. de Luca, *Relatio curiae romanae,* disc. 5. For details of the ceremonies and costume, Grimaldi, *Les Congrégations romaines* (Sienna, 1890), p. 99 et seq.; Barbier de Montault,*Le Costume et les usages ecclésiastiques* (Paris), s.d. For a list of the names of the cardinals, according to their titles, see De Mas-Latrie, *Trésor de chronologie,* col. 2219-2264; and in the chronological order of their promotion, from St Leo IX. to Benedict XIV., ibid. 1177-1242; also*Dictionnaire des cardinaux* (Paris, 1856).

(A. Bo.*)

324

CARDINAL VIRTUES (Lat. *cardo,* a hinge; the fixed point on which anything turns), a phrase used for the principal virtues on which conduct in general depends. Socrates and Plato (see *Republic,* iv. 427) take these to be Prudence, Courage (or Fortitude), Temperance and Justice. It is noticeable that the virtue of Benevolence, which has played so important a part in Christian ethics and in modern altruistic and sociological theories, is omitted by the ancients. Further, against the Platonic list it may be urged (1) that it is arbitrary, and (2) that the several virtues are not specifically distinct, that the basis of the division is unsound, and that there is overlapping. It is said that St Ambrose was the first to adapt the Platonic classification to Christian theology. By the Roman Catholic Church these virtues are regarded as *natural* as opposed to the*theological* virtues, Faith, Hope and Charity. Some authors, combining the two lists, have spoken of the Seven Cardinal Virtues. In English literature the phrase is found as far back as the *Cursor Mundi* (1300) and the *Ayenbite of Inwit*(1340).

See B. Jowett, *Republic of Plato* (Eng. trans., Oxford, 1887, Introd. p. lxiii); Plato, *Protagoras* (329-330); Aristotle, *Nicomachean Ethics,* vi. 13. 6; Th. Ziegler, *Gesch. d. chr. Eth.* (2nd ed.); H. Sidgwick, *History of Ethics*(5th ed.), pp. 44, 133, 143; and *Methods of Ethics,* p. 375.

CARDING, the process of using the "card" (Lat. *carduus,* a thistle or teasel) for combing textile fibrous materials. The practice of carding is of such great antiquity that its origin cannot be traced. It consists in combing or brushing fibres until they are straight and placed in parallel lines; in doing this, imperfect fibres are separated from perfect ones, all impurities are removed, and the sound fibres are in condition for further treatment. The teasels once used have long given place to hand cards, and these in turn to what, in the rudest form, were known as "stock cards," namely, two wire brushes, each 4 in. broad by 12 in. long, and having teeth bent at a uniform angle. One was nailed upon a bench with the teeth sloping from the operator, the other was similarly secured upon a two-handled bar with the teeth sloping towards the operator. The material to be treated was thinly spread upon the fixed card, and the movable one drawn by hand to and fro over it. When sufficiently carded, a rod furnished with parallel projecting needles, called a "needle stick," was pushed amongst the card teeth to strip the fibres from the comb. The strip thus procured was rolled into a sliver and spun. James Hargreaves, the inventor of the spinning jenny, suspended the movable comb by passing two cords over pulleys fixed in the ceiling and attached balance weights to opposite ends of the cords. This enabled him to lengthen the cards, to apply two or three to the same stock and to manipulate the top one with less labour, as well as to produce more and better work. In May of 1748, Daniel Bourn, of Leominster, patented a machine in which four parallel rollers were covered with cards, and set close together. Fibres were fed to the first rotating roller, each in turn drew them from the preceding one, and a grid was employed to remove the carded material from the last roller. This introduced the principle of carding with revolving cylinders whose surfaces were clothed with cards working point to point. In December of the same year Lewis Paul, of Birmingham, the inventor of drawing rollers, patented two types of carding engines. In one, parallel rows of spaced cards were nailed upon a cylinder which was revolved by a winch handle. Beneath the cylinder a concave trough had a card fixed on the inside, so that as the fibres passed between the two series of teeth they were combed. This was the origin of "flat-carding," namely, nailing strips of stationary cards upon transverse pieces of wood and adjusting the strips or flats by screws to the cylinder. In 1762, the father of Sir Robert Peel, with the assistance of Hargreaves, erected and used a cylinder carding engine which differed in some important particulars from Bourn's invention. But although roller-carding and flat-carding are the only principles in use at the present time, to Sir Richard Arkwright belongs the merit of introducing an automatic carding engine, for between the years 1773 and 1775 he combined the various improvements of his predecessors, entirely remodelled the machine, and added parts which made the operation continuous. So successful were these cards that some of them were in use at the beginning of the present century. Notwithstanding the numerous and important changes that have been made since Arkwright's time, carding remains essentially the same as established by him. (See COTTON-SPINNING MACHINERY.)

(T. W. F.)

CARDIOID, a curve so named by G.F.M.M. Castillon (1708-1791), on account of its heart-like form (Gr. καρδία, heart). It was mathematically treated by Louis Carré in 1705 and Koersma in 1741. It is a particular form of the limaçon (*q.v.*) and is generated in the same way. It may be regarded as an epicycloid in which the rolling and fixed circles are equal in diameter, as the inverse of a parabola for its focus, or as the caustic produced by the reflection at a spherical surface of rays emanating from a point on the circumference. The polar equation to the cardioid is $r = a(1 + \cos\theta)$. There is symmetry about the initial line and a cusp at the origin. The area is $3/2\pi a^2$, *i.e.* 1½ times the area of the generating circle; the length of the curve is 8a. (For a figure see LIMAÇON.)

CARDONA (perhaps the anc. *Udura*), a town of north-eastern Spain, in the province of Barcelona; about 55 m. N.W. of Barcelona, on a hill almost surrounded by the river Cardoner, a branch of the Llobregat. Pop. (1900) 3855. Cardona is a picturesque and old-fashioned town, with Moorish walls and citadel, and a 14th-century church. It is celebrated for the extensive deposit of rock salt in its vicinity. The salt forms a mountain mass about 300 ft. high and 3 m. in circumference, covered by a thick bed of a reddish-brown clay, and apparently resting on a yellowish-grey sandstone. It is generally more or less translucent, and large masses of it are quite transparent. The hill is worked like a mine; pieces cut from it are carved by artists in Cardona into images, crucifixes and many articles of an ornamental kind.

CARDOON, *Cynara cardunculus* (natural order Compositae), a perennial plant from the south of Europe and Barbary, a near relation of the artichoke. The edible part, called the *chard*, is composed of the blanched and crisp stalks of the inner leaves. Cardoons are found to prosper on light deep soils. The seed is sown annually about the middle of May, in shallow trenches, like those for celery, and the plants are thinned out to 10 or 12 in. from each other in the lines. In Scotland it is preferable to sow the seed singly in small plots, placing them in a mild temperature, and transplanting them into the trenches after they have attained a height of 8 or 10 in. Water must be copiously supplied in dry weather, both to prevent the formation of flower-stalks and to increase the succulence of the leaves. In autumn the leaf-stalks are applied close to each other, and wrapped round with bands of hay or straw, only the points being left free. Earth is then drawn up around them to the height of 15 or 18 in. Sometimes cardoons are blanched by a more thorough earthing up, in the manner of celery, but in this case the operation must be carried on from the end of summer. During severe frost the tops of the leaves should be defended with straw or litter. Besides the common and Spanish cardoons, there are the prickly-leaved Tours cardoon, the red-stemmed cardoon and the Paris cardoon, all of superior quality, the Paris being the largest and most tender. The common artichoke is also used for the production of chard.

CARDS, PLAYING. As is the case with all very ancient pastimes, the origin of playing-cards is obscure, many nations having been credited with the invention, but the generally accepted view is that they come from Asia. In the Chinese dictionary, *Ching-tsze-tung* (1678), it is said that cards were invented in the reign of Sèun-ho, 1120 A.D., for the amusement of his concubines. There is a tradition that cards have existed in India from time immemorial—very ancient ones, round in form, are preserved in museums—and that they were invented by the Brahmans. Their invention has also been assigned to the Egyptians, with whom they were said to have had a religious meaning, and to the Arabs. A very ingenious theory, founded on numerous singular resemblances to the ancient game of chess 325(*chaturanga*, the four *angas* or members of an army), has been advanced that they were suggested by chess (see "Essay on the Indian Game of Chess," by Sir William Jones, in his *Asiatic Researches*, vol. ii.).

The time and manner of the introduction of cards into Europe are matters of dispute. The 38th canon of the council of Worcester (1240) is often quoted as evidence of cards having been known in England in the middle of the 13th century; but the games *de rege et regina* there mentioned are now thought to have been a kind of mumming exhibition (Strutt says chess). No queen is found in the earliest European cards. In the wardrobe accounts of Edward I. (1278), Walter Stourton is paid 8s. 3d. *ad opus regis ad ludendum ad quatuor reges*, a passage which has been thought to refer to cards, but it is now supposed to mean chess, which may have been called the "game of four kings," as was the case in India (*chaturaji*). If cards were generally known in Europe as early as 1278, it is very remarkable that Petrarch, in his dialogue that treats of gaming, never once mentions them; and that, though Boccaccio, Chaucer and other writers of that time notice various games, there is not a single passage in them that can be fairly construed to refer to cards. Passages have been quoted from various works, of or relative to this period, but modern research leads to the supposition that the word rendered *cards* has often been mistranslated or interpolated. An early mention of a distinct series of playing cards is the entry of Charles or Charbot Poupart, treasurer of the household of Charles VI. of France, in his book of accounts for 1392 or 1393, which runs thus: *Donné à Jacquemin Gringonneur, peintre, pour trois jeux de cartes, à or et à diverses couleurs, ornés de plusieurs devises, pour porter devers le Seigneur Roi, pour son ébatement, cinquante-six sols parisis*. This, of course, refers only to the painting of a set or pack of cards, which were evidently already well known. But, according to various conjectural interpretations of documents, the earliest date of the mention of cards has been pushed farther back by different authorities. For instance, in the account-books of Johanna, duchess of Brabant, and her husband, Wenceslaus of Luxemburg, there is an entry, under date of the 14th of May 1379, as follows: "Given to Monsieur and Madame four peters, two florins, value eight and a half moutons, wherewith to buy a pack of cards" (*Quartspel met te copen*). This proves their introduction into the Netherlands at least as early as 1379. In a British Museum MS. (Egerton, 2, 419) mention is made of a game of cards (*qui ludus cartarum appellatur*) in Germany in 1377. The safe conclusion with regard to their introduction is that, though they may possibly have been known to a few persons in Europe about the middle of the 14th century, they did not come into general use until about a half-century later. Whence they came is another question that has not yet been answered satisfactorily. If we may believe the evidence of Covelluzzo of Viterbo (15th century) cards were introduced into Italy from Arabia. On the authority of a chronicle of one of his ancestors he writes: "In the year 1379 was brought into Viterbo the game of cards, which comes from the country of the Saracens, and is with them called *naib*." The Crusaders, who were inveterate gamblers, may have been the instruments of their

152

introduction (see *Istoria della città di Viterbo*, by F. Bussi, Rome, 1743). According to other authorities, cards came first to Spain from Africa with the Moors, and it is significant that, to this day, playing cards are called in Spain *naipes* (probably a corruption of the Arabic *Nabi*, prophet). Taken in connexion with the statement of Covelluzzo, this fact would seem to prove the wide popularity of the game of *naib*, or cards, among the Arab tribes. The meaning of the word (prophet) has been suggested to refer to the fortune-telling function of cards, and the theory has been advanced that they were used by the Moorish gypsies for that purpose. Gypsies are, however, not known to have appeared in Spain before the 15th century, at a time when cards were already well known. In regard to the word *naib*, the Italian language still preserves the name *naibi*, playing cards.

Towards the end of the 14th century cards seem to have become common, for in an edict of the provost of Paris, 1397, working-people are forbidden to play at tennis, bowls, dice, cards or nine-pins on working days. From an omission of any mention of cards in an ordonnance of Charles V. in 1369, forbidding certain other games, it may be reasonably concluded that cards became popular in France between that date and the end of the century. In Italy it is possible that they were generally known at a somewhat earlier date. In the 15th century they were often the object of the attacks of the clergy. In 1423 St Bernardino of Siena preached a celebrated sermon against them at Bologna, in which, like the English Puritans after him, he attributed their invention to the devil. Cards in Germany are referred to in a manuscript of Nuremberg about 1384, which illustrates the rapid spread of the new game throughout Europe. In form the earliest cards were generally rectangular or square, though sometimes circular.

Not long after their introduction, cards began to be used for other purposes than gaming. In 1509 a Franciscan friar, Thomas Murner, published an exposition of logic in the form of a pack of cards, and a pack invented in 1651 by Baptist Pendleton purported to convey a knowledge of grammar. These were soon followed by packs teaching geography and heraldry, the whole class being called "scientiall cards." Politics followed, and in England satirical and historical sets appeared, one of them designed to reveal the plots of the Popish agitators. The first mention of cards in the New World is found in the letters of Herrera, a companion of Cortes, who describes the interest manifested by the Aztecs in the card games of the Spanish soldiers.

Early in the 15th century the making of cards had become a regular trade in Germany, whence they were sent to other countries. Cards were also manufactured in Italy at least as early as 1425, and in England before 1463; for by an act of parliament of 3 Edw. IV. the importation of playing cards is forbidden, in consequence, it is said, of the complaints of manufacturers that importation obstructed their business. No cards of undoubted English manufacture of so early a date have been discovered; and there is reason to believe, notwithstanding the act of Edward IV., that the chief supplies came from France or the Netherlands. In the reign of Elizabeth the importation of cards was a monopoly; but from the time of James I. most of the cards used in this country were of home manufacture. A duty was first levied on cards in the reign of James I.; since when they have always been taxed.

It has been much disputed whether the earliest cards were printed from wood-blocks. If so, it would appear that the art of wood-engraving, which led to that of printing, may have been developed through the demand for the multiplication of implements of play. The belief that the early card-makers or card-painters of Ulm, Nuremberg and Augsburg, from about 1418-1450, were also wood-engravers, is founded on the assumption that the cards of that period were printed from wood-blocks. It is, however, clear that the earliest cards were executed by hand, like those designed for Charles VI. Many of the earliest wood-cuts were coloured by means of a stencil, so it would seem that at the time wood-engraving was first introduced, the art of depicting and colouring figures by means of stencil plates was well known. There are no playing cards engraved on wood to which so early a date as 1423 (that of the earliest dated wood-engraving generally accepted) can be fairly assigned; and as at this period there were professional card-makers established in Germany, it is probable that wood-engraving was employed to produce cuts for sacred subjects before it was applied to cards, and that there were hand-painted and stencilled cards before there were wood-engravings of saints. The German *Briefmaler* or card-painter probably progressed into the wood-engraver; but there is no proof that the earliest wood-engravers were the card-makers.

It is undecided whether the earliest cards were of the kind now common, called *numeral* cards, or whether they were *tarocchi* or *tarots*, which are still used in some parts of France, Germany and Italy, but the probability is that the tarots were the earlier. A pack of tarots consists of seventy-eight cards, four suits of 326numeral cards and twenty-two emblematic cards, called *atutti* or *atouts* (= trumps). Each suit consists of fourteen cards, ten of which are the pip cards, and four court (or more properly *coat* cards), viz. king, queen, chevalier and valet. The *atouts* are numbered from 1 to 21; the unnumbered card, called the *fou*, has no positive value, but augments that of the other *atouts* (see *Académie des jeux*, Corbet, Paris, 1814, for an account of the mode of playing tarocchino or tarots).

The marks of the suits on the earliest cards (German) are hearts, bells, leaves and acorns. No ace corresponding to the earliest known pack has been discovered; but other packs of about the same date have aces, and it seems unlikely that the suits commenced with the deuces.

Next in antiquity to the marks mentioned are swords, batons, cups and money. These are the most common on Italian cards of the late 15th century, and are used both in Italy and in Spain. French cards of the 16th century bear the marks now generally used in France and England, viz. *coeur* (hearts), *trèfle* (clubs), *pique* (spades) and *carreau* (diamonds).

The French *trèfle*, though so named from its resemblance to the trefoil leaf, was in all probability copied from the acorn; and the *pique* similarly from the leaf (*grün*) of the German suits, while its name is derived from the sword of the Italian suits. It is not derived from its resemblance to a pike head, as commonly supposed. In England the French marks are used, and are named—hearts, clubs (corresponding to *trèfle*, the French symbol being joined to the Italian name, *bastoni*), spades (corresponding to the French *pique*, but having the Italian name, *spade*=swords) and diamonds. This confusion of names and symbols is accounted for by Chatto thus—"If cards were actually known in Italy and Spain in the latter part of the 14th century, it is not unlikely that the game was introduced into this country by some of the English soldiers who had served, under Hawkwood and other free captains, in the wars of Italy and Spain. However this may be, it seems certain that the earliest cards commonly used in this country were of the same kind, with respect to the marks of the suits, as those used in Italy and Spain."

About the last quarter of the 15th century, packs with animals, flowers and human figures, for marks of the suits, were engraved upon copper; and later, numerous variations appeared, dictated by the caprice of individual card-makers; but they never came into general use.

The court cards of the early packs were king, chevalier and knave. The Italians were probably the first to substitute a queen for the chevalier, who in French cards is altogether superseded by the queen. The court cards of French packs received fanciful names, which varied from time to time.

AUTHORITIES.—Abbé Rive, *Éclaircissements sur l'invention des cartes à jouer* (Paris, 1780); J.G.I. Breitkopf, *Versuch den Ursprung der Spielkarten zu erforschen* (Leipzig, 1784); Samuel Weller Singer, *Researches into the History of Playing Cards, with Illustrations of the Origin of Printing and Engraving on Wood* (London, 1816); G. Peignot, *Analyse critique et raisonnée de toutes les recherches publiées jusqu'à ce jour, sur l'origine des cartes à jouer* (Dijon, 1826); M.C. Leber, *Études historiques sur les cartes à jouer, principalement sur les cartes françaises* (Paris, 1842); William Andrew Chatto, *Facts and Speculations on the Origin and History of Playing Cards* (London, 1848); P. Boiteau D'Ambly, *Les Cartes à jouer et la cartomancie* (Paris, 1854), translated into English with additions under the title of *The History of Playing Cards, with Anecdotes of their use in Conjuring, Fortune-telling, and Card-sharping*, edited by the Rev. E.S. Taylor, B.A. (London, 1865); W. Hughes Willshire, M.D., *A Descriptive Catalogue of Playing and other Cards in the British Museum*, printed by order of the trustees (London, 1876); *Origine des cartes à jouer*, by R. Merlin (Paris, 1869); *The Devil's Picture Books*, by Mrs J.K. Van Rensselaer (New York, 1890); *Bibliography of Works in English on Playing Cards and Gaming*, by F. Jessel (London, 1905); and especially *Les Cartes à jouer*, by Henri René d'Allemagne (Paris, 1906) (an exhaustive account).

CARDUCCI, BARTOLOMMEO (1560-1610), Italian painter, better known as CARDUCHO, the Spanish corruption of his Italian patronymic, was born in Florence, where he studied architecture and sculpture under Ammanati, and painting under Zuccaero. The latter master he accompanied to Madrid, where he painted the ceiling of the Escorial library, assisting also in the production of the frescos that adorn the cloisters of that famous palace. He was a great favourite with Philip III., and lived and died in Spain, where most of his works are to be found. The most celebrated of them is a Descent from the Cross, in the church of San Felipe el Real, in Madrid.

His younger brother VINCENZO (1568-1638), was born in Florence, and was trained as a painter by Bartolommeo, whom he followed to Madrid. He worked a great deal for Philip III. and Philip IV., and his best pictures are those he executed for the former monarch as decorations in the Prado. Examples of his work are preserved at Toledo, at Valladolid, at Segovia, and at several other Spanish cities. For many years he laboured in Madrid as a teacher of his art, and among his pupils were Giovanni Ricci, Pedro Obregon, Vela, Francisco Collantes, and other distinguished representatives of the Spanish school during the 17th century. He was also author of a treatise or dialogue, *De las Excelencias de la Pintura*, which was published in 1633.

CARDUCCI, GIOSUÈ (1836-1907), Italian poet, was born at Val-di-Castello, in Tuscany, on the 27th of July 1836, his father being Michele Carducci, a physician, of an old Florentine family, who in his youth had suffered imprisonment for his share in the revolution of 1831. Carducci received a good education. He began life as a public teacher, but soon took to giving private lessons at Florence, where he became connected with a set of young men, enthusiastic patriots in politics, and in literature bent on overthrowing the reigning romantic taste by a return to classical models. These aspirations always constituted the mainsprings of Carducci's poetry. In 1860 he became professor at Bologna, where, after in 1865 astonishing the public by a defiant *Hymn to Satan*, he published in 1868 *Levia Gravia*, a volume of lyrics which not only gave him an indisputable position at the head of contemporary Italian poets, but made him the head of a school of which the best Italian men of letters have been disciples, and which has influenced all. Several other volumes succeeded, the most important of which were the *Decennalia* (1871), the *Nuove Poesie* (1872), and the three series of the *Odi Barbare* (1877-1889).

Carducci had been brought into more fraternal contact with the aims of the younger generation by the efforts of Angelo Sommaruga who became, about 1880, the publisher of a group of young unknown writers all destined to some, and a few to great, accomplishment. The period of his prosperity was a strange one for Italy. The first ten years of the newly constituted kingdom had passed more in stupor than activity; original contributions to literature had been scarce, and publishers had preferred bringing out inferior translations of not always admirable French authors to encouraging the original work of Italians—work which it must be confessed was generally mediocre and entirely lifeless. Sommaruga's creation, a literary review called *La Cronaca Bizantina*, gathered together such beginners as Giovanni Marradi, Matilde Serao, Edoardo Scarfoglio, Guido Magnoni and Gabriele d'Annunzio. In order to obtain the sanction of what he considered an enduring name, the founder turned to Giosuè Carducci, then living in retirement at Bologna, discontented with his fate, and still not generally known by the public of his own country. The activity of Sommaruga exercised a great influence on Giosuè Carducci. Within the next few years he published the three admirable volumes of his *Confessioni e Battaglie*, the *Ça Ira* sonnets, the *Nuove Odi Barbare*, and a considerable number of articles, pamphlets and essays, which in their collected edition form the most living part of his work. His lyrical production, too, seemed to reach its perfection in those five years of tense, unrelenting work; for the *Canzone di Legnano*, the Odes to Rome and to Monte Mario, the Elegy on the urn of Percy Bysshe Shelley, the ringing rhymes of the *Intermezzo*, in which he happily blended the satire of Heine with the lyrical form of his native poetry—all belong to this period, together with the essays on Leopardi and on Parini, the admirable discussions in defence of his *Ça Ira*, and the pamphlet called *Eterno Femminino regale*, a kind of self-defence, undertaken to explain the origin of the Alcaic metre to the queen of Italy, which marks the beginning of the last evolution in Carducci's work (1881). The revolutionary spirits of the day, who had always ³²⁷looked upon Giosuè Carducci as their bard and champion, fell away from him after this poem written in honour of a queen, and the poet, wounded by the attitude of his party, wrote what he intended to be his defence and his programme for the future in pages that will remain amongst the noblest and most powerful of contemporary literature. From that time Carducci appears in a new form, evolved afterwards in his last Odes, *Il Piemonte, Li Bicocca di San Giacomo*, the Ode to the daughter of Francesco Crispi on her marriage, and the one to the church where Dante once prayed, *Alla Chiesetta dei Polenta*, which is like the withdrawing into itself of a warlike soul weary of its battle.

For a few months in 1876 Carducci had a seat in the Italian Chamber. In 1881 he was appointed a member of the higher council of education. In 1890 he was made a senator. And in 1906 he was awarded the Nobel prize for literature. He died at Bologna on the 16th of February 1907. By his marriage in 1859 he had two daughters, who survived him, and one son, who died in infancy.

The same qualities which placed Carducci among the classics of Italy in his earlier days remained consistently with him in later life. His thought flows limpid, serene, sure of itself above an undercurrent of sane and vigorous if pagan philosophy. Patriotism, the grandeur of work, the soul-satisfying power of justice, are the poet's dominant ideals. For many years the national struggle for liberty had forced the best there was in heart and brain into the atmosphere of political intrigue and from one battlefield to another; Carducci therefore found a poetry emasculated by the deviation into other channels of the intellectual virility of his country. On this mass of patriotic doggerel, of sickly, languishing sentimentality as insincere as it was inane, he grafted a poetry not often tender, but always violently felt and thrown into a mould of majestic form; not always quite expected or appreciated by his contemporaries, but never commonplace in structure; always high in tone and free in spirit. The adaptation of various kinds of Latin metres to the somewhat sinewless language he found at his disposal, whilst it might have been an effort of mere pedantry in another, was a life-giving and strengthening inspiration in his case. Another of his characteristics, which made him peculiarly precious to his countrymen, is the fact that his poems form a kind of lyric record of the Italian struggle for independence. The tumultuous vicissitudes of all other nations, however, and the pageantry of the history of all times, have in turns touched his particular order of imagination. The more important part of his critical work which belongs to this later period consists of his *Conversazioni critiche*, his *Storia filosofica della letteratura Italiana*, and a masterly edition of Petrarch. That he should have had the faults of his qualities is not remarkable. Being almost a pioneer in the world of criticism, his essays on the authors of other countries, though appearing in the light of discoveries to his own country, absorbed as it had hitherto been in its own vicissitudes, have little of value to the general student beyond the attraction of robust style. And in his unbounded admiration for the sculptural lines of antique Latin poetry he sometimes relapsed into that fascination by mere sound which is the snare of his language, and against which his own work in its great moments is a reaction.

CARDWELL, EDWARD (1787-1861), English theologian, was born at Blackburn in Lancashire in 1787. He was educated at Brasenose College, Oxford (B.A. 1809; M.A. 1812; B.D. 1819; D.D. 1831), and after being for several years tutor and lecturer, was appointed, in 1814, one of the examiners to the university. In 1825 he was chosen Camden professor of ancient history; and during his five years' professorship he published an edition of the *Ethics* of Aristotle, and a course of his lectures on *The Coinage of the Greeks and Romans*. In 1831 he succeeded Archbishop Whately as principal of St Alban's Hall. He published in 1837 a student's edition of the Greek Testament, and an edition of the Greek and Latin texts of the *History of the Jewish War*, by Josephus, with illustrative notes. But his most important labours were in the field of English church history. He projected an extensive work, which was to embrace the entire synodical history of the church in England, and was to be founded on David Wilkins's *Concilia Magnae Britanniae et Hiberniae*. Of this work he executed some portions only. The first published was *Documentary Annals of the Reformed Church of England from 1546 to 1716*, which appeared in 1839. It was followed by a *History of Conferences, &c., connected with the Revision of the Book of Common Prayer* (1840). On 1842 appeared *Synodalia, a Collection of*

Articles of Religion, Canons, and Proceedings of Convocation from 1547 to 1717, completing the series for that period. Closely connected with these works is the *Reformatio Legum Ecclesiasticarum* (1850), which treats of the efforts for reform during the reigns of Henry VIII., Edward VI., and Elizabeth. Cardwell also published in 1854 a new edition of Bishop Gibson's *Synodus Anglicana*. He was one of the best men of business in the university, and held various important posts, among which were those of delegate of the press, curator of the university galleries, manager of the Bible department of the press, and private secretary to successive chancellors of the university. He established the Wolvercot paper mill. He died at Oxford on the 23rd of May 1861.

CARDWELL, EDWARD CARDWELL, VISCOUNT (1813-1886), English statesman, was the son of a merchant of Liverpool, where he was born on the 24th of July 1813. After a brilliant career at Oxford, where he gained a double first-class, he entered parliament as member for Clitheroe in 1842, and in 1845 was made secretary to the treasury. He supported Sir Robert Peel's free-trade policy, and went out of office with him. In 1847 he was elected for Liverpool, but lost his seat in 1852 for having supported the repeal of the navigation laws. He soon found another constituency at Oxford, and upon the formation of Lord Aberdeen's coalition ministry became president of the Board of Trade, although debarred by the jealousy of his Whig colleagues from a seat in the cabinet. In 1854 he carried, almost without opposition, a most important and complicated act consolidating all existing shipping laws, but in 1855 resigned, with his Peelite colleagues, upon the appointment of Mr Roebuck's Sevastopol inquiry committee, declining the offer of the chancellorship of the Exchequer pressed upon him by Lord Palmerston. In 1858 he moved the famous resolution condemnatory of Lord Ellenborough's despatch to Lord Canning on the affairs of Oude, which for a time seemed certain to overthrow the Derby government, but which ultimately dissolved into nothing. He obtained a seat in Lord Palmerston's cabinet of 1859, and after filling the uncongenial posts of secretary for Ireland and chancellor of the duchy of Lancaster (1861), became secretary for the colonies in 1864. Here he reformed the system of colonial defence, refusing to keep troops in the colonies during time of peace unless their expense was defrayed by the colonists; he also laid the foundation of federation in Canada and, rightly or wrongly, censured Sir George Grey's conduct in New Zealand. Resigning with his friends in 1866, he again took office in 1868 as secretary for war. In this post he performed the most memorable actions of his life by the abolition of purchase and the institution of the short service system and the reserve in the army, measures which excited more opposition than any of the numerous reforms effected by the Gladstone government of that period, but which were entirely justified by their successful working afterwards. On the resignation of the Gladstone ministry in 1874 he was raised to the peerage as Viscount Cardwell of Ellerbeck, but took no further prominent part in politics. His mental faculties, indeed, were considerably impaired during the last few years of his life, and he died at Torquay on the 15th of February 1886. He was not a showy, hardly even a prominent politician, but effected far more than many more conspicuous men. The great administrator and the bold innovator were united in him in an exceptional degree, and he allowed neither character to preponderate unduly.

CARDWELL, a town of Cardwell county, Queensland, Australia, on Rockingham Bay, about 800 m. direct N.W. by N. of Brisbane. Pop. of town and district (1901) 3435. It has one of the best harbours in the state, easy of access in all weathers, with a depth ranging from 4 to 10 fathoms. Various minerals, including gold and tin, exist in the district; and there are preserve and sauce 328factories, and works for meat extract and tinning. The dugong fishery is carried on, and the oil is extracted. There are large timber forests in the district, and much cedar is exported.

CAREW, GEORGE (d. about 1613), English diplomatist and historian, second son of Sir Wymond Carew of Antony, was educated at Oxford, entered the Inns of Court, and passed some years in continental travel. At the recommendation of Queen Elizabeth, who conferred on him the honour of knighthood, he was appointed secretary to Sir Christopher

157

Hatton, and afterwards, having been promoted to a mastership in chancery, was sent as ambassador to the king of Poland. In the reign of James he was employed in negotiating the treaty of union with Scotland, and for several years was ambassador to the court of France. On his return he wrote a *Relation of the State of France*, with sketches of the leading persons at the court of Henry IV. It is written in the classical style of the Elizabethan age, and was appended by Dr Birch to his *Historical View of the Negotiations between the Courts of England, France and Brussels, from 1592 to 1617*. Much of the information regarding Poland contained in De Thou's *History of His Own Times* was furnished by Carew.

CAREW, RICHARD (1555-1620), English poet and antiquary, was born on the 17th of July 1555, at Antony House, East Antony, Cornwall. At the age of eleven, he entered Christ Church, Oxford, and when only fourteen was chosen to carry on an extempore debate with Sir Philip Sidney, in presence of the earls of Leicester and Warwick and other noblemen. From Oxford he removed to the Middle Temple, where he spent three years, and then went abroad. By his marriage with Juliana Arundel in 1577 he added Coswarth to the estates he had already inherited from his father. In 1586 he was appointed high-sheriff of Cornwall; he entered parliament in 1584; and he served under Sir Walter Raleigh, then lord lieutenant of Cornwall, as treasurer. He became a member of the Society of Antiquaries in 1589, and was a friend of William Camden and Sir Henry Spelman. His great work is the *Survey of Cornwall*, published in 1602, and reprinted in 1769 and 1811. It still possesses interest, apart from its antiquarian value, for the picture it gives of the life and interests of a country gentleman of the days of Elizabeth. Carew's other works are:—a translation of the first five Cantos of Tasso's *Gerusalemme* (1594), printed in the first instance without the author's knowledge, and entitled *Godfrey of Balloigne, or the Recouerie of Hierusalam*; The *Examination of Men's Wits* (1594), a translation of an Italian version of John Huarte's *Examen de Ingenios*; and *An Epistle concerning the Excellences of the English Tongue* (1605). Carew died on the 6th of November 1620.

His son, Sir RICHARD CAREW (d. 1643?), was the author of a *True and Readie Way to learn the Latine Tongue*, by writers of three nations, published by Samuel Hartlib in 1654.

CAREW, THOMAS (1595-1645?), English poet, was the son of Sir Matthew Carew, master in chancery, and his wife, Alice Ingpenny, widow of Sir John Rivers, lord mayor of London. The poet was probably the third of the eleven children of his parents, and was born at West Wickham in Kent, in the early part of 1595, for he was thirteen years of age in June 1608, when he matriculated at Merton College, Oxford. He took his degree of B.A. early in 1611, and proceeded to study at the Middle Temple. Two years later his father complained to Sir Dudley Carleton that he was doing little at the law. He was in consequence sent to Italy, as a member of Sir Dudley's household, and when the ambassador returned from Venice, he seems to have kept Thomas Carew with him, for he is found in the capacity of secretary to Sir Dudley Carleton, at the Hague, early in 1616. From this office he was dismissed in the autumn of that year for levity and slander; he had great difficulty in finding another situation. In August 1618 his father died, and Carew entered the service of Lord Herbert of Cherbury, in whose train he started for France in March 1619, and it is believed that he travelled in Herbert's company until that nobleman returned to England, at the close of his diplomatic missions, in April 1624. Carew "followed the court before he was of it," not receiving the definite appointment of gentleman of the privy chamber until 1628. While Carew held this office, he displayed his tact and presence of mind by stumbling and extinguishing the candle he was holding to light Charles I. into the queen's chamber, because he saw that Lord St Albans had his arm round her majesty's neck. The king suspected nothing, and the queen heaped favours on the poet. Probably in 1630, Carew was made "server" or taster-in-ordinary to the king. To this period may be attributed his close friendship with Sir John Suckling, Ben Jonson and Clarendon; the latter says that Carew was "a person of pleasant and facetious wit." Donne, whose celebrity as a court-preacher lasted until his death in 1631, exercised a powerful if not entirely healthful influence over the genius of Carew. In February 1633 a masque by the latter, entitled *Coelum Britanicum*, was acted in the banqueting-house at Whitehall, and was printed in 1634. The close of Carew's life is absolutely obscure. It was long supposed that he died in 1639, and this has been thought to be confirmed by the fact that the first edition of his *Poems*, published in 1640, seems to have a posthumous character. But Clarendon tells us that "after fifty years of life spent with less severity and exactness than it ought to have been, he died with the greatest remorse for that licence." If Carew was more than fifty years of age, he must have died in or after 1645, and in fact there were final additions made to his *Poems* in the third edition of 1651. Walton tells us that Carew in his last illness, being afflicted with the horrors, sent in great haste to "the ever-memorable" John Hales (1584-1656); Hales "told him he should have his prayers, but would by no means give him then either the sacrament or absolution."

Carew's poems, at their best, are brilliant lyrics of the purely sensuous order. They open to us, in his own phrase, "a mine of rich and pregnant fancy." His metrical style was influenced by Jonson and his imagery still more clearly by Donne, for whom he had an almost servile admiration. His intellectual power was not comparable with Donne's, but Carew had a lucidity and directness of lyrical utterance unknown to Donne. It is perhaps his greatest distinction that he is the earliest of the Cavalier song-writers by profession, of whom Rochester is the latest, poets who turned the disreputable incidents of an idle court-life into poetry which was often of the rarest delicacy and the purest melody and colour. The longest and best of Carew's poems, "A Rapture," would be more widely appreciated if the rich flow of its imagination were restrained by greater reticence of taste.

The best edition of Carew's *Poems* is that prepared by Arthur Vincent in 1899.

(E. G.)

CAREY, HENRY (d. 1743), English poet and musician, reputed to be an illegitimate son of George Savile, marquess of Halifax, was born towards the end of the 17th century. His mother is supposed to have been a schoolmistress, and Carey himself taught music at various schools. He owed his knowledge of music to Olaus Linnert, and later he studied with Roseingrave and Geminiani. He wrote the words and the music of *The Contrivances; or More Ways than One*, a farce produced at Drury Lane in 1715. His *Hanging and Marriage; or The Dead Man's Wedding* was acted at Lincoln's Inn Fields in 1722.*Chrononhotonthologos* (1734), described as "The most Tragical Tragedy that ever was tragedized by any Company of Tragedians," was a successful burlesque of the bombast of the contemporary stage. The best of his other pieces were *A Wonder; or the Honest Yorkshireman* (1735), a ballad opera, and the*Dragon of Wantley* (1737), a burlesque opera, the music of which was by J.F. Lampe. He was the author of *Namby-Pamby*, a once famous parody of Ambrose Philips's verses to the infant daughter of the earl of Carteret. Carey is best remembered by his songs. "Sally in our Alley" (printed in his *Musical Century*) was a sketch drawn after following a shoemaker's 'prentice and his sweetheart on a holiday. The present tune set to these words, however, is not the one written by Carey, but is borrowed from an earlier song, "The Country Lasse," which is printed in *The Merry Musician* (vol. iii., c. 1716). It has been claimed for him that he was the author of "God save the King" (see NATIONAL ANTHEMS). He died in London on the 4th of 329October 1743, and it was asserted, without justification, that he had committed suicide. Edmund Kean, the tragedian, was one of his great-grandchildren.

The completest edition of his poems is *Poems on Several Occasions*(1729). His dramatic works were published by subscription in 1743.

CAREY, HENRY CHARLES (1793-1879), American economist, was born in Philadelphia on the 15th of December 1793. At the age of twenty-eight he succeeded his father, Mathew Carey (1760-1839)—an influential economist, political reformer, editor, and publisher, of Irish birth, but for many years a resident of Philadelphia—as a member of the publishing firm of Carey & Lea, which was long the most conspicuous in America. He died in Philadelphia on the 13th of October 1879.

Among Mathew Carey's many writings had been a collection (1822) of*Essays on Political Economy*, one of the earliest of American treatises favouring protection, and Henry C. Carey's life-work was devoted to the propagation of the same theory. He retired from business in 1838, almost simultaneously with the appearance (1837-1840) of his *Principles of*

Political Economy. This treatise, which was translated into Italian and Swedish, soon became the standard representative in the United States of the school of economic thought which, with some interruptions, has since dominated the tariff system of that country. Carey's first large work on political economy was preceded and followed by many smaller volumes on wages, the credit system, interest, slavery, copyright, &c.; and in 1858-1859 he gathered the fruits of his lifelong labours into *The Principles of Social Science*, in three volumes. This work is a most comprehensive as well as mature exposition of his views. In it Carey sought to show that there exists, independently of human wills, a natural system of economic laws, which is essentially beneficent, and of which the increasing prosperity of the whole community, and especially of the working classes, is the spontaneous result—capable of being defeated only by the ignorance or perversity of man resisting or impeding its action. He rejected the Malthusian doctrine of population, maintaining that numbers regulate themselves sufficiently in every well-governed society, and that their pressure on subsistence characterizes the lower, not the more advanced, stages of civilization. He denied the universal truth, for all stages of cultivation, of the law of diminishing returns from land.

His fundamental theoretic position relates to the antithesis of wealth and value. Carey held that land, as we are concerned with it in industrial life, is really an instrument of production which has been formed as such by man, and that its value is due to the labour expended on it in the past—though measured, not by the sum of that labour, but by the labour necessary under existing conditions to bring new land to the same stage of productiveness. He studied the occupation and reclamation of land with peculiar advantage as an American, for whom the traditions of first settlement were living and fresh, and before whose eyes the process was indeed still going on. The difficulties of adapting a primitive soil to the work of yielding organic products for man's use can be lightly estimated only by an inhabitant of a country long under cultivation. It is, in Carey's view, the overcoming of these difficulties by arduous and continued effort that entitles the first occupier of land to his property in the soil. Its present value forms a very small proportion of the cost expended on it, because it represents only what would be required, with the science and appliances of our time, to bring the land from its primitive into its present state. Property in land is therefore only a form of invested capital—a quantity of labour or the fruits of labour permanently incorporated with the soil; for which, like any other capitalist, the owner is compensated by a share of the produce. He is not rewarded for what is done by the powers of nature, and society is in no sense defrauded by his sole possession. The so-called Ricardian theory of rent is a speculative fancy, contradicted by all experience. Cultivation does not in fact, as that theory supposes, begin with the best, and move downwards to the poorer soils in the order of their inferiority. The light and dry higher lands are first cultivated; and only when population has become dense and capital has accumulated, are the low-lying lands, with their greater fertility, but also with their morasses, inundations, and miasmas, attacked and brought into occupation. Rent, regarded as a proportion of the produce, sinks, like all interest on capital, in process of time, but, as an absolute amount, increases. The share of the labourer increases, both as a proportion and an absolute amount. And thus the interests of these different social classes are in harmony. But, Carey proceeded to say, in order that this harmonious progress may be realized, what is taken from the land must be given back to it. All the articles derived from it are really separated parts of it, which must be restored on pain of its exhaustion. Hence the producer and the consumer must be close to each other; the products must not be exported to a foreign country in exchange for its manufactures, and thus go to enrich as manure a foreign soil. In immediate exchange value the landowner may gain by such exportation, but the productive powers of the land will suffer.

Carey, who had set out as an earnest advocate of free trade, accordingly arrived at the doctrine of protection: the "coordinating power" in society must intervene to prevent private advantage from working public mischief. He attributed his conversion on this question to his observation of the effects of liberal and protective tariffs respectively on American prosperity. This observation, he says, threw him back on theory, and led him to see that the intervention referred to might be necessary to remove (as he phrases it) the obstacles to the progress of younger communities created by the action of older and wealthier nations. But it seems probable that the influence of List's writings, added to his

160

own deep-rooted and hereditary jealousy and dislike of English predominance, had something to do with his change of attitude (see PROTECTION).

CAREY, WILLIAM (1761-1834), English Oriental scholar, and the pioneer of modern missionary enterprise, was born at Paulerspury, Northamptonshire, on the 17th of August 1761. When a youth he worked as a shoemaker; but having joined the Baptists when he was about twenty-one, he devoted much of his time to village preaching. In 1787 he became pastor of a Baptist church in Leicester, and began those energetic movements among his fellow religionists which resulted in the formation of the Baptist Missionary Society, Carey himself being one of the first to go abroad. On reaching Bengal in 1793, he and his companions lost all their property in the Hugli; but having received the charge of an indigo factory at Malda, he was soon able to prosecute the work of translating the Bible into Bengali. In 1799 he quitted Malda for Serampore, where he established a church, a school, and a printing-press for the publication of the Scriptures and philological works. In 1801 Carey was appointed professor of Oriental languages in a college founded at Fort William by the marquess of Wellesley. From this time to his death he devoted himself to the preparation of numerous philological works, consisting of grammars and dictionaries in the Mahratta, Sanskrit, Punjabi, Telinga, Bengali and Bhotanta dialects. The Sanskrit dictionary was unfortunately destroyed by a fire which broke out in the printing establishment. From the Serampore press there issued in his lifetime over 200,000 Bibles and portions in nearly forty different languages and dialects, Carey himself undertaking most of the literary work. He died on the 9th of June 1834.

See *Lives* by J. Culross (1881) and G. Smith (1884).

CARGILL, DONALD (1610-1681), Scottish Covenanter, was born in 1610. He was educated at St Andrews, and afterwards attached himself to the Protesters. After his appointment to one of the churches in Glasgow, he openly resisted the measures of the government. Compelled to remain at a distance from his charge, he ventured back to celebrate the Communion, and was arrested, but was liberated at the instance of some of his private friends. He was afterwards wounded at the battle of Bothwell Bridge, and fled to Holland, where he remained a few months. On his return he joined Richard Cameron in publishing the Sanquhar declaration, and boldly excommunicated the king and his officials. He was soon afterwards apprehended, and brought to Edinburgh, where he was beheaded on the 27th of July 1681.

330
CARGO (Span. for "loading," from Lat. *carrus*, car), a shipload, or the goods (or even, less technically, persons) carried on board a ship; and so, by analogy, a term used for any large amount. The maritime law affecting the cargo of a ship is dealt with in the articles AVERAGE, AFFREIGHTMENT, INSURANCE, SALVAGE, BOTTOMRY, LIEN; and the specialities of cargo-ships under SHIP.

CARIA, an ancient district of Asia Minor, bounded on the N. by Ionia and Lydia, on the W. and S. by the Aegean Sea, and on the E. by Lycia and a small part of Phrygia. The coast-line consists of a succession of great promontories alternating with deep inlets. The most important inlet, the Ceramic Gulf, or Gulf of Cos, extends inland for 70 m., between the great mountain promontory terminating at Myndus on the north, and that which extends to Cnidus and the remarkable headland of Cape Krio on the south. North of this is the deep bay called in ancient times the Gulf of Iasus (now known as the Gulf of Mendeliyah), and beyond this again was the deeper inlet which formerly extended inland between Miletus and Priene, but of which the outer part has been entirely filled up by the alluvial deposits of the Maeander, while the innermost arm, the ancient Latmic Gulf, is now a lake. South of Cape Krio again is the gulf known as the Gulf of Doris, with several subordinate inlets, bounded on the south by the rugged promontory of Cynossema (mod. Cape Alupo). Between this headland and the frontier of Lycia is the sheltered bay of Marmarice, noted in modern times as one of the finest harbours of the Mediterranean.

Almost the whole of Caria is mountainous. The two great masses of Cadmus (Baba-dagh) and Salbacum (Boz-dagh), which are in fact portions of the great chain of Taurus (see ASIA MINOR), form the nucleus to which the whole physical framework of the country is attached. From these lofty ranges there extends a broad tableland (in many parts more than 3000 ft. high), while it sends down offshoots on the north towards the Maeander, and on the west towards the Aegean. Of these ranges the summit of Mt Latmus alone reaches 4500 ft.

The coast is fringed by numerous islands, in some instances separated only by narrow straits from the mainland. Of these the most celebrated are Rhodes and Cos. Besides these are Syme, Telos, Nisyros, Calymnos, Leros and Patmos, all of which have been inhabited, both in ancient and modern times, and some of which contain excellent harbours. Of these Nisyros alone is of volcanic origin; the others belong to the same limestone formation with the rocky headlands of the coast. The country known as Caria was shared between the Carians proper and the Caunians, who were a wilder people, inhabiting the district between Caria and Lycia. They were not considered to be of the same blood as the Carians, and were, therefore, excluded from the temple of the Carian Zeus at Mylasa, which was common to the Carians, Lydians and Mysians, though their language was the same as that of the Carians proper. Herodotus (i. 172) believed the Caunians to have been aborigines, the Carians having been originally called Leleges, who had been driven from the Aegean islands by the invading Greeks. This seems to have been a prevalent view among the Greek writers, for Thucydides (i. 8) states that when Delos was "purified" more than half the bodies found buried in it were those of "Carians." Modern archaeological discovery, however, is against this belief; and the fact that Mysus, Lydus and Car were regarded as brothers indicates that the three populations who worshipped together in the temple of Mylasa all belonged to the same stock. Homer (*Il.* x. 428-429) distinguishes the Leleges (*q.v.*) from the Carians, to whom is ascribed the invention of helmet-crests, coats of arms, and shield handles.

A considerable number of short Carian inscriptions has been found, most of them in Egypt. They were first noticed by Lepsius at Abu-Simbel, where he correctly inferred that they were the work of the Carian mercenaries of Psammetichus. The language, so far as it has been deciphered, is "Asianic" and not Indo-European.

The excavations of W.R. Paton at Assarlik (*Journ. Hell. Studies*, 1887) and of F. Winter at Idrias have resulted in the discovery of Late-Mycenaean and Geometric pottery. Caria, however, figured but little in history. It was absorbed into the kingdom of Lydia, where Carian troops formed the bodyguard of the king. Cnidus and Halicarnassus on the coast were colonized by Dorians. At Halicarnassus (*q.v.*) the Mausoleum, the monument erected by Artemisia to her husband Mausolus, about 360 B.C., was excavated by Sir C.T. Newton in 1857-1858. Cnidus (*q.v.*) was excavated at the same time, when the "Cnidian Lion," now in the British Museum, was found crowning a tomb near the site of the old city (C.T. Newton, *History of Discoveries at Cnidus, Halicarnassus and Branchidae*). On the border-land between Caria and Lydia lay other Greek cities, Miletus, Priene, and Magnesia (see articles *s.v.*), colonized in early times by the Ionians. Inland was Tralles (mod. Aidin), which also had an Ionic population, though it never belonged to the Ionic confederacy (see TRALLES). The excavations of the English in 1868-1869, of the French under O. Rayet and A. Thomas in 1873, and more recently of the Germans under Th. Wiegand and Schrader in 1895-1898 have laid bare the site of the Greek Priene, and the same has been done for the remains of Magnesia ad Maeandrum by French excavators in 1842-1843 and the German expedition under K. Humann in 1891-1893. A German expedition under Th. Wiegand carried on excavations at Miletus (see articles on these towns).

In the Persian epoch, native dynasts established themselves in Caria and even extended their rule over the Greek cities. The last of them seems to have been Pixodarus, after whose death the crown was seized by a Persian, Orontobates, who offered a vigorous resistance to Alexander the Great. But his capital, Halicarnassus, was taken after a siege, and the principality of Caria conferred by Alexander on Ada, a princess of the native dynasty. Soon afterwards the country was incorporated into the Syrian empire and then into the kingdom of Pergamum.

162

See W.M. Ramsay, "Historical Geography of Asia Minor" (*R.G.S.* iv., 1890); W. Ruge and E. Friedrich, *Archäologische Karte von Kleinasien*(1899); Perrot and Chipiez, *History of Art in Phrygia, Lydia, Caria and Lycia* (Eng. trans., 1892); A.H. Sayce, "The Karian Language and Inscriptions" (*T.S.B.A.* ix. 1, 1887); P. Kretschmer, *Einleitung in die Geschichte der griechischen Sprache*, pp. 376-384 (1896). For the coinage see NUMISMATICS.

(A. H. S.)

CARIACO, or SAN FELIPE DE AUSTRIA, a town on the north coast of Venezuela, 40 m. east of the city of Cumaná at the head of the gulf bearing the same name. Pop. (1908, estimate) 7000. It stands a short distance up the Cariaco river and its port immediately on the coast is known as Puerto Sucre. The surrounding district produces cotton, tobacco, cacáo, cattle and fruit, and there is considerable trade through Puerto Sucre, although that port has no regular connexion with foreign ports.

CARIBBEE ISLANDS, a name chiefly of historical importance, sometimes applied to the whole of the West Indies, but strictly comprehending only the chain of islands stretching from Porto Rico to the coast of South America. These are also known as the Lesser Antilles, and the bulk of them are divided into the two groups of the Leeward and Windward Islands.

CARIBS, the name, used first by Columbus (from *Cariba*, said to mean "a valiant man"), of a South American people, who, at the arrival of the Spanish, occupied parts of Guiana and the lower Orinoco and the Windward and other islands in what is still known as the Caribbean Sea. They were believed to have had their original home in North America, spreading thence through the Antilles southward to Venezuela, the Guianas, and north-east Brazil. This view has been abandoned, as Carib tribes, the Bakairi and Nahuquas, using an archaic type of Carib speech and primitive in habits, have been met by German explorers in the very heart of Brazil. It may thus be assumed that the cradle of the race was the centre of South America; their first migrating movements being to Guiana and the Antilles. A cruel, ferocious and warlike people, they made a stout resistance to the Spaniards. They were cannibals, and it is to them that we owe that word, Columbus's *Caribal* being transformed into *Cannibal* in apparent reference to the *canine* voracity of the Caribs. They are physically by no means a powerful race, being distinguished by slight figures with limbs well formed but lacking muscle, and with a tendency to be pot-bellied, due apparently to their habit of drinking *paiwari* (liquor prepared from the cassava plant) in great quantities. Their colour is a red cinnamon, but varies with different tribes. Their hair is thick, long, very black, and generally cut to an even edge, at right angles to the neck, round the head. The features are strikingly Mongoloid. Among the true Caribs a 2-in. broad belt of cotton is knitted round each ankle, and just below each knee of the young female children. All body-hair in both sexes is pulled out, even to the eye-brows. Among the women the lower lips are often pierced, pins of wood being passed through and forming a sort of *chevaux de frise* round the mouth. Sometimes a bell-shaped ornament is hung by men to a piece of string passed through the lower lip. The Carib government was patriarchal. Though the women did most of the hard work, they were kindly treated. Polygamy prevailed. Very little ceremony attended death. The Caribs of the West Indies, known as "Red" and "Black," the first pure, the second mixed with negro blood, after a protracted war with the British were transported in 1796 to the number of 5000 from Dominica and St Vincent to the island of Ruatan near the coast of Honduras. A few were subsequently allowed back to St Vincent, but the majority are settled in Honduras and Nicaragua.

CARICATURE (Ital. *caricatura, i.e. "ritratto ridicolo,"* from *caricare*, to load, to charge; Fr. *charge*), a general term for the art of applying the grotesque to the purposes of satire, and for pictorial and plastic ridicule and burlesque. The word, "caricatura" was first used as English by Sir Thomas Browne (1605-1682), in his *Christian Morals*, a posthumous work; it is next found, still in its Italian form, in No. 537 of the *Spectator*; it was adopted by Johnson in his dictionary (1757), but does not appear in Bailey's dictionary, for example, as late as 1773;

and it only assumed its modern guise towards the end of the 18th century, when its use and comprehension became general.

Little that is not conjectural can be written concerning caricature among the ancients. Few traces of the comic are discoverable in Egyptian art—such papyri of a satirical tendency as are known to exist appearing to belong rather to the class of ithyphallic drolleries than to that of the ironical grotesque. Among the Greeks, though but few and dubious data are extant, it seems possible that caricature may not have been altogether unknown. Their taste for pictorial parody, indeed, has been sufficiently proved by plentiful discoveries of pottery painted with burlesque subjects. Aristotle, moreover, who disapproved of grotesque art, condemns in strong terms the pictures of a certain Pauson, who, alluded to by Aristophanes, and the subject of one of Lucian's anecdotes, is hailed by Champfleury as the *doyen* of caricaturists. That the grotesque in graphic art conceived in the true spirit of intentional caricature was practised by the Romans is evident from the curious frescoes uncovered at Pompeii and Herculaneum; from the mention in Pliny of certain painters celebrated for burlesque pictures; from the curious fantasies graven in gems and called Grylli; and from the number of ithyphallic caprices that have descended to modern times. But in spite of these evidences of Greek and Roman humour, in spite of the famous comic statuette of Caracalla, and of the more famous *graffito* of the Crucifixion, the caricaturists of the old world must be sought for, not among its painters and sculptors, but among its poets and dramatists. The comedies of Aristophanes and the epigrams of Martial were, to the Athens of Pericles and the Rome of Domitian, what the etchings of Gillray and the lithographs of Daumier were to the London of George III. and the Paris of the Citizen King.

During the middle ages a vast mass of grotesque material was accumulated, but selection becomes even more difficult than with the scarce relics of antiquity. With the building of the cathedrals originated a new style of art; a strange mixture of memories of paganism and Christian imaginings was called into being for the adornment of those great strongholds of urban Catholicism, and in this the coarse and brutal materialism of the popular humour found its largest and freest expression. On missal-marge and sign-board, on stall and entablature, in gargoyle and initial, the grotesque displayed itself in an infinite variety of forms. The import of this inextricable tangle of imagery, often obscene and horrible, often quaint and fantastic, is difficult, if not impossible, to determine. We recognize the prevalence of three great popular types or figures, each of which may be credited with a satirical intention—of Reynard the Fox, the hero of the famous medieval romance; of the Devil, that peculiarly medieval antithesis of God; and of Death, the sarcastic and irreverent skeleton. The popularity of the last is evidenced by the fact that no fewer than forty-three towns in England, France and Germany are enumerated as possessing sets of the Dance of Death, that grandiose all-levelling series of caprices in the contemplation of which the middle ages found so much consolation. It was reserved for Holbein (1498-1554), seizing the idea and resuming all that his contemporaries thought and felt on the subject, to produce, in his fifty-three magnificent designs of the Danse Macabre, the first and perhaps the greatest set of satirical moralities known to the modern world.

It is in the tumult of the Renaissance, indeed, that caricature in its modern sense may be said to have been born. The great popular movements required some such vehicle of comment or censure; the perfection to which the arts of design were attaining supplied the means; the invention of printing ensured its dissemination. The earliest genuine piece of graphic irony that has been discovered is a caricature (1499) relating to Louis XII. and his Italian war. But it was the Reformation that produced the first full crop of satirical ephemerae, and the heads of Luther and Alexander VI. are therefore the direct ancestors of the masks that smirk and frown from the "cartoons" of *Punch* and the *Charivari*. Fairly started by Lucas Cranach, a friend of Luther, in his *Passionale of Christ and Antichrist* (1521), caricature was naturalized in France under the League, but only to pass into the hands of the Dutch, who supplied the rest of Europe with satirical prints during the whole of the next century. A curious reaction is visible in the work of Pieter Breughel (1510-1570) towards the grotesque*diablerie* and macaberesque morality of medieval art, the last original and striking note of which is caught in the compositions of Jacques Callot (1593-1635), and, in a less degree, in those of his followers, Stefano della Bella (1610-1664) and Salvator Rosa (1615-

1673). On the other hand, however, Callot, one of the greatest masters of the grotesque that ever lived, in certain of his *Caprices*, and in his two famous sets of prints, the *Misères de la guerre*, may be said to anticipate certain productions of Hogarth and Goya, and so to have founded the modern school of ironic *genre*.

In England one of the earliest caricatures extant is that in the margin of the Forest Roll of Essex, 5, ed. 1, now at the Record Office; it is a grotesque portrait of "Aaron fil Diabole" (Aaron, son of the devil), probably representing Cok, son of Aaron. It is dated 1277. Another caricature, undated, appears on a Roll containing an account of the tallages and fines paid by Jews, 17. Henry III., belonging to 1233 (Exch. of Receipt, Jews' Roll, No. 8). It is an elaborate satirical design of Jews and devils, arranged in a pediment. During the 16th century, caricature can hardly be said to have existed at all,—a grotesque of Mary Stuart as a mermaid, a pen and ink sketch of which is yet to be seen in the Rolls Office, being the only example of it known. The Great Rebellion, however, acted as the Reformation had done in Germany, and Cavaliers and Roundheads caricatured each other freely. At this period satirical pictures usually did duty as the title-pages of scurrilous pamphlets; but one instance is known of the employment during the war of a grotesque allegory as a banner, while the end of the Commonwealth produced a satirical pack of playing cards, probably of Dutch origin. The Dutch, indeed, as already has been stated, were the great purveyors of pictorial satire at this time and during the early part of the next century. In England the wit of the victorious party was rather vocal than pictorial; in France the spirit of caricature was sternly repressed; and it was from Holland, bold in its republican freedom, and rich in painters and etchers, that issued the flood of prints and medals which illustrate, through cumbrous allegories and elaborate 332symbolization, the principal political passages of both the former countries, from the Restoration (1660) to the South Sea Bubble (1720). The most distinguished of the Dutch artists was Romain de Hooghe (1638-1720), a follower of Callot, who, without any of the weird power of his master, possessed a certain skill in grouping and faculty of grotesque suggestiveness that made his point a most useful weapon to William of Orange during the long struggle with Louis XIV.

The 18th century, however, may be called emphatically the age of caricature. The spirit is evident in letters as in art; in the fierce grotesques of Swift, in the coarser *charges* of Smollett, in the keen ironies of Henry Fielding, in the Aristophanic tendency of Foote's farces, no less than in the masterly moralities of Hogarth and the truculent satires of Gillray. The first event that called forth caricatures in any number was the prosecution (1710) of Dr Sacheverell; most of these, however, were importations from Holland, and only in the excitement attendant on the South Sea Bubble, some ten years later, can the English school be said to have begun. Starting into active being with the ministry of Walpole (1721), it flourished under that statesman for some twenty years,—the "hieroglyphics," as its prints were named, graphically enough, often circulating on fans. It continued to increase in importance and audacity till the reign of Pitt (1757-1761), when its activity was somewhat abated. It rose, however, to a greater height than ever during the rule of Bute (1761-1763), and since that time its influence has extended without a check. The artists whose combinations amused the public during this earlier period are, with few exceptions, but little known and not greatly esteemed. Among them were two amateurs, Dorothy, wife of Richard Boyle, 3rd earl of Burlington, and General George Townshend (afterwards 1st Marquess Townshend); Goupy, Boitard and Liotard were Frenchmen; Vandergucht and Vanderbank were Dutchmen. This period witnessed also the rise of William Hogarth (1697-1764). As a political caricaturist Hogarth was not successful, save in a few isolated examples, as in the portraits of Wilkes and Churchill; but as a moralist and social satirist he has not yet been equalled. The publication, in 1732, of his *Modern Midnight Conversation* may be said to mark an epoch in the history of caricature. Mention must also be made of Paul Sandby (1725-1809), who was not a professional caricaturist, though he joined in the pictorial hue-and-cry against Hogarth and Lord Bute, and who is best remembered as the founder of the English school of water-colour; and of John Collet (1723-1788), said to have been a pupil of Hogarth, a kindly and industrious humorist, rarely venturing into the arena of politics. During the latter half of the century, however, political caricature began to be somewhat more skilfully handled than of old by James Sayer, a satirist in the pay of the younger Pitt, while social grotesques were pleasantly treated by Henry William Bunbury (1750-1811) and George Moutard Woodward. These personalities, however, interesting as they are, are dwarfed into insignificance by the great figure of James Gillray (1757-1815), in whose hands political caricature became almost epic for grandeur of conception and far-reaching suggestiveness. It is to the works of this man of genius, indeed, and (in a less degree) to those of his contemporary, Thomas Rowlandson (1756-1827), an artist of great and varied powers, that historians must turn for the popular reflection of all the political notabilia of the end of the 18th and the beginning of the 19th centuries. England may be said to have been the chosen home of caricature during this period. In France, timid and futile under the Monarchy, it had assumed an immense importance under the Revolution, and a cloud of hideous pictorial libels was the result; but even the Revolution left no such notes through its own artists, though Fragonard (1732-1806) himself was of the number, as came from the gravers of Gillray and Rowlandson. In Germany caricature did not exist. Only in Spain was there to be found an artist capable of entering into competition with the masters of the satirical grotesque of whom England could boast. The works of Francesco Goya y Lucientes (1746-1828) are described by Théophile Gautier as "a mixture of those of Rembrandt, Watteau, and the comical dreams of Rabelais," and Champfleury discovers analogies between him and Honoré Daumier, the greatest caricaturist of modern France.

The satirical grotesque of the 18th century had been characterized by a sort of grandiose brutality, by a certain vigorous obscenity, by a violence of expression and intention, that appear monstrous in these days of reserve and restraint, but that doubtless sorted well enough with the strong party feelings and fierce political passions of the age. After the downfall of Napoleon (1815), however, when strife was over and men were weary and satisfied, a change in matter and manner came over the caricature of the period. In connection with this change, the name of George Cruikshank (1792-1878), an artist who stretches hands on the one side towards Hogarth and Gillray, and on the other towards Leech and Tenniel, deserves honourable mention. Those of Cruikshank's political caricatures which were designed for the squibs of William Hone (1779-1842) are, comparatively speaking, uninteresting; his ambition was that of Hogarth—the production of "moral comedies." Much of his work, therefore, may be said to form a link in the chain of development through which has passed that ironical *genre* to which reference has already been made. In 1829, however, began to appear the famous series of lithographs, signed H.B., the work of John Doyle (1798-1868). These jocularities are interesting otherwise than politically; thin and weakly as they are, they inaugurated the style of later political caricature. In France, meanwhile, with the farcical designs of Edme Jean Pigal (b. 1794) and the realistic sketches of Henri Monnier (1805-1872), the admirable portrait-busts of Jean Pierre Dantan the younger (1800-1869) and the fine military and low-life drolleries of Nicolas Toussaint Charlet (1792-1845) were appearing. Up to this date, though journalism and caricature had sometimes joined hands (as in the case of the *Craftsman* and the *Anti-Jacobin*, and particularly in *Les Révolutions de France et de Brabant* and *Les Actes des Apôtres*), the alliance had been but brief; it was reserved for Charles Philipon (1802-1862), who may be called the father of comic journalism, to make it lasting. The foundation of *La Caricature*, by Philipon in 1831, suppressed in 1835 after a brief but glorious career, was followed by *Le Charivari* (December 1832), which is perhaps the most renowned of the innumerable enterprises of this extraordinary man. Among the artists he assembled round him, the highest place is held by Honoré Daumier (1808-1879), a draughtsman of great skill, and a caricaturist of immense vigour and audacity. Another of Philipon's band was Sulpice Paul Chevalier (1801-1866), better known as Gavarni, in whose hands modern social caricature, advanced by Cruikshank and Charlet, assumed its present guise and became elegant. Mention must also be made of Grandville (J.I.I. Gérard) (1803-1847), the illustrator of La Fontaine, and a modern patron of the medieval skeleton; of Charles Joseph Traviès de Villers, the father of the famous hunchback "Mayeux"; and of Amedée de Noé, or "Cham," the wittiest and most ephemeral of pictorial satirists. In 1840 the pleasantries of "H.B." having come to an end, there was founded, in imitation of this enterprise of Philipon, the comic journal which, under the title of *Punch, or the London Charivari*, has since become famous all over the world. Among its early illustrators were John Leech (1817-1864) and Richard Doyle (1824-1883), whose drawings were full of the richest grotesque humour.

In 1862 Carlo Pellegrini, in *Vanity Fair*, began a series of portraits of public men, which may be considered the most remarkable instances of personal caricature in England.

For the later developments of caricature, it is convenient to take them by countries in the following sections:—

Great Britain.—During the later 19th century the term caricature, somewhat loosely used at all times, came gradually to cover almost every form of humorous art, from the pictorial wit and wisdom of Sir John Tenniel to the weird grotesques of Mr S.H. Sime, from the gay pleasantries of Randolph Caldecott to the graceful but sedate fancies of Mr Walter Crane. It is made to embrace alike the social studies, satirical and sympathetic, of Du Maurier and Keene, the political cartoons of Mr Harry Furniss and Sir F.C. Gould, the unextenuating likenesses of "Ape," and "Spy," and "Max," the 333subtle conceits of Mr Linley Sambourne, the whimsicalities of Mr E.T. Reed, the exuberant burlesques of Mr J.F. Sullivan, the frank buffooneries of W.G. Baxter, Of these diverse forms of graphic humour, some have no other object than to amuse, and therefore do not call for serious notice. The work of Mr Max Beerbohm ("Max") has the note of originality and extravagance too; while that of "Spy" (Mr Leslie Ward) in *Vanity Fair*, if it does not rival the occasional brilliancy of his predecessor "Ape" (Carlo Pellegrini, 1839-1889), maintains a higher average of merit. The pupil, too, is much more genial than the master, and he is content if his pencil evokes the comment, "How ridiculously like!" Caricature of this kind is merely an entertainment. Here we are concerned rather with those branches of caricature which, merrily or mordantly, reflect and comment upon the actual life we live. In treating of recent caricature of this kind, we must give the first place to*Punch*. Mr Punch's outlook upon life has not changed much since the 'seventies of the last century. His influence upon the tone of caricature made itself felt most appreciably in the days of John Leech and Richard Doyle. Their successors but follow in their steps. In their work, says a clever German critic, is to be found no vestige of the "sour bilious temper of John Bull" that pervaded the pictures of Hogarth and Rowlandson. Charles Keene (1823-1891) and Du Maurier (1834-1896), he declares, are not caricaturists or satirists, but amiable and tenderly grave observers of life, friendly optimists. The characterization is truer of Keene, perhaps, than of Du Maurier. Charles Keene's sketches are almost always cheerful; almost without exception they make you smile or laugh. In many of Du Maurier's, on the other hand, there is an underlying seriousness. While Keene looks on at life with easy tolerance, an amused spectator, Du Maurier shows himself sensitive, emotional, sympathetic, taking infinite delight in what is pretty and gay and charming, but hurt and offended by the sordid and the ugly. Thus while Keene takes things dispassionately as they come, seeing only the humorous side of them, we find Du Maurier ever and anon attacking some new phase of snobbishness or philistinism or cant. For all his kindliness in depicting congenial scenes, he is at times as unrelenting a satirist as Rowlandson. The other *Punch* artists, whose work is in the same field, resemble Keene in this respect rather than Du Maurier. Mr Leonard Raven-Hill recalls Charles Keene not merely in temperament but in technique; like Keene, too, he finds his subjects principally in *bourgeois* life. Mr J. Bernard Partridge, though, like Du Maurier, he has an eye for physical beauty, is a spectator rather than a critic of life, yet he has made his mark as a "cartoonist." Phil May (d. 1903), a modern Touchstone, is less easily classified. Though he wears the cap and bells, he is alive to the pity of things; he sees the pathos no less than the humour of his street-boys and "gutter-snipes." He is, however, a jester primarily: an artist, too, of high achievement. Two others stand out as masters of the art of social caricature—Frederick Barnard and Mr J.F. Sullivan. Barnard's illustrations to Dickens, like his original sketches, have a lively humour—the humour of irrepressible high spirits—and endless invention. High spirits and invention are characteristics also of Mr Sullivan. It is at the British artisan and petty tradesman—at the grocer given to adulteration and the plumber who outstays his welcome—that he aims his most boisterous fun. He rebels, too, delightfully, against red tape and all the petty tyrannies of officialdom. In political caricature Sir John Tenniel (*q.v.*) remained the leading artist of his day. The death of Abraham Lincoln, Bismarck's fall from power, the tragedy of Khartum—to subjects such as these, worthy of a great painter, Tenniel

167

has brought a classic simplicity and a sense of dignity unknown previously to caricature. It is hard to say in which field Tenniel most excels—whether in those ingenious parables in which the British Lion and the Russian Bear, John Chinaman, Jacques Bonhomme and Uncle Sam play their part—or in the ever-changing scenes of the great parliamentary Comedy—or in sombre dramas of Anarchy, Famine or Crime—or in those London extravaganzas in which the symbolic personalities of Gog and Magog, Father Thames and the Fog Fiend, the duke of Mudford and Mr Punch himself, have become familiar. Subjects similar to these have been treated also for many years by Mr Linley Sambourne in his fanciful and often beautiful designs. In the field of humorous portraiture also, as in cartoon-designing, Mr Sambourne has made his mark, and he may be said almost to have originated, in a small way, that practice of illustrating the doings of parliament with comic sketches in which Mr Furniss, Mr E.T. Reed and Sir F.C. Gould were his most notable successors. Mr Furniss satirized the Royal Academy as effectively as the Houses of Parliament, but he has been above all the illustrator of parliament—the creator of Mr Gladstone's collars, the thief of Lord Randolph Churchill's inches, the immortalizer of so many otherwise obscure politicians who has worked the House of Commons and its doings into so many hundreds of eccentric designs. But Mr Furniss was never, like Sir F.C. Gould (of the *Westminster Gazette*), a politician first and a caricaturist afterwards. Gould is an avowed partisan, and his caricatures became the most formidable weapons of the Radical party. Caustic, witty and telling, not specially well drawn, but drawn well enough—the likenesses unfailingly caught and recognizable at a glance—his "Picture Politics" won him a place unique in the ranks of caricaturists. There is no evidence of such strenuousness in the work of Mr E.T. Read (of*Punch*). In his parliamentary sketches, as in his "Animal Land" and "Prehistoric Peeps," Mr Reed is a wholly irresponsible humorist and parodist. One finds keen satire, however, in those "Ready-made Coats of Arms," in which he turned at once his heraldic lore and his insight into character to excellent account. In his more serious picture in which he has drawn a parallel between the *tricoteuses* awaiting with grim enjoyment the fall of the guillotine and those modern English gentlewomen who flock to the Old Bailey as to the play, we have the true Hogarthian touch. Mr Gunning King, Mr F.H. Townshend, Mr C.E. Brock, Mr Tom Browne, are among the younger humorists who have advanced to the front rank. Though there have been some notable competitors with *Punch*, there has never been a really "good second." In Matt Morgan the *Tomahawk* (1865-1867) could boast an original cartoonist after Tenniel's style, but without Tenniel's power and humour. Morgan's *Tomahawk* cartoons gained in effect from an ingenious method of printing in two colours. In Fred Barnard, W.G. Baxter, and Mr J.F. Sullivan, *Judy* (founded in 1867) possessed a trio of pictorial humorists of the first rank, and in W. Bowcher a political cartoonist thoroughly to the taste of those hot and strong Conservatives to whom*Punch's* faint Whiggery was but Radicalism in disguise. His successor, Mr William Parkinson, was not less loyal to Tory ideas, though more urbane in his methods. *Fun* has had cartoonists of high merit in Mr Gordon Thomson and in Mr John Proctor, who worked also for *Moonshine* (founded in 1879, now extinct). *Moonshine* afterwards enlisted the services of Alfred Bryan, to whose clever pencil the Christmas number of the *World* was indebted for many years. *Ally Sloper*, founded in 1884, is notable only as the widely circulated medium for W.G. Baxter's wild humours, kept up in the same spirit by Mr W.F. Thomas, his successor. *Pick-me-up* could once count a staff which rivalled at least the social side of *Punch*; Mr Raven-Hill, Phil May, Mr Maurice Greiffenhagen and Mr Dudley Hardy all contributed in their time to its sprightly pages, while Mr S.H. Sime made it the vehicle for his "squint-brained" imaginings. The *Will o' the Wisp*, the *Butterfly* and the*Unicorn*, kindred ventures, though on different lines, all met with an early death. *Lika Joko*, founded in 1894 by Mr Harry Furniss, who in that year abandoned *Punch*, and afterwards *Fair Game*, were also short-lived. To this brief list of purely comic or satirical journals should be added the names of several daily and weekly publications—and among monthlies the *Idler*, with its caricatures by Mr Scott Rankin, Mr Sime and Mr Beerbohm—which have made a special feature of humorous art. Among these are the *Graphic*, whose Christmas numbers were first brightened by Randolph Caldecott; the*Daily Graphic*, enlivened sometimes by Phil May and Mr A.S. Boyd; *Vanity Fair*, with its grotesque portraits; *Truth*, to whose Christmas numbers Sir F.C. Gould contributed some of his best and most ambitious work, printed in colours; the *Sketch*, with Phil May and others; *Black and White*, with Mr Henry Meyer; the *Pall Mall Gazette*, first with Sir F.C. Gould, and later with Mr G.R. Halkett. The *St Stephen's Review*, whose crudely powerful cartoons, the work of Tom Merry, were so popular, ceased publication in 1892. A tribute should be paid in conclusion to the coloured cartoons of the *Weekly Freeman* and other Irish papers, often remarkable for their humour and talent. (See also CARTOON and ILLUSTRATION.)

France.—In that peculiar branch of art which is based on irony, fun, oddity and wit, and in which Honoré Daumier (1808-1879), next to "Gavarni" (1804-1866), remains the undisputed master, France—as has already been shown—can produce an unbroken series of draughtsmen of strong individuality. Though "Cham" died in 1879, Eugène Giraud in 1881, "Randon" in 1884, "André Gill" in 1885, "Marcelin" in 1887, Edouard de Beaumont in 1888, Lami in 1891, Alfred Grévin in 1892, and "Stop" in 1899, a new group arose under the leadership of "Nadar" (b. 1820) and Etienne Carjat (b. 1828). Mirthful or satirical, and less philosophical than of yore, neglecting history for incident, and humanity for the puppets of the day, their drawings, which illustrate daily events, will perpetuate the manner and anecdotes of the time, though the illustrations to newspapers, or prints which need a paragraph of explanation, show nothing to compare with the *Propos de Thomas Virelocque* by "Gavarni." Quantity perhaps makes up for quality, and some of these artists deserve special mention. "Draner" (b. 1833) and "Henriot" (b. 1857) are journalists, carrying on the method first introduced by "Cham" in the *Univers Illustré*: realistic sketches, with no purpose beyond the droll illustration of facts, amusing at the time, but of no value to the print-collector. M. J.L. Forain, born at Reims in 1852, studied at the École des Beaux Arts under Jean Léon Gérôme and J.B. Carpeaux. He first worked for the *Courrier Français* in 1887, and afterwards for *Figaro*; he was then drawn into the polemical work of politics. Though he has created some great types of flunkeydom, the explanatory story is more to him than the picture, which is often too sketchy, though masterly. Reduced reproductions of his work have been issued in volumes, a common form of popularity never attempted with Daumier's fine lithographs. M. A.L. Willette, born at Châlons-sur-Marne in 1857, a son of Colonel Willette, the aide-de-camp to Marshal Bazaine, worked for four years in Alexandre Cabanel's studio, and so gained an artistic training which alone would have distinguished him from his fellows, even without the delightful poetical fancy and Watteau-like grace which are somewhat unexpected amid the ugliness of 334modern life. His work has the value, no doubt, of deep and various meaning, but it has also intrinsic artistic worth. M. Willette is, in fact, the ideal delineator of the more voluptuous and highly spiced aspects of contemporary life. "Caran d'Ache," a native of Moscow, born in 1858, borrowed from the German caricaturists— mainly from W. Busch—his methods of illustrating "a story without words." He makes fun even of animals, and is a master of canine physiognomy. His simple and unerring outline is a method peculiarly his own; now and again his wit rises to grandiloquence, as in his *Bellona*, rushing on an automobile through massacre and conflagrations, and in his *Épopée* (Epic) of shadows thrown on a sheet. Among his followers may be included A. Guillaume and Gerbault. M.C.L. Léandre, born at Champsecret (Orne), in 1862, is, like "André Gill," a draughtsman of monstrosities; he can get a perfect likeness of a face while exaggerating some particular feature, gives his figure a hump-back, as Dantan did in his statuettes, and has a facial dexterity which sometimes does scant justice to his very original wit. At the same time he has a true sense of beauty. M. Théophile A. Steinlen, born at Lausanne in 1859, went to Paris in 1881. He should be studied in his illustrations to *Bruant*. He knows the inmost core of the Butte-Montmartre, and depicts it with realistic and brutal relish. M. Albert Robida, born at Compiègne in 1848, collaborated with Decaux in 1871 to found *La Caricature*; he is a paradoxical seer of the possible future and a curiosity-hunter of the past. Old Paris has no secrets from him; he knows all the old stones and costumes of the middle ages, and has illustrated Rabelais; and for fertility of fancy he reminds us of Gustave Doré, but with a sense of movement so vibrant as to be almost distressing. "Bac," born at Vienna in 1859, has infused a strain of the Austrian woman into the Parisienne; representing her merely as a pleasure- and love-seeking creature, as the toy of an evening, he has recorded her peccadilloes, her witcheries and her vices. Others who have shot folly as it flies are M. Albert Guillaume, who illustrated the Exhibition of 1900 in a series of remarkable silhouettes;

"Mars"; "Henri Somm"; Gerbault; and Grün. M. Huard depicts to perfection the country townsfolk in their elementary psychology. M. Hermann Paul, M. Forain's not unworthy successor on the *Figaro*, is a cruel satirist, who in a single face can epitomize a whole class of society, and could catalogue the actors of the *comédie humaine* in a series of drawings. M. Jean Veber loves fantastic subjects, the gnomes of fairy-tales and myths; but he has a biting irony for contemporary history, as in the *Butcher's Shop*, where Bismarck is the blood-stained butcher. M. Abel Faivre, a refined and charming painter, is a whimsical humorist with the pencil. He shows us monstrous women, fabulously hideous, drawing them with a sort of realism which is droll by sheer ugliness. Henri de Toulouse-Lautrec startles us by extraordinary dislocations, scrawled limbs and inexplicable anatomy; he has left an inimitable series of sketches of Mme Yvette Guilbert when she was at her thinnest. M. Felix Vallotton reproduces crows in blots of black with a Japanese use of the brush. M. G. Jeanniot, a notable illustrator, sometimes amuses himself by contributing to *Le Rire, Le Sourire, Le Pompon, L'Assiette au Beurre*, &c., drawing the two types he most affects: the fashionable world and soldiers. M. Ibels, Capiello and many more might be enumerated, but it is impossible to chronicle all the clever humorous artists of the illustrated papers.

It is the frequent habit of French caricaturists to employ a *nom-de-guerre*. We therefore give here a list of the genuine names represented by the pseudonyms used above, together with others familiar to the public:—

"André Gill"	= L.A. Gosset de Guine (1840-1885).
"Bac" ("Cab" and "Saro")	= Ferdinand Bach (b. 1859).
"Caran d'Ache"	= Emmanuel Poiré.
"Cham"	= Comte Amédée de Noé (b. 1818).
"Crafty"	= Victor Gérusez (b. 1840).
"Draner" (and "Paf")	= Jules Renard (b. 1833).
"Faustin"	= Faustin Betbeder (b. 1847).
"Gavarni"	= S.G. Chevalier (1804-1866).
"Gédéon"	= Gédéon Baril (b. 1832).
"Grandville"	= J.I.I. Gérard (1803-1847).
"Henriot" (and "Piff")	= Henri Maigrot (b. 1857).
"Henri Somm"	= Henri Sommier (b. 1844).
"Job"	= J.O. de Bréville (b. 1858).
"Marcelin"	= Émile Planat (1825-1887).
"Mars"	= Maurice Bonvoisin (b. 1849).
"Moloch"	= Colomb (b. 1849).
"Montbard"	= C.A. Loye (1841-1905).
"Nadar"	= Félix Tournachon (b. 1820).
"Pasquin"	= Georges Coutan (b. 1853).
"Pépin"	= Ed. Guillaume (b. 1842).
"Randon"	= Gilbert (1814-1845).
"Sahib"	= L.E. Lesage (b. 1847).
"Said"	= Alphonse Lévy (b. 1845).
"Sem"	= George Goursat.
"Stop"	= L.P. Morel-Retz (b. 1825).

Germany.—During the later 19th century German caricature flourished principally in the comic papers *Kladderadatsch* of Berlin and *Fliegende Blätter* of Munich; the former a political paper with little artistic value, in which the ideas alone are clever, whilst the illustrations are merely a more or less clumsy adjunct to the text, while the *Fliegende Blätter*, on the contrary, has artistic merit as well as wit. Wilhelm Busch (b. 1832), the most brilliant German draughtsman of the last generation, made his *début* with an illustrated poem "The Peasant and the Miller," and won a world-wide reputation with the following works: *Pater Filucius, Die Fromme Helene, Max und Moritz, Der heilige Antonius, Maler Kleksel, Balduin Bählamm, Die Erlebnisse Knopps des Junggesellen.* Busch stands alone among the caricaturists of his nation, inasmuch as he is both the author and the illustrator of these works, his witty doggerel supplying Germany with household words. The drawings that accompany the text are amazing for the skill and directness with which he hits the vital mark. A flourish or two and a few touches are enough to set before us figures of intensely comical aspect. This distinguishes Busch from Adolf Oberländer (1845), who became the chief draughtsman on *Fliegende Blätter*. Busch's drawings would have no meaning apart from the humorous words. Oberländer works with the pencil only. Men, animals, trees, objects, are endowed by him with a mysterious life of their own. Without the help of any verbal joke, he achieves the funniest results simply by seeing and accentuating the comical side of everything. His drawings are caricature in the strict sense of the word, its principle being the exaggeration of some natural characteristic. The new generation of contributors to *Fliegende Blätter* do not work on these lines. Busch and Oberländer were both offshoots of the romantic school; they made fun of modern novelties. Hermann Schlittgen, Meggendorfer, H. Vogel-Plauen, Réne Reinicke, Adolf Hengeler and Fritz Wahle are the sons of a self-satisfied time, triumphing in its own *chic*, elegance and grace; hence they do not parody what they see, but simply depict it. The wit lies exclusively in the text; the illustrations aim merely at a direct representation of street or drawing-room scenes. It is this which gives to *Fliegende Blätter* its value as a pictorial record of the history of German manners. Its pages are a permanent authority on the subject for those who desire to see the social aspects of Germany during the last quarter of the 19th century onwards. At the same time a falling-off in the brilliancy of this periodical was perceptible. Its fun became domestic and homely; it has faithfully adhered to the old technique of wood-engraving, and made no effort to keep pace with the modern methods of reproduction. German caricature, to live and flourish, was not keeping pace with the development of the art; it had to take into its service the gay effects of colour, and derive fresh inspiration from the sweeping lines of the ornamental draughtsman. This led to the appearance of three new weekly papers: *Jugend, Das Narrenschiff* and *Simplicissimus*. *Jugend*, started in 1896 by Georg Hirth in Munich, collected from the first a group of gifted young artists, more especially Thöny, Bernhard Pankok and Julius Diez, who based their style on old German wood-engraving; Fidus, who lavished the utmost beauty of line in unshaded pen-and-ink work; Rudolf Wilke, whose grotesques have much in common with Forain's clever drawings; Angelo Jank and R.M. Eichler, who work with a delightful *bonhomie*. Among the draughtsmen on the *Narrenschiff* (The Ship of Fools), Hans Baluschek is worthy of mention as having made the types of Berlin life all his own; and while this paper gives us for the most part inoffensive satire on society, *Simplicissimus*, first printed at Munich and then at Zurich, under the editorship of Albert Langen, shows a marked Socialist and indeed Anarchist tendency, subjecting to ridicule and mockery everything that has hitherto been held as unassailable by such weapons; it reminds us of the scathing satire of Honoré Daumier in *La Caricature* at the time of Louis Philippe. Thomas Theodor Heine (1867) is unsurpassed in this style for his power of expression and variety of technique. We must admire his delicate draughtsmanship, or again, his drawing of the figure with the heavy line of heraldic ornament, and his broad and monumental grasp of the grotesque. His laughter is often insolent, but he is more often the preacher, scourge in hand, who ruthlessly unveils all the dark side of life. Next to him come Paul, an incomparable limner of student life and the manners and customs of the Bavarian populace; E. Thöny, a wonderfully clever caricaturist of the airs and assumption of the Prussian *Junker* and the Prussian subaltern; J.C. Eugh and F. von Regnieck, who make fun of the townsman and political spouter in biting and searching satire. The standard of caricature is at the present time a high one in Germany;

indeed, the modern adoption of the pen-line, which has arisen since the impressionists in oil-painting repudiated line, had its origin in the influence of caricature.

United States.—The proverbial irreverence of the American mind even towards its most cherished personages and ideals has made it particularly responsive to the appeal of caricature. At first an importation, it developed but slowly; then it burst into luxuriant growth, sometimes exceeding the limits of wise and careful cultivation. In the early period of American caricature, almost the only native is F.O.C. Darley (1822-1888), an illustrator of some importance; the other names include the engraver Paul Revere (chiefly famous for a picturesque exploit in the War of Independence); a Scotsman, William Charles; the Englishmen, Matt Morgan and E.P. Bellew; and the Germans, Thomas Nast and Joseph Keppler.

The name of Thomas Nast overshadows and sums up American political caricature. Nast, who was born in Bavaria in 1840, was 335brought to America at the age of six; and his training and all his interests were strongly American. At fourteen he was an illustrator on *Leslie's Weekly*, and was sent at twenty to England to illustrate the famous Sayers-Heenan prize-fight. He then went as recorder of Garibaldi's campaign of 1860. He returned to America known only as an illustrator. The Civil War did not awaken his latent genius till 1864, when he published a cartoon of fierce irony against the political party which opposed Lincoln's re-election and advocated peace measures with the Southern confederacy. This cartoon not only made Nast famous, but may be said to contain the germ of American caricature; for all that had gone before was too crude in technique to pass muster even as good caricature.

The magnificent corruption of Tammany Hall under the leadership of William M. Tweed, the first of the great municipal "bosses," gave Nast a subject worth attacking. Siegfried, earnest but light-hearted, armed with the mightier sword of the pen of ridicule, assailed the monster ensconced in his treasure-cave, and after a long battle won a brilliant victory. Nast did not always rely on a mere picture to carry his thrust; often his cartoon consisted of only a minor figure or two looking at a large placard on which a long and poignantly-worded attack was delivered in cold type. At other times the most ingenious pictorial subtlety was displayed. This long series sounds almost the whole gamut of caricature, from downright ridicule to the most lofty denunciation. A very happy device was the representation of Tweed's face by a money-bag with only dollar marks for features, a device which, strangely enough, made a curiously faithful likeness of the "boodle"-loving despot. When, finally, Tweed took to flight, to escape imprisonment, he was recognized and caught, it is said, entirely through the wide familiarity given to his image in Nast's cartoons.

When Nast retired from *Harper's Weekly*, he was succeeded by Charles Green Bush (born 1842; died 1909). With even greater technical resources, he poured forth a series of cartoons of remarkable evenness of skill and interest; he soon left weekly for daily journalism. He never won, single-handed, such a battle as Nast's, but his drawings have a more general, perhaps a more lasting interest. When he left *Harper's Weekly* he was succeeded by W.A. Rogers, who composed many ingenious and telling cartoons.

The vogue which, through Nast, *Harper's Weekly* gave to caricature, prepared the way for the first purely comic weekly paper, *Puck*, founded by two Germans, and for long published in a German as well as an English edition—a journal which has cast its influence generally in favour of the Democratic party. It is worth noting that not only the founders but the spirit of American caricature have been rather German than English, the American comic papers more closely resembling *Fliegende Blätter*, for example, than*Punch*. One of the founders of *Puck* was Joseph Keppler (1838-1894), long its chief caricaturist.

The Republican party soon found a champion in *Judge*, a weekly satirical paper which resembles *Puck* closely in its crudely coloured pages, though somewhat broader and less ambitious in the spirit and execution of its black-and-white illustrations. These two papers have kept rather strictly to permanent staffs, and have furnished the opening for many popular draughtsmen, such as Bernhard Gillam (d. 1896), and his brother, Victor; J.A. Wales (d. 1886); E. Zimmerman, whose extremely plebeian and broadly treated types often obscure the observation and Falstaffian humour displayed in them; Grant Hamilton; Frederick Opper, for many years devoted to the trials of suburban existence, and later concerned in

172

combating the trusts; C.J. Taylor, a graceful technician; H. Smith; Frank A. Nankivell, whose pretty athletic girls are prone to attitudinizing; J. Mortimer Flagg; F.M. Howarth; Mrs Frances O'Neill Latham, whose personages are singularly well modelled and alive; and Miss Baker Baker, a skilful draughtswoman of animals.

A stimulus to genuine art in caricature was given by the establishment (1883) of the weekly *Life*, edited by J.A. Mitchell, a clever draughtsman as well as an original writer. It is to this paper that America owes the discovery and encouragement of its most remarkable artist humorist, Charles Dana Gibson, whose technique has developed through many interesting phases from exceeding delicacy to a sculpturesque boldness of line without losing its rich texture, and without becoming monotonous. Mr Gibson is chiefly beloved by his public for his almost idolatrous realizations of the beautiful American woman of various types, ages and environments. His works are, however, full of the most subtle character-observations, and American men of all walks of life, and foreigners of every type, impart as much importance and humour to his pages as his "Gibson girls" give radiance. His admitted devotion to Du Maurier, in reverence for the beautiful woman beautifully attired, has led some critics to set him down as a mere disciple, while his powerful individuality has led others to accuse him of monotony; but a serious examination of his work has seemed to reveal that he has gone beyond the genius of Du Maurier in sophistication, if not in variety, of subjects and treatment. As much as any other artist Mr Gibson has studiously tried new experiments in the new fields opened by modernized processes of photo-engraving, and has been an important influence in both English and American line-illustration.

Among other students of society, particular success has been achieved by C.S. Reinhart (1844-1896), Charles Howard Johnson (d. 1895), H.W. M'Vickar, S.W. van Schaick, A.E. Sterner, W.H. Hyde, W.T. Smedley and A.B. Wenzell, each of them strongly individual in manner and often full of *verve* and truth.

Life, and other comic papers, including for many years *Truth*, also brought forward caricaturists of distinct worth and a marked tendency to specialization. F.E. Atwood (d. 1900) was ingenious in cartoons lightly allegorical; Oliver Herford has shown a fascination elusive of analysis in his drawings as in his verse; T.S. Sullivant has made a quaintly intellectual application of the old-world devices of large heads, small bodies, and the like; Peter Newell has developed individuality both in treatment and in humour; E.W. Kemble is noteworthy among the exploiters of negro life; and H.B. Eddy, Augustus Dirk, Robert L. Wagner, A. Anderson, F. Sarka and J. Swinnerton have all displayed marked individuality.

In distinction from the earlier period, the modern school of American caricature is strongly national, not only in subject, but in origin, training and in mental attitude, exception being made of a few notable figures, such as Michael Angelo Woolf, born in England, and of a somewhat Cruikshankian technique. He came to America while young, and contributed a long series of what may be called slum-fantasies, instinct alike with laughter and sorrow, at times strangely combining extravagant melodrama with a most plausible and convincing impossibility. His drawings must always lie very close to the affections of the large audience that welcomed them. American also by adoption is Henry Mayer, a German by birth, who has contributed to many of the chief comic papers of France, England, Germany and America.

Entirely native in every way is the art of A.B. Frost (b. 1851), a prominent humorist who deals with the life of the common people. His caricature (he is also an illustrator of versatility and importance) is distinguished by its anatomical knowledge, or, rather, anatomical imagination. Violent as the action of his figures frequently is, it is always convincing. Such triumphs as the tragedy of the kind-hearted man and the ungrateful bull-calf; the spinster's cat that ate rat poison, and many others, force the most serious to laughter by their amazing velocity of action and their unctuousness of expression. Frost is to American caricature what "Artemus Ward" has been to American humour, and his field of publication has been chiefly the monthly magazine.

The influence of the weekly periodicals has been briefly traced. A later development was the entrance of the omnivorous daily newspaper into the field of both the magazine and the weekly. For many years almost every newspaper has printed its daily cartoon, generally of a political nature. Few of the cartoonists have been able to keep up the pace of a daily inspiration, but C.G. Bush has been unusually successful in the attempt. Yet an occasional success atones for many slips, and the cartoonists are known and eagerly watched. The most influential has doubtless been Homer C. Davenport, whose slender artistic resources have been eked out by a vigour and mercilessness of assault rare even in American annals. He has a Rabelaisian complacency and skill in making a portrait magnificently repulsive, and his caricatures are a vivid example of the school of cartoonists who believe in slashing rather than merely prodding or tickling the object of attack. Charles Nelan (1859-1904) frequently scored, and in the wide extent of the United States one finds keen wits busily assailing the manifold evils of life. Noteworthy among them are: Thos. E. Powers, H.R. Heaton, Albert Levering, Clare Angell and R.C. Swayne.

Scandinavia.—Caricature flourishes also in the Scandinavian countries, but few names are known beyond their borders. Professor Hans Tegner of Denmark is an exception; his illustrations to Hans Andersen (English edition, 1900) have carried his name wherever that author is appreciated, yet his reputation was made in the Danish *Punch,* which was founded after the year 1870 but has long ceased to exist. Alfred Schmidt and Axel Thiess have contributed notable sketches to *Puk* and its successor *Klockhaus,* but in point of style they scarcely carry on the tradition of their predecessor, Fritz Jürgensen. Among humorous artists of Norway, Th. Kittelsen perhaps holds the leading place, and in Sweden, Bruno Liljefors, best known as a brilliant painter of bird life.

BIBLIOGRAPHY.—*Rules for Drawing Caricature, with an Essay on Comic Painting,* by Francis Grose (8vo, London, 1788); *Historical Sketch of the Art of Caricaturing,* by J. Peller Malcolm (4to, London, 1813); *History of Caricature and Grotesque in Literature and Art,* by Thomas Wright (8vo, London, 1865); *Musée de la caricature,* by Jaime; (a) *Histoire de la caricature antique,* (b) *Histoire de la caricature au moyen âge et sous la renaissance;* (c) *Histoire de la caricature sous la réforme et la ligue;* (d)*Histoire de la caricature sous la république, l'empire, et la restauration;* (e)*Histoire de la caricature moderne* (5 vols.), by Champfleury (*i.e.* Jules Fleury), (8vo, Paris); *Le Musée secret de la caricature,* by Champfleury (*i.e.*Jules Fleury), (8vo, Paris); *L'Art du rire et de la caricature,* by Arsène Alexandre (8vo, Paris); *Caricature and other Comic Art,* by James Parton (sm. 4to, New York, 1878); *Le Miroir de la vie: la Caricature,* by Robert de la Sizeranne (8vo, Paris, 1902), (tracing the aesthetic development of the art and spirit of caricature); *La Caricature à travers les siècles,* by Georges Veyrat (4to, Paris); *La Caricature et les caricaturistes,* by Émile Bagaud (with a preface by Ch. Léandre), (fo., Paris); *Le Rire et la caricature,* by Paul Gaultier (with a preface by Sully Prudhomme), (8vo, Paris, 1906), (a work of originality, dwelling not only on the aesthetic but on the essentially 336pessimistic side of satiric art); *English Caricaturists and Graphic Humorists of the Nineteenth Century,* by Graham Everitt (*i.e.* William Rodgers Richardson), (4to, London, 1886), (a careful and interesting survey); *La Caricature en Angleterre,* by Augustin Filva (8vo, Paris, 1902), (an able criticism from the point of view of psycho-sociology); *The History of Punch,* by M.H. Spielmann (8vo, London, 1895), (dealing with caricature art of England during the half-century covered by the book); *Magazine of Art,* passim, for biographies of English caricaturists—"Our Graphic Humorists";*Social Pictorial Satire,* by George du Maurier (12mo, London, 1898); *Les Moeurs et la caricature en France,* by J. Grand-Carteret (8vo, Paris, 1885);*La Caricature et l'humeur français au XIXe siècle,* by Raoul Deberdt (8vo, Paris); *Les Maîtres de la caricature française en XIXe siècle,* by Armand Dayot (Paris); *Nos humoristes,* by Ad. Brisson (4to, Paris, 1900); *Les Moeurs et la caricature en Allemagne, &c.,* by J. Grand-Carteret (8vo, Paris, 1885). See also biographies of Charles Keene, H. Daumier, John Leech, &c., indicated under those names.

(M. H. S.)

CARIGARA, a town of the province of Leyte, island of Leyte, Philippine Islands, on Carigara Bay, 22 m. W. of Tacloban, the capital. Pop. (1903) 19,488, including that of Capoocan (3106), annexed to Carigara in the same year. Carigara is open to coast trade, exports large quantities of hemp, raises much rice, and manufactures cotton and abaca fabrics. It also has important fisheries.

CARIGNANO, a town of Piedmont, Italy, in the province of Turin, 11 m. S. by steam tramway from the town of Turin. Pop. (1901) town, 4672, commune, 7104. It has a handsome church (S. Giovanni Battista) erected in 1756-1766 by the architect Benedetto Alfieri di Sostegno (1700-1767), uncle of the poet Alfieri. S. Maria delle Grazie contains the tomb of Bianca Palaeologus, wife of Duke Charles I. of Savoy, at whose court Bayard was brought up. The town passed into the hands of the counts of Savoy in 1418.

Carignano was erected by Charles Emmanuel I. of Savoy into a principality as an appanage for his third son, Thomas Francis (1596-1656), whose descendant, Charles Albert, prince of Carignano, became king of Sardinia on the extinction of the elder line of the house of Savoy with the death of Charles Felix in 1831. The house of Carignano developed two junior branches, those of Soissons and Villafranca. The first of these, which became extinct in 1734, was founded by Eugene Maurice, second son of Thomas, by his wife Marie de Condé, countess of Soissons, who received his mother's countship as his appanage. In 1662 the town of Yvois in the Ardennes was raised by Louis XIV. into a duchy in his favour, its name being changed at the same time to Carignan. The famous Prince Eugene was the second son of the first duke of Carignan. The branch of Villafranca started with Eugene Marie Louis (d. 1785), second son of Louis Victor of Carignano, whose grandson Eugene (1816-1888), afterwards an admiral in the Italian navy, was created prince of Savoy-Carignano, by King Charles Albert in 1834. He had contracted a morganatic marriage, and in 1888, on the occasion of his silver wedding, the title of countess of Villafranca was bestowed upon his wife, his eldest son, Filiberto, being at the same time created count of Villafranca, and his younger son, Vittorio, count of Soissons.

CARILLON, an arrangement for playing tunes upon a set of bells by mechanical means. The word is said to be a Fr. form of Late Lat. or Ital.*quadriglio,* a simple dance measure on four notes or for four persons (Lat.*quattuor*); and is used sometimes for the tune played, sometimes (and more commonly in England) for the set of bells used in playing it. The earliest medieval attempts at bell music, as distinct from mere noise, seem to have consisted in striking a row of small bells by hand with a hammer, and illustrations in MSS. of the 12th and 13th centuries show this process on three, four or even eight bells. The introduction of mechanism in the form either of a barrel (see BARREL-ORGAN) set with pegs or studs and revolving in connexion with the machinery of a clock, or of a keyboard struck by hand (*carillon à clavier*), made it possible largely to increase the number of bells and the range of harmonies. In Belgium, the home of the *carillon* the art of the *carillonneur* was at one time brought to great perfection and held in high esteem (see BELL); but even there it is gradually giving way to mechanism. In England manual skill has never been much employed, though keyboards on the continental model have been introduced, *e.g.* at the Manchester town hall, at Eaton Hall, and elsewhere; carillon music being mainly confined to hymn tunes at regular intervals (generally three hours), or chimes at the hours and intervening quarters. The "Cambridge" and "Westminster" chimes are very familiar; and more recently chimes have been composed by Sir John Stainer for Freshwater in the Isle of Wight ("Tennyson" Chimes), and by Sir Charles Stanford for "Bow Bells" in London.

CARINI, a town in the province of Palermo, Sicily, 13 m. by rail W.N.W. of Palermo. Pop. (1901) 13,931. On the coast are some ruins of the ancient*Hyccara*, the only Sican settlement (probably a fishing village) on the coast. It was stormed and taken by the Athenians in 415 B.C., and the inhabitants, among them the famous courtesan Lais, sold as slaves. At La Grazia Christian catacombs have been found (*Not. degli Scavi*, 1899, 362).

CARINTHIA (Ger. *Kärnten*), a duchy and crownland of Austria, bounded E. by Styria, N. by Styria and Salzburg, W. by Tirol, and S. by Italy, Görz and Gradisca and Carniola. It has an area of 4005 sq. m. Carinthia is for the most part a mountainous region, divided by the Drave, which traverses it from west to east into two parts. To the north of the valley of the Drave the duchy is occupied by the Hohe Tauern and the primitive Alps of Carinthia and Styria, which belong to the central zone of the Eastern Alps. The Hohe Tauern contains the massifs of the Gross Glockner (12,455 ft.); the Hochnarr (10,670 ft.) and the Ankogel (11,006 ft.), and is traversed by the saddles of the Hochthor and the Malnitzer Tauern, which separates these groups from one another. To the east of the Hohe

Tauern stretches the group of the primitive Alps of Carinthia and Styria, namely the Pöllaer Alps with the glacier-covered peak of the Hafner Eck (10,041 ft.); the Stang Alps with the highest peak the Eisenhut (8007 ft.); the Saualpe with the highest peak the Grosse Saualpe (6825 ft.); and finally the Koralpen chain or the Stainzer Alps (7023 ft.) separated from the preceding group by the Lavant valley. The country south of the Drave is occupied by several groups of the southern limestone zone, namely the Carnic Alps, the Julian Alps, the Karawankas and the Steiner Alps. The Carnic Alps are divided by the Gail valley into the South Carnic group and the northern Gailthal Alps. They are traversed by the Pontebba or Pontafel Pass, through which passes one of the principal Alpine roads from Italy to Austria. The road is covered by the fortress of Malborgeth, where Captain Hensel with a handful of men met with a heroic death defending the place against an overwhelming French force in the campaign of 1809. A similar fate overtook, on the same day, the 18th of May 1809, Captain Hermann von Hermannsdorf and his small garrison, who were defending the Predil fort. This fort covers the road which traverses the Predil Pass in the Julian Alps and is the principal road leading from Carinthia to the Coastland. Commemorative monuments have been erected in both places. The Gailthal Alps end with the Dobratsch or Villacher Alp (7107 ft.), situated to the south-west of Villach (*q.v.*), which is celebrated as one of the finest views in the whole eastern Alps. South of Hermagor, the principal place of the Gail valley, is the chain of mountains which is famous as being the only place where the beautiful *Wulfenia Carinthiaca* is found. The highest peaks in the Karawankas are the Grosse Mittagskogel (7033 ft.), the Och Obir (7023 ft.) and the Petzen (6934 ft.). The Ursula Berg (5563 ft.) ends the group of the Karawankas, which are continued by the Steiner Alps.

The principal river is the Drave, which flows from west to east through the length of the duchy, and receives in its course the waters of all the other streams, except the Fella, which reaches the Adriatic by its junction with the Tagliamento. Its principal tributaries are the Gail on the right, and the Möll, the Lieser, the Gurk with the Glan, and the Lavant on the left. Carinthia possesses a great number of Alpine lakes, which, unlike the other Alpine lakes, lie in the longitudinal valleys. The principal lakes are: the Millstätter-see (8½ sq. m. in extent, 908 ft. deep, at an altitude of 1902 ft.), the Wörther-see (17 sq. m. in extent, 212 ft. deep, at an altitude of 1438 ft.), the Ossiach-see (10½ sq. m. 337in extent, 150 ft. deep, at an altitude of 1599 ft.), and the elongated Weissen-see (4½ m. long, 309 ft. deep, at an altitude of 3037 ft.).

The climate is severe in the north and north-west parts, but the south and south-east districts are milder, while the most favoured part is the Lavant valley. Of the total area only 13.71% is arable land, 10.50% is occupied by meadows and gardens, 5.18% by pastures, while 44.24% is covered by forests, almost exclusively pine-forests. Cattle-rearing is well developed, and the horses bred in Carinthia enjoy a good reputation. The mineral wealth of Carinthia is great, and consists in lead, iron, zinc and coal. Iron ore is extracted in the region of the Saualpe, and is worked in the foundries of St Leonhard, St Gertraud, Prävali, Hirt, Treibach and Eberstein. About two-thirds of the total production of lead in Austria is extracted in Carinthia, the principal places being Bleiberg and Raibl. The metallurgic industries are well developed, and consist in the production of iron, steel, machinery, small-arms, lead articles, wire-cables and rails. The principal manufacturing places are Prävali, Brückl, Klagenfurt, Lippitzbach, Wolfsberg, St Veit and Buchscheiden near Feldkirchen. The manufacture of small-arms is concentrated at Ferlach. Other trades are the manufacture of paper, leather, cement and the exploitation of forests.

The population of Carinthia in 1900 was 367,344, which corresponds to 91 inhabitants per sq. m. According to nationality, 71.54% were Germans, and 28.39% Slovenes, mostly settled in the districts adjoining the Slovene province of Carniola. Over 94% of the population were Roman Catholics. The local diet, of which the bishop of Gurk is a member *ex officio*, is composed of 37 members, and Carinthia sends 10 deputies to the Reichsrat at Vienna. For administrative purposes, the province is divided into seven districts, and an autonomous municipality, Klagenfurt (pop. 24,314), the capital. Other principal places are: Villach (9690), Wolfsberg (4852), St Veit (4667), an old town, the former capital of Carinthia up to 1518, Prävali (4047), Travis (3640), a favourite summer-resort and tourist place, Bleiberg (3435), Völkermarkt (2606) and Spittal (2564).

Carinthia is so called from the Carni, a Celtic people, and in the time of Augustus it formed part of Noricum. After the fall of the Roman empire, it was the nucleus of the kingdom of Carentania, which was founded by Samo, a Frankish adventurer, but soon fell to pieces after his death. Under Charlemagne it constituted a margravate, which in 843 passed into the hands of Louis the German, whose grandson Arnulf was the first to bear the title of duke of Carinthia. The duchy was held by various families during the 11th, 12th and 13th centuries, and at length in 1335 was bestowed by Louis the Bavarian on the dukes of Austria. It was divided into Upper or Western Carinthia and Lower or Eastern; of these the former fell to France in 1809, but was reconquered in 1813. It was created a separate crownland in 1849.

See Aelschker. *Geschichte Kärntens* (Klagenfurt, 1885).

CARINUS, MARCUS AURELIUS, Roman emperor, A.D. 283-284, was the elder son of the emperor Carus, on whose accession he was appointed governor of the western portion of the empire. He fought with success against the German tribes, but soon left the defence of the Upper Rhine to his legates and returned to Rome, where he abandoned himself to all kinds of debauchery and excess. He also celebrated the *ludi Romani* on a scale of unexampled magnificence. After the death of Carus, the army in the East demanded to be led back to Europe, and Numerianus, the younger son of Carus, was forced to comply. During a halt at Chalcedon, Numerianus was murdered, and Diocletian, commander of the body-guards, was proclaimed emperor by the soldiers. Carinus at once left Rome and set out for the East to meet Diocletian. On his way through Pannonia he put down the usurper M. Aurelius Julianus, and encountered the army of Diocletian in Moesia. Carinus was successful in several engagements, and at the battle on the Margus (Morava), according to one account, the valour of his troops had gained the day, when he was assassinated by a tribune whose wife he had seduced. In another account, the battle is represented as having resulted in a complete victory for Diocletian. Carinus has the reputation of having been one of the worst of the emperors.

Vopiscus, *Carinus* (mainly the recital of his crimes); Aurelius Victor, *De Caesaribus*, 38, Epit. 38; Eutropius ix. 18-20; Zonaras xii. 30; Orosius vii. 25; Pauly-Wissowa, *Realencyclopadie*, ii. 24 ff. (Henze).

CARIPE, a small town of Venezuela in the state of Bermúdez, about 53 m. E.S.E. of Cumaná. It is the chief station of the Capuchin missions to the Chayma Indians, founded toward the close of the 17th century, and stands 2635 ft. above sea-level, in a fertile valley of the Sierra Bergantín, long celebrated for its cool, invigorating climate. The locality is also celebrated for the extensive system of caves in the limestone rocks found in its vicinity, which were described by Humboldt in his *Personal Narrative*. The principal cave, known as the Cueva del Guácharo, extends inward a distance of 2800 ft. with a height of 70-80 ft. These caves are frequented by a species of night-hawk, called *guacharo*, which nests in the recesses of the rocks. The young are killed in great numbers for their oil. Caripe itself has a population of only 580, but the valley and neighbouring stations have about ten times that number. Caripe should not be confounded with Rio Caribe, a town and port on the Caribbean coast a short distance east of Carúpano, which has a population of about 6000.

CARISBROOKE, a town in the Isle of Wight, England, 1 m. S. of Newport. Pop. (1901) 3993. The valley of the Lugley brook separates the village from the steep conical hill crowned by the castle, the existence of which has given Carisbrooke its chief fame. There are remains of a Roman villa in the valley, but no reliable mention of Carisbrooke occurs in Saxon times, though it has commonly been identified with the Saxon *Wihtgaraburh* captured by Cerdic in 530. Carisbrooke is not mentioned by name in the Domesday Survey, but Bowcombe, its principal manor, was a dependency of the royal manor of Amesbury, and was obtained from the king by William Fitz Osbern in exchange for three Wiltshire manors. The castle is mentioned in the Survey under Alvington, and was probably raised by William Fitz Osbern, who was made first lord of the Isle of Wight. From this date lordship of the Isle of Wight was always associated with ownership of the castle, which thus became the seat of government of the island. Henry I. bestowed it on Richard de Redvers, in whose family it continued until Isabella de Fortibus sold it to Edward I., after which the government was entrusted to wardens as representatives of the crown. The keep was added to the castle in the reign of Henry I., and in the reign of Elizabeth, when the Spanish Armada was expected, it was surrounded by an elaborate pentagonal fortification. The castle was garrisoned by Baldwin de Redvers for the empress Maud in 1136, but was captured by Stephen. In the reign of Richard II. it was unsuccessfully attacked by the French; Charles I. was imprisoned here for fourteen months before his execution. Afterwards his two youngest children were confined in the castle, and the Princess Elizabeth died there. In 1904 the chapel of St Nicholas in the castle was reopened and reconsecrated, having been rebuilt as a national memorial of Charles I. The remains of the castle are extensive and imposing, and the keeper's house and other parts are inhabited, but the king's apartments are in ruins. Within the walls is a well 200 ft. deep; and another in the centre of the keep is reputed to have been still deeper. The church of St Mary, Carisbrooke, has a beautiful Perpendicular tower, and contains transitional Norman portions. Only the site can be traced of the Cistercian priory to which it belonged. This was founded shortly after the Conquest and originated from the endowment which the monks of Lyre near Evreux held in Bowcombe, including the church, mill, houses, land and tithes of the manor. Richard II. bestowed it on the abbey of Mountgrace in Yorkshire. It was restored by Henry IV., but was dissolved by act of parliament in the reign of Henry V., who bestowed it on his newly-founded charter-house at Sheen. Carisbrooke formerly had a considerable market, several mills, and valuable fisheries, but it never acquired municipal or representative rights, and was important only as the site of the castle.

See *Victoria County History—Hampshire*; William Westall, *History of Carisbrooke Castle* (1850).

338

CARISSIMI, GIACOMO (c. 1604-1674), one of the most celebrated masters of the Italian, or, more accurately, the Roman school of music, was born about 1604 in Marino (near Rome). Of his life almost nothing is known. At the age of twenty he became chapel-master at Assisi, and in 1628 he obtained the same position at the church of St Apollinaris belonging to the Collegium Germanicum in Rome, which he held till his death on the 12th of January 1674, at Rome. He seems never to have left Italy. The two great achievements generally ascribed to him are the further development of the recitative, lately introduced by Monteverde, and of infinite importance in the history of dramatic music; and the invention of the chamber-cantata, by which Carissimi superseded the madrigals formerly in use. His position in the history of church music and vocal chamber music is somewhat similar to that of Cavalli in the history of opera. It is impossible to say who was really the inventor of the chamber-cantata; but Carissimi and Luigi Rossi were the composers who first made this form the vehicle for the most intellectual style of chamber-music, a function which it continued to perform until the death of Alessandro Scarlatti, Astorga and Marcello. Of his oratorios *Jephthah* has been published by Novello & Co., and is well known; this work and others are important as definitely establishing the form of oratorio unaccompanied by dramatic action, which has maintained its hold to the present day. He also may claim the merit of having given greater variety and interest to the instrumental accompaniments of vocal compositions. Dr Burney and Sir John Hawkins published specimens of his compositions in their works on the history of music; and Dr Aldrich collected an almost complete set of his compositions, at present in the library of Christ Church, Oxford. The British Museum also possesses numerous valuable works by this great Italian master. Most of his oratorios are in the Bibliothèque Nationale at Paris.

CARLETON, WILLIAM (1794-1869), Irish novelist, was born at Prillisk, Clogher, Co. Tyrone, on the 4th of March 1794. His father was a tenant farmer, who supported a family of fourteen children on as many acres, and young Carleton passed his early life among scenes precisely similar to those he afterwards delineated with so much power and truthfulness. His father was remarkable for his extraordinary memory, and had a thorough acquaintance with Irish folklore; the mother was noted throughout the district for the sweetness of her voice. The beautiful character of Honor, the miser's wife, in *Fardorougha*, is said to have been drawn from her.

The education received by Carleton was of a very humble description. As his father removed from one small farm to another, he attended at various places the hedge-schools, which used to be a notable feature of Irish life. The admirable little picture of one of these schools is given in the sketch called "The Hedge School" included in *Traits and Stories of Irish Peasantry*. Most of his learning was gained from a curate named Keenan, who taught a classical school at Donagh (Co. Monaghan), which Carleton attended from 1814 to 1816. Before this Carleton had resolved to prosecute his education as a poor scholar at Munster, with a view to entering the church; but in obedience to a warning dream, the story of which is told in the *Poor Scholar*, he returned home, where he received the unbounded veneration of the neighbouring peasantry for his supposed wonderful learning. An amusing account of this phase of his existence is given in the little sketch, "Denis O'Shaughnessy." About the age of nineteen he undertook one of the religious pilgrimages then common in Ireland. His experiences as a pilgrim, narrated in "The Lough Derg Pilgrim," made him resign for ever the thought of entering the church, and he eventually became a Protestant. His vacillating ideas as to a mode of life were determined in a definite direction by the reading of *Gil Blas*. He resolved to cast himself boldly upon the world, and try what fortune had in store for him. He went to Killanny, Co Louth, and for six months acted as tutor in the family of a farmer named Piers Murphy, and after some other experiments he set out for Dublin, and arrived in the metropolis with 2s 9d. in his pocket. He first sought occupation as a bird-stuffer, but a proposal to use potatoes and meal as stuffing failed to recommend him. He then determined to become a soldier, but the colonel of the regiment in which he desired to enlist persuaded him—Carleton had applied in Latin—to give up the idea. He obtained some teaching and a clerkship in a Sunday School office, began to contribute to the journals, and his paper "The Pilgrimage to Lough Derg," which was published in the *Christian Examiner*, excited great attention. In 1830 appeared the first series of *Traits and Stories of the Irish Peasantry* (2 vols.), which at once placed the author in the first rank of Irish novelists. A second series (3 vols.), containing, among other stories, "Tubber Derg, or the Red Well," appeared in 1833, and *Tales of Ireland* in 1834. From that time till within a few years of his death Carleton's literary activity was incessant. "Fardorougha the Miser, or the Convicts of Lisnamona" appeared in 1837-1838 in the *Dublin University Magazine*. Among his other famous novels are: *Valentine McClutchy, the Irish Agent, or Chronicles of the Castle Cumber Property* (3 vols., 1845); *The Black Prophet, a Tale of the Famine*, in the *Dublin University Magazine* (1846), printed separately in the next year; *The Emigrants of Ahadarra* (1847); *Willy Reilly and his dear Colleen Bawn* (in *The Independent*, London, 1850); and *The Tithe Proctor* (1849), the violence of which did his reputation harm among his own countrymen. Some of his later stories, *The Squanders of Castle Squander* (1852) for instance, are defaced by the mass of political matter with which they are overloaded. In spite of his very considerable literary production Carleton remained poor, but his necessities were relieved in 1848 by a pension of £200 a year granted by Lord John Russell in response to a memorial on Carleton's behalf signed by numbers of distinguished persons in Ireland. He died at Sandford, Co. Dublin, on the 30th of January 1869.

Carleton's best work is contained in the *Traits and Stories of the Irish Peasantry*. He wrote from intimate acquaintance with the scenes he described; and he drew with a sure hand a series of pictures of peasant life, unsurpassed for their appreciation of the passionate tenderness of Irish home life, of the buoyant humour and the domestic virtues which would, under better circumstances, bring prosperity and happiness. He alienated the sympathies of many Irishmen, however, by his unsparing criticism and occasional exaggeration of the darker side of Irish character. He was in his own words the "historian of their habits and manners, their feelings, their prejudices, their superstitions and their crimes." (Preface to *Tales of Ireland*.)

During the last months of his life Carleton began an autobiography which he brought down to the beginning of his literary career. This forms the first part of *The Life of William Carleton* ... (2 vols., 1896), by D.J. O'Donoghue, which contains full information about his life,

179

and a list of his scattered writings. A selection from his stories (1889), in the "Camelot Series," has an introduction by Mr W.B. Yeats. He must not be confused with Will Carleton (b. 1845), the American author of *Farm Ballads* (1873).

CARLETON PLACE, a town and port of entry of Lanark county, Ontario, Canada, 28 m. S.W. of Ottawa, on the Mississippi river, and at the junction of the main line and Brockville branch of the Canadian Pacific railway. It has abundant water-power privileges, and extensive railway-repair shops and woollen mills. Pop. (1901) 4059.

CARLILE, RICHARD (1790-1843), English freethinker, was born on the 8th of December 1790, at Ashburton, Devonshire, the son of a shoemaker. Educated in the village school, he was apprenticed to a tinman against whose harsh treatment he frequently rebelled. Having finished his apprenticeship, he obtained occupation in London as a journeyman tinman. Influenced by reading Paine's *Rights of Man*, he became an uncompromising radical, and in 1817 started pushing the sale of the *Black Dwarf*, a new weekly paper, edited by Jonathan Wooler, all over London, and in his zeal to secure the dissemination of its doctrines frequently walked 30 m. a day. In the same year he also printed and sold 25,000 copies of Southey's *Wat Tyler*, reprinted the suppressed *Parodies* of Hone, and wrote himself, in imitation of them, the *Political Litany*. This work cost him eighteen weeks imprisonment. In 1818 he published Paine's works, for which 339and for other publications of a like character he was fined £1500, and sentenced to three years' imprisonment in Dorchester gaol. Here he published the first twelve volumes of his periodical the *Republican*. The publication was continued by his wife, who was accordingly sentenced to two years' imprisonment in 1821. A public subscription, headed by the duke of Wellington, was now raised to prosecute Carlile's assistants. At the same time Carlile's furniture and stock-in-trade in London were seized, three years were added to his imprisonment in lieu of payment of his fine, his sister was fined £500 and imprisoned for a year for publishing an address by him, and nine of his shopmen received terms of imprisonment varying from six months to three years. In 1825 the government decided to discontinue the prosecutions. After his release in that year Carlile edited the *Gorgon*, a weekly paper, and conducted free discussions in the London Rotunda. For refusing to give sureties for good behaviour after a prosecution arising out of a refusal to pay church rates, he was again imprisoned for three years, and a similar resistance cost him ten weeks' more imprisonment in 1834-1835. He died on the 10th of February 1843, after having spent in all nine years and four months in prison.

CARLINGFORD, CHICHESTER SAMUEL FORTESCUE, BARON(1823-1898), British statesman, son of Chichester Fortescue (d. 1826), M.P. for Louth in the Irish parliament, was born in January 1823. He came of an old family settled in Ireland since the days of Sir Faithful Fortescue (1581-1666), whose uncle, Lord Chichester, was lord deputy. The history of the family was written by his elder brother Thomas (1815-1887), who in 1852 was created Baron Clermont. The future Lord Carlingford, then Mr Chichester Fortescue, went to Christ Church, Oxford, where he took a first in classics (1844) and won the chancellor's English essay (1846); and in 1847 he was elected to parliament for Louth as a Liberal. He became a junior lord of the treasury in 1854, and subsequently held minor offices in the Liberal administrations till in 1865 he was made chief secretary for Ireland under Lord Russell, a post which he again occupied under Gladstone in 1868-1870; he then became president of the Board of Trade (1871-1874), and later lord privy seal (1881-1885) and president of the council (1883-1885). He was raised to the peerage in 1874. He parted from Gladstone on the question of Irish Home Rule, but in earlier years he was his active supporter on Irish questions. His influence in society was due largely to his wife, Frances (1821-1879), previously the wife of the 7th Earl Waldegrave, whom he married in 1863. In 1887 his brother, Lord Clermont, died, and Carlingford inherited his peerage; but on his own death without issue on the 30th of January 1898 both titles became extinct.

CARLINGFORD, a small market town and port of Co. Louth, Ireland, in the north parliamentary division. Pop. (1901) 606. It is beautifully situated on the western shore of

Carlingford Lough, at the foot of Carlingford Mountain (1935 ft.), facing the fine heights of the Mourne Mountains across the lough in Co. Down. It has a station on the railway connecting Greenore and Newry, owned by the London & North-Western railway of England. It was formerly a place of great importance, as attested by numerous remains. King John's Castle (1210) commands the lough from an isolated rock. There are other remains of the castellated houses erected during the Elizabethan and previous wars. A Dominican monastery was founded in 1305, and combines ecclesiastical and military remains. The town received several charters between the reigns of Edward II. and James II., was represented in the Irish parliament until the Union, and possessed a mint from 1467. The lough is a typical rock-basin hollowed out by glacial action, about 4 fathoms deep at its entrance, but increasing to four times that depth within. The oyster-beds are valuable.

CARLI-RUBBI, GIOVANNI RINALDO, COUNT OF (1720-1795), Italian economist and antiquarian, was born at Capo d'Istria, in 1720. At the age of twenty-four he was appointed by the senate of Venice to the newly established professorship of astronomy and navigation in the university of Padua, and entrusted with the superintendence of the Venetian marine. After filling these offices for seven years with great credit, he resigned them, in order to devote himself to the study of antiquities and political economy. His principal economic works are his *Delle monete, e della instituzione delle zecche d' Italia*; his *Ragionamento sopra i bilanci economici delle nazioni* (1759), in which he maintained that what is termed the balance of trade between two nations is no criterion of the prosperity of either, since both may be gainers by their reciprocal transactions; and his *Sul libero commercio dei grani* (1771), in which he argues that free trade in grain is not always advisable. Count Carli's merits were appreciated by Leopold of Tuscany, afterwards emperor, who in 1765 placed him at the head of the council of public economy and of the board of public instruction. In 1769 he became privy councillor, in 1771 president of the new council of finances. He died at Milan in February 1795. During his leisure he completed and published his *Antichità Italiche*, in which the literature and arts of his country are ably discussed. Besides the above, he published many works on antiquarian, economic and other subjects, including *L' Uomo libero*, in confutation of Rousseau's *Contrat Social*; an attack upon the abbé Tartarotti's assertion of the existence of magicians; *Osservazioni sulla musica antica e moderna*; and several poems.

CARLISLE, EARLS OF. This English title has been held by two families, being created for James Hay in 1622, and being extinct in that line on the death of his son in 1660, and then being given in 1661 to Charles Howard, and descending to the present day in the Howard family.

JAMES HAY, 1st earl of Carlisle (d. 1636), was the son of Sir James Hay of Kingask (a member of a younger branch of the Erroll family), and of Margaret Murray, cousin of George Hay, afterwards 1st earl of Kinnoull. He was knighted and taken into favour by James VI. of Scotland, brought into England in 1603, treated as a "prime favourite" and made a gentleman of the bedchamber. In 1604 he was sent on a mission to France and pleaded for the Huguenots, which annoyed Henry IV. and caused a substantial reduction of the present made to the English envoy. On the 21st of June 1606 he was created by patent a baron for life, with precedence next to the barons, but without a place or voice in parliament, no doubt to render his advancement less unpalatable to the English lords. The king bestowed on him numerous grants, paid his debts, and secured for him a rich bride in the person of Honora, only daughter and heir of Edward, Lord Denny, afterwards earl of Norwich. In 1610 he was made a knight of the Bath, and in 1613 master of the wardrobe, while in 1615 he was created Lord Hay of Sawley, and took his seat in the House of Lords. He was sent to France next year to negotiate the marriage of Princess Christina with Prince Charles, and on his return, being now a widower, married in 1617 Lady Lucy Percy (1599-1660), daughter of the 9th earl of Northumberland, and was made a privy councillor. In 1618 he resigned the mastership of the wardrobe for a large sum in compensation. He was created Viscount Doncaster, and in February 1619 was despatched on a mission to Germany, where he identified himself with the cause of the elector palatine and urged James to make war in his support. In 1621 and 1622 he was sent to France to obtain peace for the Huguenots from Louis XIII., in which he was unsuccessful, and in September 1622 was created earl of Carlisle. Next year he went to Paris on the occasion of Prince Charles's journey to Madrid, and again in 1624 to join Henry Rich, afterwards Lord Holland, in negotiating the prince's marriage with Henrietta Maria, when he advised James without success to resist Richelieu's demands on the subject of religious toleration. On the 2nd of July 1627 Lord Carlisle obtained from the king a grant of all the Caribbean Islands, including Barbados, this being a confirmation of a former concession given by James I. He was also a patentee and councillor of the plantation of New England, and showed great zeal and interest in the colonies. He became gentleman of the bedchamber to King Charles I. after his accession. In 1628, after the failure of the expedition to Rhé, he was sent to make a diversion against Richelieu in Lorraine and Piedmont; he counselled peace with Spain and the 340vigorous prosecution of the war with France, but on his return home found his advice neglected. He took no further part in public life, and died in March 1636. Carlisle was a man of good sense and of accommodating temper, with some diplomatic ability. His extravagance and lavish expenditure, his "double suppers" and costly entertainments, were the theme of satirists and wonder of society, and his debts were said at his death to amount to more than £80,000. "He left behind him," says Clarendon, "a reputation of a very fine gentleman and a most accomplished courtier, and after having spent, in a very jovial life, above £400,000, which upon a strict computation he received from the crown, he left not a house or acre of land to be remembered by."

The charms and wit of his second wife, Lucy, countess of Carlisle, which were celebrated in verse by all the poets of the day, including Carew, Cartwright, Herrick and Suckling, and by Sir Toby Matthew in prose, made her a conspicuous figure at the court of Charles I. There appears no foundation for the scandal which made her the mistress successively of Strafford and of Pym. Strafford valued highly her sincerity and services, but after his death, possibly in consequence of a revulsion of feeling at his abandonment by the court, she devoted herself to Pym and to the interests of the parliamentary leaders, to whom she communicated the king's most secret plans and counsels. Her greatest achievement was the timely disclosure to Lord Essex of the king's intended arrest of the five members, which enabled them to escape. But she appears to have served both parties simultaneously, betraying communications on both sides, and doing considerable mischief in inflaming political animosities. In 1647 she attached herself to the interests of the moderate Presbyterian party, which assembled at her house, and in the second Civil War showed great zeal and activity in the royal cause, pawned her pearl necklace for £1500 to raise money for Lord Holland's troops, established communications with Prince Charles during his blockade of the Thames, and made herself the intermediary between the scattered bands of royalists and the queen. In consequence her arrest was ordered on the 21st of March 1649, and she was imprisoned in the Tower, whence she maintained a correspondence in cipher with the king through her brother, Lord Percy, till Charles went to Scotland. According to a royalist newsletter, while in the Tower she was threatened with the rack to extort information. She was released on bail on the 25th of September 1650, but appears never to have regained her former influence in the royalist counsels, and died soon after the Restoration, on the 5th of November 1660.

The first earl was succeeded by JAMES, his only surviving son by his first wife, at whose death in 1660 without issue, the peerage became extinct in the Hay family.

CHARLES HOWARD, 1st earl of Carlisle in the Howard line (1629-1685), was the son and heir of Sir William Howard, of Naworth in Cumberland, by Mary, daughter of William, Lord Eure, and great-grandson of Lord William Howard, "Belted Will" (1563-1640), and was born in 1629. In 1645 he became a Protestant and supported the government of the commonwealth, being appointed high sheriff of Cumberland in 1650. He bought Carlisle Castle and became governor of the town. He distinguished himself at the battle of Worcester on Cromwell's side, was made a member of the council of state in 1653, chosen captain of the protector's body-guard and selected to carry out various public duties. In 1655 he was given a regiment, was appointed a commissioner to try the northern rebels, and a deputy major-general of Cumberland, Westmorland and Northumberland. In the parliament of

1653 he sat for Westmorland, in those of 1654 and 1656 for Cumberland. In 1657 he was included in Cromwell's House of Lords and voted for the protector's assumption of the royal title the same year. In 1659 he urged Richard Cromwell to defend his government by force against the army leaders, but his advice being refused he used his influence in favour of a restoration of the monarchy, and after Richard's fall he was imprisoned. In April 1660 he sat again in parliament for Cumberland, and at the Restoration was made *custos rotulorum* of Essex and lord-lieutenant of Cumberland and Westmorland. On the 20th of April 1661 he was created Baron Dacre of Gillesland, Viscount Howard of Morpeth, and earl of Carlisle; the same year he was made vice-admiral of Northumberland, Cumberland and Durham, and in 1662 joint commissioner for the office of earl marshal. In 1663 he was appointed ambassador to Russia, Sweden and Denmark, and in 1668 he carried the Garter to Charles XI. of Sweden. In 1667 he was made lieutenant-general of the forces and joint commander-in-chief of the four northernmost counties. In 1672 he became lord-lieutenant of Durham, and in 1673 deputy earl marshal. In 1678 he was appointed governor of Jamaica, and reappointed governor of Carlisle. He died on the 24th of February 1685, and was buried in York Minster. He married Anne (d. 1696), daughter of Edward, 1st Lord Howard of Escrick; his eldest son EDWARD (*c.* 1646-1692) succeeded him as 2nd earl of Carlisle, the title descending to his son CHARLES (1674-1738) and grandson HENRY (1694-1758).

FREDERICK HOWARD, 5th earl (1748-1825), son of the 4th earl, was born in 1748. During his youth he was chiefly known as a man of pleasure and fashion; and after he had reached thirty years of age, his appointment on a commission sent out by Lord North to attempt a reconciliation with the American colonies was received with sneers by the opposition. The failure of the embassy was not due to any incapacity on the part of the earl, but to the unpopularity of the government from which it received its authority. He was, indeed, considered to have displayed so much ability that he was entrusted with the vice-royalty of Ireland in 1780. The time was one of the greatest difficulty; for while the calm of the country was disturbed by the American rebellion, it was drained of regular troops, and large bands of volunteers not under the control of the government had been formed. Nevertheless, the two years of Carlisle's rule passed in quietness and prosperity, and the institution of a national bank and other measures which he effected left permanently beneficial results upon the commerce of the island. In 1789, in the discussions as to the regency, Carlisle took a prominent part on the side of the prince of Wales. In 1791 he opposed Pitt's policy of resistance to the dismemberment of Turkey by Russia; but on the outbreak of the French Revolution he left the opposition and vigorously maintained the cause of war. In 1815 he opposed the enactment of the Corn Laws; but from this time till his death, in 1825, he took no important part in public life. Carlisle was the author of some political tracts, a number of poems, and two tragedies, *The Father's Revenge* and *The Stepmother*, which received high praise from his contemporaries. His mother was a daughter of the 4th Lord Byron, and in 1798 he was appointed guardian to Lord Byron, the poet, who lampooned him in *English Bards and Scotch Reviewers.*

GEORGE HOWARD, 6th earl (1773-1848), eldest son of the 5th earl, entered parliament as Lord Morpeth in 1795 as a Whig. He was appointed to the Indian board in 1806, when the "Ministry of all the Talents" took office, but resigned in 1807, though he remained prominent in the House of Commons. After his elevation to the House of Lords (1825), he held various cabinet offices under Canning and Grey. He made some minor contributions to literature and left the reputation of an amiable scholar.

GEORGE WILLIAM FREDERICK HOWARD, 7th earl (1802-1864), was born in London on the 18th of April 1802. He was the eldest son of the 6th earl by his wife Lady Georgiana Cavendish, eldest daughter of the duke of Devonshire. He was educated at Eton and Christ Church, Oxford, where (as Lord Morpeth) he earned a reputation as a scholar and writer of graceful verse, obtaining in 1821 both the chancellor's and the Newdigate prizes for a Latin and an English poem. In 1826 he accompanied his uncle, the duke of Devonshire, to Russia, to attend the coronation of the tsar Nicholas, and became a great favourite in society at St Petersburg. At the general election of the same year he was returned to parliament as member for the family borough of Morpeth. In one of his earliest speeches he undertook, 341at the risk of forfeiting the good opinion of the Liberal party, the defence of the Russian emperor against severe attacks made on him in reference to the suppression of the Polish insurrection of 1830. In the agitation for parliamentary reform he took the side of Earl Grey; and after the dissolution of parliament, which took place about that time, he was elected member for Yorkshire. This seat he held till after the passing of the Reform Bill in 1832. He was then returned for the West Riding; and in 1835 he was appointed by Lord Melbourne chief secretary for Ireland, a position at that time of great difficulty, O'Connell being then at the height of his reputation. This post he held for about six years (being included in the cabinet in 1839), winning great popularity by his amiable manners and kindly disposition. Losing his seat at the election of 1841, he visited the United States, but in 1846 he was again returned for the West Riding, and was made chief commissioner of woods and forests in Lord John Russell's cabinet. Succeeding to the peerage in 1848, he became chancellor of the duchy of Lancaster in 1850. The great event of his life, however, was his appointment by Lord Palmerston to the lord-lieutenancy of Ireland in 1855. This office he continued to hold till February 1858, and again from June 1859 till within a few months of his death. His literary tastes and culture were displayed in various popular lectures and in several published works. Among these may be mentioned a lecture on *The Life and Writings of Pope* (1851); *The Last of the Greeks*, a tragedy (1828); a *Diary in Turkish and Greek Waters* (1854), the fruit of travels in the East in 1853 and 1854; and a volume of *Poems*, published after his death. In 1866 appeared his *Viceregal Speeches*, collected and edited by J. Gaskin. He took warm interest in the reformation of juvenile criminals, and established on his own estate one of the best conducted reformatories in the country. Lord Carlisle died at Castle Howard on the 5th of December 1864. He was never married, and was succeeded in the peerage by his brother, the REV. WILLIAM GEORGE HOWARD (d. 1889), as 8th earl.

GEORGE JAMES HOWARD, 9th earl, born in 1843, was the son of Charles, fourth son of the 6th earl. He was educated at Eton and Trinity, Cambridge, and, then being only Mr Howard, married in 1864 Rosalind, daughter of the 2nd Lord Stanley of Alderley. He sat in parliament as a Liberal in 1879-1880, and again from 1881 to 1885; and succeeded his uncle in the peerage in 1889. His wife, a more active Liberal politician than himself, took a prominent part in the temperance movement and other advanced causes; and Lord Carlisle became best known as an art patron and an artist of considerable ability, whose landscape painting had considerable affinity to the work of Giovanni Costa. His position as a connoisseur was recognized by his being made one of the trustees of the National Gallery. His son, Viscount Morpeth (b. 1867), had a distinguished career at Oxford, and after various defeats in other constituencies was returned to parliament for South Birmingham as a Unionist supporter of Mr Chamberlain in 1904.

CARLISLE, a city, municipal and parliamentary borough, and the county town of Cumberland, England, 299 m. N.N.W. of London, and 8 m. S. of the Scottish border. Pop. (1901) 45,480. It lies on the south bank of the river Eden, a little below the point where it debouches upon the Solway Plain, 8 m. above its mouth in the Solway Firth, at the junction of two tributaries from the south, the Caldew and the Petteril. The city grew up originally on and about the two slight eminences of the peninsula enclosed between these three streams. To the north of the Eden lies the suburb of Stanwix, connected with the city by a handsome bridge (1812-1815). The rivers are not navigable, and a canal opened in 1823, connecting the city with Port Carlisle on the Solway Firth, was unsuccessful, and was converted into a railway. Silloth, on the Irish Sea, is the nearest port of importance (21 m.). Carlisle, however, is one of the principal railway centres in Great Britain. The London & North-Western and the Midland railways of England, and the Caledonian, North British and Glasgow & South-Western of Scotland, here make a junction for through traffic between England and Scotland; and the city is further served by the North Eastern (from Newcastle) and the Maryport & Carlisle railways.

Carlisle is the seat of a bishop. Bede, in his life of St Cuthbert, alludes to a monastery here, and the saint was also believed to have founded a convent and school. But all was swept away by the Northmen, and though William Rufus, who rehabilitated the town, doubtless made provision for an ecclesiastical foundation, it was left for Henry I., in 1133, to create a bishopric out of the house of Augustinian canons, founded in 1102. This was the sole episcopal chapter of regular canons of St Augustine in England. It was dissolved in 1540. Between 1156 and 1204 the bishop's throne was unoccupied, but thereafter there was a continuous succession. The diocese covers the whole of Westmorland, and practically of Cumberland, with Furness and the adjacent district in the north of Lancashire. The cathedral as it stands is a fine cruciform building with a central tower, but it is incomplete. Of the Norman nave, built by Aethelwold, the first prior and bishop, only two bays are standing, the remainder having been destroyed by the Parliamentarians in 1646. The south transept, and the lower part of the tower piers, are also of this period. Remarkable distortion is seen in the nave arches, owing to the sinking of the foundations. The thinness of the aisle walls, and the rude masonry of the foundations of the original apse which have been discovered, point to native, not Norman, workmanship. The choir is ornate and beautiful, and the huge Decorated east window, with its wonderful elaborate tracery, is perhaps the finest of its kind extant. The reconstruction of the Norman choir was begun in the middle of the 13th century, but the work was almost wholly destroyed by fire in 1292. The north transept and the tower also suffered. Building began again c. 1352, and the present tower, erected with some difficulty on the weak foundations of the Norman period, dates from 1400-1419. The conventual buildings are scanty, including little more than a Perpendicular gateway and refectory. A stone inscribed with runes, and a well, are among the objects of interest within the cathedral. Among the numerous memorials is one to Archdeacon Paley; and a stained-glass window commemorates the five children of Archibald Campbell Tait, dean of the cathedral, and afterwards archbishop of Canterbury. Of the two eminences within the three rivers, the cathedral occupies one, the castle the other. It was moated and very strong; but has been so far altered that only the keep is of special interest. A tower in which Mary, queen of Scots, was imprisoned was taken down in 1835. The castle serves as barracks. Fragments of the old city walls are seen on the western side over against the river Caldew. At Carlisle are the county gaol and the Cumberland infirmary, in connexion with which there is a seaside convalescent institution at Silloth. Other notable public buildings are the city hall, the court-houses, museum and art gallery. The grammar school, of very early foundation, received endowment from Henry VIII. Industries include the manufacture of cotton and woollen goods, and there are iron foundries, breweries, tanneries and large railway works. There is also a considerable agricultural trade. The parliamentary borough returns one member. The municipal borough is under a mayor, 10 aldermen and 30 councillors. Area, 2025 acres.

This was the Romano-British *Luguvallium*, probably rather a town than a fort, being one of the few towns as distinct from forts in the north of Britain. It lay a mile south of Hadrian's wall. There are no traces above ground *in situ*; but many inscriptions, potsherds, coins and other such-like relics have been discovered.

Carlisle (*Caer Luel, Karliol*) is first mentioned in 685, when under the name of Luel it was bestowed by Ecgfrith on St Cuthbert to form part of his see of Lindisfarne. It was then a thriving and populous city, and when St Cuthbert visited it in 686 he was shown with pride the ancient walls and a Roman fountain of marvellous construction. Nennius, writing in the 9th century, mentions it in a list of British cities under the name of Caer Luadiit, Caer Ligualid or Caer Lualid, but about this time it was either wholly or in part destroyed by the Danes, and vanishes completely from history until in 1092 it was re-established as the political centre of the district by William Rufus, 342who built the castle and sent husbandmen to dwell there and till the land. During the centuries of border-strife which followed, the history of Carlisle centres round that of the castle, which formed the chief bulwark against the Scots on the western border, and played an important part in the history of the country down to the rebellion of the young Pretender in 1745. In 1292 a great fire destroyed nearly all the buildings and muniments of the city, so that no original charter is extant before that date. A charter from Edward I., dated 1293, however, exemplifies two earlier grants. The first, from Henry II., confirmed the liberties and customs which the city had theretofore enjoyed, granting in addition a free gild merchant, with other privileges. This grant is exemplified in the second charter, from Henry III., dated 1251. By a writ dated 5 Henry III. the citizens were allowed to hold the city direct from the king, paying a fee-farm rent of £60, instead of the former rent of £50, paid by the medium of the sheriff. A charter from Edward II., dated 1316, grants to the citizens the city, the king's mills in the city, and the fishery in the Eden, at a fee-farm rent of £80 a year. A charter from Edward III. in 1352 enumerates the privileges and liberties hitherto enjoyed by the citizens, including a market twice a week, on Wednesday and Saturday; a fair for sixteen days at the feast of the Assumption of the Virgin (15th of August); free election of a mayor, bailiffs and two coroners; and the right to hold their markets in the place called "Battailholm." It also mentions that the city was greatly impoverished by reason of the devastations of the Scots and by pestilence. Confirmations of former privileges were issued by Richard II., Henry IV. and Henry VI. A charter from Edward IV. in 1461, after reciting the damage sustained by the city through fire, reduced the fee-farm rent from £80 to £40, and granted to the citizens the fishery called the sheriff's net, free of rent. Further confirmations were granted by later sovereigns. Although the city had been under the jurisdiction of a mayor and bailiffs at least as early as 1290, the first charter of incorporation was granted by Elizabeth in 1566; it established a corporation under the style of "a mayor, eleven worshipful persons, and twenty-four able persons." A charter of James I. confirmed former liberties, and in 1638 Charles I. granted a charter under which the town continued to be governed until 1835. It declared Carlisle a city by itself, and established a corporation consisting of a mayor, 11 aldermen, 24 capital citizens, 2 bailiffs, 2 coroners and a recorder; the mayor, the recorder and 2 senior aldermen to be justices of the peace, and the mayor to be clerk of the market; other officers were a common clerk, a sword-bearer and three serjeants-at-mace. Two charters from Charles II. in 1664 and 1684 were never accepted. The latter granted a three days' fair or market on the first Wednesday in June. Much valuable information relating to the early history and customs of Carlisle is furnished both by the Dormont Book, which contains an elaborate set of bye-laws dated 1561, and by the records of the eight craft gilds—weavers, smiths, tailors, tanners, shoemakers, skinners, butchers and merchants. The defensive and offensive warfare in which the citizens were constantly engaged until the union of the crowns of England and Scotland left little time for the development of commercial pursuits, and Fuller, writing in the 17th century, says that the sole manufacture, that of fustian, though established shortly after the Restoration, had met with scant encouragement. In 1750 the manufacture of coarse linen cloth was established, and was followed in a few years by the introduction of calico stamperies. The commercial prosperity of Carlisle, however, began with the railway development of the 19th century. In 1283 the citizens of Carlisle were summoned to send two representatives to parliament, but no return is recorded. From 1295 Carlisle continued to return two members until the Redistribution Act of 1885. At the time of the Scottish wars Edward I. held two parliaments at Carlisle—in 1300 and in 1307.

See *Victoria County History, Cumberland*; R.S. Ferguson, *Some Municipal Records of the City of Carlisle* (Cumberl. and Westm. Antiq. and Archaeol. Soc., Carlisle and London, 1887), and *Royal Charters of Carlisle* (ditto, Carlisle, &c., 1894); Mandell Creighton, *Carlisle* in "Historic Towns" series (London, 1889).

CARLISLE, a borough and the county-seat of Cumberland county, Pennsylvania, U.S.A., 18 m. W. by S. of Harrisburg and 118 m. W. by N. of Philadelphia. Pop. (1890) 7620; (1900) 9626 (1148 being negroes); (1910) 10,303. It is served by the Cumberland Valley (controlled by the Pennsylvania railway) and the Gettysburg & Harrisburg railways. The borough is pleasantly situated in the central part of the fertile Cumberland Valley, which is here 12 m. wide. Mount Holly Springs and Boiling Springs are near, and are important summer attractions. In Carlisle is Dickinson College, founded in 1783 by Presbyterians, and named in honour of John Dickinson (*q.v.*), a benefactor of the college; it was reorganized in 1833 as a Methodist Episcopal College, and is now divided into the college, the school of law (founded in 1834) and Conway Hall, the preparatory department. President James Buchanan and Chief Justice R.B. Taney were graduates. Here are also Metzger College for young ladies, and a well-known United States Indian industrial school, established in 1879 through the efforts of Lieutenant (later Brigadier-General) Richard Henry Pratt (b. 1840), its superintendent until 1904; the school pays especial attention to industrial and agricultural training, and its athletic organizations are famous. A great effort is made to preserve and develop Indian arts and crafts; the instruction given by Mrs Angel Decora Dietz, a Winnebago, in colour work and design, decorating leather, making beadwork and weaving rugs, is particularly noteworthy. On the initiative of the pupils the Leupp Indian Art School was built on the campus in 1906-1907, all materials being purchased with the funds of the athletic association and all work being done by the students. The building is named in honour of Francis Ellington Leupp (b. 1849), U.S. commissioner of Indian affairs in 1905. Carlisle is prominent for the manufacture of boots and shoes, and has machine shops and manufactories of carriages, ribbons, railway frogs and switches, carpets and paper boxes. In 1905 the value of all the factory products was $1,985,743, of which $1,078,401 was the value of boots and shoes. The place was laid out as a town in 1751, was named from Carlisle, Cumberland, England, and was incorporated as a borough in 1872. In 1753 Benjamin Franklin, with two other commissioners, negotiated a treaty with the Ohio Indians here. During the War of Independence the Americans kept here for secure confinement a number of British prisoners, among them Major John André, and in 1794 Carlisle was the headquarters of George Washington during the Whisky Rebellion. On the night of the 1st of July 1863 Carlisle was bombarded by Confederate troops.

CARLOFORTE, a town of Sardinia, in the province of Cagliari, the capital of the small island (6 by 5 m.) of San Pietro (anc. *Accipitrum* or Ἱερακοννῆσος) off the west coast of Sardinia. Pop. (1901) 7693. It lies on the east coast of the island, 6 m. west by sea from Portoscuso, which is 47 m. west by rail from Cagliari. It was founded in 1737 by Charles Emmanuel III. of Savoy, who planted a colony of Genoese, whose dialect and costume still prevail. In 1798 it was attacked by the Tunisians and 933 inhabitants taken away as slaves. They were ransomed after five years and the place fortified. It is now a centre of the tunny fishery, and there are manganese mines also. The coral banks, which were once important, are now exhausted. Three m. to the south-east is the island of S. Antioco.

CARLOMAN (828-880), king of Bavaria and Italy, was the eldest son of Louis the German, king of the East Franks. In 856 he undertook the defence of the eastern frontier of Bavaria against the Bohemians and Moravians, and won considerable fame in various campaigns. He married a daughter of Ernest, count of the Bohemian mark, and in conjunction with his father-in-law resisted the authority of his father in 861. For some years he alternated between rebellion and submission to his father, but in 865 an arrangement was made by which he became possessed of Bavaria and Carinthia as his expectant share of the kingdom of Louis. During the troubles between Louis and his two younger sons Carloman remained faithful to his father, and carried on the war with the Moravians so successfully that in 870 their territory was completely under the power of the 343Franks; and when peace was made at Forchheim in 874, they recognized the Frankish supremacy. In 875 the emperor Louis II. died, having named his cousin Carloman as his successor in Italy. Carloman crossed the Alps to claim his inheritance, but was cajoled into returning by the king of the West Franks, Charles the Bald. In 876, on his father's death, Carloman became actually king of Bavaria, and after a short campaign against the Moravians he went again to Italy in 877 and was crowned king of the Lombards at Pavia; but his negotiations with Pope John VIII. for the imperial crown were fruitless, and personal illness added to the outbreak of an epidemic in his army compelled him to return to Bavaria. Stricken with paralysis, Carloman was unable to prevent his brother Louis from seizing Bavaria; so making a virtue of necessity, he bequeathed the whole of his lands to Louis. He died on the 22nd of September 880 at Öttingen, where he was buried, leaving an illegitimate son, afterwards the emperor Arnulf.

See "Annales Fuldenses," "Annales Bertiniani," Reginovon Prum, "Chronicon," all in the *Monumenta Germaniae historica. Scriptores,* Bandi. (Hanover and Berlin, 1826-1892); E. Mühlbacher, *Die Regesten des Kaiserreichs unter den Karolingern* (Innsbruck, 1881); and E. Dümmler,*Geschichte des ostfrankischen Reiches* (Leipzig, 1887-1888).

CARLOMAN, the name of three Frankish princes.

CARLOMAN (d. 754), mayor of the palace under the Merovingian kings, was a son of Charles Martel, and, together with his brother, Pippin the Short, became mayor on his father's death in 741, administering the eastern part of the Frankish kingdom. He was successful in extending the power of the Franks in various wars with his troublesome neighbours, and was not less zealous in seeking to strengthen and reform the church in the lands under his rule. In 747 Carloman laid down his office and retired to a monastery which he founded on Monte Soracte, but troubled by the number of his visitors, he subsequently entered a monastery on Monte Casino. He died at Vienne on the 17th of August 754.

CARLOMAN (751-771), king of the Franks, was a son of King Pippin the Short, and consequently a brother of Charlemagne. The brothers became joint kings of the Franks on Pippin's death in 768, and some trouble which broke out between them over the conduct of the war in Aquitaine was followed by Carloman's death at Samoussy on the 4th of December 771. He married Gerberga, a daughter of Desiderius, king of the Lombards, who, together with her children, vanished from history soon after her husband's death.

CARLOMAN (d. 884), king of France, was the eldest son of King Louis II., the Stammerer, and became king, together with his brother Louis III., on his father's death in 879. Although some doubts were cast upon their legitimacy, the brothers obtained recognition and in 880 made a division of the kingdom, Carloman receiving Burgundy and the southern part of France. In 882 he became sole king owing to his brother's death, but the kingdom was in a very deplorable condition, and his power was very circumscribed. Carloman met his death while hunting on the 12th of December 884.

See E. Lavisse, *Histoire de France*, tome ii. (Paris, 1903).

CARLOS I. (1863-1908), king of Portugal, the third sovereign of Portugal of the line of Braganza-Coburg, son of King Louis I. and Maria Pia, daughter of King Victor Emmanuel of Italy, was born on the 28th of September 1863. When about twenty years of age he spent a considerable time in travelling, visiting England in 1883. On the 22nd of May 1886 he married Marie Amélie, daughter of Philippe, duc d'Orléans, comte de Paris, and on the death of his father (19th of October 1889) he succeeded to the throne of Portugal. In that year the British government found it necessary to make formal remonstrances against Portuguese encroachments in South Africa, and relations between the two countries were greatly strained for some time. The king's attitude during this critical period was one of conciliation, and his temperate, though firm, speech on opening the Cortes in January 1890 did much to strengthen the party of peace. In 1900-1901 also his friendly attitude towards Great Britain was shown by cordial toasts at a banquet to the officers of the British fleet at Lisbon. King Carlos distinguished himself as a patron of science and literature, and was himself an artist of some repute. In March 1894 he took a very active part in the celebration of the 500th anniversary of the birth of Prince Henry the Navigator, and a year later he decorated the Portuguese poet, João de Deus, with much honour at Lisbon. He took a great personal interest in deep-sea soundings and marine exploration, and published an account of some of his own investigations, the results themselves being shown at an oceanographic exhibition opened by him on the 12th of April 1897. In May 1907 the king suspended the constitution of Portugal and temporarily appointed Senhor Franco as dictator with a view to carrying out certain necessary reforms. Some discontent was aroused by this proceeding; this was increased by Franco's drastic measures, and on the 1st of February 1908 King Carlos and his elder son, Louis, duke of Braganza (1887-1908), were assassinated whilst driving through the streets of Lisbon. The king was succeeded by his only surviving son, Manuel, duke of Beja (b. 1889), who took the title of Manuel II.

See *S.M. El Rei D. Carlos I. e sua obra artistica, e scientifica* (Lisbon, 1908).

CARLOS, DON (1545-1568), prince of Asturias, was the son of Philip II. king of Spain, by his first wife Maria, daughter of John III., king of Portugal, and was born at Valladolid on the 8th of July 1545. His mother died a few days after his birth, and the prince, who was very delicate, grew up proud, wilful and indolent, and soon began to show signs of insanity. In 1559 he was betrothed to Elizabeth, daughter of Henry II., king of France, a lady who a few months later became the third wife of his father; in 1560 he was recognized as the heir to the throne of Castile, and three years later to that of Aragon. Other brides were then suggested for the prince; Mary, queen of Scots, Margaret, another daughter of Henry II., and Anne, a daughter of the emperor Maximilian II.; but meanwhile his mental derangement had become much more acute, and his condition could no longer be kept secret. In 1562 he met with an accident which was followed by a serious illness, and after his recovery he showed more obvious signs of insanity, while his conduct both in public and in private was extremely vicious and disorderly. He took a marked dislike to the duke of Alva, possibly because he wished to proceed to the Netherlands instead of the duke, and he exhibited a morbid antipathy towards his father, whose murder he even contemplated. At length in January 1568, when he had made preparations for flight from Spain, he was placed in confinement by order of Philip, and on the 24th of July of the same year he died. This event is still enveloped in some mystery. Philip has been accused of murdering his son, and from what is known of the king's character this supposition is by no means improbable. It is known that the king appointed commissioners to try the prince, and he may have been put to death for treason in accordance with their verdict. It has also been suggested that his crime was heresy, and that his death was due to poison, and other solutions of the mystery have been put forward. On the other hand, it should be remembered that the health of Carlos was very poor, and that his outrageous behaviour in captivity would have undermined a much stronger constitution than his own. Consequently there is nothing strange or surprising in his death from natural causes, and while no decisive verdict upon this question can be given, Philip may perhaps be granted the benefit of the doubt. By some writers the sad fate and early death of Carlos have been connected with the story of his unlawful attachment to his promised bride, Elizabeth, who soon became his stepmother, and whose death followed so quickly upon his own. There is circumstantial evidence for this tale. The loss of an affianced bride, followed by hatred between supplanted and supplanter, who were father and son, then the increasing infirmity of the slighted prince, and finally the almost simultaneous deaths of the pair. But mature historical research dismisses this story as a fable. It has, however, served as the subject for romance. Schiller and Alfieri, J.G. de Campristron in *Andronic*, and Lord John Russell have made it the subject of dramas, and other dramas based upon the life of Don Carlos have been written by Thomas Otway, M.A. Chénier, J.P. de Montalvan, and D.N. de Enciso.

344

See C.V. de Saint Réal, *Don Carlos, nouvelle historique* (Paris, 1672). This gives the story of the attachment of Carlos and Elizabeth, which has been refuted by L. von Ranke, *Zur Geschichte des don Carlos* (Vienna, 1829); and J.A. Llorente, *Histoire critique de l'Inquisition* (French translation, Paris, 1817). See also L.P. Gachard, *Don Carlos et Philippe II*(Brussels, 1863); C. de Moüy, *Don Carlos et Philippe II* (Paris, 1863); M. Büdinger, *Don Carlos, Haft und Tod* (Vienna, 1891); L.A. Warnkönig, *Don Carlos, Leben, Verhaftung und Tod* (Stuttgart, 1864); W. Maurenbrecher,*Don Carlos* (Berlin, 1876); and W.H. Prescott, *History of the Reign of Philip II.* vol. ii. (London, 1855, 1859).

CARLOS, DON (1788-1855), the first of the Carlist claimants of the throne of Spain, was the second surviving son of King Charles IV. and his wife, Louisa Maria of Parma. He was born on the 29th of March 1788, and was christened Carlos Maria Isidro. From 1808 till 1814 he was a prisoner in France at Valençay with his brothers, who had been imprisoned by Napoleon when he seized the whole royal family of Spain at Bayonne. After his return he lived quietly as a prince at Madrid. In September 1816 he married Maria Francesca de Asis, daughter of King John VI. of Portugal, and sister of the second wife of his elder brother King Ferdinand VII. Though he took no part in the government of Spain, except to hold a few formal offices, Don Carlos was known for the rigid orthodoxy of his religious opinions, the piety of his life, and his firm belief in the divine right of kings to govern despotically. During the revolutionary troubles of 1820-1823 he was threatened by the extreme radicals, but no attack was made on him. When the revolutionary agitation was put down by French intervention in 1823, Don Carlos continued to behave as the affectionate brother and loyal subject of Ferdinand VII. The family affection between them was undoubtedly sincere, and was one of the very few amiable traits in the character of the elder brother. Towards the close of Ferdinand's reign Don Carlos was forced against his own will into the position of a party leader, or rather into the position of a prince whom a great party was forced to take as its leader. The extreme clericals among the Spaniards, who were the partisans of despotism because they rightly considered it as most favourable to the church, began to be discontented with King Ferdinand, who seemed wanting in energy. When the king showed his intention to alter the law of succession in order to secure the crown for his daughter Isabella, the clericals (in the Spanish phrase, "apostólicos") banded to protect the rights of Don Carlos. There can be no question that if he had been disposed to place himself at the head of an insurrection he would have been followed, and might have put Ferdinand under restraint. But Don Carlos held his principles honestly. He considered rebellion as a sin in a prince as much as in other men, and as wicked when made by "apostólicos" as by liberals. He would do no more than assert his rights, and those of his children, in words. His wife and her sister, the princess of Beira, widow of his first cousin the infante Pedro, were less scrupulous. They were actively engaged in intrigues with the "apostólicos." In March 1833 the princess of Beira was informed by the king that her brother Don Miguel, then regent in Portugal, desired her presence, and that she must pay him a visit. On the 16th of March Don Carlos left for Portugal with his wife, in company with the princess, after an interview with his brother the king which is said to have been friendly. In the following month he was called upon by the king to swear allegiance to the infanta Isabella, afterwards queen. Don Carlos refused, in respectful terms but with great firmness, to renounce his rights and those of his sons, in a public letter dated the 29th of April. The death of his brother on the 29th of September 1833 gave him an opportunity to vindicate his claims without offence to his principles, for in his own opinion and that of his partisans he was now king. But he was entangled in the civil war of Portugal and was shut off from Spain. He did, and perhaps could do, nothing to direct the Spaniards who rose on his behalf, and had proclaimed him king as Charles V. When the Miguelite party was beaten in Portugal, Don Carlos escaped to England on the 1st of June 1834 in H.M.S. "Donegal." His stay in England was short. On the 2nd of July he passed over to France, where he was actively aided by the legitimist party, and on the 11th he joined his partisans at Elizondo in the valley of Bastan, in the western Pyrenees. On the 27th of October of this year he was deprived of his rights as infante by a royal decree, confirmed by the Cortes on the 15th of January 1837. Don Carlos remained in Spain till the defeat of his party, and then escaped to France on the 14th of September 1839. During these years he accompanied his armies, without displaying any of the qualities of a general or even much personal courage. But he endured a good deal of hardship, and was often compelled to take to hiding in the hills. On these occasions he was often carried over difficult places on the back of a stout guide commonly known as the royal jackass (*burro real*). The semblance of a court which he maintained was torn by incessant personal intrigues, and by conflicts between his generals and the ecclesiastics who exercised unbounded influence over his mind. The defeat of his cause, which had many chances of success, was unquestionably due to a very large extent to his want of capacity, his apathy, and his increasing absorption in practices of puerile piety. His first wife having died in England, Don Carlos married her elder sister, the princess of Beira, in Biscay in October 1837. After his flight from Spain, Don Carlos led a life of increasing insignificance. He abdicated in May 1845, took a title of count of Molina, and died at Trieste on the 10th of March 1855.

By his first marriage, Don Carlos had three sons, Charles (1818-1861), John (1822-1887), and Ferdinand (1824-1861). Charles succeeded to the claims of his father, and was known to his partisans as Don Carlos VI., but was more commonly known as the count of Montemolin. In 1846, when the marriage of queen Isabella was being negotiated, the Austrian government endeavoured to arrange an alliance between her and the count of Montemolin. But as he insisted on the complete recognition of his rights, the Spanish government refused to hear of him as a candidate. The Carlists took up arms on his behalf between 1846 and 1848, but the count, who had been expelled from France by the police, did not join them in the field. In April 1860 he and his brother Ferdinand landed at San Carlos de la Rápita, at the mouth of the Ebro, in company with a feather-headed officer named Ortega, who held a command in the Balearic islands. They hoped to profit by the fact that the bulk of the Spanish army was absent in a war with Morocco. But no Carlist rising took place. The men who had been brought from the islands by Ortega deserted him. Montemolin and his brother, together with their devoted partisan General Elio, who had accompanied them from exile, lurked in hiding for a fortnight and were then captured. Ortega was shot, but the princes saved their lives, and that of Elio, by making an abject surrender of their claims. When he had been allowed to escape and had reached Cologne, the count of Montemolin publicly retracted his renunciation on the 15th of June, on the ignominious ground that it had been extorted by fear. Montemolin and his brother Ferdinand died within a fortnight of one another in January 1861 without issue.

The third brother, John, who had advanced his own claims before his brother's retraction, now came forward as the representative of the legitimist and Carlist cause. As he had shown a disposition to accept liberalism, and to make concessions to the spirit of the age, he was unpopular with the party. On the 3rd of October 1868 he made a formal renunciation in favour of his son Charles (Don Carlos VII.), who is separately noticed below.

See Hermann Baumgarten, *Geschichte Spaniens* (Leipzig, 1861); H. Butler Clarke, *Modern Spain* (Cambridge, 1906), which contains a useful bibliography.

CARLOS, DON (CHARLES MARIA DE LOS DOLORES JUAN ISIDORE JOSEPH FRANCIS QUIRIN ANTONY MICHAEL GABRIEL RAPHAEL) (1848-1909), prince of Bourbon, claimant, as Don Carlos VII., to the throne of Spain, was born at Laibach on the 30th of March 1848, being the eldest surviving son of Don Juan (John) of Bourbon and of the archduchess Maria Beatrix, daughter of Francis IV., duke of Modena. Don Carlos was the grandson of the first pretender, noticed above. He married in February 1867, at Frohsdorf, Princess Marguerite, daughter of the duke of Parma and niece of the comte de Chambord, who was born on the 1st ³⁴⁵of January 1847, and who bore him a son, Don Jaime, in 1870, and three daughters. Don Carlos boldly asserted his pretensions to the throne of Spain two years after the revolution of 1868 had driven Queen Isabella II. and the other branch of the Bourbons into exile. His manifesto, addressed to his brother Alphonso, namesake of his rival, Alphonso XII., found an echo in the fanatical priesthood and peasantry of many provinces of the Peninsula, but little support among the more enlightened middle classes, especially in the towns. The first rising was started in Catalonia by the brother of the pretender, who himself entered Spain by way of Vera, in the Basque provinces, on the 21st of May 1872. The troops of King Amadeus under General Moriones, a progressist officer, who was one of Spain's ablest and most popular commanders, surprised and very nearly captured the pretender at Oroquista, sending him a fugitive to France in headlong flight with a few followers. For more than a year he loitered about in the French Pyrenees, the guest of old noble houses who showed him much sympathy, while the French authorities winked at the fact that he was fomenting civil war in Spain, where his guerilla bands, many of them led by priests, committed atrocities, burning, pillaging, shooting prisoners of war, and not unfrequently ill-using even foreign residents and destroying their property. When the Federal Republic was proclaimed on the abdication of King Amadeus, the Carlists had overrun Spain to such an extent that they held all the interior of Navarre, the three Basque provinces, and a great part of Catalonia, Lower Aragon, and Valencia, and had made raids into the provinces of Old Castile and Estremadura. Don Carlos re-entered Spain on the 15th of July 1873, just before the Carlists took Estella, in Navarre, which became, with Tolosa and Durango in the Basque provinces, his favourite residence. He displayed very lax morals and an apathy which displeased his staff and partisans. Don Carlos was present at some fights around Estella, and was in the neighbourhood of Bilbao during its famous siege of three months in 1874 until its relief by Marshals Serrano and Concha on the 2nd of May. He was also present at the battle near Estella on the 27th of June 1874, in which Marshal Concha was killed and the liberals were repulsed with loss. Twice he lost golden opportunities of making a rush for the capital—in 1873, during the Federal Republic, and after Concha's death. From the moment that his cousin Alphonso XII. was proclaimed king at Sagunto, at Valencia, in Madrid, and at Logroño, by General Campos, Daban, Jovellar, Primo de Rivera, and Laserna, the star of the pretender was on the wane. Only once, a few weeks after the Alphonsist restoration, the army of Don Carlos checked the Liberal forces in Navarre, and surprised and made prisoners half a brigade, with guns and colours, at Lacar, almost under the eyes of the new king and his headquarters. This was the last Carlist success. The tide of war set in favour of Alphonso XII., whose armies swept the Carlist bands out of central Spain and Catalonia in 1875, while Marshal Quesada, in the upper Ebro valley, Navarre, and Ulava, prepared by a series of successful operations the final advance of 180,000 men, headed by Quesada and the king, which defeated the Carlists at Estella, Peña Plata, and Elgueta, thus forcing Don Carlos with a few thousand faithful Carlists to retreat and surrender to the French frontier authorities in March 1876.

The pretender went to Pau, and there, singularly enough, issued his proclamations bidding temporary adieu to the nation and to his volunteers from the same chateau where Queen Isabella, also a refugee, had issued hers in 1868. From that date Don Carlos became an exile and a wanderer, travelling much in the Old and New World, and raising some scandal by his mode of life. He fixed his residence for a time in England, then in Paris, from which he was expelled at the request of the Madrid government, and next in Austria, before he took up his abode at Viarreggio in Italy. Like all pretenders, he never gave in, and his pretensions, haughtily reasserted, often troubled the courts and countries whose hospitality he enjoyed. His great disappointment was the coldness towards him of Pope Leo XIII., and the favour shown by that pontiff for Alphonso XII. and his godson, Alphonso XIII. Don Carlos had two splendid chances of testing the power of his party in Spain, but failed to profit by them. The first was when he was invited to unfurl his flag on the death of Alphonso XII., when the perplexities and uncertainties of Castilian politics reached a climax during the first year of a long minority under a foreign queen-regent. The second was at the close of the war with the United States and after the loss of the colonies, when the discontent was so widespread that the Carlists were able to assure their prince that many Spaniards looked upon his cause as the one untried solution of the national difficulties. Don Carlos showed his usual lack of decision; he wavered between the advice of those who told him to unfurl his standard with a view to rally all the discontented and disappointed, and of those who recommended him to wait until a great *pronunciamiento*, chiefly military, should be made in his favour—a day-dream founded upon the coquetting of General Weyler and other officers with the Carlist senators and deputies in Madrid. Afterwards the pretender continued to ask his partisans to go on organizing their forces for action some day, and to push their propaganda and preparations, which was easy enough in view of the indulgence shown them by all the governments of the regency and the open favour exhibited by many of the priesthood, especially in the rural districts, the religious orders, and the Jesuits, swarming all over the kingdom. After the death of his first wife in 1893, Don Carlos married in the following year Princess Marie Bertha of Rohan. He died on the 18th of July 1909. His son by his first wife, Don Jaime, was educated in Austrian and British military schools before he entered the Russian army, in which he became a colonel of dragoons.

CARLOW, a county of Ireland in the province of Leinster, bounded N. by the counties Kildare and Wicklow, E. by Wicklow and Wexford, S. by Wexford, and W. by Queen's county and Kilkenny. Excepting Louth, it is the smallest county in Ireland, having an area of 221,424 acres, or about 346 sq. m. The surface of the county is in general level or gently undulating, and of pleasing appearance, except the elevated tract of land known as the ridge of Old Leighlin (Gallows Hill Bog, 974 ft.), forming the beginning of the coal-measures of Leinster, and the south-eastern portion of the county bordering on Wexford, where the wild and barren granitic elevations of Knockroe (1746 ft.) and Mount Leinster (2610 ft.) present a bolder aspect. Glacial deposits, which overspread the lower grounds, sometimes afford good examples of the ridge-forms known as eskers, as in the neighbourhood of Bagenalstown. There are no lakes nor canals in the county, nor does it contain the source of any important river; but on its western side it is intersected from north to south by the Barrow, which is navigable throughout the county and affords means of communication with the port of Waterford; while on the eastern border the Slaney, which is not navigable in any part of its course through the county, passes out of Carlow into Wexford at Newtownbarry.

Carlow is largely a granite county; but here the Leinster Chain does not form a uniform moorland. The mica-schists and Silurian slates of its eastern flank are seen in the diversified and hilly country on the pass over the shoulder of Mt. Leinster, between Newtownbarry and Borris. The highland drops westward to the valley of the Barrow, Carlow and Bagenalstown lying on Carboniferous Limestone, which here abuts upon the granite. On the west of the hollow, the high edge of the Castle-comer coalfields rises, scarps of limestone, grit, and coal-measures succeeding one another on the ascent. Formerly clay-ironstone was raised from the Upper Carboniferous strata.

The soil is of great natural richness, and the country is among the most generally fertile in the island. Agriculture is the chief occupation of the inhabitants, but is not so fully developed as the capabilities of the land would suggest; in effect, the extent of land under tillage shows a distinctly retrograde movement, being rather more than half that under pasture. The pasture land is of excellent quality, and generally occupied as dairy farms, the butter made in this county maintaining a high reputation in the Dublin market. The farms are frequently large, and care is given to the breeding of cattle. Sheep and poultry, however, receive the greatest attention. The staple trade of the county is 346in corn, flour, meal, butter and provisions, which are exported in large quantities. There are no manufactures. The sandstone of the county is frequently of such a nature as to split easily into layers, known in commerce as Carlow flags.

Porcelain clay exists in the neighbourhood of Tullow; but no attempt is made to turn this product to use.

The Great Southern & Western railway from Kildare to Wexford follows the river Barrow through the county, with a branch from Bagenalstown to Kilkenny, while another branch from the north terminates at Tullow.

As regards population (41,964 in 1891; 37,748 in 1901), the county shows a decrease among the more serious of Irish counties, and correspondingly heavy emigration returns. Of the total, about 89% are Roman Catholics, and nearly the whole are rural. Carlow (pop. 6513), Bagenalstown (1882), and Tullow (1725) are the only towns. The county is divided into seven baronies, and contains forty-four civil parishes and parts of parishes. It belongs to the Protestant diocese of Dublin and the Roman Catholic diocese of Kildare and Leighlin. The assizes are held at Carlow, and quarter sessions at that town and also at Bagenalstown and Tullow. One member is returned to parliament.

Carlow, under the name of Catherlogh, is among the counties generally considered to have been created in the reign of John. Leinster was confirmed as a liberty to William Marshal, earl of Pembroke, by John, and Carlow, among other counties in this area, had the privileges of a palatinate on descending to one of the earl's heiresses. The relics of antiquity in the county comprise large cromlechs at Browne's Hill near Carlow and at Hacketstown, and a rath near Leighlin Bridge, in which were found several urns of baked earth, containing only small quantities of dust. Some relics of ecclesiastical and monastic buildings exist, and also the remains of several castles built after the English settlement. Old Leighlin, where the 12th century cathedral of St Lazerian is situated, is merely a village, although until the Union it returned two members to the Irish parliament.

CARLOW, the county town of Co. Carlow, Ireland, on the navigable river Barrow. Pop. of urban district (1901) 6513. It is 56 m. S.W. of Dublin by the Great Southern & Western railway. The castle (supposed to have been founded by Hugh de Lacy, appointed governor of Ireland in 1179, but sometimes attributed to King John), situated on an eminence overlooking the river, is still a chief feature of attraction in the general view of the town, although there is not much of the original building left. It consisted of a hollow quadrangle, with a massive round tower at each angle. The principal buildings are the Roman Catholic College of St Patrick (1793), a plain but spacious building in a picturesque park adjoining the Roman Catholic cathedral of the diocese of Kildare and Leighlin; the Protestant parish church, with a handsome steeple of modern erection; the court-house, where the assizes are held, an octagonal stone building with a handsome Ionic portico; and other county buildings. The cathedral, in the Perpendicular style, has a highly ornamented west front, and a monument to Bishop James Doyle (d. 1834). The Wellington Bridge over

193

the river Barrow connects Carlow with the suburb of Graigue. Two m. N.E. of the town is one of the finest cromlechs in Ireland, and 3 m. to the west is the notable church, of Norman and pre-Norman date, of Killeshin in Queen's county. The industries of Carlow consist of brewing and flour-milling, and a considerable trade is carried on in the sale of butter and eggs.

Carlow was of early importance. In the reign of Edward III. the king's exchequer was removed thither, and £500, a large sum at that period, applied towards surrounding the town with a strong wall. In the early part of the reign of Queen Elizabeth the castle was taken, and the town burned by the Irish chieftain, Rory Oge O'More. When summoned to surrender by Ireton, the Commonwealth general, during the war of 1641, Carlow submitted without resistance. In the insurrection of 1798 the castle was attacked by an undisciplined body of insurgents. They were speedily repulsed, and suffered severe loss, no quarter being given; and, in the confusion of their flight, many of the insurgents took refuge in houses, which the king's troops immediately set on fire. Carlow obtained a charter of incorporation as early as the 13th century, and was reincorporated, with enlarged privileges, by James I. The corporation, which was styled "The Sovereign, Free Burgesses and Commonalty of the Borough of Catherlogh," was authorized to return two members to the Irish parliament. The town returned one member to the Imperial parliament until 1885.

CARLSBAD, or KAISER-KARLSBAD (Czech, *Karlovy Vary*), a town and celebrated watering-place of Bohemia, Austria, 116 m. W.N.W. of Prague by rail. Pop. (1900) 14,640. It is situated at an altitude of 1227 ft. and lies in the beautiful narrow and winding valley of the Tepl at its junction with the Eger, being hemmed in by precipitous granite hills, covered with magnificent forests of pine. The town is spread on both banks of the river and in the valley of the Eger, its houses being built up the mountain sides in tier above tier of terraces approached by long flights of steps or steep and tortuous roads. This irregularity of site and plan, together with the varied form and high-pitched roofs of the houses, makes the place very picturesque. Among the principal buildings of Carlsbad are the Catholic parish church, built in 1732-1736 in rococo style; the gorgeous Russian church, finished in 1897; the English church; and a handsome synagogue. In the first rank of the other buildings stands the famous Mühlbrunnen Colonnade, erected between 1871 and 1878, which, with its 103 monolithic granite Corinthian columns, is a fine example of modern classical architecture; the *Kurhaus* (1865); the magnificent *Kaiserbad*, built in 1895 in the French Renaissance style, and several other bathing establishments; the Sprudel Colonnade, an imposing iron and glass structure, built in 1879, within which rises the Sprudel, the principal spring of Carlsbad; and several hospitals and hospices for poor patients. Both banks of the Tepl are provided with *quais*, planted with trees, which constitute the chief promenades of the centre of the town; and there are, besides, a municipal park and several public gardens.

The mineral springs, to which Carlsbad owes its fame, rise from beneath a very hard kind of rock, known as Sprudelschale or Sprudeldecke, beneath which it is believed that there exists a large common reservoir of the hot mineral water, known as the Sprudelkessel. Several artificial apertures in the rock have been made for the escape of the steam of this subterranean cauldron, which, owing to the incrustations deposited by the water, require to be cleared at regular intervals. Altogether there are seventeen warm springs, with a temperature varying from 164° F. to 107.7° F., and two cold ones. The oldest, best-known, and at the same time the most copious spring is the Sprudel, a hot geyser with a temperature of 164° F., which gushes up in jets of 1½ ft. thick to a height of about 3½ ft., and delivers about 405 gallons of water per minute. Other springs are the Mühlbrunnen, with a temperature of 121° F., which is after the Sprudel the most used spring; the Neubrunnen (138° F.); the Kaiser-Karl-Quelle (112° F.); the Theresienbrunnen (134° F.), &c. The warm springs belong to the class of alkaline-saline waters and have all the same chemical composition, varying only in their degree of temperature. The chemical composition of the Sprudel, taken to a thousand parts of water, is: 2.405 sulphate of soda, 1.298 bicarbonate of soda, 1.042 chloride of soda, 0.186 sulphate of potash, 0.166 bicarbonate of magnesia, 0.012 bicarbonate of lithium, and 0.966 carbonic acid gas. They contain also traces of arsenic, antimony, selenium, rubidium, tin and organic substances. The water is colourless and odourless, with a slightly acidulated and salt taste, and has a specific gravity of 1.0053 at 64.4° F. The waters are used both for drinking and bathing, and are very beneficent in cases of liver affections, biliary and renal calculi, diabetes, gout, rheumatism, and uric acid troubles. They are very powerful in their effect and must not be used except under medical direction, and during the cure, a carefully-regulated diet must be observed, coupled with a moderate amount of exercise in the open air. The number of visitors in 1901 was 51,454; in 1756 it was only 257; in 1828 it was 3713; and it attained 14,182 in 1869, and 34,396 in 1890.

Carlsbad is encircled by mountains, covered with beautiful forests of pine, which are made accessible by well-kept paths. Just above the town towers the Hirschensprung (1620 ft.), a little farther the Freundschaftshöhe (1722 ft.); the Franz-Josefs-Höhe (1663 ft.); and the Aberg (1980 ft.). On the opposite bank of the Tepl lies the Rudolfshöhe (1379 ft.); the Dreikreuzberg (1805 ft.); the König Otto's Höhe (1960 ft); and the Ewiges Leben (2086 ft.), with the Stephaniewarte, a tower, 98 ft. high, built in 1889, which commands a superb view. The town is the centre of the porcelain and stoneware industry of Bohemia, and manufactures a special liqueur (*Karlsbader Bitter*), besides various objects from the Sprudel rock and confectionery. It exported, in 1901, 2¼ millions of bottles of mineral water, and 160,000 ℔ of Sprudel salt, *i.e.* salt obtained by evaporation from the water of the Sprudel.

Many interesting places are to be found near Carlsbad. To the north is the village of Dallwitz, with a porcelain factory, a handsome castle and beautiful oaks extolled by Theodor Körner, under which he composed in 1812 his touching elegy on the downfall of Germany. To the east is the watering-place of Giesshübl-Puchstein with celebrated springs, which contain alkaline waters impregnated with carbonic acid gas. To the west in the valley of the Eger, the village of Aich, with a porcelain factory, and a little farther the much-visited Hans Heiling's Rock, a wild and romantic spot, with which a very touching legend is connected. To the south-east the ruined castle of Engelhaus, situated on a rock of phonolite, 2340 ft. high, built probably in the first part of the 13th century and destroyed by the Swedes in 1635. At the foot of the mountain lies the actual village of Engelhaus.

According to legend the springs of Carlsbad were discovered during a hunting expedition by the emperor Charles IV., who built the town, which derives its name from him, on both banks of the Tepl. But the hot springs were already known two centuries before, as is indicated by the name of the river *Tepl*(warm), under which name the river was known in the 12th century. Besides, on the same spot stood already in the 13th century a place called *Vary*, which means the Sprudel. The truth is, that the emperor Charles IV., after being cured here, built about 1358 a castle in the neighbourhood and accorded many privileges to the town. It obtained its charter as a town in 1370; the fame of the waters spread and it was created a royal free town in 1707 by the emperor Joseph I. The waters were used only for bathing purposes until 1520, when they began to be prescribed also for drinking. The first *Kurhaus* was erected in 1711 near the Mühlbrunnen, and was replaced by a larger one, built in 1761 by the empress Maria Theresa. Carlsbad was nearly completely destroyed by fire in 1604, and another great fire raged here in 1759. It also suffered much from inundations, especially in 1582 and 1890. In August 1819 a meeting of the ministers of the German courts took place here under the presidency of Prince Metternich, when many reactionary measures, embodied in the so-called "Carlsbad Decrees" (see below), were agreed upon and introduced in the various states of the German Confederation.

Among the extensive literature of the place see Mannl, *Carlsbad and its Mineral Springs* (Leipzig, 1850); Cartellieri, *Karlsbad als Kurort* (Karlsbad, 1888); Friedenthal, *Der Kurort Karlsbad Topographisch und Medizinisch*(Karlsbad, 1895).

CARLSBAD DECREES (*Karlsbader Beschlüsse*), the name usually given to a series of resolutions (*Beschlüsse*) passed by a conference of the ministers and envoys of the more important German states, held at Carlsbad from the 6th to the 31st of August 1819. The occasion of the meeting was the desire of Prince Metternich to take advantage of the consternation caused by recent revolutionary outrages (especially the murder of the dramatist Kotzebue by Karl Sand) to persuade the German governments to combine in a system for the suppression of the Liberal agitation in Germany. The pretended urgency of the case served as the excuse for only inviting to the conference those states whose ministers happened to be visiting Carlsbad at the time. The conferences were, therefore, actually attended by the representatives of Austria, Prussia, Saxony, Bavaria, Württemberg, Hanover, Baden, Nassau and Mecklenburg; at the fourth conference (August 9th) Baron von Fritsch, minister of state for Saxe-Weimar, who "happened to be present" at Carlsbad on that day, attended by special invitation. Prince Metternich presided over the conferences, and Friedrich von Gentz acted as secretary.

The business to be discussed, as announced in Metternich's opening address, was twofold: (1) Matters of urgent importance necessitating immediate action; (2) Questions affecting the fundamental constitution of the German Confederation, demanding more careful and prolonged discussion. To the first class belonged (a) the urgent necessity for a uniform system of press regulation in Germany; (b) the most urgent measures in regard to the supervision of universities and schools; (c) measures in view of the already discovered machinations of the political parties. To the second class belonged (a) the more clear definition of article XIII. of the Act of Confederation (*i.e.* state constitutions); (b) the creation of a permanent federal supreme court; (c) the creation of a federal executive organization (*Bundes-Executions Ordnung*) armed with power to make the decrees of the diet and the judgments of the high court effective; (d) the facilitation of commercial intercourse within the confederation in accordance with article XIX. of the Act of Confederation (*Beilage A. zum ersten Protokoll*, Martens, iv. p. 74).

These questions were debated in twenty-three formal conferences. On the issues raised by the first class there was practical unanimity. All were agreed that the state of Germany demanded disciplinary measures, and as the result of the deliberations it was determined to lay before the federal diet definite proposals for (1) a uniform press censorship over all periodical publications; (2) a system of "curators" to supervise the education given in universities and schools, with disciplinary enactments against professors and teachers who should use their position for purposes of political propaganda; (3) the erection of a central commission at Mainz, armed with inquisitorial powers, for the purpose of unmasking the widespread revolutionary conspiracy, the existence of which was assumed.

On the questions raised under the second class there was more fundamental difference of opinion, and by far the greater part of the time of the conference was occupied in discussing the burning question of the due interpretation of article XIII. The controversy raged round the distinction between "assemblies of estates," as laid down in the article, and "representative assemblies," such as had been already established in several German states. Gentz, in an elaborate memorandum (*Nebenbeilage zum siebenten Protokoll*, iv. p. 102), laid down that representation by estates was the only system compatible with the conservative principle, as the "outcome of a well-ordered civil society, in which the relations and rights of the several estates are due to the peculiar position of the classes and corporations on which they are based, which have been from time to time modified by law without detracting from the essentials of the sovereign power"; whereas representative assemblies are based on "the sovereignty of the people." In answer to this, Count Wintzingerode, on behalf of the king of Württemberg, placed on record (*Nebenbeilage 2 zum neunten Protokoll*, p. 147) a protest, in which he urged that to insist on the system of estates would be to stereotype caste distinctions foreign to the whole spirit of the age, would alienate public opinion from the governments, and—if enforced by the central power—would violate the sovereign independence of those states which, like Württemberg, had already established representative constitutions.

Though the majority of the ministers present favoured the Austrian interpretation of article XIII. as elaborated by Gentz, they were as little prepared as the representative of Württemberg to agree to any hasty measures for strengthening the federal government at the expense of the jealously guarded prerogatives of the minor sovereignties. The result was that the constitutional questions falling under the second class were reserved for further discussion at a general conference of German ministers to be summoned at Vienna later in the year. The 348effective Carlsbad resolutions, subsequently issued as laws by the federal diet, were therefore only those dealing with the curbing of the "revolutionary" agitation. For the results of their operation see GERMANY:*History*.

The acts, protocols and resolutions of the conference of Carlsbad are given in M. de Martens's *Nouveau Recueil général de traités*, &c., t. 4, pp. 8-166 (Göttingen, 1846). An interesting criticism of the Carlsbad Decrees is appended (p. 166), addressed by Baron Hans von Gagern, Luxemburg representative in the federal diet, to Baron von Plessen, Mecklenburg plenipotentiary at the conference of Carlsbad.

(W. A. P.)

CARLSTADT, KARLSTADT or KAROLOSTADT (1480-1541), German reformer, whose real name was Andreas Rudolf Bodenstein, was born at Carlstadt in Bohemia. He entered the university of Erfurt in the winter term of 1499-1500, and remained there till 1503, when he went to Cologne. In the winter term of 1504-1505 he transferred himself to the newly founded university of Wittenberg, where he soon established his reputation as a teacher of philosophy, and a zealous champion of the scholastic system of Thomas Aquinas, against the revised nominalism associated with the name of Occam. In 1508 he was made canon of the *Allerheiligenstift*, a collegiate church incorporated in the university; and in 1510 he became doctor of theology and archdeacon, his duties being to preach, to say mass once a week and to lecture before the university; in 1513 he was appointed ordinary professor of theology. In 1515 he went to Rome, where with a view to becoming provost of the *Allerheiligenstift* he studied law, taking his degree as *doctor juris utriusque*. His experiences in the papal city produced upon him the same effect as upon Luther, and when in 1516 he returned to Germany it was as an ardent opponent of the Thomist philosophy and as a champion of the Augustinian doctrine of the impotence of the human will and salvation through Divine grace alone. The 151 theses of Carlstadt, dated the 16th of September 1516, discovered by Theodor Kolde ("*Wittenberger Disputationsthesen*" in *Zeitschrift für Kirchengeschichte*, xi. p. 448, &c.), prove that, so far from owing his change of view to Luther's influence, he was at this time actually in advance of Luther. The two reformers were, in fact, never friends; though from the end of 1516 onwards the development of each was considerably influenced by the other.

In the spring of 1518, in reply to Eck's *Obelisci*, an attack on Luther's 95 theses, Carlstadt published a series of theses, maintaining the supremacy of the Holy Scriptures (which he regarded as verbally inspired) over ecclesiastical tradition and the authority of the fathers, and asserting the liability of general councils to error. Eck challenged him to a public disputation, in which Luther also took part, and which lasted from the 27th of June to the 15th of July 1519. In this dialectical warfare Carlstadt was no match for Eck; but the dispute only served to confirm him in his revolt from the dominant theology, and in three violent polemical treatises against Eck he proclaimed the doctrine of the exclusive operation of grace in the justification of believers.

This attitude led him in 1520, by a logical development, to an open attack on all those ecclesiastical practices in which the doctrine of justification by works had become crystallized; *e.g.* indulgences and the abuse of holy water and consecrated salt. At the same time he appeared as the first of modern biblical critics, denying the Mosaic authorship of the Pentateuch and classing the Scriptures into three categories of different value in accordance with the degrees of certainty as to their traditional origin. He still, however, maintained the doctrine of verbal inspiration, and attacked Luther for rejecting the epistle of James. In 1520 Carlstadt's name was included in the papal bull excommunicating Luther; after a momentary hesitation he decided to remain firm in his protestant attitude, published an appeal from the pope to a general council, and attacked the corruptions of the papacy itself in a treatise on "the holiness of the pope" (*Von päpstlicher Heiligkeit*, October 17th, 1520).

In May 1521 Carlstadt went to Denmark, on the invitation of King Christian II., to assist in the reform of the church; but his disposition was anything but conciliatory, and, though his influence is traceable in the royal law of the 26th of May 1521 abolishing the celibacy of the clergy, he was forced, by the hostility of nobles and clerics alike, to leave after a few weeks' stay. In June he was back in Wittenberg, busy with tracts on the Holy Sacrament (he still believed in the corporeal presence) and against the celibacy of the clergy (*de coelibatu*). Carlstadt has been unjustly accused of being responsible for the riots against the Mass fomented by the Augustinian friars and the students; as a matter of fact, he did his best to keep the peace, pending a decision by the elector of Saxony and the authorities of the university, and it was not till Christmas day that he himself publicly communicated the laity under both species. The next day he announced his engagement to a young lady of noble family, Anna von Mochau.

From this moment Carlstadt was accepted as the leader of Protestantism in Wittenberg; and, at his instance, auricular confession, the elevation of the Host and the rules for fasting were abolished. On the 19th of January he was married, in the presence of many of the university professors and city magistrates. A few days later the property of the religious corporations was confiscated by the city and, after pensions had been assigned to their former members, was handed over to charitable foundations. A pronouncement of Carlstadt's against pictures and images, supported by the town, also led to iconoclastic excesses.

The return of Luther early in March, however, ended Carlstadt's supremacy. The elector Frederick the Wise was strenuously opposed to any alteration in the traditional services, and at his command Luther restored communion in one kind and the elevation of the Host. Carlstadt himself, though still professor, was deprived of all influence in practical affairs, and devoted himself entirely to theological speculation, which led him ever nearer to the position of the mystics. He now denied the necessity for a clerical order at all, called himself "a new layman," doffed his ecclesiastical dress, and lived for a while as a peasant with his wife's relations at Segrena. In the middle of 1523, however, he went to Orlamünde, a living held by him with his canonry, and there in the parish church reformed the services according to his ideas, abolishing the Mass and even preaching against the necessity for sacraments at all. He still continued occasionally to lecture at Wittenberg and to fulminate against Luther's policy of compromise.

All this brought him into violent conflict with the elector, the university and Luther himself. His professorship and living were confiscated and, in September 1524, he went into exile with his wife and child. He was now exposed to great privations and hardships, but found opportunity for polemical writing, proclaiming for the first time his disbelief in the "Real Presence." He preached wherever he could gain a hearing, and visited Strassburg, Heidelberg, Zürich, Basel, Schweinfurth, Kitzingen and Nördlingen, before he found a more permanent resting-place at Rothenburg on the Tauber. He was here when the Peasants' War broke out, and was sent as a delegate to reason with the insurgents. His admonitions were unsuccessful, and he only succeeded in bringing himself under suspicion of being in part responsible for their excesses. When Rothenburg was taken by the margrave of Anspach (28th June 1525) Carlstadt had to fly for his life. His spirit was now broken, and from Frankfort he wrote to Luther humbly praying him to intercede for him with the elector. Luther agreed to do so, on receiving from Carlstadt a recantation of his heterodox views on the Lord's Supper, and as the result the latter was permitted to return to Wittenberg (1525). He was not, however, allowed to lecture, and he lived as a peasant, first at Segrena and afterwards at Bergwitz, cultivating small properties, in which he had invested the remnant of his fortune, with such poor success that at the end of 1526 he had to eke out a living as a pedlar in the little town of Kemberg. This was endurable; but not so the demand presently made upon him to take up the cudgels against Zwingli and Oecolampadius. Once more he revolted; to agree with "Dr Martin's opinions on the sacrament" was as difficult as flying like a bird; he appealed to the elector to allow him to leave Saxony; but the elector's conscience was in Luther's 349keeping, and Carlstadt had to fly ignominiously in order to avoid imprisonment. He escaped to Holstein, where in March 1529 he stayed with the Anabaptist Melchior Hofmann. Expelled by the authorities, he took refuge in East Friesland, where he remained till the beginning of 1530 under the protection of a nobleman in sympathy with the Helvetic reformers. His preaching gave him great influence, but towards the close of the year persecution again sent him on his travels. He ultimately reached Zürich, where the recommendations of Bucer and Oecolampadius secured him a friendly reception by Zwingli, who procured him employment. After Zwingli's death he remained in close intercourse with the Zürich preachers, who defended him against renewed attacks on Luther's part; and finally, in 1534, on Bullinger's recommendation, he was called to Basel as preacher at the church of St Peter and professor at the university. Here he remained till his death on the 24th of December 1541.

During these latter years Carlstadt's attitude became more moderate. His championship of the town council against the theocratic claims of Antistes Myconius and the ecclesiastical council, in the matter of the control of the university, was perhaps in consonance with his earlier views on the relations of clergy and laity. He was, however, also instrumental in restoring the abolished doctorate of theology and other degrees; and, despatched on a mission to Strassburg in 1536, to take part in a discussion on a proposed compromise in the matter of the Lord's Supper between the theologians of Strassburg and Wittenberg, he displayed a conciliatory attitude which earned him the praise of Bucer. Carlstadt's historical significance lies in the fact that he was one of the pioneers of the Reformation. But he was a thinker and dreamer rather than a man of affairs, and though he had the moral and physical courage to carry his principles to their logical conclusions (he was the first priest to write against celibacy, and the first to take a wife), he lacked the balance of mind and sturdy common sense that inspired Luther's policy of consideration for "the weaker brethren" and built up the Evangelical Church on a conservative basis. But though Carlstadt was on friendly terms, and corresponded with Münzer and other Anabaptists, he did not share their antinomian views, nor was he responsible for their excesses. His opinion as to the relation of faith and "good works" was practically that expressed in articles XI. and XII. of the Church of England. In reply to Luther's violent onslaught on him in his *Wider die himmlischen Propheten* he issued from Rothenburg his *Anzeig etlicher Hauptartikel christlicher Lehre*, a compendious exposition of his views, in which he says: "Those who urge to good works do so, not that the conscience may be justified by works, but that their freedom may redound to God's glory and that their neighbours may be fired to praise God."

See C.F. Jaeger, *Andreas Bodenstein von Karlstadt* (Stuttgart, 1856); Hermann Barge, *Andreas Bodenstein von Karlstadt*, vol. i. (Leipzig, 1905).

CARLYLE, ALEXANDER (1722-1805), Scottish divine, was born on the 26th of January 1722, in Dumfriesshire, and passed his youth and early manhood at Prestonpans, where he witnessed the battle of 1745. He was educated at Edinburgh (M.A. 1743), Glasgow and Leiden. From 1748 until his death on the 28th of August 1805 he was minister at Inveresk in Midlothian, and during this long career rose to high eminence in his church not only as leader of the moderate or "broad" Church section, but as moderator of the General Assembly 1770 and dean of the Chapel Royal in 1789. His influence was enhanced by his personal appearance, which was so striking as to earn him the name of "Jupiter Carlyle"; and his autobiography (published 1860), though written in his closing years and not extending beyond the year 1770, is abundantly interesting as a picture of Scottish life, social and ecclesiastical, in the 18th century. Carlyle's memory recalled the Porteous Riots of 1736, and less remotely his friendship with Adam Smith, David Hume, and John Home, the dramatist, for witnessing the performance of whose tragedy *Douglas* he was censured in 1757. He was distinctly a *bon vivant*, but withal an upright, conscientious and capable minister.

CARLYLE, JOSEPH DACRE (1759-1804), British orientalist, was born in 1759 at Carlisle, where his father was a physician. He went in 1775 to Cambridge, was elected a fellow of Queens' College in 1779, taking the degree of B.D. in 1793. With the assistance of a native of Bagdad known in England as David Zamio, then resident at Cambridge, he attained great proficiency in Arabic literature; and after succeeding Dr Paley in the chancellorship of Carlisle, he was appointed, in 1795, professor of Arabic in Cambridge University. His translation from the Arabic of Yusuf ibn Taghri Birdi, the *Rerum Egypticarum Annales*, appeared in 1792, and in 1796 a volume of *Specimens of Arabic Poetry*, from the earliest times to the fall of the Caliphate, with some account of the authors. Carlyle was appointed chaplain by Lord Elgin to the embassy at Constantinople in 1799, and prosecuted his researches in Eastern literature in a tour through Asia Minor, Palestine, Greece and Italy, collecting in his travels several valuable Greek and Syriac MSS. for a projected critical edition of the New Testament, collated with the Syriac and other versions—a work, however, which he did not live to complete. On his return to England in 1801 he was presented by the bishop of Carlisle to the living of Newcastle-on-Tyne, where he died on the 12th of April 1804. After his death there appeared a volume of poems descriptive of the scenes of his travels, with prefaces extracted from his journal. Among other works which he left unfinished was an edition of the Bible in Arabic, completed by H. Ford and published in 1811.

CARLYLE, THOMAS (1795-1881), British essayist, historian and philosopher, born on the 4th of December 1795 at Ecclefechan, in Annandale, was the eldest of the nine children of James Carlyle by his second wife, Janet Aitken. The father was by trade a mason, and afterwards a small farmer. He had joined a sect of seceders from the kirk, and had all the characteristics of the typical Scottish Calvinist. He was respected for his integrity and independence, and a stern outside covered warm affections. The family tie between all the Carlyles was unusually strong, and Thomas regarded his father with a reverence which found forcible expression in his *Reminiscences*. He always showed the tenderest love for his mother, and was the best of brothers. The narrow means of his parents were made sufficient by strict frugality. He was sent to the parish school when seven, and to Annan grammar-school when ten years old. His pugnacity brought him into troubles with his fellows at Annan; but he soon showed an appetite for learning which induced his father to educate him for the ministry. He walked to Edinburgh in November 1809, and entered the university. He cared little for any of the professors, except Sir John Leslie, from whom he learned some mathematics. He acquired a little classical knowledge, but the most valuable influence was that of his contemporaries. A few lads in positions similar to his own began to look up to him as an intellectual leader, and their correspondence with him shows remarkable interest in literary matters. In 1814 Carlyle, still looking forward to the career of a minister, obtained the mathematical mastership at Annan. The salary of £60 or £70 a year enabled him to save a little money. He went to Edinburgh once or twice, to deliver the discourses required from students of divinity. He does not seem, however, to have taken to his profession very earnestly. He was too shy and proud to see many of the Annan people, and found his chief solace in reading such books as he could get. In 1816 he was appointed, through the recommendation of Leslie, to a school at Kirkcaldy, where Edward Irving, Carlyle's senior by three years, was also master of a school. Irving's severity as a teacher had offended some of the parents, who set up Carlyle to be his rival. A previous meeting with Irving, also a native of Annan, had led to a little passage of arms, but Irving now welcomed Carlyle with a generosity which entirely won his heart, and the rivals soon became the closest of friends. The intimacy, affectionately commemorated in the *Reminiscences*, was of great importance to Carlyle's whole career. "But for Irving," he says, "I had never known what the communion of man with man means." Irving had a library, in which Carlyle devoured Gibbon and much French literature, and they made various excursions 350together. Carlyle did his duties as a schoolmaster punctiliously, but found the life thoroughly uncongenial. No man was less fitted by temperament for the necessary drudgery and worry. A passing admiration for a Miss Gordon is supposed to have suggested the "Blumine" of *Sartor Resartus*; but he made no new friendships, and when Irving left at the end of 1818 Carlyle also resigned his post.

He had by this time resolved to give up the ministry. He has given no details of the intellectual change which alienated him from the church. He had, however, been led, by whatever process, to abandon the dogmatic system of his forefathers, though he was and always remained in profound sympathy with the spirit of their teaching. A period of severe struggle followed. He studied law for a time, but liked it no better than schoolmastering. He took a pupil or two, and wrote articles for the *Edinburgh Encyclopaedia* under the editorship of Brewster. He occasionally visited his family, and their unfailing confidence helped to keep up his courage. Meanwhile he was going through a spiritual crisis. Atheism seemed for a time to be the only alternative to his old creed. It was, however, profoundly repugnant to him. At last, one day in June 1821, after three weeks' total sleeplessness, he went through the crisis afterwards described quite "literally" in *Sartor Resartus*. He cast out the spirit of negation, and henceforth the temper of his misery was changed to one, not of "whining," but of "indignation and grim fire-eyed defiance." That, he says, was his spiritual new-birth, though certainly not into a life of serenity. The conversion was coincident with Carlyle's submission to a new and very potent influence. In 1819 he had begun to study German, with which he soon acquired a very remarkable familiarity. Many of his contemporaries were awakening to the importance of German thought, and Carlyle's knowledge enabled him before long to take a conspicuous part in diffusing the new intellectual light. The chief object of his reverence was Goethe. In many most important respects no two men could be more unlike; but, for the present, Carlyle seems to have seen in Goethe a proof that it was possible to reject outworn dogmas without sinking into materialism. Goethe, by singularly different methods, had emerged from a merely negative position into a lofty and coherent conception of the universe. Meanwhile, Carlyle's various anxieties were beginning to be complicated by physical derangement. A rat, he declared, was gnawing at the pit of his stomach. He was already suffering from the ailments, whatever their precise nature, from which he never escaped. He gave vent to his irritability by lamentations so grotesquely exaggerated as to make it difficult to estimate the real extent of the evil.

Irving's friendship now became serviceable. Carlyle's confession of the radical difference of religious opinion had not alienated his friend, who was settling in London, and used his opportunities for promoting Carlyle's interest. In January 1822 Carlyle, through Irving's recommendation, became tutor to Charles and Arthur Buller, who were to be students at Edinburgh. Carlyle's salary was £200 a year, and this, with the proceeds of some literary work, enabled him at once to help his brother John to study medicine and his brother Alexander to take up a farm. Carlyle spent some time with the elder Bullers, but found a life of dependence upon fashionable people humiliating and unsatisfactory. He employed himself at intervals upon a life of Schiller and a translation of *Wilhelm Meister*. He received £50 for a translation of Legendre's *Geometry*; and an introduction, explaining the theory of proportion, is said by De Morgan to show that he could have gained distinction as an expounder of mathematical principles. He finally gave up his tutorship in July 1824, and for a time tried to find employment in London. The impressions made upon him by London men of letters were most unfavourable. Carlyle felt by this time conscious of having a message to deliver to mankind, and his comrades, he thought, were making literature a trade instead of a vocation, and prostituting their talents to frivolous journalism. He went once to see Coleridge, who was then delivering his oracular utterances at Highgate, and the only result was the singularly vivid portrait given in a famous chapter in his life of Sterling. Coleridge seemed to him to be ineffectual as a philosopher, and personally to be a melancholy instance of genius running to waste. Carlyle, conscious of great abilities, and impressed by such instances of the deleterious effects of the social atmosphere of London, resolved to settle in his native district. There he could live frugally and achieve some real work. He could, for one thing, be the interpreter of Germany to England. A friendly letter from Goethe, acknowledging the translation of *Wilhelm Meister*, reached him at the end of 1824 and greatly encouraged him. Goethe afterwards spoke warmly of the life of Schiller, and desired it to be translated into German. Letters occasionally passed between them in later years, which were edited by Professor Charles Eliot Norton in 1887. Goethe received Carlyle's homage with kind complacency. The gift of a seal to Goethe on his birthday in 1831 "from fifteen English friends," including Scott and Wordsworth, was suggested and carried out by Carlyle. The interest in German, which Carlyle did so much to promote, suggested to him other translations and reviews during the next few years, and he made some preparations for a history of German literature. British curiosity, however, about such matters seems to have been soon satisfied, and the demand for such work slackened.

Carlyle was meanwhile passing through the most important crisis of his personal history. Jané Baillie Welsh, born 1801, was the only child of Dr Welsh of Haddington. She had shown precocious talent, and was sent to the school at Haddington where Edward Irving (*q.v.*) was a master. After her father's death in 1819 she lived with her mother, and her wit and beauty attracted many admirers. Her old tutor, Irving, was now at Kirkcaldy, where he became engaged to a Miss Martin. He visited Haddington occasionally in the following years, and a strong mutual regard arose between him and Miss Welsh. They contemplated a marriage, and Irving endeavoured to obtain a release from his previous engagement. The Martin family held him to his word, and he took a final leave of Miss Welsh in 1822.

Meanwhile he had brought Carlyle from Edinburgh and introduced him to the Welshes. Carlyle was attracted by the brilliant abilities of the young lady, procured books for her and wrote letters to her as an intellectual guide. The two were to perform a new variation upon the theme of Abelard and Héloïse. [A good deal of uncertainty long covered the precise character of their relations. Until 1909, when Mr. Alexander Carlyle published his edition of the "love-letters," the full material was not accessible; they had been read by Carlyle's biographer, Froude, and also by Professor Charles Norton, and Norton (in his edition of Carlyle's *Early Letters*, 1886) declared that Froude had distorted the significance of this correspondence in a sense injurious to the writers. The publication of the letters certainly seems to justify Norton's view.] Miss Welsh's previous affair with Irving had far less importance than Froude ascribes to it; and she soon came to regard her past love as a childish fancy. She recognized Carlyle's vast intellectual superiority, and the respect gradually deepened into genuine love. The process, however, took some time. Her father had bequeathed to her his whole property (£200 to £300 a year). In 1823 she made it over to her mother, but left the whole to Carlyle in the event of her own and her mother's death. She still declared that she did not love him well enough to become his wife. In 1824 she gradually relented so far as to say that she would marry if he could achieve independence. She had been brought up in a station superior to that of the Carlyles, and could not accept the life of hardship which would be necessary in his present circumstances. Carlyle, accustomed to his father's household, was less frightened by the prospect of poverty. He was determined not to abandon his vocation as a man of genius by following the lower though more profitable paths to literary success, and expected that his wife should partake the necessary sacrifice of comfort. The natural result of such discussions followed. The attraction became stronger on both sides, in spite of occasional spasms of doubt. 351An odd incident precipitated the result. A friend of Irving's, Mrs Basil Montague, wrote to Miss Welsh, to exhort her to suppress her love for Irving, who had married Miss Martin in 1823. Miss Welsh replied by announcing her intention to marry Carlyle; and then told him the whole story, of which he had previously been ignorant. He properly begged her not to yield to the impulse without due consideration. She answered by coming at once to his father's house, where he was staying; and the marriage was finally settled. It took place on the 17th of October 1826.

Carlyle had now to arrange the mode of life which should enable him to fulfil his aspiration. His wife had made over her income to her mother, but he had saved a small sum upon which to begin housekeeping. A passing suggestion from Mrs Carlyle that they might live with her mother was judiciously abandoned. Carlyle had thought of occupying Craigenputtock, a remote and dreary farm belonging to Mrs Welsh. His wife objected to his utter incapacity as a farmer; and they finally took a small house at Comely Bank, Edinburgh, where they could live on a humble scale. The brilliant conversation of both attracted some notice in the literary society of Edinburgh. The most important connexion was with Francis, Lord Jeffrey, still editor of the *Edinburgh Review*. Though Jeffrey had no intellectual sympathy with Carlyle, he accepted some articles for the *Review* and became warmly attached to Mrs Carlyle. Carlyle began to be known as leader of a new "mystic" school, and his earnings enabled him to send his brother John to study in Germany. The public appetite, however, for "mysticism" was not keen. In spite of support from Jeffrey and other friends, Carlyle failed in a candidature for a professorship at St Andrews. His brother, Alexander, had now taken the farm at Craigenputtock, and the Carlyles decided to settle at the separate dwelling-house there, which would bring them nearer to Mrs Welsh. They went there in 1828, and began a hard struggle. Carlyle, indomitably determined to make no concessions for immediate profit, wrote slowly and carefully, and turned out some of his most finished work. He laboured "passionately" at *Sartor Resartus*, and made articles out of fragments originally intended for the history of German literature. The money difficulty soon became more pressing. John, whom he was still helping, was trying unsuccessfully to set up as a doctor in London; and Alexander's farming failed. In spite of such drawbacks, Carlyle in later years looked back upon the life at Craigenputtock as on the whole a comparatively healthy and even happy period, as it was certainly one of most strenuous and courageous endeavour. Though often absorbed in his work and made both gloomy and irritable by his anxieties, he found relief in rides with his wife, and occasionally visiting their relations. Their letters during temporary separations are most affectionate. The bleak climate, however, the solitude, and the necessity of managing a household with a single servant, were excessively trying to a delicate woman, though Mrs Carlyle concealed from her husband the extent of her sacrifices. The position was gradually becoming untenable. In the autumn of 1831 Carlyle was forced to accept a loan of £50 from Jeffrey, and went in search of work to London, whither his wife followed him. He made some engagements with publishers, though no one would take *Sartor Resartus*, and returned to Craigenputtock in the spring of 1832. Jeffrey, stimulated perhaps by his sympathy for Mrs Carlyle, was characteristically generous. Besides pressing loans upon both Thomas and John Carlyle, he offered to settle an annuity of £100 upon Thomas, and finally enabled John to support himself by recommending him to a medical position.1Carlyle's proud spirit of independence made him reject Jeffrey's help as long as possible; and even his acknowledgment of the generosity (in the *Reminiscences*) is tinged with something disagreeably like resentment. In 1834 he applied to Jeffrey for a post at the Edinburgh Observatory. Jeffrey naturally declined to appoint a man who, in spite of some mathematical knowledge, had no special qualification, and administered a general lecture upon Carlyle's arrogance and eccentricity which left a permanent sense of injury.

In the beginning of 1833 the Carlyles made another trial of Edinburgh. There Carlyle found materials in the Advocates' Library for the article on the *Diamond Necklace*, one of his most perfect writings, which led him to study the history of the French Revolution. *Sartor Resartus* was at last appearing in *Fraser's Magazine*, though the rate of payment was cut down, and the publisher reported that it was received with "unqualified dissatisfaction." Edinburgh society did not attract him, and he retreated once more to Craigenputtock. After another winter the necessity of some change became obvious. The Carlyles resolved to "burn their ships." They went to London in the summer of 1834, and took a house at 5 (now 24) Cheyne Row, Chelsea, which Carlyle inhabited till his death; the house has since been bought for the public. Irving, who had welcomed him on former occasions, was just dying,—a victim, as Carlyle thought, to fashionable cajoleries. A few young men were beginning to show appreciation. J.S. Mill had made Carlyle's acquaintance in the previous visit to London, and had corresponded with him. Mill had introduced Ralph Waldo Emerson, who visited Craigenputtock in 1833. Carlyle was charmed with Emerson, and their letters published by Professor Norton show that his regard never cooled. Emerson's interest showed that Carlyle's fame was already spreading in America. Carlyle's connexion with Charles Buller, a zealous utilitarian, introduced him to the circle of "philosophical radicals."

Carlyle called himself in some sense a radical; and J.S. Mill, though not an intellectual disciple, was a very warm admirer of his friend's genius. Carlyle had some expectation of the editorship of the *London Review*, started by Sir W. Molesworth at this time as an organ of philosophical radicalism. The combination would clearly have been explosive. Meanwhile Mill, who had collected many books upon the French Revolution, was eager to help Carlyle in the history which he was now beginning. He set to work at once and finished the first volume in five months. The manuscript, while entrusted to Mill for annotation, was burnt by an accident. Mill induced Carlyle to accept in compensation £100, which was urgently needed. Carlyle took up the task again and finished the whole on the 12th of January 1837. "I can tell the world," he said to his wife, "you have not had for a hundred years any book that comes more direct and flamingly from the heart of a living man. Do what you like with it, you—"

The publication, six months later, of the *French Revolution* marks the turning-point of Carlyle's career. Many readers hold it to be the best, as it is certainly the most characteristic, of Carlyle's books. The failure of *Sartor Resartus* to attract average readers is quite intelligible. It contains, indeed, some of the most impressive expositions of his philosophical position, and some of his most beautiful and perfectly written passages. But there is something forced and clumsy, in spite of the flashes of grim humour, in the machinery of the *Clothes Philosophy*. The mannerism, which has been attributed to an imitation of Jean Paul, appeared to Carlyle himself to be derived rather from the phrases current in his father's house, and in any case gave an appropriate dialect for the expression of his peculiar idiosyncrasy. But it could not be appreciated by readers who would not take the trouble to learn a new language. In the *French Revolution* Carlyle had discovered his real strength. He was always at his best when his imagination was set to work upon a solid framework of fact. The book shows a unique combination: on the one hand is the singularly shrewd insight into character and the vivid realization of the picturesque; on the other is the "mysticism" or poetical philosophy which relieves the events against a background of mystery. The contrast is marked by the humour which seems to combine a cynical view of human folly with a deeply pathetic sense of the sadness and suffering of life. The convictions, whatever their value, came, as he said, "flamingly from the heart." It was, of course, impossible for Carlyle to satisfy modern requirements of matter-of-fact accuracy. 352He could not in the time have assimilated all the materials even then extant, and later accumulations would necessitate a complete revision. Considered as a "prose epic," or a vivid utterance of the thought of the period, it has a permanent and unique value.

The book was speedily successful. It was reviewed by Mill in the *Westminster* and by Thackeray in *The Times*, and Carlyle, after a heroic struggle, was at last touching land. In each of the years 1837 to 1840 he gave a course of lectures, of which the last only (upon "Hero Worship") was published; they materially helped his finances. By Emerson's management he also received something during the same period from American publishers. At the age of forty-five he had thus become independent. He had also established a position among the chief writers of the day. Young disciples, among whom John Sterling was the most accepted, were gathering round him, and he became an object of social curiosity. Monckton Milnes (Lord Houghton), who won universal popularity by the most genuine kindliness of nature, became a cordial friend. Another important intimacy was with the Barings, afterwards Lord and Lady Ashburton. Carlyle's conversational powers were extraordinary; though, as he won greater recognition as a prophet, he indulged too freely in didactic monologue. In his prophetic capacity he published two remarkable books: *Chartism* (1829), enlarged from an article which Lockhart, though personally approving, was afraid to take for the *Quarterly*; and *Past and Present* (1843), in which the recently published *Mediaeval Chronicle* was taken as a text for the exposure of modern evils. They may be regarded as expositions of the doctrine implicitly set forth in the *French Revolution*. Carlyle was a "radical" as sharing the sentiments of the class in which he was born. He had been profoundly moved by the widely-spread distresses in his earlier years. When the yeomanry were called out to suppress riots after the Peace, his sympathies were with the people rather than with the authorities. So far he was in harmony with Mill and the "philosophical radicals." A fundamental divergence of principle, however, existed and was soon indicated by his speedy separation from the party and alienation from Mill himself. The Revolution, according to him, meant the sweeping away of effete beliefs and institutions, but implied also the necessity of a reconstructive process. *Chartism* begins with a fierce attack upon the *laissez faire* theory, which showed blindness to this necessity. The prevalent political economy, in which that theory was embodied, made a principle of neglecting the very evils which it should be the great function of government to remedy. Carlyle's doctrines, entirely opposed to the ordinary opinions of Whigs and Radicals, found afterwards an expositor in his ardent disciple Ruskin, and have obvious affinities with more recent socialism. At the time he was as one crying in the wilderness to little practical purpose. Liberals were scandalized by his apparent identification of "right" with "might," implied in the demand for a strong government; and though he often declared the true interpretation to be that the right would ultimately become might, his desire for strong government seemed too often to sanction the inverse view. He came into collision with philanthropists, and was supposed to approve of despotism for its own sake.

His religious position was equally unintelligible to the average mind. While unequivocally rejecting the accepted creeds, and so scandalizing even liberal theologians, he was still more hostile to simply sceptical and materialist tendencies. He was, as he called himself, a "mystic"; and his creed was too vague to be put into any formula beyond a condemnation of atheism. One corollary was the famous doctrine of "hero worship" first expounded in his lectures. Any philosophy of history which emphasized the importance of general causes seemed to him to imply a simply mechanical doctrine and to deny the efficacy of the great spiritual forces. He met it by making biography the essence of history, or attributing all great events to the "heroes," who are the successive embodiments of divine revelations. This belief was implied in his next great work, the *Life and Letters of Oliver Cromwell*, published in 1845. The great Puritan hero was a man after his own heart, and the portrait drawn by so sympathetic a writer is not only intensely vivid, but a very effective rehabilitation of misrepresented character. The "biographical" view of history, however, implies the weakness, not only of unqualified approval of all Cromwell's actions, but of omitting any attempt to estimate the Protector's real relation to the social and political development of the time. The question, what was Cromwell's real and permanent achievement, is not answered nor distinctly considered. The effect may be partly due to the peculiar form of the book as a detached series of documents and comments. The composition introduced Carlyle to the "Dryasdust" rubbish heaps of which he here and ever afterwards bitterly complained. A conscientious desire to unearth the facts, and the effort of extracting from the dullest records the materials for graphic pictures, made the process of production excessively painful. For some years after *Cromwell* Carlyle wrote little. His growing acceptance by publishers, and the inheritance of her property by Mrs Carlyle on her mother's death in 1842, finally removed the stimulus of money pressure. He visited Ireland in 1846 and again in 1849, when he made a long tour in company with Sir C. Gavan Duffy, then a young member of the Nationalist party (see Sir C.G. Duffy's *Conversations with Carlyle*, 1892, for an interesting narrative). Carlyle's strong convictions as to the misery and misgovernment of Ireland recommended him to men who had taken part in the rising of 1848. Although the remedies acceptable to a eulogist of Cromwell could not be to their taste, they admired his moral teaching; and he received their attentions, as Sir C.G. Duffy testifies, with conspicuous courtesy. His aversion from the ordinary radicalism led to an article upon slavery in 1849, to which Mill replied, and which caused their final alienation. It was followed in 1850 by the *Latterday Pamphlets*, containing "sulphurous" denunciations of the do-nothing principle. They gave general offence, and the disapproval, according to Froude, stopped the sale for years. The *Life* of Sterling (d. 1844), which appeared in 1851, was intended to correct the life by Julius Hare, which had given too much prominence to theological questions. The subject roused Carlyle's tenderest mood, and the *Life* is one of the most perfect in the language.

Carlyle meanwhile was suffering domestic troubles, unfortunately not exceptional in their nature, though the exceptional intellect and characters of the persons concerned have given them unusual prominence. Carlyle's constitutional irritability made him intensely sensitive to petty annoyances. He suffered the torments of dyspepsia; he was often sleepless, and the crowing of "demon-fowls" in neighbours' yards drove him wild. Composition meant for him intense absorption in his work; solitude and quiet were essential; and he resented interruptions by grotesque explosions of humorously exaggerated wrath. Mrs Carlyle had to pass many hours alone, and the management of the household and of devices intended to shield him from annoyances was left entirely to her. House-cleanings and struggles with builders during the construction of a "sound-proof room" taxed her energy, while Carlyle was hiding himself with his family in Scotland or staying at English country houses. Nothing could be more affectionate than his behaviour to his wife on serious occasions, such as the death of her mother, and he could be considerate when his attention was called to the facts. But he was often oblivious to the strain upon her energies, and had little command of his temper. An unfortunate aggravation of the difficulty arose from his intimacy with the Ashburtons. Lady Ashburton, a woman of singular social charm and great ability, appreciated the author, but apparently accepted the company of the author's wife rather as a necessity than as an additional charm. Mrs Carlyle was hurt by the fine lady's condescension and her husband's accessibility to aristocratic blandishments. Carlyle, as a wise man, should have yielded to his wife's wishes; unluckily, he was content to point out that her jealousy was unreasonable, and, upon that very insufficient ground, to disregard it and to continue his intimacy with the Ashburtons on the old terms. Mrs Carlyle bitterly resented his conduct. She had been willing to renounce any aspirations of her own and to sink herself in his glory, but she 353 naturally expected him to recognize her devotion and to value her society beyond all others. She had just cause of complaint, and a remarkable power, as her letters prove, of seeing things plainly and despising sentimental consolations. She was childless, and had time to brood over her wrongs. She formed a little circle of friends, attached to her rather than to her husband; and to one of them, Giuseppe Mazzini, she confided her troubles in 1846. He gave her admirable advice; and the alienation from her husband, though it continued still to smoulder, led to no further results. A journal written at the same time gives a painful record of her sufferings, and after her death made Carlyle conscious for the first time of their full extent. The death of Lady Ashburton in 1857 removed this cause of jealousy; and Lord Ashburton married a second wife in 1858, who became a warm friend of both Carlyles. The cloud which had separated them was thus at last dispersed. Meanwhile Carlyle had become absorbed in his best and most laborious work. Soon after the completion of the *Cromwell* he had thought of Frederick for his next hero, and had in 1845 contemplated a visit to Germany to collect materials. He did not, however, settle down finally to the work till 1851. He shut himself up in his study to wrestle with the Prussian Dryasdusts, whom he discovered to be as wearisome as their Puritan predecessors and more voluminous. He went to Scotland to see his mother, to whom he had always shown the tenderest affection, on her deathbed at the end of 1853. He returned to shut himself up in the "sound-proof room." He twice visited Germany (1852 and 1858) to see Frederick's battlefields and obtain materials; and he occasionally went to the Ashburtons and his relations in Scotland. The first two volumes of *Frederick the Great* appeared in 1858, and succeeding volumes in 1862, 1864 and 1865. The success was great from the first, though it did little to clear up Carlyle's gloom. The book is in some respects his masterpiece, and its merits are beyond question. Carlyle had spared no pains in research. The descriptions of the campaigns are admirably vivid, and show his singular eye for scenery. These narratives are said to be used by military students in Germany, and at least convince the non-military student that he can understand the story. The book was declared by Emerson to be the wittiest ever written. Many episodes, describing the society at the Prussian court and the relations of Frederick to Voltaire, are unsurpassable as humorous portraiture. The effort to fuse the masses of raw material into a well-proportioned whole is perhaps not quite successful; and Carlyle had not the full sympathy with Frederick which had given interest to the *Cromwell*. A hero-worshipper with half-concealed doubts as to his hero is in an awkward position. Carlyle's general conception of history made him comparatively blind to aspects of the subject which would, to writers of other schools, have a great importance. The extraordinary power of the book is undeniable, though it does not show the fire which animated the *French Revolution*. A certain depression and weariness of spirit darken the general tone.

During the later labours Mrs Carlyle's health had been breaking. Carlyle, now that happier relations had been restored, did his best to give her the needed comforts; and in spite of his immersion in *Frederick*, showed her all possible attention in later years. She had apparently recovered from an almost hopeless illness, when at the end of 1865 he was elected to the rectorship of the university of Edinburgh. He delivered an address there on the 2nd of April 1866, unusually mild in tone, and received with general applause. He was still detained in Scotland when Mrs Carlyle died suddenly while driving in her carriage. The immediate cause was the shock of an accident to her dog. She had once hurt her mother's feelings by refusing to use some wax candles. She had preserved them ever since, and by her direction they were now lighted in the chamber of death. Carlyle was overpowered by her loss. His life thenceforward became more and more secluded, and he gradually became incapable of work. He went to Mentone in the winter of 1866 and began the *Reminiscences*. He afterwards annotated the letters from his wife, published (1883) as *Letters and Memorials*. He was, as Froude says, impressed by the story of Johnson's "penance" at Uttoxeter, and desired to make a posthumous confession of his shortcomings in his relations to his wife. A few later utterances made known his opinions of current affairs. He joined the committee for the defence of Governor Eyre in 1867; he also wrote in 1867 an article upon "shooting Niagara," that is, upon the tendency of the Reform Bill of that year; and in 1870 he wrote a letter defending the German case against France. The worth of his *Frederick* was acknowledged by the Prussian Order of Merit in 1874. In the same year Disraeli offered him the Grand Cross of the Bath and a pension. He declined very courteously, and felt some regret for previous remarks upon the minister. The length of his literary career was now softening old antipathies, and he was the object of general respect. His infirmities enforced a very retired life, but he was constantly visited by Froude, and occasionally by his disciple Ruskin. A small number of other friends paid him constant attention. His conversation was still interesting, especially when it turned upon his recollections, and though his judgments were sometimes severe enough, he never condescended to the scandalous. His views of the future were gloomy. The world seemed to be going from bad to worse, with little heed to his warnings. He would sometimes regret that it was no longer permissible to leave it in the old Roman fashion. He sank gradually, and died on the 4th of February 1881. A place in Westminster Abbey was offered, but he was buried, according to his own desire, by the side of his parents at Ecclefechan. He left Craigenputtock, which had become his own property, to found bursaries at the university of Edinburgh. He gave his books to Harvard College.

Carlyle's appearance has been made familiar by many portraits, none of them, according to Froude, satisfactory. The statue by Boehm on the Chelsea Embankment, however, is characteristic; and there is a fine painting by Watts in the National Portrait Gallery. J. McNeill Whistler's portrait of him is in the possession of the Glasgow corporation.

During Carlyle's later years the antagonism roused by his attacks upon popular opinions had subsided; and upon his death general expression was given to the emotions natural upon the loss of a remarkable man of genius. The rapid publication of the *Reminiscences* by Froude produced a sudden revulsion of feeling. Carlyle became the object of general condemnation. Froude's biography, and the *Memorials* of Mrs Carlyle, published soon afterwards, strengthened the hostile feeling. Carlyle had appended to the *Reminiscences* an injunction to his friends not to publish them as they stood, and added that no part could ever be published without the strictest editing. Afterwards, when he had almost forgotten what he had written, he verbally empowered Froude to use his own judgment: Froude accordingly published the book at once, without any editing, and with many inaccuracies. Omissions of a few passages written from memory at a time of profound nervous depression would have altered the whole character of the book. Froude in this and the later publications held that he was giving effect to Carlyle's wish to imitate Johnson's "penance." No one, said Boswell, should persuade him to make his lion into a cat. Froude intended, in the same spirit, to give the shades as well as the lights in the portrait of his hero. His admiration for Carlyle probably led him to assume too early that his readers would approach the story from the same point of view, that is, with an admiration too warm to be repelled by the admissions. Moreover, Froude's characteristic desire for picturesque effect, unchecked by any painstaking accuracy, led to his reading preconceived impressions into his documents. The result was that Carlyle was too often judged by his defects, and regarded as a selfish and eccentric misanthrope with flashes of genius, rather than as a man with many of the highest qualities of mind and character clouded by constitutional infirmities. Yet it would be difficult to speak too strongly of the great qualities which underlay the superficial defects. Through long years of poverty and obscurity Carlyle showed unsurpassed fidelity to his vocation and superiority to the lower temptations which have ruined so many literary careers, His ambition might be interpreted as selfishness, but certainly 354showed no coldness of heart. His unstinted generosity to his brothers during his worst times is only one proof of the singular strength of his family affections. No one was more devoted to such congenial friends as Irving and Sterling. He is not the only man whom absorption in work and infirmity of temper have made into a provoking husband, though few wives have had Mrs Carlyle's capacity for expressing the sense of injustice. The knowledge that the deepest devotion underlies misunderstandings is often a very imperfect consolation; but such devotion clearly existed all through, and proves the defect to have been relatively superficial.

The harsh judgments of individuals in the *Reminiscences* had no parallel in his own writings. He scarcely ever mentions a contemporary, and was never involved in a personal controversy. But the harshness certainly reflects a characteristic attitude of mind. Carlyle was throughout a pessimist or a prophet denouncing a backsliding world. His most popular contemporaries seemed to him to be false guides, and charlatans had ousted the heroes. The general condemnation of "shams" and cant had, of course, particular applications, though he left them to be inferred by his readers. Carlyle was the exponent of many of the deepest convictions of his time. Nobody could be more in sympathy with aspirations for a spiritual religion and for a lofty idealism in political and social life. To most minds, however, which

207

cherish such aspirations the gentler optimism of men like Emerson was more congenial. They believed in the progress of the race and the triumph of the nobler elements. Though Carlyle, especially in his earlier years, could deliver an invigorating and encouraging, if not a sanguine doctrine, his utterances were more generally couched in the key of denunciation, and betrayed a growing despondency. Materialism and low moral principles seemed to him to be gaining the upper hand; and the hope that religion might survive the "old clothes" in which it had been draped seemed to grow fainter. The ordinary mind complained that he had no specific remedy to propose for the growing evils of the time; and the more cultivated idealist was alienated by the gloom and the tendency to despair. To a later generation it will probably appear that, whatever the exaggerations and the misconceptions to which he was led, his vehement attacks at least called attention to rather grave limitations and defects in the current beliefs and social tendencies of the time. The mannerisms and grotesque exaggerations of his writings annoyed persons of refinement, and suggest Matthew Arnold's advice to flee "Carlylese" as you would flee the devil. Yet the shrewd common-sense, the biting humour, the power of graphic description and the imaginative "mysticism" give them a unique attraction for many even who do not fully sympathize with the implied philosophy or with the Puritanical code of ethics. The letters and autobiographical writings, whether they attract or repel sympathy, are at least a series of documents of profound interest for any one who cares to study character, and display an almost unique idiosyncrasy.

(L. S.)

The chief authorities for Carlyle's life are his own *Reminiscences*, the *Letters of Jane Welsh Carlyle*, the *Love Letters of Thomas Carlyle and Jane Welsh* (ed. A. Carlyle), and the four volumes of J.A. Froude's biography; Froude was Carlyle's literary executor. Prof. C.E. Norton's edition of the *Reminiscences* and his collection of Carlyle's *Early Letters* correct some of Froude's inaccuracies. A list of many articles upon Carlyle is given by Mr Ireland in *Notes and Queries*, sixth series, vol. iv. Among other authors may be noticed Henry James, sen., in *Literary Remains*; Prof. Masson, *Carlyle, Personally and in his Writings*; Conway, *Thomas Carlyle*; Larkin, *The Open Secret of Carlyle's Life*; Mrs Oliphant in *Macmillan's Magazine* for April 1881; G.S. Venables in *Fortnightly Review* for May 1883 and November 1884. A good deal of controversy has arisen relating to Froude's treatment of the relations between Carlyle and his wife, and during 1903-1904 this was pushed to a somewhat unsavoury extent. Those who are curious to pry into the question of Carlyle's marital capacity, and the issues between Froude's assailants and his defenders, may consult *New Letters and Memorials of Jane Welsh Carlyle*, with introduction by Sir James Crichton-Browne; *My Relations with Carlyle*, by J.A. Froude; *The Nemesis of Froude*, by Sir J. Crichton-Browne and Alexander Carlyle; and articles in the *Contemporary Review* (June, July, August, 1903), and *Nineteenth Century and After* (May, July, 1903). See also Herbert Paul's *Life of Froude* (1905). The precise truth in these matters is hardly recoverable, even if it concerns posterity: and though Froude was often inaccurate, he was given full authority by Carlyle, he had all the unpublished material before him, and he was dead and unable to reply to criticism when the later attacks were made.

1John Aitken Carlyle (1801-1879) finally settled near the Carlyles in Chelsea. He began an English prose version of Dante's *Divine Comedy*—which has earned him the name of "Dante Carlyle"—but only completed the translation of the *Inferno* (1849). The work included a critical edition of the text and a valuable introduction and notes.

CARMAGNOLA, FRANCESCO BUSSONE, COUNT OF (1390-1432), Italian soldier of fortune, was born at Carmagnola near Turin, and began his military career when twelve years old under Facino Cane, a *condottiere* then in the service of Gian Galeazzo Visconti, duke of Milan. On the death of the latter his duchy was divided among his captains, but his son and heir, Filippo Maria, determined to reconquer it by force of arms. Facino Cane being dead, Visconti applied to Carmagnola, then in his thirtieth year, and gave him command of the army. That general's success was astonishingly rapid, and soon the whole duchy was brought once more under Visconti's sway. But Filippo Maria, although he rewarded Carmagnola generously, feared that he might become a danger to himself, and instead of giving him further military commands made him governor of Genoa. Carmagnola

208

felt greatly aggrieved, and failing to obtain a personal interview with the duke, threw up his commission and offered his services to the Venetians (1425). He was well received in Venice, for the republic was beginning to fear the ambitions of the Visconti, and the new doge, Francesco Foscari, was anxious to join the Florentines and go to war with Milan. Carmagnola himself represented the duke's forces as much less numerous than they were supposed to be, and said that the moment was an opportune one to attack him. These arguments, combined with the doge's warlike temper, prevailed; Carmagnola was made captain-general of St Mark in 1426, and war was declared. But while the republic was desirous of rapid and conclusive operations, it was to the interest of Carmagnola, as indeed to all other soldiers of fortune, to make the operations last as long as possible, to avoid decisive operations, and to liberate all prisoners quickly. Consequently the campaign dragged on interminably, some battles were won and others lost, truces and peace treaties were made only to be broken, and no definite result was achieved. Carmagnola's most important success was the battle of Maclodio (1427), but he did not follow it up. The republic, impatient of his dilatoriness, raised his emoluments and promised him immense fiefs including the lordship of Milan, so as to increase his ardour, but in vain. At the same time Carmagnola was perpetually receiving messengers from Visconti, who offered him great rewards if he would abandon the Venetians. The general trifled with his past as with his present employers, believing in his foolish vanity that he held the fate of both in his hand. But the Venetians were dangerous masters to trifle with, and when they at last lost all patience, the Council of Ten determined to bring him to justice. Summoned to Venice to discuss future operations on the 29th of March 1432, he came without suspicion. On his arrival at the ducal palace he was seized, imprisoned and brought to trial for treason against the republic. Although the doge befriended him he was condemned to death and beheaded on the 5th of May. A man of third-rate ability, his great mistake was that he failed to see that he could not do with a solvent and strong government what he could with bankrupt tyrants without military resources, and that the astute Visconti meant to ruin him for his abandonment.

BIBLIOGRAPHY.—The best account of Carmagnola is Horatio Brown's essay in his *Studies in Venetian History* (London, 1907); see also A. Battistella, *Il Conte di Carmagnola* (Genoa, 1889); E. Ricotti, *Storia delle Compagnie di Ventura* (Turin, 1845). Alessandro Manzoni (*q.v.*) made this episode the subject of a poetical drama, *Il Conte di Carmagnola* (1826).

(L. V.*)

CARMAGNOLA, a town of Italy, in the province of Turin, 18 m. by rail S. of Turin. Pop. (1901) 2447 (town), 11,721 (commune). It is the junction where the lines for Savona and Cuneo diverge; it is also connected with Turin by a steam tramway via Carignano. Carmagnola is a place of medieval origin. The town was captured by the French in 1796.

CARMAGNOLE (from Carmagnola, the town in Italy), a word first applied to a Piedmontese peasant costume, well known in the south of France, and brought to Paris by the revolutionaries 355of Marseilles in 1798. It consisted of a short skirted coat with rows of metal buttons, a tricoloured waistcoat and red cap, and became the popular dress of the Jacobins. The name was then given to the famous revolutionary song, composed in 1792, the tune of which, and the wild dance which accompanied it, may have also been brought into France by the Piedmontese. The original first verse began:—

"Monsieur Veto (*i.e.* Louis XVI.) avait promis
D'être fidèle à sa patrie."

and each verse ends with the refrain:—

"Vive le son, vive le son,
Dansons   la Carmagnole,
Vive le son

Du Canon."

The words were constantly altered and added to during the Terror and later; thus the well-known lines,

"Madame Veto avait promis
De faire égorger tout Paris

    .   .   .

On lui coupa la tête," &c.,

were added after the execution of Marie Antoinette. Played in double time the tune was a favourite march in the Revolutionary armies, until it was forbidden by Napoleon, on becoming First Consul.

CARMARTHEN (*Caerfyrddin*), a municipal borough, contributory parliamentary borough (united with Llanelly since 1832), and county town of Carmarthenshire, and a county of itself, finely situated on the right bank of the Towy, which is here tidal and navigable for small craft. Pop. (1901) 10,025. It is the terminal station of a branch of the London & North-Western railway coming southward from Shrewsbury, and is a station on the main line of the Great Western running to Fishguard; it is also the terminus of a branch-line of the Great Western running to Newcastle-Emlyn. The station buildings lie on the left bank of the river, which is here spanned by a fine old stone bridge. There are works for the manufacture of woollens and ropes, also tanneries, but it is as the central market of a large and fertile district that Carmarthen is most important. The weekly Saturday market is well attended, and affords interesting scenes of modern Welsh agricultural life. From the convenient and accessible position of the town, the gaol and lunatic asylum serving for the three south-western counties of Wales—Cardigan, Pembroke and Carmarthen—have been fixed here. Although historically one of the most important towns in South Wales, Carmarthen can boast of very few ancient buildings, and the general aspect of the town is modern. A well-preserved gateway of red sandstone and portions of two towers of the castle are included in the buildings of the present gaol, and the old parish church of St Peter contains some interesting monuments, amongst them being the altar tomb (of the 16th century) of Sir Rhys ap Thomas, K.G., and his wife, which was removed hither for safety at the Reformation from the desecrated church of the neighbouring Priory of St John. Some vestiges of this celebrated monastic house, which formerly owned the famous Welsh MS. known as the "Black Book of Carmarthen," are visible between the present Priory Street and the river. Of the more recent erections in the town, mention may be made of the granite obelisk in memory of General Sir Thomas Picton (1758-1815) and the bronze statue of General Sir William Nott (1784-1846).

Carmarthen is commonly reputed to occupy the site of the Roman station of Maridunum, and its present name is popularly associated with the wizard-statesman Merlin, or Merddyn, whose memory and prophecies are well remembered in these parts of Wales and whose home is popularly believed to have been the conspicuous hill above Abergwili, known as Merlin's Hill. Another derivation of the name is to be found in *Caer-môr-din*, signifying "a fortified place near the sea." In any case, the antiquity of the town is undisputed, and it served as the seat of government for Ystrad Tywi until the year 877, when Prince Cadell of South Wales abandoned Carmarthen for Dinefawr, near Llandilo, probably on account of the maritime raids of the Danes and Saxons. Towards the close of the 11th century a castle was built here by the Normans, and for the next two hundred years town and castle were frequently taken and retaken by Welsh or English. On the annexation of Wales, Edward I. established here his courts of chancery and exchequer and the great sessions for South Wales. Edward III., by the Statute Staple of 1353, declared Carmarthen the sole staple for Wales, ordering that every bale of Welsh wool should be sealed or "cocketed" here before it left the Principality. The earliest charter recorded was granted in 1201 under King John; a charter of James I. in 1604 constituted Carmarthen a county of itself; and under a charter by George III. in 1764, which had been specially petitioned for by the citizens, the two separate jurisdictions of Old and New Carmarthen were fused and henceforth "called by the name of Our Borough of Carmarthen." In 1555 Bishop Farrar of St David's was publicly burned for heresy under Queen Mary at the Market Cross, which was ruthlessly destroyed in 1846 to provide a site for General Nott's statue. In 1646 General Laugharne took and demolished the castle in the name of the parliament, and in 1649 Oliver Cromwell resided at Carmarthen on his way to Ireland. In 1684 the duke of Beaufort with a numerous train made his state entry into Carmarthen as lord-president of Wales and the Marches. With the rise of Llanelly the industrial importance of Carmarthen has tended to decline; but owing to its central position, its close connexion with the bishops of St David's and its historic past the town is still the chief focus of all social, political and ecclesiastical movements in the three counties of Cardigan, Pembroke and Carmarthen. Carmarthen was created a parliamentary borough in 1536.

CARMARTHENSHIRE. (*Sîr Gaerfyrddin*, colloquially known as *Sîr Gâr*), a county of South Wales bounded N. by Cardigan, E. by Brecon and Glamorgan, W. by Pembroke and S. by Carmarthen Bay of the Bristol Channel. The modern county has an area of 918 sq. m., and is therefore the largest in size of the South Welsh counties. Almost the whole of its surface is hilly and irregular, though the coast-line is fringed with extensive stretches of marsh or sandy burrows. Much of the scenery in the county, particularly in the upper valley of the Towy, is exceedingly beautiful and varied. On its eastern borders adjoining Breconshire rises the imposing range of the Black Mountains (*Mynydd Dû*), sometimes called the Carmarthenshire Beacons, where the Carmarthen Van attains an elevation of 2632 ft. Mynydd Mallaen in the wild districts of the north-east corner of the county is 1430 ft. in height, but otherwise few of the numberless rounded hills with which Carmarthenshire is thickly studded exceed 1000 ft. The principal river is the Towy (*Tywi*), which, with its chief tributaries, the Gwili, the Cothi and the Sawdde, drains the central part of the county and enters the Bay at Llanstephan, 9 m. below Carmarthen. Coracles are frequently to be observed on this river, as well as on the Teifi, which separates Carmarthenshire from Cardiganshire on the north. Other streams are the Tâf, which flows through the south-western portion of the county and reaches the sea at Laugharne; the Gwendraeth, with its mouth at Kidwelly; and the Loughor, or Llwchwr, which rises in the Black Mountains and forms for several miles the boundary between the counties of Carmarthen and Glamorgan until it falls into Carmarthen Bay at Loughor. All these rivers contain salmon, sewin (*gleisiad*) and trout in fair numbers, and are consequently frequented by anglers. With the exception of the Van Pool in the Black Mountains the lakes of the county are inconsiderable in size.

Geology.—The oldest rocks in Carmarthenshire come to the surface in the Vale of Towy at Llanarthney and near Carmarthen; they consist of black shales of Tremadoc (Cambrian) age, and are succeeded by conglomerates, sandstones and shales, with beds of volcanic ash and lava, of Arenig (Ordovician) age, which have been brought up along a belt of intense folding and faulting which follows the Towy from Llangadock to Carmarthen and extends westwards to the edge of the county at Whitland. The Llandeilo shales, flags and limestones and occasional volcanic ashes, which follow, are well developed at Llangadock and Llandeilo and near Carmarthen, and are famed for their trilobites, *Asaphus tyrannus* and *Ogygia Buchi*. Shales and mudstones and impersistent limestones of Bala age come next in order, and, bounding the Vale of Towy on the north, extend as a narrow belt north-westwards towards the Presley hills. Except for the foregoing deposits the great area between the Teifi and the Towy, of which little is known, is made up of a monotonous succession of greatly folded slates and shales with interbedded conglomerates and sandstones which give rise to scarps, ridges and moorlands; they appear to be of Llandovery age.

South of the Towy a narrow belt of steeply dipping and even inverted Silurian sandstones and mudstones (Upper Llandovery, Wenlock and Ludlow) extends south-westwards from Llandovery to Llanarthney, where they disappear under the Old Red Sandstone. This formation, which consists of red marls and sandstones with occasional thin impure limestones (cornstones), extends from near Llandovery to beyond Carmarthen Bay; its upper conglomeratic beds cap the escarpment of the Black Mountains (2460 ft.) on the south-eastern borders of the county. To the south the scarps and moorlands of the

Carboniferous Limestone and Millstone Grit form the north-western rim of the South Wales coalfield. The rest of the county is occupied by the rich Coal-Measures of the Gwendraeth Valley and Llanelly districts. All the rocks in the county are affected by powerful folds and faults. Glacial deposits are plentiful in the valleys south of the Towy, striae abound on the Millstone Grit and show that the ice-sheet rose far up the slopes of the Black Mountains. Coal is the chief mineral, the iron-ore is no longer worked; the Carboniferous Limestone is burnt at Llandybie; fire-bricks are manufactured from the Millstone Grit, and a few lead-veins are found in the Ordovician rocks.

Industries.—The climate is mild, except in the upland regions, but the annual rainfall is very heavy. With the exception of its south-eastern portion, which forms part of the great South Welsh coalfield, Carmarthenshire may be considered wholly as an agricultural county. The attention of the farmers is devoted to stock-raising and dairy-farming rather than to the growth of cereals, whilst the large tracts of unenclosed hill-country form good pastures for sheep and ponies. The soil varies much, but in the lower valleys of the Towy and Tâf it is exceedingly fertile. Outside agriculture the gathering of cockles at the estuaries of the Towy and Tâf gives employment to a large number of persons, principally women; Ferryside and Laugharne being the chief centres of the cockling industry. The local textile factories at Pencader, Penboyr, Llangeler, and in the valley of the Loughor are of some importance. Gold has been found near Caio in the Cothi valley, but the yield is trifling. There are lead-mines in various places, but none of great value. The really important industries are restricted to the populous south-eastern district, where coal-mining, iron-founding and the smelting of tin and copper are carried on extensively at Llanelly, Pembrey, Tirydail, Garnant, Pontardulais, Ammanford and other centres.

Communications.—The Great Western railway traverses the lower part of the county, whilst a branch of the London & North-Western enters it at its extreme north-eastern point by a tunnel under the Sugar Loaf Mountain, and has its terminal station at Carmarthen. A branch line of the Great Western connects Llanelly with Llandilo by way of Ammanford, and another branch of the same railway runs northward from Carmarthen to Newcastle-Emlyn on the Teifi, joining the Aberystwyth branch, formerly the Manchester & Milford line, at Pencader.

Population and Administration.—The area of the county is 587,816 acres, and the population in 1891 was 130,566 and in 1901 it was 135,325. The municipal boroughs are Carmarthen (pop. 9935), Kidwelly (2285) and Llandovery (1809). Urban districts are Ammanford, Llanelly, Burry Port, Llandilo and Newcastle-Emlyn. The principal towns are Carmarthen, Llanelly (25,617), Llandilo or Llandeilo Fawr (1934), Llangadock (1578), Llandovery, Kidwelly, Pembrey (7513) and Laugharne (1439). The county is in the South Wales circuit, and assizes are held at Carmarthen. The borough of Carmarthen has a commission of the peace and separate quarter sessions. The county is divided into two parliamentary divisions, the eastern and western, and it also includes the united boroughs of Carmarthen and Llanelly, thus returning three members in all to parliament. The ancient county, which contains 75 parishes and part of another, is wholly in the diocese of St David's.

History.—Carmarthenshire originally formed part of the lands of the Dimetae conquered by the Romans, who constructed military roads and built on the Via Julia the important station of Maridunum upon or near the site of the present county town. After the retirement of the Roman forces this fortified town became known in course of time as Caerfyrddin, anglicized into Carmarthen, which subsequently gave its name to the county. During the 5th and 6th centuries Carmarthenshire, or Ystrad Tywi, was the scene of the labours of many Celtic missionaries, notably of St David and St Teilo, who brought the arts of civilization as well as the doctrines of Christianity to its rude inhabitants. In the 9th century the whole of Ystrad Tywi was annexed to the kingdom of Roderick the Great (*Rhodri Mawr*), who at his death in 877 bequeathed the principality of South Wales to his son, Cadell. The royal residence of the South Welsh princes was now fixed at Dynevor (*Dinefawr*) on the Towy near Llandilo. Cadell's son, Howell the Good (*Hywel Dda*), was the first to codify the ancient laws of Wales at his palace of Ty Gwyn Ar Dâf, the White Lodge on the banks of the Tâf, near the modern Whitland. In 1080, during the troubled reign of Rhys ap Tudor, the

Normans first appeared on the shores of Carmarthen Bay, and before the end of King Henry I.'s reign had constructed the great castles of Kidwelly, Carmarthen, Laugharne and Llanstephan near the coast. From this period until the death of Prince Llewelyn (1282) the history of Carmarthenshire is national rather than local. By the Statutes of Rhuddlan (1284) Edward I. formed the counties of Cardigan and Carmarthen out of the districts of Ceredigion and Ystrad Tywi, the ancient possessions of the house of Dinefawr, which were now formally annexed to the English crown. Nearly a third of the present county, however, still remained under the jurisdiction of the Lords Marchers, and it was not until the Act 27 Henry VIII. that these districts, including the commots of Kidwelly, Iscennen and Carnwillion, were added to Edward I.'s original shire. The prosperity of the new county increased considerably under Edward III., who named Carmarthen the chief staple-town in Wales for the wool trade. The revolt of Owen Glendower had the effect of disturbing the peace of the county for a time, and the French army, landed at Milford on his behalf, was warmly received by the people of Carmarthenshire. In the summer of 1485 Sir Rhys ap Thomas, of Abermarlais and Dinefawr, marched through the county collecting recruits for Henry of Richmond, for which service he was created a knight of the Garter and made governor of all Wales. At the Reformation the removal of the episcopal residence from distant St David's to Abergwili, a village barely two miles from Carmarthen, brought the county into close touch with the chief Welsh diocese, and the new palace at Abergwili will always be associated with the first Welsh translations of the New Testament and the Prayer Book, made by Bishop Richard Davies (1500-1581) and his friend William Salesbury, of Llanrwst (16th century). In the early part of the 17th century the county witnessed the first religious revival recorded in Welsh annals, that led by Rhys Prichard (d. 1644), the Puritan vicar of Llandovery, whose poetical works, the *Canwyll y Cymry* ("the Welshman's Candle") are still studied in the principality. At the time of the Civil Wars, Richard Vaughan, earl of Carbery, the patron of Jeremy Taylor, was in command of the royal fortresses and troops, but made a very feeble and half-hearted resistance against the parliamentarian forces. During the following century the great Welsh spiritual and educational movement, which later spread over all Wales, had its origin in the quiet and remote parish of Llanddowror, near Laugharne, where the vicar, the celebrated and pious Griffith Jones (1684-1761), had become the founder of the Welsh circulating charity schools. Other prominent members of this important Methodist revival, likewise natives of Carmarthenshire, were William Williams of Pantycelyn, the well-known hymn-writer (1716-1791), and Peter Williams, the Welsh Bible commentator (1722-1796). The county was deeply implicated in the Rebecca Riots of 1842-1843.

Foremost amongst the county families of Carmarthenshire is Rhys, or Rice, of Dynevor Castle, near Llandilo, a modern castellated house standing in a beautiful park which contains the historic ruin of the old Dinefawr fortress. The present Lord Dynevor, the direct lineal descendant of the princes of South Wales, is the head of this family. Almost opposite Dynevor 357Castle (formerly known as Newtown), on the left bank of the Towy, stands Golden Grove (*Gelli Aur*), once the seat of the Vaughans, earls of Carbery, whose senior line and titles became extinct early in the 18th century. The famous old mansion has been replaced by a modern Gothic structure, and is now the property of Earl Cawdor. Golden Grove contains the "Hirlas Horn," the gift of King Henry VII. to Dafydd ap Evan of Llwyndafydd, Cardiganshire, perhaps the most celebrated of Welsh historical relics. Other families of importance, extinct or existing, are Johnes, formerly of Abermarlais and now of Dolaucothi; Williams (now Drummond) of Edwinsford; Lloyd of Forest; Lloyd of Glansevin; Stepney of Llanelly and Gwynne of Taliaris.

Antiquities.—Carmarthenshire contains few memorials of the Roman occupation, but it possesses various camps and tumuli of the British period, and also a small but perfect cromlech near Llanglydwen on the banks of the Tâf. Of its many medieval castles the most important still in existence are: Kidwelly; Laugharne; Llanstephan, a fine pile of the 12th century on a hill at the mouth of the Towy; Carreg Cennen, an imposing Norman fortress crowning a cliff not far from Llandilo; and Dynevor Castle, the ancient seat of Welsh royalty, situated on a bold wooded height above the Towy. The remains of the castles at Carmarthen, Drysllwyn, Llandovery and Newcastle-Emlyn are inconsiderable. Of the monastic houses Talley Abbey (Tal-y-Llychau, a name drawn from the two small lakes in the neighbourhood of its site) was founded by Rhys ap Griffith, prince of South Wales, towards the close of the 12th century for Benedictine monks; Whitland, or Albalanda, also a Benedictine house, was probably founded by Bishop Bernard of St David's early in the 12th century, on a site long associated with Welsh monastic life; and the celebrated Augustinian Priory of St John at Carmarthen was likewise established in the 12th century. Very slight traces of these three important religious houses now exist. The parish churches of Carmarthenshire are for the most part small and of no special architectural value. Of the more noteworthy mention may be made of St Peter's at Carmarthen, and of the parish churches at Laugharne, Kidwelly, Llangadock, Abergwili and Llangathen, the last named of which contains a fine monument to Bishop Anthony Rudd (d. 1615). Many of these churches are distinguished by tall massive western towers, usually of the 12th or 13th centuries. Besides Golden Grove and Dynevor the county contains some fine historic houses, prominent amongst which are Abergwili Palace, the official residence of the bishops of St David's since the Reformation, burnt down in 1902, but rebuilt on the old lines; Aberglasney, a mansion near Llangathen, erected by Bishop Rudd and once inhabited by the poet John Dyer (1700-1758); Court Henry, an ancient seat of the Herbert family; and Abermarlais, once the property of Sir Rhys ap Thomas.

Customs, &c.—The old Welsh costume, folklore and customs have survived longer in Carmarthenshire than perhaps in any other county of Wales. The steeple-crowned beaver hat, now practically extinct, was often to be seen in the neighbourhood of Carmarthen as late as 1890, and the older women often affect the *pais-a-gŵn bâch*, the frilled mob-cap and the small plaid shawl of a previous generation. Curious instances of old Welsh superstitions are to be found amongst the peasantry of the more remote districts, particularly in the lovely country in the valleys of the Towy and Teifi, where belief in fairies, fairy-rings, goblins and "corpse-candles" still lingers. The curious mumming, known as "Mari Lwyd" (Blessed Mary), in which one of the performers wears a horse's skull decked with coloured ribbands, was prevalent round Carmarthen as late as 1885. At many parish churches the ancient service of the "Pylgain" (a name said to be a corruption of the Latin *pulli cantus*) is held at daybreak or cock-crow on Christmas morning. A species of general catechism, known as *pwnc*, is also common in the churches and Nonconformist chapels. The old custom of receiving New Year's gifts of bread and cheese, or meal and money (*calenig*), still flourishes in the rural parishes. The "bidding" before marriage (as in Cardiganshire) was formerly universal and is not yet altogether discontinued, and bidding papers were printed at Llandilo as late as 1900. The horse weddings (*priodas ceffylau*) were indulged in by the farmer class in the neighbourhood of Abergwili as late as 1880.

AUTHORITIES.—T. Nicholas, *Annals and Antiquities of the Counties of Wales* (London, 1872); W. Spurrell, *Carmarthen and its Neighbourhood*(Carmarthen, 1879); J.B.D. Tyssen and Alcwyn C. Evans, *Royal Charters, &c., relating to the Town and County of Carmarthen* (Carmarthen, 1878).

CARMATHIANS (QARMATHIANS, KARMATHIANS), a Mahommedan sect named after Hamdān Qarmat, who accepted the teaching of the Isma'īlites (see MAHOMMEDAN RELIGION: *Sects*) from Ḥosain ul-Ahwāzī, a missionary of Ahmed, son of the Persian Abdallah ibn Maimūn, toward the close of the 9th century. This was in the Sawād of Irak, which was inhabited by a people little attached to Islam. The object of Abdallah ibn Maimūn had been to undermine Islam and the Arabian power by a secret society with various degrees, which offered inducements to all classes and creeds and led men on from an interpretation of Islam to a total rejection of its teaching and a strict personal submission to the head of the society. For the political history of the Carmathians, their conquests and their decay, see ARABIA: *History*; CALIPHATE (sect. C. §§ 16, 17, 18, 23); and EGYPT: *History* (Mahommedan period).

In their religious teaching they claimed to be Shi'ites; *i.e.* they asserted that the imamate belonged by right to the descendants of Ali. Further, they were of the Isma'īlite branch of these, *i.e.* they acknowledged the claim to the imamate of Isma'īl the eldest son of the sixth imam. The claim of Isma'īl had been passed over by his father and many Shi'ites because he had been guilty of drinking wine. The Isma'īlites said that as the imam could do no wrong, his action only showed that wine-drinking was not sinful. Abdallah taught that from the creation of man there had always been an imam sometimes known, sometimes hidden. Isma'īl was the last known; a new one was to be looked for. But while the imam was hidden, his doctrines were to be taught by his missionaries (dā'īs). Hamdān Qarmat was one of these, Ahmed ibn Abdallah being nominally the chief. The adherents of this party were initiated by degrees into the secrets of its doctrines and were divided into seven (afterwards nine) classes. In the first stage the convert was taught the existence of mystery in the Koran and made to feel the necessity of a teacher who could explain it. He took an oath of complete submission and paid a sum of money. In the second stage the earlier teachers of Islam were shown to be wrong in doctrine and the imams alone were proved to be infallible. In the third it was taught that there were only seven imams and that the other sects of the Shi'ites were in error. In the fourth the disciple learnt that each of the seven imams had a prophet, who was to be obeyed in all things. The prophet of the last imam was Abdallah. The doctrine of Islam was that Mahomet was the last of the prophets. In the fifth stage the uselessness of tradition and the temporary nature of the precepts and practices of Mahomet were taught, while in the sixth the believer was induced to give up these practices (prayer, fasting, pilgrimage, &c.). At this point the Carmathian had completely ceased to be a Moslem. In the remaining degrees there was more liberty of opinion allowed and much variety of belief and teaching existed.

The last contemporary mention of the Carmathians is that of Nāsir ibn Khosrau, who visited them in A.D. 1050. In Arabia they ceased to exercise influence. In Persia and Syria their work was taken up by the Assassins (q.v.). Their doctrines are said, however, to exist still in parts of Syria, Persia, Arabia and India, and to be still propagated in Zanzibar.

See *Journal asiatique* (1877), vol. i. pp. 377-386.

(G. W. T.)

CARMAUX, a town of southern France, in the department of Tarn, on the left bank of the Cérou, 10 m. N. of Albi by rail. Pop. (1906) 8618. The town gives its name to an important coal-basin, and carries on the manufacture of glass.

CARMEL, the mountain promontory by which the seacoast of Palestine is interrupted south of the Bay of Acre, 32° 50' N., 35° E. It continues as a ridge of oolitic limestone, broken by ravines and honeycombed by caves, running for about 20 m. in a south-easterly direction, and finally joining the mountains of Samaria. Its maximum height is at 'Esfia, 1760 ft. It was included in the territory of the tribe of Asher. No great political event is recorded in connexion with it; it appears throughout the Old Testament "either as a symbol or as a sanctuary"; its name means "garden-land." Its fruitfulness is referred to by Isaiah and by Amos; Micah describes it as wooded, to which was no doubt due its value as a hiding-place (Amos ix. 3). It is now wild, only a few patches being cultivated; most of the mountain is covered with a thick brushwood of evergreens, oaks, myrtles, pines, &c., which is gradually being cleared away. That the cultivation was once much more extensive is indicated by the large number of rock-hewn wine and olive presses. Vines and olives are now found at 'Esfia only. The outstanding position of Carmel, its solitariness, its visibility over a wide area of country, and its fertility, marked it out as a suitable place for a sanctuary from very ancient times. It is possibly referred to in the Palestine lists of Thothmes III. as *Rosh Kodsu*, "the holy headland." An altar of Jehovah existed here from early times; it was destroyed when the Phoenician Baal claimed the country under Jezebel, and repaired by Elijah (1 Kings xviii. 30) before the great sacrifice which decided the claims of the contending deities. The traditional site of this sacrifice is at *El-Muhraka*, at the eastern end of the ridge. The Druses still visit this site, where is a dilapidated structure of stones, as a holy place for sacrifice. On the bank of the Kishon below is a mound known as *Tell el-Kusīs*, "the Priest's mound," but the connexion that has been sought between this name and the slaughter of the priests of Baal is hardly justifiable. Other sites on the hill are traditionally connected with Elijah, and some melon-like fossils are explained as being fruits refused to him by its owner, who was punished by having them turned to stone. Elisha was stationed here for a time. Tacitus describes the hill as the site of an oracle, which Vespasian consulted. Iamblichus in his life of Pythagoras speaks of it as a place of great sanctity forbidden to the vulgar. A grove of trees, called the "Trees of the Forty" [Martyrs], still remains, no doubt in former times a sacred grove. So early as the 4th century Christian hermits began to settle here, and in 1207 the Carmelite order was organized. The monastery, founded at the fountain of Elijah in 1209, has had many vicissitudes: the monks were slaughtered or driven to Europe in 1238 and the building decayed; it was visited and refounded by St Louis in 1252; again despoiled in 1291; once more rebuilt in 1631, and, in 1635 (when the monks were massacred), sacked and turned into a mosque. Once more the monks established themselves, only to be murdered after Napoleon's retreat in 1799. The church and the monastery were entirely destroyed in 1821 by 'Abd Allah, pasha of Acre, on the plea that the monks would favour the revolting Greeks; but it was shortly afterwards rebuilt by order from the Porte, partly at 'Abd Allah's expense and partly by contributions raised in Europe, Asia and Africa by Brother Giovanni Battista of Frascati. The villages with which the mountain was once covered have been to a large extent depopulated by the Druses.

(R. A. S. M.)

CARMELITES, in England called White Friars (from the white mantle over a brown habit), one of the four mendicant orders. The stories concerning the origin of this order, seriously put forward and believed in the 17th and 18th centuries, are one of the curiosities of history. It was asserted that Elias established a community of hermits on Mount Carmel, and that this community existed without break until the Christian era and was nothing else than a Jewish Carmelite order, to which belonged the Sons of the Prophets and the Essenes. Members of it were present at St Peter's first sermon on Pentecost and were converted, and built a chapel on Mount Carmel in honour of the Blessed Virgin Mary, who, as well as the apostles, enrolled herself in the order. In 1668 the Bollandist Daniel Papenbroek (1628-1714), in the March volumes of the *Acta Sanctorum*, rejected these stories as fables. A controversy arose and the Carmelites had recourse to the Inquisition. In Spain they succeeded in getting the offending volumes of the *Acta* censured, but in Rome they were less successful, and so hot did the controversy become that in 1698 a decree was issued imposing silence upon both parties, until a formal decision should be promulgated—which has not yet been done.

The historical origin of the Carmelites must be placed at the middle of the 12th century, when a crusader from Calabria, named Berthold, and ten companions established themselves as hermits near the cave of Elias on Mount Carmel. A Greek monk, Phocas, who visited the Holy Land in 1185, gives an account of them, and says that the ruins of an ancient building existed on Mount Carmel; but though it is likely enough that there had previously been Christian monks and hermits on the spot, it is impossible to place the beginning of the Carmelite institute before Berthold. About 1210 the hermits on Carmel received from Albert, Latin patriarch of Jerusalem, a rule comprising sixteen articles. This was the primitive Carmelite rule. The life prescribed was strictly eremitical: the monks were to live in separate cells or huts, devoted to prayer and work; they met only in the oratory for the liturgical services, and were to live a life of great silence, seclusion, abstinence and austerity. This rule received papal approbation in 1226. Soon, however, the losses of the Christian arms in Palestine made Carmel an unsafe place of residence for western hermits, and so, c. 1240, they migrated first to Cyprus and thence to Sicily, France and England. In England the first establishment was at Alnwick and the second at Aylesford, where the first general chapter of the order was held in 1247, and St Simon Stock, an English anchorite who had joined the order, was elected general. During his generalate the institute was adapted to the conditions of the western lands to which it had been transplanted, and for this purpose the original rule had to be in many ways altered: the austerities were mitigated, and the life was turned from eremitical into cenobitical, but on the mendicant rather than the monastic model. The polity and government were also organized on the same lines, and the Carmelites were turned into mendicants and became one of the four great orders of Mendicant Friars, in England distinguished as the "White Friars" from the white mantle worn over the dark brown habit. This change was made and the new rule approved in 1247, and under this form the Carmelites spread all over western Europe and became exceedingly popular, as an order closely analogous to the Dominicans and Franciscans. In the course of time, further relaxations of the rule were introduced, and during the Great Schism the Carmelites were divided between the two papal obediences, rival generals being elected,—a state of things that caused still further relaxations. To cope with existing evils Eugenius IV. approved in 1431 of a rule notably milder than that of 1247, but many houses clung to the earlier rule; thus arose among the Carmelites the same division into "observants" and "conventuals" that wrought such mischief among the Franciscans. During the 15th and 16th centuries various attempts at reform arose, as among other orders, and resulted in the formation of semi-independent congregations owing a titular obedience to the general of the order. The Carmelite friars seem to have flourished especially in England, where at the dissolution of the monasteries there were some 40 friaries. (See F.A. Gasquet, *English Monastic Life*, table and maps; *Catholic Dictionary*, art. "Carmelites.") There were no Carmelite nunneries in England, and indeed until the middle of the 15th century there were no nuns at all anywhere in the order.

Of all movements in the Carmelite order by far the most important and far-reaching in its results has been the reform initiated by St Teresa. After nearly thirty years passed in a Carmelite convent in Avila under the mitigated rule of 1431, she founded in the same city a small convent wherein a rule stricter than that of 1247 was to be observed. This was in 1562. In spite of opposition and difficulties of all kinds, she succeeded in establishing a number, not only of nunneries, but (with the co-operation of St John of the Cross, *q.v.*) also of friaries of the strict observance; so that at her death in 1582 there were of the reform 15 monasteries of men and 17 of women, all in Spain. The interesting and dramatic story of the movement should be sought for in the biographies of the two protagonists; as also 359an account of the school of mystical theology founded by them, without doubt the chief contribution made by the Carmelites to religion (see MYSTICISM). Here it must suffice to say that the idea of the reform was to go behind the settlement of 1247 and to restore and emphasize the purely contemplative character of primitive Carmelite life: indeed provision was made for the reproduction, for such as desired it, of the eremitical life led by Berthold and his companions. St Teresa's additions to the rule of 1247 made the life one of extreme bodily austerity and of prolonged prayer for all, two hours of private prayer daily, in addition to the choral canonical office, being enjoined. From the fact that those of the reform wore sandals in place of shoes and stockings, they have come to be called the Discalced, or bare-footed, Carmelites, also Teresians, in distinction to the Calced or older branch of the order. In 1580 the reformed monasteries were made a separate province under the general of the order, and in 1593 this province was made by papal act an independent order with its own general and government, so that there are now two distinct orders of Carmelites. The Discalced Carmelites spread rapidly all over Catholic Europe, and then to Spanish America and the East, especially India and Persia, in which lands they have carried on to this day extensive missionary undertakings. Both observances suffered severely from the various revolutions, but they both still exist, the Discalced being by far the most numerous and thriving. There are in all some 2000 Carmelite friars, and the nuns are much more numerous. In England and Ireland there are houses, both of men and of women, belonging to each observance.

AUTHORITIES.—A full account is given by Helyot, *Hist, des ordres religieux* (1792), i. cc. 40-52; shorter accounts, continued to the end of the 19th century and giving references to all literature old and new, may be found in Max Heimbucher, *Orden u. Kongregationen* (1897), ii. §§ 92-96; Wetzer u. Welte, *Kirchenlexicon* (ed. 2), art. "Carmelitenorden"; Herzog-Hauck, *Realencyklopädie* (ed. 3), art. "Karmeliter." The story of St Teresa's reform will be found in lives of St Teresa and in her writings, especially the *Foundations*. Special reference may be made to the works of Zimmerman, a Carmelite friar, *Carmel in England* (1899), and *Monumenta historica Carmelitana*, i. (1905 foll.).

(E. C. B.)

CARMICHAEL, GERSHOM (c. 1672-1729), Scottish philosopher, was born probably in London, the son of a Presbyterian minister who had been banished by the Scottish privy council for his religious opinions. He graduated at Edinburgh University in 1691, and became a regent at St Andrews. In 1694 he was elected a master in the university of Glasgow—an office that was converted into the professorship of moral philosophy in 1727, when the system of masters was abolished at Glasgow. Sir William Hamilton regarded him as "the real founder of the Scottish school of philosophy." He wrote *Bremuscula Introductio ad Logicam*, a treatise on logic and the psychology of the intellectual powers;*Synopsis Theologiae Naturalis*; and an edition of Pufendorf, *De Officio Hominis et Civis*, with notes and supplements of high value. His son Frederick was the author of *Sermons on Several Important Subjects* and *Sermons on Christian Zeal*, both published in 1753.

CARMINE, a pigment of a bright red colour obtained from cochineal (*q.v.*). It may be prepared by exhausting cochineal with boiling water and then treating the clear solution with alum, cream of tartar, stannous chloride, or acid oxalate of potassium; the colouring and animal matters present in the liquid are thus precipitated. Other methods are in use; sometimes white of egg, fish glue, or gelatine are added before the precipitation. The quality of carmine is affected by the temperature and the degree of illumination during its preparation—sunlight being requisite for the production of a brilliant hue. It differs also according to the amount of alumina present in it. It is sometimes adulterated with cinnabar, starch and other materials; from these the carmine can be separated by dissolving it in ammonia. Good carmine should crumble readily between the fingers when dry. Chemically, carmine is a compound of carminic acid with alumina, lime and some organic acid. Carmine is used in the manufacture of artificial flowers, water-colours, rouge, cosmetics and crimson ink, and in the painting of miniatures. "Carmine lake" is a pigment obtained by adding freshly precipitated alumina to decoction of cochineal.

CARMONA, a town of south-western Spain, in the province of Seville; 27 m. N.E. of Seville by rail. Pop. (1900) 17,215. Carmona is built on a ridge overlooking the central plain of Andalusia, from the Sierra Morena, on the north, to the peak of San Cristobal, on the south. It has a thriving trade in wine, olive oil, grain and cattle; and the annual fair, which is held in April, affords good opportunity of observing the costumes and customs of southern Spain. The citadel of Carmona, now in ruins, was formerly the principal fortress of Peter the Cruel (1350-1369), and contained a spacious palace within its defences. The principal entrance to the town is an old Moorish gateway; and the gate on the road to Cordova is partly of Roman construction. Portions of the ancient college of San Teodomir are of Moorish architecture, and the tower of the church of San Pedro is an imitation of the Giralda at Seville.

In 1881 a large Roman necropolis was discovered close to the town, beside the Seville road. It contains many rock-hewn sepulchral chambers, with niches for the cinerary urns, and occasionally with vestibules containing stone seats (*triclinia*). In 1881 an amphitheatre, and another group of tombs, all belonging to the first four centuries A.D., were disinterred near the original necropolis, and a small museum, maintained by the Carmona archaeological society, is filled with the mosaics, inscriptions, portrait-heads and other antiquities found here.

Carmona, the Roman *Carmo*, was the strongest city of Further Spain in the time of Julius Caesar (100-44 B.C.), and its strength was greatly increased by the Moors, who surrounded it with a wall and ornamented it with fountains and palaces. In 1247 Ferdinand III. of Castile took the city, and bestowed on it the motto *Sicut Lucifer lucet in Aurora, sic in Wandalia Carmona* ("As the Morning-star shines in the Dawn, so shines Carmona in Andalusia").

For an account of the antiquities of Carmona, see *Estudios arqueologicos e historicos*, by M. Sales y Ferré (Madrid, 1887).

CARNAC, a village of north-western France, in the department of Morbihan and arrondissement of Lorient, 9 m. S.S.W. of Auray by road. Pop. (1906) 667, Carnac has a handsome church in the Renaissance style of Brittany, but it owes its celebrity to the stone monuments in its vicinity, which are among the most extensive and interesting of their kind (see STONE MONUMENTS). The most remarkable consist of long avenues of menhirs or standing stones; but there is also a profusion of other erections, such as dolmens and barrows, throughout the whole district. About half a mile to the north-west of the village is the Menec system, which consists of eleven lines, numbers 874 menhirs, and extends a distance of 3376 ft. The terminal circle, whose longest diameter is 300 ft., is somewhat difficult to make out, as it is broken by the houses and gardens of a little hamlet. To the east-north-east there is another system at Kermario (Place of the Dead), which consists of 855 stones, many of them of great size—some, for example, 18 ft. in height —arranged in ten lines and extending about 4000 ft. in length. Still further in the same direction is a third system at Kerlescan (Place of Burning), composed of 262 stones, which are distributed into thirteen lines, terminated by an irregular circle, and altogether extend over a distance of 1000 ft. or more. These three systems seem once to have formed a continuous series; the menhirs, many of which have been broken up for road-mending and other purposes, have diminished in number by some thousands in modern times. The alignment of Kermario points to the dolmen of Kercado (Place of St Cado), where there is also a barrow, explored in 1863; and to the south-east of Menec stands the great tumulus of Mont St Michel, which measures 377 ft. in length, and has a height of 65 ft. The tumulus, which is crowned with a chapel, was excavated by René Galles in 1862; and the contents of the sepulchral chamber, which include several jade and fibrolite axes, are preserved in the museum at Vannes. About a mile east of the village is a small piece of moorland called the Bossenno, from the *bocenieu* or mounds with which it is covered; and here, in 1874, the explorations of 360James Miln, a Scottish antiquary, brought to light the remains of a Gallo-Roman town. The tradition of Carnac is that there was once a convent of the Templars or Red Cross Knights on the spot; but this, it seems, is not supported by history. Similar traces were also discovered at Mane Bras, a height about 3 m. to the east. The rocks of which these various monuments are composed is the ordinary granite of the district, and most of them present a strange appearance from their coating of white lichens. Carnac has an interesting museum of antiquities.

See W.C. Lukis, *Guide to the Principal Chambered Barrows and other Prehistoric Monuments in the Islands of the Morbihan, &c.* (Ripon, 1875); René Galles, *Fouilles du Mont Saint Michel en Carnac* (Vannes, 1864); A. Fouquet, *Des monuments celtiques et des ruines romaines dans le Morbihan*(Vannes, 1853); James Miln, *Archaeological Researches at Carnac in Brittany: Kermario* (Edinburgh, 1881); and *Excavations at Carnac: The Bossenno and the Mont St Michel* (Edinburgh, 1877).

CARNARVON, EARLDOM OF. The earldom of Carnarvon was created in 1628 for Robert Dormer, Baron Dormer of Wyng (c. 1610-1643), who was killed at the first battle of Newbury whilst fighting for Charles I., and it became extinct on the death of his son Charles, the 2nd earl, in 1709. From 1714 to 1789 it was held by the family of Brydges, dukes of Chandos and marquesses of Carnarvon, and in 1793 Henry Herbert, Baron Porchester (1741-1811), was created earl of Carnarvon.

His great-grandson, HENRY HOWARD MOLYNEUX HERBERT, 4th earl of Carnarvon (1831-1890), was born on the 24th of June 1831. He succeeded to the title in 1849, on the death of his father, Henry John George, the 3rd earl (1800-1849). Soon after taking his degree at Oxford he began to play a prominent part in the deliberations of the House of Lords. In 1858 he was under secretary for the colonies, and in 1866 secretary of state. In this capacity he introduced in 1867 the bill for the federation of the British North American provinces which set so many political problems at rest; but he had not the privilege of passing it, having, before the measure became law, resigned, owing to his distaste for Disraeli's Reform Bill. Resuming office in 1874, he endeavoured to confer a similar boon on South Africa, but the times were not ripe. In 1878 he again resigned, out of opposition to Lord Beaconsfield's policy on the Eastern question; but on his party's return to power in 1885 he became lord-lieutenant of Ireland. His short period of office, memorable for a conflict on a question of personal veracity between himself and Mr Parnell as to his negotiations with the latter in respect of Home Rule, was terminated by another premature resignation. He never returned to office, and died on the 29th of June 1890. As a statesman his career was marred by extreme sensitiveness; but he was beloved as a man of worth and admired as a man of culture. He was high steward of the university of Oxford, and president of the Society of Antiquaries. The 4th earl was succeeded by his son, George Edward Stanhope Molyneux (b. 1866).

CARNARVON, a market town and municipal borough, and the county town of Carnarvonshire, north Wales, 68½ m. W. of Chester by the London & North-Western railway. Pop. (1901) 9760. It stands very nearly on the site of Caer Seint, capital of the Segontiaci, and was fortified in 1098 by Hugh Lupus, earl of Chester, after Roman occupation, a fort, baths and villa, with coins and pottery, having been exhumed here. As the castle was begun only in 1284, Edward II., supposed to have been born in its Eagle Tower on the extreme west, can only have been born outside. The castle is an irregular oblong building on the west of the town, surrounded by walls and having thirteen polygonal towers. There is still much of the town wall extant. The parish church (Llanbeblig) is some half-mile out of the town, the institutions of which include a town and county hall, a training college, and a gaol for Anglesey and Carnarvonshire jointly. Manufactures in the town are scanty, but Llanberis and Llanllyfni export hence slates, "sets" and copper ore. A steam ferry unites Carnarvon and Tan y foel, Anglesey, while a summer service of steamers runs to Menai Bridge, Bardsey, &c. The borough forms part of a district returning a member to parliament since 1536. To this district the Reform Act added Bangor. The county quarter sessions and assizes are held in the town, which has a separate commission of the peace, but no separate court of quarter sessions. Three weekly Welsh (besides English) newspapers are published here.

CARNARVONSHIRE (Welsh *Caer'narfon*, for *Caer yn Arfon*), a county of north Wales, bounded N. by the Irish Sea, E. by the county of Denbigh, S.E. by Merioneth, S. by Tremadoc and Cardigan Bays, S.W. by Carnarvon Bay, W. by the Menai Straits (separating the county from Anglesey), and N.W. by Conway Bay. Area, 565 sq. m. There is, owing to the changed bed of the Conwy stream, a small detached part of the county on the north coast of Denbighshire, stretching inland for some 2½ m. between Old Colwyn and Llandulas. About half the whole length of the county is a peninsula, Lleyn, running south-west into the Irish Sea, and forming Cardigan Bay on the south and Carnarvon Bay on the north. The county is rich in minerals, *e.g.* lead, copper, some gold. Its slate quarries are many and good. Its mountains include the highest in England and Wales, the summit of Snowdon (Wyddfa or Eryri) being 3560 ft. The principal mountains occupy the middle of the county and include Carnedd Llewelyn (3484 ft.), Carnedd Dafydd (3426), Glydyr Fawr (3279) and Glydyr Fach (3262), Elidr Fawr (3029), Moel Siabod (2860), Moel Hebog or Hebawg (2566). The valleys vary from the wildness of Pont Aberglaslyn gorge to the quiet of Nant Gwynnant. Those of Beddgelert and Llanberis—at the south and north base of Snowdon respectively—are famous, while that of the Conwy, from Llanrwst to Conway (Conwy), is well set off by the background of Snowdonia.

The largest stream is the Conwy, tidal and navigable for some 12 m. from Deganwy; this rises in Llyn Conwy, in the south-east, divides Carnarvon from Denbigh (running nearly due north) for some 30 m., and falls into the sea at Deganwy. The Seint (wrongly spelled Seiont) is a small stream rising in Snowdon and falling into the sea at Carnarvon, to which it gave its old name Segontium (Kaer Seint yn Arvon in the *Mabinogion*). The Swallow Falls are near Nant Ffrancon (the stream of the Beaver or Afanc, a mythological animal). Nant Ffrancon leads north-west from near Capel Curig and Bettws y coed and past Bethesda, reaching the sea in Beaumaris Bay. The lakes, numerous and occasionally large, include: Llyn Peris and Llyn Padarn at Llanberis, north of Snowdon; Llyn Ogwen, north of Glydyr Fawr; Llyn Cowlyd and Llyn Eigiau, both north of Capel Curig; Llyn Llydaw, on Snowdon; Llyn Cwellyn, west of Snowdon; Llyn Gwynnant, east of Snowdon; Llyniau (Nant y llef or) Nantlle, near Llanllyfni; Llyn Conway.

The greater part of the county, including the mountainous Snowdon district and nearly all the eastern portion of the promontory of Lleyn, is occupied by rocks of Ordovician age, the Arenig, Bala and Llandeilo series. These are dark slates and thin-bedded grits with enormous masses of interbedded igneous rocks, lavas and ashes, the product of contemporaneous volcanoes. At the base of Snowdon are Bala grits and slates, above them lie three beds of felspathic porphyry, which are in turn succeeded by a great mass of calcareous and sandy volcanic ashes, while upon the summit are the remnants of a lava sheet. The whole mountain is part of a syncline, the beds dipping into it from the north-west and south-east.

Next to the Ordovician, the Cambrian rocks are the most important; they are found in three separate areas; the largest is in the north-west, and extends from Bangor to Bethesda, through Llyn Cwellyn and Llanwada to the coast near Clynnogfawr. The second area lies west of Tremadoc, which has given its name to the upper division of the Cambrian system. The third forms the promontory south of Llanenga. Cambrian slates are extensively quarried at Penrhyn, Llanberis and Dinorwic. Pre-Cambrian schists and igneous rocks occupy a strip, from 2 to 3 m. wide, along the coast from Neirn to Bardsey Island. A very small area of the Denbighshire Silurian enters this county near Conway near the eastern border; it comprises Tarannon shale and Wenlock beds with graptolites.

The striking headland of the Great Orme as well as Little Orme's Head is composed of carboniferous limestone, containing corals and large *Productus* shells. A narrow strip of the same formation runs along the Menai Straits for several miles south of the tubular bridge. At the southern extremity of the limestone a small patch of coal measures is found.

Glacial drift—gravel, boulders and clay—is abundant along the northern coast, and in the neighbourhood of Snowdon it is an important feature in the landscape; massive moraines, perched blocks, striated stones and other evidences of ice action are common. On 361 Moel Trygarn and on the western flanks of Snowdon marine shells have been found in the drift up to an elevation of 1400 ft. above sea-level. Blown sand occurs along the coast near Conway, south-west of Carnarvon and on the south coast. Several hollows and pipes in the carboniferous limestone about Orme's Head contain clays and sands of mixed origin, including Upper Carboniferous, Triassic and drift materials. The igneous rocks, especially those of volcanic origin, constitute one of the most striking geological features of the county; they comprise felsites, rhyolites, quartz porphyries, enstatite diabases, andesite tuffs, diabases and granite.

The climate is cold and damp in winter, except in the peninsula, Lleyn, and on the mild coast. Arable land, but a small proportion of the surface, is mostly in the Conwy valley or near the sea. Principal crops are oats, barley and potatoes, with some little wheat. The valley soil (alluvial) is often fertile, chiefly as meadow and enclosed pasture. Dairy and sheep-farming occupy most farmers. The small mountain ponies, especially of Llanbedr (Conwy Vale), are famous, and Welsh ponies were known for staying power even to Arrian (*Cynegetics*). Agriculture still too much follows the old routine, besides losing by the influx of labour into the towns or to the mining industry and "set works" (stone).

The county is served by the London & North-Western railway; its terminus is Afon Wen, within 4 m. of Pwllheli. Between these stations plies the Cambrian, which runs along the Cardigan Bay coast and terminates at Pwllheli. The North Wales Narrow Gauge line runs from Dinas, south of Carnarvon, to Snowdon Ranger, 4 m. from Beddgelert. The main line of the London & North-Western runs along the northern coast, with branches from Llandudno junction to Blaenau Festiniog, along the Denbighshire side of the Conwy stream; from Menai Bridge to Carnarvon (thence continuing to Llanberis, or, by another line, to Afon Wen). The chief ports are Portmadoc, Pwllheli, Carnarvon, Port Dinorwic and Bangor. Near Portmadoc is Criccieth, with a castle resorted to by visitors; Pwllheli is also a summer resort, and a tramway runs thence to within a short distance of Abersoch, another favourite watering-place. Nefyn (some 6 m. from Pwllheli), still unserved by rail or tram, was the scene of a royal tournament in the 15th century, and is another bathing resort; near are Carreg Llam and Pistyll farm (see BARDSEY).

The area of the ancient county is 361,156 acres, with a population in 1901 of 126,883. The area of the administrative county is 365,986 acres. The inhabitants practically all speak

Welsh (slightly differing, especially in Lleyn, from that of Anglesey). Over 80 is the percentage in Carnarvonshire, as against over 90 for Anglesey. The county is divided into two parliamentary divisions, south (Eifion) and north (Arfon).

The Carnarvon district of boroughs is formed of Bangor city, Carnarvon, Conway, Criccieth, Nefyn and Pwllheli. There are four municipal boroughs: Bangor (pop. 11,269), Carnarvon (9760), Conway (4681) and Pwllheli (3675). Other urban districts are: Bethesda (5281), Bettws y coed (1070), Criccieth (1406), Llandudno (9279), Llanfairfechan (2769), Penmaenmawr (3503) and Ynyscynhaiarn (4883). Carnarvon, where assizes are held, is in the north Wales circuit. Except a few parishes (in and near Llandudno) in St Asaph diocese, Carnarvonshire is in the diocese of Bangor, and contains sixty-one ecclesiastical parishes or districts, with parts of four others. Bangor, Carnarvon, Pwllheli and Llandudno are the principal towns, with Criccieth, Nefyn, Portmadoc and Tremadoc.

Carnarvonshire was occupied by the Segontiaci, with difficulty subdued by Ostorius Scapula and C. Suetonius Paulinus (Paullinus). From here Agricola crossed to conquer Anglesey. Relics of British forts and camps have been discovered. Caerhun (Caer Rhun) and Carnarvon (Caer Seint) are respectively the old Conovium and Segontium of Britannia Secunda. The county was part of Gwynedd kingdom, until Edward I. in 1277 restricted that to Snowdon proper. The early fortresses at Deganwy, Dinorwic, Dinas Dinlle, &c., and the later castles of Conwy (Conway), Carnarvon, Criccieth and Dolbadarn, bear witness to the warlike character of its inhabitants.

See Edw. Breese, *Kalendar of Gwynedd* (London, 1874).

CARNATIC, or KARNATAK (Kannada, Karnata, Karnatakadesa), a name given by Europeans to a region of southern India, between the Eastern Ghats and the Coromandel coast, in the presidency of Madras. It is ultimately derived, according to Bishop Caldwell (*Grammar of the Dravidian Languages*), from *kar,* "black," and *nadu,* "country," *i.e.* "the black country," "a term very suitable to designate the 'black cotton soil,' as it is called, of the plateau of the Southern Deccan." Properly the name is, in fact, applicable only to the country of the Kanarese extending between the Eastern and Western Ghats, over an irregular area narrowing northwards, from Palghat in the south to Bidar in the north, and including Mysore. The extension of the name to the country south of the Karnata was probably due to the Mahommedan conquerors who in the 16th century overthrew the kingdom of Vijayanagar, and who extended the name which they found used of the country north of the Ghats to that south of them. After this period the plain country of the south came to be called Karnata Payanghat, or "lowlands," as distinguished from Karnata Balaghat, or "highlands." The misapplication of the name Carnatic was carried by the British a step further than by the Mahommedans, it being confined by them to the country below the Ghats, Mysore not being included. Officially, however, this name is no longer applied, "the Carnatic" having become a mere geographical term. Administratively the name Carnatic (or rather Karnatak) is now applied only to the Bombay portion of the original Karnata, viz. the districts of Belgaum, Dharwar and Bijapur, part of North Kanara, and the native states of the Southern Mahratta agency and Kolhapur.

The region generally known to Europeans as the Carnatic, though no longer a political or administrative division, is of great historical importance. It extended along the eastern coast about 600 m. in length, and from 50 to 100 m. in breadth. It was bounded on the north by the Guntur circar, and thence it stretched southward to Cape Comorin. It was divided into the Southern, Central and Northern Carnatic. The region south of the river Coleroon, which passes the town of Trichinopoly, was called the Southern Carnatic. The principal towns of this division were Tanjore, Trichinopoly, Madura, Tranquebar, Negapatam and Tinnevelly. The Central Carnatic extended from the Coleroon river to the river Pennar; its chief towns were Madras, Pondicherry, Arcot, Vellore, Cuddalore, Pulicat, Nellore, &c. The Northern Carnatic extended from the river Pennar to the northern limit of the country; and the chief town was Ongole.[1] The Carnatic, as above defined, comprehended within its limits the maritime provinces of Nellore, Chingleput, South Arcot, Tanjore, Madura and Tinnevelly, besides the inland districts of North Arcot and Trichinopoly. The population of this region consists chiefly of Brahmanical Hindus, the

222

Mahommedans being but thinly scattered over the country. The Brahmans rent a great proportion of the land, and also fill different offices in the collection of the revenue and the administration of justice. Throughout the country they appropriate to themselves a particular quarter in every town, generally the strongest part of it. Large temples and other public monuments of civilization abound. The temples are commonly built in the middle of a square area, and enclosed by a wall 15 or 20 ft. high, which conceals them completely from the public view, as they are never raised above it.

At the earliest period of which any records exist, the country known as the Carnatic was divided between the Pandya and Chola kingdoms, which with that of Chera or Kerala formed the three Tamil kingdoms of southern India. The Pandya kingdom practically coincided in extent with the districts of Madura and Tinnevelly; that of the Cholas extended along the Coromandel coast from Nellore to Pudukottai, being bounded on the north by the Pennar river and on the south by the Southern Vellaru. The government of the country was shared for centuries with these dynasties by numerous independent or semi-independent chiefs, evidence of whose perennial internecine conflicts is 362preserved in the multitudes of forts and fortresses the deserted ruins of which crown almost all the elevated points. In spite, however, of this passion of the military classes for war the Tamil civilization developed in the country was of a high type. This was largely due to the wealth of the country, famous in the earliest times as now for its pearl fisheries. Of this fishery Korkai (the Greek Κόλχοι), now a village on the Tambraparni river in Tinnevelly, but once the Pandya capital, was the centre long before the Christian era. In Pliny's day, owing to the silting up of the harbour, its glory had already decayed and the Pandya capital had been removed to Madura (*Hist. Nat.* vi. cap. xxiii. 26), famous later as a centre of Tamil literature. The Chola kingdom, which four centuries before Christ had been recognized as independent by the great Maurya king Asoka, had for its chief port Kaviripaddinam at the mouth of the Cauvery, every vestige of which is now buried in sand. For the first two centuries after Christ a large sea-borne trade was carried on between the Roman empire and the Tamil kingdoms; but after Caracalla's massacre at Alexandria in A.D. 215 this ceased, and with it all intercourse with Europe for centuries. Henceforward, until the 9th century, the history of the country is illustrated only by occasional and broken lights. The 4th century saw the rise of the Pallava power,2 which for some 400 years encroached on, without extinguishing, the Tamil kingdoms. When in A.D. 640 the Chinese traveller Hsüan Tsang visited Kanchi (Conjevaram), the capital of the Pallava king, he learned that the kingdom of Chola (Chu-li-ya) embraced but a small territory, wild, and inhabited by a scanty and fierce population; in the Pandya kingdom (Malakuta), which was under Pallava suzerainty, literature was dead, Buddhism all but extinct, while Hinduism and the naked Jain saints divided the religious allegiance of the people, and the pearl fisheries continued to flourish. The power of the Pallava kings was shaken by the victory of Vikramaditya Chalukya in A.D. 740, and shattered by Aditya Chola at the close of the 9th century. From this time onward the inscriptional records are abundant. The Chola kingdom, which in the 9th century had been weak, now revived, its power culminating in the victories of Rajaraja the Great, who defeated the Chalukyas after a four years' war, and, about A.D. 994, forced the Pandya kings to become his tributaries. A magnificent temple at Tanjore, once his capital, preserves the records of his victories engraved upon its walls. His career of conquest was continued by his son Rajendra Choladeva I., self-styled Gangaikonda owing to his victorious advance to the Ganges, who succeeded to the throne in A.D. 1018. The ruins of the new capital which he built, called Gangaikonda Cholapuram, still stand in a desolate region of the Trichinopoly district. His successors continued the eternal wars with the Chalukyas and other dynasties, and the Chola power continued in the ascendant until the death of Kulottunga Chola III. in 1278, when a disputed succession caused its downfall and gave the Pandyas the opportunity of gaining for a few years the upper hand in the south. In 1310, however, the Mahommedan invasion under Malik Kafur overwhelmed the Hindu states of southern India in a common ruin. Though crushed, however, they were not extinguished; a period of anarchy followed, the struggle between the Chola kings and the Mussulmans issuing in the establishment at Kanchi of a usurping Hindu dynasty which ruled till the end of the 14th century, while in 1365 a branch of the Pandyas succeeded in re-establishing itself in part of the kingdom of Madura, where it survived till 1623. At the beginning of the 15th century the whole country had come under the rule of the kings of Vijayanagar; but in the anarchy that followed the overthrow of the Vijayanagar empire by the Mussulmans in the 16th century, the Hindu viceroys (*nayakkas*) established in Madura, Tanjore and Kanchi made themselves independent, only in their turn to become tributary to the kings of Golconda and Bijapur, who divided the Carnatic between them. Towards the close of the 17th century the country was reduced by the armies of Aurangzeb, who in 1692 appointed Zulfikar Ali nawab of the Carnatic, with his seat at Arcot. Meanwhile, the Mahratta power had begun to develop; in 1677 Sivaji had suppressed the last remnants of the Vijayanagar power in Vellore, Gingee and Kurnool, while his brother Ekoji, who in 1674 had overthrown the Nayakkas of Tanjore, established in that city a dynasty which lasted for a century. The collapse of the Delhi power after the death of Aurangzeb produced further changes. The nawab Saadet-allah of Arcot (1710-1732) established his independence; his successor Dost Ali (1732-1740) conquered and annexed Madura in 1736, and his successors were confirmed in their position as nawabs of the Carnatic by the nizam of Hyderabad after that potentate had established his power in southern India. After the death of the nawab Mahommed Anwar-ud-din (1744-1749), the succession was disputed between Mahommed Ali and Husein Dost. In this quarrel the French and English, then competing for influence in the Carnatic, took opposite sides. The victory of the British established Mahommed Ali in power over part of the Carnatic till his death in 1795. Meanwhile, however, the country had been exposed to other troubles. In 1741 Madura, which the nawab Dost Ali (1732-1740) had added to his dominions in 1736, was conquered by the Mahrattas; and in 1743 Hyder Ali of Mysore overran and ravaged the central Carnatic. The latter was reconquered by the British, to whom Madura had fallen in 1758; and, finally, in 1801 all the possessions of the nawab of the Carnatic were transferred to them by a treaty which stipulated that an annual revenue of several lakhs of pagodas should be reserved to the nawab, and that the British should undertake to support a sufficient civil and military force for the protection of the country and the collection of the revenue. On the death of the nawab in 1853 it was determined to put an end to the nominal sovereignty, a liberal establishment being provided for the family.

The southern Carnatic, when it came into the possession of the British, was occupied by military chieftains called poligars, who ruled over the country, and held lands by doubtful tenures. They were unquestionably a disorderly race; and the country, by their incessant feuds and plunderings, was one continued scene of strife and violence. Under British rule they were reduced to order, and their forts and military establishments were destroyed.

See INDIA: *History*. For the various applications of the name Carnatic see the *Imperial Gazetteer of India* (Oxford, 1908), *s.v.*; for the results of the latest researches in the early history of the country see V.A. Smith, *Early History of India* (2nd ed., Oxford, 1908), and Robert Sewell, *A Forgotten Empire* (Vijayanagar), (London, 1900).

1As a geographical term, Carnatic is not now applied to the district north of Pennar.

2The Pallavas are supposed by some authorities to be identical with the Pahlavas (Parthians of Persia), who, with the Sakas and Yayanas, settled in western India about A.D. 100. Mr Vincent Smith, however, who in the 1st edition (1904) of his *Early History of India* maintained this view, says in the 2nd edition (1908, p. 423) that "recent research does not support this hypothesis," and that "it seems more likely that the Pallavas were a tribe, clan or caste which was formed in the northern part of the existing Madras Presidency." The evidence points to their having been a race distinct from the Tamils.

CARNATION (*Dianthus Caryophyllus*, natural order Caryophyllaceae), a garden flower, a native of southern Europe, but occasionally found in an apparently wild state in England. It has long been held in high estimation for the beauty and the delightful fragrance of its blossoms. The varieties are numerous, and are ranged under three groups, called *bizarres*, *flakes* and *picotees*. The last, from their distinctness of character, are now generally looked upon as if they were a different plant, whereas they are, in truth, but a seminal development from the carnation itself, their number and variety being entirely owing to the assiduous endeavours of the modern florist to vary and to improve them.

The true carnations, as distinguished from picotees, are those which have the colours arranged in longitudinal stripes or bars of variable width on each petal, the ground colour being white. The *bizarres* are those in which stripes of two distinct colours occur on the white ground, and it is on the purity of the white ground and the clearness and evenness of the striping that the technical merit of each variety rests. There are scarlet bizarres 363marked with scarlet and maroon, crimson bizarres marked with crimson and purple, and pink and purple bizarres marked with those two colours. The *flakes* have stripes of only one colour on the white ground; purple flakes are striped with purple, scarlet flakes with scarlet, and rose flakes with rose colour. The *selfs*, those showing one colour only, as white, yellow, crimson, purple, &c., are commonly called *cloves*.

The *picotee* has the petals laced instead of striped with a distinct colour; the subgroups are red-edged, purple-edged, rose-edged and scarlet-edged, all having white grounds; each group divides into two sections, the heavy-edged and the light-edged. In the heavy-edged the colour appears to be laid on in little touches, passing from the edge inwards, but so closely that they coalesce into one line of colour from 1/12 to 1/16 of an inch broad, and more or less feathered on the inner edge, the less feathered the better; the light-edged display only a fine edge, or "wire" edge, of colour on the white ground. Yellow picotees are a group of great beauty, but deficient in correct marking.

During the decade 1898-1908 a new American race of carnations became very popular with British growers. As the plants flower chiefly during the winter—from October till the end of March—they are known as "winter flowering" or "perpetual"; they are remarkable for the charming delicacy and colouring of the blossoms and for the length of the flower-stalks. This enables them to be used with great effect during the dullest months of the year for all kinds of floral decorations. These varieties are propagated by layers or cuttings or "pipings."

"Marguerite" carnations are lovely annuals remarkable for their beautifully fringed blossoms. They are easily raised from seeds every year, and should be treated like half-hardy annuals.

What trade growers call "jacks" are seedling carnations with single flowers of no great value or beauty. Thousands of these are raised every year for supplying "grass" (as the foliage is called) to put with choicer varieties. Costermongers take advantage of the ordinary householders' ignorance of plants by selling "jacks" as choice varieties at a high price.

Carnations are usually propagated by "layering" the non-flowering shoots about the second or third week in July, in the open air; but almost at any period when proper shoots can be obtained under glass. Cuttings or "pipings" are also inserted in rich but very gritty soil in cold frames, or in beds with gentle bottom heat in greenhouses. The rooted layers may be removed and potted or planted out towards the end of September, or early in October, the choice sorts being potted in rather small pots and kept in a cold frame during winter, when damp is dangerous.

New varieties can only be obtained from carefully saved seeds, or when a "sport" is produced—*i.e.* when a shoot with a flower differing entirely in colour from that of the parent plant appears unexpectedly. "Malmaison" carnations arose in this way, and are largely cultivated in greenhouses.

The soil for carnations and picotees should be a good turfy loam, free from wireworm, and as fibry as it can be obtained; to four parts of this add one part of rotten manure and one of leaf-mould, with sufficient sharp sand to keep it loose. A moderate addition of old lime rubbish will also be an advantage. This should be laid up in a dry place, and frequently turned over so as to be in a free friable condition for use towards the end of February or early in March.

Carnations are subject to several diseases, the worst being the "rust" (*Uromyces Caryophilinus*), "leaf-spot" and maggot. The first two are checked or prevented by spraying the plants with sulphide of potassium (1 oz. to 10 gallons of water), taking care to avoid the painted woodwork; while the only way to deal with the carnation maggot is to pierce the centre of attacked plants with a needle, and to destroy the eggs whenever they are observed.

Descriptive lists of the best varieties may be had from all the leading nurserymen.

CARNEA, one of the great national festivals of Sparta, held in honour of Apollo Carneus. Whether Carneus (or Carnus) was originally an old Peloponnesian divinity subsequently identified with Apollo, or merely an "emanation" from him, is uncertain; but there seems no reason to doubt that Carneus means "the god of flocks and herds" (Hesychius, *s.v.* Κάρνος), in a wider sense, of the harvest and the vintage. The chief centre of his worship was Sparta, where the Carnea took place every year from the 7th to the 15th of the month Carneus (= Metageitnion, August). During this period all military operations were suspended. The Carnea appears to have been at once agrarian, military and piacular in character. In the last aspect it is supposed to commemorate the death of Carnus, an Acarnanian seer and favourite of Apollo, who, being suspected of espionage, was slain by one of the Heraclidae during the passage of the Dorians from Naupactus to Peloponnesus. By way of punishment, Apollo visited the army with a pestilence, which only ceased after the institution of the Carnea. The tradition is probably intended to explain the sacrifice of an animal (perhaps a later substitute for a human being) as the representative of the god.

The agrarian and military sides of the festival are clearly distinguished. (1) Five unmarried youths (Καρνεᾶται) were chosen by lot from each [tribe] for four years, to superintend the proceedings, the officiating priest being calledἀγητής ("leader"). A man decked with garlands (possibly the priest himself) started running, pursued by a band of young men called σταφυλοδρόμοι("running with bunches of grapes in their hands"); if he was caught, it was a guarantee of good fortune to the city; if not, the reverse. (2) In the second part of the festival nine tents were set up in the country, in each of which nine citizens, representing the phratries (or *obae*), feasted together in honour of the god (for huts or booths extemporized as shelters compare the Jewish feast of Tabernacles; and see W. Warde Fowler in *Classical Review*, March 1908, on the country festival in Tibullus ii. 1). According to Demetrius of Scepsis (in Athenaeus iv. 141), the Carnea was an imitation of life in camp, and everything was done in accordance with the command of a herald. In regard to the sacrifice, which doubtless formed part of the ceremonial, all that is known is that a ram was sacrificed at Thurii. Other indications point to the festival having assumed a military character at an early date, as might have been expected among the warlike Dorians, although some scholars deny this. The general meaning of the agrarian ceremony is clear, and has numerous parallels in north European harvest-customs, in which an animal (or man disguised as an animal) was pursued by the reapers, the animal if caught being usually killed; in any case, both the man and the animal represent the vegetation spirit. E.H. Binney in*Classical Review* (March 1905) suggests that the story of Alcestis was performed at the Carnea (to which it may have become attached with the name of Apollo) as a vegetation drama, and "embodied a Death and Resurrection ceremony."

The great importance attached to the festival and its month is shown in several instances. It was responsible for the delay which prevented the Spartans from assisting the Athenians at the battle of Marathon (Herodotus vi. 106), and for the despatch of a small advance guard under Leonidas to hold Thermopylae instead of the main army (Herodotus vii. 206). Again, when Epidaurus was attacked in 419 by Argos, the movements of the Spartans under Agis against the latter were interrupted until the end of the month, while the Argives (on whom, as Dorians, the custom was equally binding), by manipulating the calendar, avoided the necessity of suspending operations (see Grote, *Hist, of Greece,* ch. 56; Thucydides v. 54).

See S. Wide, *Lakonische Kulte* (1893), and article "Karneios" in Roscher's *Lexikon;* L. Couve in Daremberg and Saglio's *Dictionnaire des antiquites;* W. Mannhardt, *Mythologische Forschungen* (1883), p. 170, and*Wald- und Feldkulte* (2nd ed., 1905), ii. 254; L.R. Farnell, *Cults of the Greek States,* iv. (1907); G. Schömann, *Griechische Altertümer* (ed. J.H. Lipsius, 1902); J.G. Frazer on Pausanias, iii. 13, 3; H. Usener in *Rheinisches Museum,* liii. (1898), p. 377; J. Vürtheim in *Mnemosyne,* xxxi. (1903), p. 234.

CARNEADES (214-129 B.C.), Greek philosopher, founder of the Third or New Academy, was born at Cyrene. Little is known of his life. He learned dialectics under Diogenes the Stoic, and under Hegesinus, the third leader, of the Academy in descent from Arcesilaus. The chief objects of his study, however, 364were the works of Chrysippus, opposition to whose views is the mainspring of his philosophy. "If Chrysippus had not been," he is reported to have said, "I had not been either." In 155, together with Diogenes the Stoic and Critolaus the Peripatetic, he was sent on an embassy to Rome to justify certain depredations committed by the Athenians in the territory of Oropus. On this occasion he delivered two speeches on successive days, one in favour of justice, the other against it. His powerful reasoning excited among the Roman youth an enthusiasm for philosophical speculations, and the elder Cato insisted on Carneades and his companions being dismissed from the city.

Carneades, practically a 5th-century sophist, is the most important of the ancient sceptics. Negatively, his philosophy is a polemic against the Stoic theory of knowledge in all its aspects. All our sensations are relative, and acquaint us, not with things as they are, but only with the impressions that things produce upon us. Experience, he says, clearly shows that there is no true impression. There is no notion that may not deceive us; it is impossible to distinguish between false and true impressions; therefore the Stoic φαντασία καταληπτική (see STOICS) must be given up. There is no criterion of truth. Carneades also assailed Stoic theology and physics. In answer to the doctrine of final cause, of design in nature, he points to those things which cause destruction and danger to man, to the evil committed by men endowed with reason, to the miserable condition of humanity, and to the misfortunes that assail the good man. There is, he concludes, no evidence for the doctrine of a divine superintending providence. Even if there were orderly connexion of parts in the universe, this may have resulted quite naturally. No proof can be advanced to show that this world is anything but the product of natural forces. Carneades further attacked the very idea of God. He points out the contradiction between the attributes of infinity and individuality. Like Aristotle, he insists that virtue, being relative, cannot be ascribed to God. Not even intelligence can be an attribute of the divine Being. Nor can he be conceived of as corporeal or incorporeal. If corporeal, he must be simple or compound; if a simple and elementary substance, he is incapable of life and thought; if compound, he contains in himself the elements of dissolution. If incorporeal, he can neither act nor feel. In fact, nothing whatever can be asserted with certainty in regard to God. The general line of argument followed by Carneades anticipates much in modern thought.

The positive side of his teaching resembles in all essentials that of Arcesilaus (*q.v.*). Knowledge being impossible, a wise man should practise ἐποχή(suspension of judgment). He will not even be sure that he can be sure of nothing. Ideas or notions are never true, but only probable; nevertheless, there are degrees of probability, and hence degrees of belief, leading to action. According to Carneades, an impression may be probable in itself; probable and uncontradicted (ἀπερίσπαστος, lit. "not pulled aside," not distracted by synchronous sensations, but shown to be in harmony with them) when compared with others; probable, uncontradicted, and thoroughly investigated and confirmed. In the first degree there is a strong persuasion of the propriety of the impression made; the second and third degrees are produced by comparisons of the impression with others associated with it, and an analysis of itself. His views on the *summum bonum* are not clearly known even to his disciple and successor Clitomachus. He seems to have held that virtue consisted in the direction of activity towards the satisfaction of the natural impulses. Carneades left no written works; his opinions seem to have been systematized by Clitomachus.

See A. Geffers, *De Arcesilae Successoribus* (1845); C. Gouraud, *De Carneadis Vita et Placitis* (1848); V. Brochard, *Les Sceptiques grecs* (1887); C. Martha, "Le Philosophe Carneade a Rome," in *Revue des deux mondes,*xxix. (1878), and the histories of philosophy; also ACADEMY, GREEK.

www.ingramcontent.com/pod-product-compliance
Lightning Source LLC
Chambersburg PA
CBHW070106290526
45789CB00005B/1948